THE GREAT HUNGER

The
Great Hunger
Ireland 1845-9

CECIL WOODHAM-SMITH

NEW ENGLISH LIBRARY
TIMES MIRROR

Once again to G.I.W-S.

First published in Great Britain by Hamish Hamilton Ltd. in 1962
Second impression November 1962
Third impression December 1962
Fourth impression September 1963
© 1962 by Cecil Woodham-Smith

❀

Published as a Four Square edition in 1965
Reprinted February 1965
Reissued in this NEL edition April 1968
Reprinted April 1969

❀

*NEL Books are published by The New English Library Limited from Barnard's Inn,
Holborn, London, EC1. Made and printed in Great Britain by Love & Malcomson Ltd.,
Brighton Road, Redhill, Surrey*

45000013 3

A Map of Ireland in the 1840s Showing Most of the Places Named is on pp. vi-vii

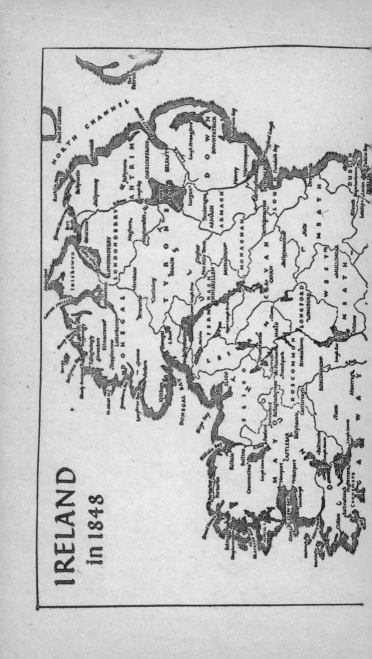

IRELAND
in 1848

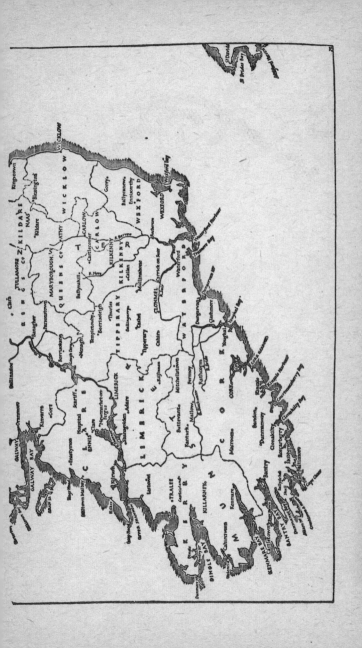

Chapter I

AT THE beginning of the year 1845 the state of Ireland was, as it had been for nearly seven hundred years, a source of grave anxiety to England. Ireland had first been invaded in 1169; it was now 1845, yet she had been neither assimilated nor subdued. The country had been conquered not once but several times, the land had been confiscated and redistributed over and over again, the population had been brought to the verge of extinction—after Cromwell's conquest and settlement only some half million Irish survived—yet an Irish nation still existed, separate, numerous and hostile.

Indeed, during the last few years it had seemed that Irish affairs were moving towards a new and alarming crisis.

On January 1, 1801, an event of enormous importance had taken place—the Act of Union between Ireland and England became operative. The two countries were made one, the economy of Ireland was assimilated into the economy of England, the Irish Parliament at Dublin disappeared and the Parliament at Westminster henceforward legislated for both countries. It was as if a marriage between England and Ireland had been celebrated, with the clauses of the Act of Union as the terms of the marriage settlement.

At first sight it seemed that Ireland had everything to gain. Free Trade between Ireland and England meant that the discrimination hitherto practised by England against Irish industry would come to an end; united with English riches Ireland would gain the capital she desperately needed for development, while the hundred Irish Members who were to sit at Westminster would give Ireland, for the first time, a voice in Imperial affairs. Further, an impression had been created that when the Union became law Catholic emancipation would immediately follow. Catholics (and three-quarters of the population of Ireland were Catholics) would be assured of justice from the wide and unprejudiced views of the Imperial Parliament, and the laws which, amongst other restrictions, prevented Catholics from becoming Members of Parliament or Judges or being appointed King's Counsel would be repealed.

The reality, however, was very different. The primary object of the Union was not to assist and improve Ireland but to bring her more completely into subjection.

Two years earlier, in 1798, the Irish had rebelled. England at that moment was in extreme danger, passing through the darkest days of her struggle with revolutionary France, and the rebels of '98 were assisted by French troops and with French money. The rebellion was put down with savagery, the strength of the army in Ireland was increased to a hundred thousand men, and the Union followed. England tightened her hold over Ireland; rebellious action, it was hoped, would henceforth become impossible.

The Union was bitterly opposed; contemporaries described it not as a marriage but as a "brutal rape," and Ireland was compared to an heiress whose chambermaid and trustees have been bribed, while she herself is dragged, protesting, to the altar. Nevertheless, after bribery on a scale such as history has seldom witnessed, and a generous distribution of places of profit and titles, "Union titles," the Act of Union became law.

As the years passed, however, no happiness resulted. The hope of English investment proved a delusion. Free Trade between the two countries enabled England to use Ireland as a market for surplus English goods; Irish industry collapsed, unemployment was widespread, and Dublin, now that an Irish Parliament sat no longer in College Green, became a half-dead city. Above all, Catholic emancipation, expected to follow immediately on the Union, was only achieved, after a desperate struggle, in 1829.

Ireland besought a repeal of the Union, and by 1843 the strength of the demand was seriously disquieting to the British Government. The Catholic peasantry was becoming organized, the commercial classes were being drawn in, substantial sums of money were being raised. All this was the work of one man, Daniel O'Connell, who gave up a brilliant career at the bar to devote his life to Ireland.

Adopted by a Catholic uncle living at Derrynane, County Kerry, a fluent speaker of the Irish language, with a magnificent voice and presence, a quick wit, a superb gift of invective, and a flamboyance his enemies called vulgarity, he was nicknamed "Swaggering Dan." Self-government, not separation from England, was O'Connell's aim; and he cherished a romantic admiration for Queen Victoria, "the darling little Queen." He had a lawyer's respect for the law, with a horror of armed rebellion which derived from his personal recollection of the hangings, torturings and floggings that had followed the '98; his followers were pledged to obtain repeal only by legal and constitutional means.

Nevertheless, the Repeal movement was felt by the Government to be menacing. From March, 1843, O'Connell held huge mass meetings, "monster" meetings, demanding repeal, and tens of thousands, hundreds of thousands, flocked to hear him. At the historic hill of Tara, the ancient seat of Irish sovereignty in Meath, a quarter of a million persons gathered; and Sir Edward Sugden, Lord Chancellor of Ireland, wrote "The peaceable demeanour of the assembled multitudes is one of the most alarming symptoms." At forty monster meetings the only disturbance which could be discovered, after searching scrutiny by the Government, was the accidental overturning of a gingerbread stall.

An Irish people united and controlled was an ominous spectacle, and the British Government, seized with something near panic, began to prepare "as if in hourly expectation of civil war." Troops were hastily brought from England, barracks were fortified and provisioned to withstand a siege, Justices of the Peace who were repealers were dismissed, and in the courtyard of Dublin Castle a regiment of infantry was kept drawn up and under arms, in readiness to suppress a revolt.

In the autumn of 1843 O'Connell announced that a monster meeting, the greatest of all, would be held on Sunday, October 8, on the fields of Clontarf, near Dublin, where eight hundred years before the Irish hero, Brian Boru, had defeated the Norsemen and driven them into the sea. The Government, convinced that a rising would follow, decided to "proclaim" the Clontarf meeting, that is, to forbid it, in a proclamation issued by the Lord Lieutenant. Later, O'Connell himself was to be arrested.

The subsequent conduct of the Government was, as Greville wrote in his diary, "certainly most extraordinary." Instead of "proclaiming" the meeting at once, nothing was done until the eleventh hour, on the Saturday afternoon before the Sunday. Then the guns of the Pigeon House, the fort

commanding Dublin Bay, were trained on Clontarf, warships
entered Dublin Bay, and troops occupied the approaches to
the meeting place when tens of thousands of people were
massing. Had it not been for O'Connell's creed that "human
blood is no cement for the temple of liberty" a massacre
might have taken place; but O'Connell ordered the people to
go home and, directed by his lieutenants, the vast multitude
quietly dispersed. No monster meeting took place, no disturbance occurred.

Nevertheless, O'Connell was arrested a week later on a
charge of trying to alter the constitution by force. Convicted
by a "packed jury," a partisan jury on which no Catholic or
repealer was allowed to sit, he was sent to prison. The verdict
was reversed by the House of Lords on September 24, 1844,
and he was released. But for the movement the psychological
moment had passed: the iron of Repeal had cooled and
O'Connell himself was a changed man, while in prison he had
"lost his nerve." He was nearly seventy, and the strain of the
monster meetings, followed by arrest, trial and imprisonment,
even though he had been treated with consideration in
prison, had broken his health.

Constitutional methods having failed, as armed rebellion
had previously failed, Ireland relapsed into helpless hostility.
No outbreak took place in 1844, the year immediately preceding the famine, but the anxiety of the Government continued to be acute, and on the eve of the famine, the
Government of Ireland was admittedly a military occupation,
and the garrison of Ireland was larger than the garrison of
India. "How do you govern it?" demanded Macaulay in the
House of Commons on February 19, 1844. "Not by love but
by fear . . . not by the confidence of the people in the laws
and their attachment to the Constitution but by means of
armed men and entrenched camps."

∞

The hostility between England and Ireland, which six centuries had failed to extinguish, had its roots first of all in
race. After the first invasions, the first conquests, the Irish
hated the English with the hatred of the defeated and the
dispossessed. Nevertheless, eventually the English and the
Irish might have fused, as the English and the Scots, the
English and the Welsh have, for practical purposes, fused,

had it not been that in the sixteenth century racial animosity was disastrously strengthened by religious enmity.

The crucial event was the Reformation. The ideas of liberty which the English cherish and the history of their country's rise to greatness are bound up with Protestantism, while Ireland, alone among the countries of northern Europe, was scarcely touched by the Reformation. The gulf which resulted could never be bridged. In the political division of Europe which followed the Reformation, England and Ireland were on opposing sides. Henceforward, Irish aspirations could only be fulfilled, Irish faith could only flourish, through the defeat of England and the triumph of her enemies.

Freedom for Ireland meant Philip of Spain and the Inquisition in place of Elizabeth I, it meant James II instead of William III, it even meant, since misery and oppression make strange bedfellows, the victory of Napoleon.

So completely is the history of the one country the reverse of the history of the other that the very names which to an Englishman mean glory, victory and prosperity to an Irishman spell degradation, misery and ruin. In Ireland the name of Elizabeth I stands only for the horrors of her Irish conquest; in the defeat of the Armada, Ireland's hopes of independence went down; above all, with the name of William III and the glorious revolution of 1688, the very foundation of British liberties, the Catholic Irishman associates only the final subjugation of his country and the degradation and injustice of the penal laws. Freedom for the one meant slavery for the other; victory for the one meant defeat for the other; the good of the one was the evil of the other. Ireland, resentful and hostile, lying only a day's sail, in fine weather, from Britain's coasts, for centuries provided a refuge for enemy agents, a hatching-ground for enemy plots; her motto was "England's difficulty is Ireland's opportunity," and in every crisis of England's history she seized the moment of weakness to stab her enemy in the back. It is the explanation, if not the excuse, for the ferocity with which the English have treated Ireland.

In the eighteen-forties, after nearly seven hundred years of English domination, Irish poverty and Irish misery appalled the traveller. The Frenchman de Beaumont found in Ireland the extreme of human misery, worse than the Negro in his chains; the German traveller Kohl wrote that no mode of life in Europe could seem pitiable after one had seen Ireland. He

used, he said, to pity the poor Letts in Livonia: "Well, Heaven
pardon my ignorance! Now I have seen Ireland, it seems to
me that the poorest among the Letts, the Esthonians and the
Finlanders, lead a life of comparative comfort."

Exceptions were to be found in Ulster, particularly the
northeast portion, which includes Belfast. Throughout the
first half of the nineteenth century, while Dublin was decaying, Belfast was growing into a leading industrial town and
port, and the linen manufacture in which Ulster was to lead
the world was rapidly developing; Belfast was the headquarters and distributing centre, and flax growing and weaving
were carried on in the surrounding districts. A large part of
Ulster differed from most of Ireland because it had been
"planted." In the "plantation of Ulster," at the beginning of
the seventeenth century, the original Irish owners of the soil
had been driven out and mainly Scottish Protestants put in
their place. The descendants of the plantation had not been
dispossessed; they shared the religion of their rulers, had
rights, seldom found elsewhere, relating to the occupation of
land, and their standard of life, assisted by the rise of the
linen industry, was somewhat higher than in the south and
south-west.

Better conditions, however, were by no means universal in
Ulster. Donegal, not then separated from the rest of Ulster,
was one of the poorest and most backward counties in Ireland
and, nearer Belfast, in districts like the Fews, in County
Armagh, the standard of living was as low as anywhere in
the country.

"There never was," said the Duke of Wellington, a native
of County Meath, "a country in which poverty existed to the
extent it exists in Ireland." Housing conditions were wretched
beyond words. The census of 1841 graded "houses" in Ireland
into four classes; the fourth and lowest class consisted of
windowless mud cabins of a single room, ". . . nearly half
of the families of the rural population," reported the Census
Commissioners, ". . . are living in the lowest state." In parts
of the west of Ireland more than three-fifths of the "houses"
were one-roomed, windowless mud cabins, and west of a
line drawn from Londonderry to Cork the proportion was
two-fifths.

Furniture was a luxury; the inhabitants of Tullahobagly,
County Donegal, numbering about 9,000, had in 1837 only
10 beds, 93 chairs and 243 stools between them. Pigs slept

with their owners, manure heaps choked doors, sometimes even stood inside; the evicted and unemployed put roofs over ditches, burrowed into banks, existed in bog holes.

∼∽

All this wretchedness and misery could, almost without exception, be traced to a single source—the system under which land had come to be occupied and owned in Ireland, a system produced by centuries of successive conquests, rebellions, confiscations and punitive legislation.

In 1843, in the midst of the Repeal agitation, the British Government, recognizing that the land question was at the root of Irish discontent, set up a Royal Commission "to inquire into the law and practice with regard to the occupation of land in Ireland." This Commission, called the Devon Commission, after its chairman, the Earl of Devon, visited every part of Ireland, examined 1,100 witnesses, printed three huge volumes of evidence, and reported in February, 1845, a few months before the outbreak of the famine. Its secretary was an able and "improving" landlord, John Pitt Kennedy, who had gained some celebrity as the author of a pamphlet on the Irish question entitled "Instruct: Employ: Don't Hang Them." It adds to the weight of its conclusions that the Commission was a landlords' Commission; every member who sat on it was a landowner, and O'Connell declared, "It is perfectly one-sided, all landlords and no tenants."

The Report of the Devon Commission stated that the principal cause of Irish misery was the bad relations between landlord and tenant. Ireland was a conquered country, the Irish peasant a dispossessed man, his landlord an alien conqueror. There was no paternalism, such as existed in England, no hereditary loyalty or feudal tie. "Confiscation is their common title," said the Earl of Clare, the famous Tory Lord Chancellor, speaking of Irish landlords, "and from the first settlements they have been hemmed in on every side by the original inhabitants of the island, brooding over their discontent in sullen indignation."

With some notable exceptions—whose names survive and are regarded with affection in Ireland today—the successive owners of the soil of Ireland regarded it merely as a source from which to extract as much money as possible, and since a hostile, backward country is neither a safe nor an agreeable place in which to live, from the first conquests the absentee landlord was common in Ireland. The absentee evil was "a very great one" as early as 1377. Rents were spent in England or on the Continent; in 1842 it was estimated that £6,000,000 of rents were being remitted out of Ireland, and Kohl, the German traveller, commented on the mansions of absentee landlords, standing "stately, silent, empty." Absentee estates, however, were by no means always the worst managed, and some, in particular the properties of great English territorial magnates, for instance, the estates of the Duke of Devonshire, were models. But too often owners visited property in Ireland only once or twice in a lifetime, sometimes not at all; as Colonel Conolly, of Kildare and Donegal, told a Select Committee of the House of Lords in 1846, "Where the landlords have never seen their estates, you can hardly suppose that their sympathies are very strong for sufferings they have never witnessed." Meanwhile, almost absolute power was left in the hands of an agent, whose ability was measured by the amount of money he could contrive to extract.

During the eighteenth century a new method of dealing with Irish property was adopted. Large tracts of land were let at a fixed rent to a single individual on a long lease, and he sub-let as he chose. This "middleman system" produced misery: the landlord rid himself of responsibility and assured himself of a regular income, but the tenants were handed over to exploitation. Profit was the only motive, and contemporary observers denounce middlemen as "land sharks," "bloodsuckers," "the most oppressive species of tyrant that ever lent assistance to the destruction of a country." Moreover, the middlemen degraded the land because, as the slum landlord finds it more profitable to let out a house room by room, so they split farms into smaller and smaller holdings for the sake of increased rents.

Yet whether he held under a middleman, a resident, or an absentee landlord, the terms on which the Irish peasant occupied his land were harsh, and two provisions in particular, the two "monster grievances" of Ireland deprived him of incentive and security.

First, any improvement he made to his holding became, when his lease expired or was terminated, the property of the landlord, without compensation. Second, he very seldom had any security of tenure; the majority of tenants in Ireland were tenants "at will," that is, the will of the landlord, who could turn them out whenever he chose.

Under a practice known as "tenant right," found mainly in Ulster, compensation for improvements was paid, and where the practice existed it was jealously guarded. ". . . It is one of the sacred rights of the country which cannot be touched with impunity," the agent for Lord Lurgan's property in County Armagh told the Devon Commission; "and if systematic efforts were made among the proprietors of Ulster to invade tenant right, I do not believe there is a force at the disposal of the Horse Guards [the War Office] sufficient to keep the peace of the province."

The Devon Commission stated that the superior prosperity and tranquillity of Ulster, compared with the rest of Ireland, were due to tenant right.

The annexation of improvements was made more inequitable by the bare state in which land was customarily let, so destitute of every aid to cultivation taken for granted in England or Scotland that it was often impossible for the tenant to work it until he had made "improvements" destined to enrich his landlord.

Even so, had the tenant possessed some degree of security, for instance held a reasonable lease, he might have been encouraged to exert himself. But leases were the exception not the rule, stated Lord Stanley, himself an Irish landowner, in the House of Lords on June 9, 1845, the eve of the famine. In many cases the landlord refused a lease because he had the tenant more completely under his control; in others, the tenant declined because recent legislation had so greatly increased the cost of the stamp on a lease that he could not find the necessary £10 or so.

In most cases, however, even a lease did not give security, owing to a deplorable and "very prevalent" Irish practice known as the "hanging gale"—"gale" being the term used for a periodical payment of rent. The hanging gale allowed an incoming tenant to leave his rent in arrear, that is "hanging," for six, twelve, or fifteen months. Tenants were almost invariably without capital, land was let bare, frequently even a dwelling had to be erected, and it was useless for the landlord to look for his rent until at least one harvest had given the tenant a chance to gain something.

But, once the tenant owed rent, any security his lease might give vanished. Edward Wakefield, a well-known economist of the period, described the "hanging gale" as "one of the great levers of oppression . . . the lower classes are kept

in a kind of perpetual bondage . . . this debt hangs over
their heads . . . and keeps them in a continual state of
anxiety and terror."

There were, of course, good landlords in Ireland, and on
Lord Monteagle's estate at Mount Trenchard, the Duke of
Leinster's at Carton, Mr. Guinness's at Stillorgan, Lord Bessborough's at Bessborough, to name only a few, farm buildings
were erected by the landlord, cabins were tidy, and the
people contented. In such cases a lease was often felt to be
superfluous. A tenant of Lord Mountcashel's told the Devon
Commission: "From the unbending integrity and honesty of
Mr. Joy [the agent] we are considered as safe at will as under
a lease. I have expended £500 without the scratch of a pen."
He added, however: "But Lord Mountcashel may be gathered to his fathers and Mr. Joy may die, and another Pharaoh
may arise who knew not Joseph."

Too often the powers given to the landlord, "the most
powerful the law can create," were remorselessly used. "The
dread of landlords was such that people trembled before
them," recorded the writer of a manuscript in Donegal, just
before the famine. "In Ireland alone," wrote John Stuart Mill,
"the whole agricultural population can be evicted by the
mere will of the landlord, either at the expiration of a lease
or, in the far more common case of their having no lease,
at six months' notice. In Ireland alone, the bulk of a population wholly dependent on the land cannot look forward to a
single year's occupation of it."

In these circumstances industry and enterprise were ex-
tinguished and a peasantry created which was one of the
most destitute in Europe. "It would be impossible adequately
to describe," stated the Devon Commission in its Report,
"the privations which they [the Irish labourer and his family]
habitually and silently endure . . . in many districts their only
food is the potato, their only beverage water . . . their cabins
are seldom a protection against the weather . . . a bed or a
blanket is a rare luxury . . . and nearly in all their pig and
a manure heap constitute their only property." The Commissioners could not "forbear expressing our strong sense of
the patient endurance which the labouring classes have exhibited under sufferings greater, we believe, than the people
of any other country in Europe have to sustain."

꧁꧂

Wretched though their condition might be, the pre-famine Irish peasants were not gloomy. "Their natural condition," wrote Sir Walter Scott during his visit to Ireland in 1825, "is turned towards gaiety and happiness," and the Census Commissioners noted "the proverbial gaiety and lightheartedness of the peasant people."

Dancing was the universal diversion, and Lord George Hill, who owned property in Donegal, has left an account of removing a cabin with dancing and fiddling. "The custom on such occasions is for the person who has the work to be done to hire a fiddler, upon which engagement all the neighbours joyously assemble and carry in an incredibly short time the stones and timber upon their backs to the new site; men, women and children alternately dancing and working while daylight lasts, at the termination of which they adjourn to some dwelling where they finish the night, often prolonging the dance to dawn of day." Arthur Young, at the end of the eighteenth century, commented on the fine physique of the average Irishman and the good looks of Irish women, and even after the sufferings of the famine Nassau Senior, the economist, revisiting Ireland, was "struck by the beauty of the population."

The culture of the potato required little attention except at springtime and harvest, and through the long winter nights the people sat within their cabins, fiddling, talking and telling stories. Firing, in the shape of turf—peat cut from the bog and costing little or nothing—was plentiful. "Few, if any, had any reason to complain of cold," records a manuscript, and poteen, illicit whiskey, was plentiful, too. Groups of neighbours gathered for dancing to the fiddle, indoors in the winter, in summer at the cross-roads; wakes, with liberal potations of poteen, were social occasions; and crowds gaily travelled immense distances to attend markets, fairs and, above all, races. "If there be a market to attend, a fair or a funeral, a horse race, a fight or a wedding, all else is neglected and forgotten," wrote George Nicholls, the leading English Poor Law expert, when reporting on the state of the Irish people.

As the main diversion of the women was talking, they disliked living in isolated houses. In schemes of land improvement the houses were separated, since in the old-style Irish settlement of cabins in clusters the women and the men spent too much time talking and quarrelling. The change was always unpopular. Lord George Hill relates a story of an agent who observed to a tenant that he seemed to be doing much better now that he was living away from neighbours and could "attend to his farm instead of idling and gossiping." The man assured him that precisely the contrary was true, and "he could not stand it much longer on account of the expense, as he was obliged to keep a servant maid just to talk to his wife."

Good manners and hospitality were universal among the poorest Irish. "The neighbour or the stranger finds every man's door open, and to walk in without ceremony at meal time and to partake of his bowl of potatoes, is always sure to give pleasure to everyone of the house," wrote Sir John Carr, a Devonshire gentleman who toured Ireland soon after the Union; and twenty years later, Sir Walter Scott found "perpetual kindness in the Irish cabin; buttermilk, potatoes, a stool is offered, or a stone is rolled that your honour may sit down . . . and those that beg everywhere else seem desirous to exercise hospitality in their own houses."

A young lady named Elizabeth Ham came to Ballina, County Mayo, when her father, a British Army officer, was stationed there in connection with the disturbed state of the country, following the rebellion of 1798. She was astonished to find that she could roam the wild mountains without fear of molestation, while in England no girl could ramble in the woods and fields alone, even though at this time Irishmen who had taken a part in the rebellion were being hanged by the English on Ballina bridge. She would, she wrote, "have fearlessly trusted" the Irish peasantry "in any circumstances." The intelligence of the people surprised her. "I never met a solitary peasant in my rambles but I addressed him, and by this means got stores of legendary lore. One man I remember told me the subjects of most of Ossian's poems in his own version of English."

Returning to England after five years she was "greatly struck by the vulgarity of everyone." Driving from Holyhead in a chaise, "we happened to stop opposite a cottage and . . . asked for a glass of water. It was brought . . . and the woman asked for payment. An Irish woman would have considered it an insult to be offered such. The cottages were clean and neat and the country looked clean in comparison but the manners seemed far inferior."

Irish dignity, Irish hospitality and the easy good manners

which still charm the modern traveller have an historical explanation. Three times, at least, the native aristocracy was conquered and dispossessed; many fled from Ireland to exile in France or Spain, but many others remained, to be forced down by poverty and penal legislation to the economic level of the peasantry.

Until the famine, it was by no means uncommon for poor peasants in mud cabins to make wills bequeathing estates which had long ago been confiscated from their forefathers, and that figure of fun in Victorian days, the Irish beggar who claimed to be descended from kings, was very often speaking the truth. "I am descended from perhaps as good a family as any I address, though now destitute of means" runs a letter imploring assistance in the Distress papers.

∽

There was, however, a darker and more sinister side to the Irish character. They are, said a land agent on the eve of the famine, "a very desperate people, with all this degree of courtesy, hospitality and cleverness amongst them."

To understand the Irish of the nineteenth century and their blend of courage and evasiveness, tenacity and inertia, loyalty and double-dealing, it is necessary to go back to the Penal Laws.

The Penal Laws, dating from 1695, and not repealed in their entirety until Catholic emancipation in 1829, aimed at the destruction of Catholicism in Ireland by a series of ferocious enactments, provoked by Irish support of the Stuarts after the Protestant William of Orange was invited to ascend the English throne in 1688, and England faced the greatest Catholic power in Europe—France. At this critical moment the Catholic Irish took up arms in support of the Stuarts. James II's standard was raised in Ireland, and he, with an Irish Catholic army, was defeated on Irish soil, at the battle of the Boyne, near Drogheda, on July 1, 1690.

The threat to England had been alarming, and vengeance followed. Irish intervention on behalf of the Stuarts was to be made impossible for ever by reducing the Catholic Irish to helpless impotence. They were, in the words of a contemporary, to become "insignificant slaves, fit for nothing but to hew wood and draw water," and to achieve this object the Penal Laws were devised.

In broad outline, they barred Catholics from the army and

navy, the law, commerce, and from every civic activity. No Catholic could vote, hold any office under the Crown, or purchase land, and Catholic estates were dismembered by an enactment directing that at the death of a Catholic owner his land was to be divided among all his sons, unless the eldest became a Protestant, when he would inherit the whole. Education was made almost impossible, since Catholics might not attend schools, nor keep schools, nor send their children to be educated abroad. The practice of the Catholic faith was proscribed; informing was encouraged as "an honourable service" and priest-hunting treated as a sport. Such were the main provisions of the Penal Code, described by Edmund Burke as "a machine as well fitted for the oppression, impoverishment and degradation of a people, and the debasement in them of human nature itself, as ever proceeded from the perverted ingenuity of man."

The material damage suffered through the Penal Laws was great; ruin was widespread, old families disappeared and old estates were broken up; but the most disastrous effects were moral. The Penal Laws brought lawlessness, dissimulation and revenge in their train, and the Irish character, above all the character of the peasantry, did become, in Burke's words, degraded and debased. The upper classes were able to leave the country and many middle-class merchants contrived, with guile, to survive, but the poor Catholic peasant bore the full hardship. His religion made him an outlaw; in the Irish House of Commons he was described as "the common enemy," and whatever was inflicted on him he must bear, for where could he look for redress? To his landlord? Almost invariably an alien conqueror. To the law? Not when every person connected with the law, from the jailer to the judge, was a Protestant who regarded him as "the common enemy."

In these conditions suspicion of the law, of the ministers of the law and of all established authority "worked into the very nerves and blood of the Irish peasant," and, since the law did not give him justice, he set up his own law. The secret societies which have been the curse of Ireland became widespread during the Penal period, and a succession of underground associations, Oak Boys, White Boys and Ribbon Men, gathering in bogs and lonely glens, flouted the law and dispensed a people's justice in the terrible form of revenge. The informer, the supplanter of an evicted tenant, the landlord's man, were punished with dreadful savagery, and since animals were wealth their unfortunate animals suffered, too. Cattle were "clifted," driven over the edge of a cliff, horses hamstrung, dogs clubbed to death, stables fired and the animals within burned alive. Nor were lawlessness, cruelty and revenge the only consequences. During the long Penal period, dissimulation became a moral necessity and evasion of the law the duty of every god-fearing Catholic. To worship according to his faith, the Catholic must attend illegal meetings; to protect his priest, he must be secret, cunning, and a concealer of the truth.

These were dangerous lessons for any government to compel its subjects to learn, and a dangerous habit of mind for any nation to acquire.

It is a curious contradiction, not very often remembered by England, that for many generations the private soldiers of the British Army were largely Irish; the Irish have natural endowments for war, courage, daring, love of excitement and conflict; Macaulay described Ireland as "an inexhaustible nursery of the finest soldiers."

Poverty and lack of opportunity at home made the soldier's shilling a day, and the chance of foreign service, attractive to the Irishman; and the armies of which England is proud, the troops which broke the power of Napoleon in the Peninsula and defeated him at Waterloo, which fought on the scorching plains of India, stormed the heights of the Alma in the Crimean campaign, and planted the British flag in every quarter of the globe in a hundred forgotten engagements. were largely, indeed in many cases mainly, Irish.

A hostile, lawless, oppressed and poverty-striken population in Ireland was already giving signs of future tragedy when a new development made catastrophe inevitable.

Between sixty and seventy years before the famine the population of Ireland began and continued to increase at a rate previously unknown in the history of Europe. Why this took place has yet to be fully explained. Demography, the science which deals with the statistics of birth, death and disease, is a relatively new science, and the waves of population growth, which from time to time pass over the world, are not yet fully understood. In the case of Ireland information is lacking; births were not compulsorily registered until 1863, and though the practice of taking a ten-yearly census began in 1821 the first figures considered reliable are those of 1841.

It is, however, agreed by all authorities that about the year 1780 the population of Ireland began to take an extraordinary upward leap. The increase between 1779 and 1841 has been placed at the almost incredible figure of 172 per cent.

During the same period a rapid increase also took place in the population of England and Wales. It is customary to ascribe this to the spread of industrialization, resulting in improved communications and more towns with better opportunities for social intercourse and early marriage, to a more general adoption of vaccination, with a consequent reduction of deaths from smallpox, and to some degree to improved cleanliness and medical care. More adults lived to old age, more babies were born and fewer died.

But this cannot apply to Ireland. Little can have been effected by medical care in a country which in 1841 possessed only 39 infirmaries, apart from hospitals for fever, venereal, ophthalmic and maternity patients, to serve a population officially calculated to have reached 8,200,000, and where the only medical aid available to the mass of the people was a limited number of dispensaries. Dublin had one dispensary to 6,286 people and Meath one to 6,545, but Down, Longford and Leitrim had only one to more than 20,000, and Mayo, which was not visited in 1841, five years previously had had a single dispensary for a population of 366,328.

Nor can the growth of towns and the improvement of communications have played much part in the bogs, the mountains and the lonely cabins of the West; yet Mayo, in Connaught, poorest and most remote of counties, had the largest rural population in Ireland. Moreover, the highest figure at which authorities estimate the increase in England and Wales is 88 per cent., almost half the increase—if 172 per cent. is correct—in backward, poverty-stricken Ireland.

Still, certain circumstances favourable to population increase were present in Ireland during this period. First, and most important, there was an abundant supply of incredibly cheap food, easily obtained, in the potato, and the standard of living of the time was such that a diet of potatoes was no great hardship. With the addition of milk or buttermilk potatoes form a scientifically satisfactory diet, as the physique of the pre-famine Irish proved. Arthur Young contrasted the Irishman's potato diet favourably with the contemporary English labourer's bread and cheese. The Irish, he wrote, "have a bellyful . . . I will not assert that potatoes are a better food than bread and cheese but I have no doubt of a bellyful of the one being much better than half a bellyful of the other."

Next, far from acting as a deterrent, the miserably low standards of Irish life encouraged young couples to marry early. No savings were necessary, no outlay was required; a cabin was erected for little or nothing in a few days, the young couple secured a scrap of land, owned a pot, perhaps a stool, not always a bed. Marriages were "daily contracted with the most reckless improvidence. Boys and girls marry literally without habitation or any means of support, trusting, as they say, to Providence as others have done before them." In fact, nothing was to be gained by waiting. Asked why the Irish married so young, the Catholic Bishop of Raphoe told the Irish Poor Enquiry of 1835: "They cannot be worse off than they are and . . . they may help each other." Women were chaste. Irish females, stated George Nicholls in his Report on Ireland, were "very correct in their conduct," and his own impressions were "highly favourable of their morals"—there was "no need to make provision for bastards." Girls married at sixteen, boys at seventeen or eighteen, and Irishwomen were exceptionally fertile; ". . . for twelve years 19 in 20 of them breed every second year. Vive la pomme de Terre!" wrote Arthur Young; and travellers in Ireland before the famine invariably comment on the troops of children to be found in every cabin. When the famine drove tens of thousands across the Atlantic, it was found that in the Irish immigrant slums of Boston, where infants under five years of age died at the rate of 61.66 per cent., the Irish nevertheless increased in numbers, because of their high birth-rate.

The Irish are fond of children, and family feeling is exceptionally strong. Moreover, in pre-famine Ireland children were a necessity. A Poor Law did not begin to operate until 1838, and then its provisions were limited; thus a man and woman's insurance against destitution in old age was their children.

There was too, barbarous and half-savage though conditions might be, one luxury enjoyed by the Irishman which

favoured the survival and rearing of children—his cabin
was usually well warmed by a turf fire. Ill-clothed though he
was, sleeping as he did on a mud floor, with his pig in the
corner, the Irish peasant did not have to endure cold, nor
did his children die of cold. They were warm, they were
abundantly fed—as long as the potato did not fail.

By 1841, when a census was taken, the population had
reached 8,175,124, and Disraeli declared that Ireland was
the most densely-populated country in Europe; on arable
land, he asserted, the population was denser than that of
China.

It seems possible, moreover, that the census figure may be
too low. Though the enumerators of 1841 were largely
members of the Irish Constabulary, superior to their predecessors and a "highly disciplined body of men," much time,
local knowledge and courage were needed to climb into the
wild mountain glens, to penetrate the bogs and track down
the communities of evicted and unemployed who existed in
caves, sod huts and under tree-roots. An intelligent relief officer wrote that the Census of 1841 was "pronounced universally to be no fair criterion of the present population." He
had tested it in Co. Clare and found the population to be
one third greater than had been recorded; therefore in 1845
when famine came the population might well have been above
nine millions.

For this closely-packed and rapidly-increasing people the
only outlet—with the exception of parts of Ulster—was the
land. Ireland had never been industrialized; such deposits of
coal and iron as she possessed were "unfortunately of more
significance to the geologist than the economist," and in 1845
the few industries she did possess were moribund. A remnant
of the famous Dublin poplin weavers worked fifteen hours a
day for about twelve shillings a week; in the once-prosperous woollen industry, production had fallen about fifty per
cent. in the last twenty years, and three-quarters of the
frieze, thick woolen cloth, worn by the peasantry, was
dumped by England. The fisheries of Ireland, too, were undeveloped, and in Galway and Mayo the herring fishermen
were too poor to buy salt with which to preserve a catch.

Even on the land, agricultural employment, as it was
understood in England, did not exist. Labourers were not
regularly employed on farms because Irish farms were too
small to require hired labour; over 93 per cent. consisted of

fewer than thirty acres. Ten years before the famine, the Poor Enquiry of 1835 stated that three-quarters of the labourers in Ireland existed without regular employment of any kind, and the economist, Nassau Senior, told the Government that for thirty weeks of the year, that is, for the whole of the year except when potatoes were being cultivated, 2,385,000 persons were without employment because there was absolutely no work to offer them. Unless an Irish labourer could get hold of a patch of land and grow potatoes on which to feed himself and his children, the family starved.

The consequence was the doom of Ireland. The land was divided and sub-divided, again and again, and holdings were split into smaller and still smaller fragments, until families were attempting to exist on plots of less than an acre, in some cases half an acre.

Farms had already been divided by middlemen and land-lords but the sub-division which preceded the famine was carried out by the people themselves, frequently against the landlord's will. As the population increased and the demand for a portion of ground grew more and more frantic, land became like gold in Ireland. Parents allowed their children to occupy a portion of their holdings because the alternative was to turn them out to starve; the children in turn allowed occupation by their children, and in a comparatively short time three, six, or even ten families were settled on land which could provide food only for one family.

The possession of a piece of land was literally the difference between life and death. "Ejectment," the House of Commons was told in April, 1846, "is tantamount to a sentence of death by slow torture." Turned off the land, evicted families wandered about begging, "miserable and turbulent." Since no employment existed they crowded the already swarming lanes and slums of the towns, lived in ditches by the roadside until, wasted by disease and hardship, "they die in a little time."

To turn out an occupier to this fate, whatever his arrears of rent or his irregularities of occupation, was to invite vengeance. On Lord Carrick's estate there was a covenant against sub-division, but it "could not be enforced for fear of outrage." The Devon Commission was told by a large land-owner that clauses against sub-division existed in most leases, but "to put them into operation is dangerous." Normally good-humoured and kind, where occupation of the land was in question the people became merciless. "I never knew them attack anyone for money," said a merchant in Tipperary, ". . . but touch the farm and turn them out and they get frantic and wild." Outrage was asserted to be the only protection of the poor; without it, said a small farmer, "landlords would hunt tenants out like rats from a cornstack"; and the Devon Commission reported, ". . . the one absorbing feeling as to the possession of land stifles all others and extinguishes the plainest principles of humanity."

In a number of districts, especially in the West, subdivision was aggravated by the system of joint tenancy known as "rundale." Land held in rundale was rented in common and divided up, so that each tenant, in what corresponded to a syndicate, received a portion of the different qualities of ground, good, bad and medium, that the property contained. Rundale, combined with sub-division, produced the merest fragments of land. One man, a tailor in Donegal, "had his land in forty-two different places and gave it up in despair." In County Mayo, the land valuator cited the case of the townland of Liscananawn, where about 167 acres of land, of three qualities, were divided into 330 portions, the 110 inhabitants having three portions each.

As a result of the desperate competition for land, rents in Ireland were enormously high, eighty per cent. to a hundred per cent. higher than in England. High rents were further encouraged by the practice, generally followed in Ireland, of letting land by advertising for "proposals" and disposing of it to the highest bidder. Only on the best-managed estates, generally those owned by large proprietors, were the character and record of the tenant taken into account. Lord Gormanston, for instance, had let land to a witness before the Devon Commission at four shillings an acre less than he was offered elsewhere. But where landlords were greedy or in debt, the people's anxiety to secure a piece of land, or the fear of losing land already occupied, was so great that offers went beyond its value. "If you ask the man why he bid so much for his farm, and more than he knew he could pay," wrote Mr. Campbell Foster of *The Times* in 1845, "his answer is, 'What could I do? Where was I to go? I know I cannot pay the rent but what could I do? Would you have me go and beg?' "

An immense and increasing number of people were too poor to make an offer to rent land, and this unfortunate class, mainly poor day-labourers, eked out an existence by means of a method of hiring land, called conacre.

Conacre was a contract by which the use of a portion of land was let, to grow one crop. Conacre was not a lease but a licence to occupy, and the relation of landlord and tenant was not created. Very small portions of land were let in conacre; in Tipperary, a quarter-acre was more common than half an acre; in Queen's County, it was reckoned that half an acre of conacre would support a labourer's family.

The owner of conacre ground manured the soil and prepared it for the reception of seed; the hirer provided the seed, planted it, and performed all subsequent operations. Rent was high; £10 or even £12 to £14 an acre on good ground, and about £6 on poor ground. But the Devon Commission did not consider conacre rents 'enormous', having regard to the crop which could be obtained in a normal season.

Demand for conacre was overwhelming; without it, said the O'Conor Don, one of the few representatives of the ancient pre-Norman Irish aristocracy, "the people would starve." But the system was not popular with landowners; the drawback was the difficulty of collecting the rent. Conacre hirers were almost invariably poor labourers, and the custom was for the rent of conacre ground to be paid after the crop was harvested. A labourer got permission to "throw up" a cabin somewhere, for which he paid in a certain number of days' work, and then took a portion of conacre. If the season was good, he derived a considerable profit; if the crop failed, he was ruined, a gambler, as a witness told the Devon Commission, playing for a stake he cannot pay. Yet on this precarious speculation the existence of the poorest Irish depended.

The 1841 census showed that sub-division of land had reached the point where 45 per cent. of holdings, taking Ireland as a whole, were of fewer than five acres; and since no holding under an acre was enumerated hundreds of thousands of patches were not taken into account. So accustomed had the people become to tiny holdings that, as the Devon Commission noted, when "consolidation," the throwing together of several small farms into a larger, more efficient unit, was discussed, the effect contemplated by witnesses was to produce farms no larger than fifteen, ten or even five acres; and Lord Stanley, called on to investigate complaints of excessive consolidation, found that a farm of 25 acres was looked on as a "monstrous grievance."

The whole of this structure, the minute subdivisions, the

closely-packed population existing at the lowest level, the high rents, the frantic competition for land, had been produced by the potato. The conditions of life in Ireland and the existence of the Irish people depended on the potato entirely and exclusively.

The potato, provided it did not fail, enabled great quantities of food to be produced at a trifling cost from a small plot of ground. Sub-division could never have taken place without the potato: an acre and a half would provide a family of five or six with food for twelve months, while to grow the equivalent grain required an acreage four to six times as large and some knowledge of tillage as well. Only a spade was needed for the primitive method of potato culture usually practised in Ireland. Trenches were dug and beds—called "lazy beds"—made; the potato sets were laid on the ground and earthed up from the trenches; when the shoots appeared, they were earthed up again. This method, regarded by the English with contempt, was in fact admirably suited to the moist soil of Ireland. The trenches provided drainage, and crops could be grown in wet ground, while cultivation by the spade enabled potatoes to be grown on mountain sides, where no plough could be used. As the population expanded, potatoes in lazy beds were pushed out into the bog and up the mountain, where no other cultivation would have been possible.

The potato was, moreover, the most universally useful of foods. Pigs, cattle and fowls could be reared on it, using the tubers which were too small for everyday use; it was simple to cook; it produced fine children; as a diet, it did not pall.

Yet it was the most dangerous of crops. It did not keep, nor could it be stored from one season to another. Thus every year the nearly two and a half million labourers who had no regular employment more or less starved in the summer, when the old potatoes were finished and the new had not come in. It was for this reason that June, July and August were called the "meal months": there was always the danger that potatoes would run out and meal would have to be eaten instead, the labourers would then have to buy it on credit, at exorbitant prices, from the petty dealer and usurer who was the scourge of the Irish village—the dreaded "Gombeen man."

More serious still, if the potato did fail, neither meal nor anything else could replace it. There could be no question of resorting to an equally cheap food, no such food existed, nor could potato cultivation be replaced, except after a long period, by the cultivation of any other food. "What hope is there for a nation that lives on potatoes!" wrote an English official.

Yet the British Government felt no apprehension about the potato crop. It was the problems arising from Ireland's perennial rebelliousness and from the swarming, poverty-stricken "surplus" population, as it was called, that absorbed the attention of Parliament, and when the exclusive dependence of the Irish on the potato was deplored it was on moral grounds, as proving the improvidence and lack of energy of the Irish people.

There were, however, voices crying in the wilderness, and contrary to the usual course of history the voices were official. The Devon Commission reported in 1845, on the eve of the famine, giving warning in grave terms of the dangerous state of Ireland. The report was dismissed on the grounds that it did not "contain anything of striking novelty" and "there was nothing in it that everyone did not know already," and a timid bill based on its recommendations giving Irish tenants a right to compensation for improvements in certain restricted circumstances was denounced as "a violation of the rights of property" and withdrawn. The Devon Commission moreover was only one of many. In the forty-five years since the Union no fewer than 114 Commissions and 61 Special Committees were instructed to report on the state of Ireland, and without exception their findings prophesied disaster; Ireland was on the verge of starvation, her population rapidly increasing, three-quarters of her labourers unemployed, housing conditions appalling and the standard of living unbelievably low.

True, an "Act for the more effectual relief of the Poor in Ireland," an Irish Poor Law Act, had been passed in 1838, but its object was not so much to mitigate the sufferings of the Irish poor as to prevent them from coming over into England. George Nicholls, who drafted it, admitted as much; the vast numbers of Irish, he wrote, who "crossed the Channel in search of the means of living . . . made it a matter of policy, as it assuredly was of humanity, to endeavour to improve their condition; and nothing seemed so equitable or so readily effective for the purpose as making property liable for the relief of the destitution in Ireland, as was the case in England —in other words establishing some kind of Poor Law."

In vain it was pointed out that the problems of poverty in England and Ireland were totally different, that the immense amount of destitution in Ireland would entail a gigantic expenditure if a poor law was to be effective. Workhouses for hundreds of thousands would have to be erected, and the annual cost would be at least five million pounds a year: there was no possibility of raising such a sum in Ireland.

The British Government's mind was made up. The property of Ireland must support the poverty of Ireland, and a menace to England be removed. George Nicholls was sent to Ireland for six weeks, his first acquaintance with the country; after that the opinion of "the most representative Irish that could be consulted" was set on one side and on July 31, 1838, the Irish Poor Law Act became law.

The British Government, however, concerned as it was with Irish disaffection, with the recent alarm of the Repeal agitation, and with religious differences—much of the last session of Parliament before the famine was spent in debating an increase in the grant to the Catholic seminary of Maynooth—continued to contemplate the condition of the Irish people with "imperturbable apathy."

Meanwhile, in 1844, a report was received that in North America a disease, hitherto unknown, had attacked the potato crop.

Chapter II

THE POTATO of the mid-nineteenth century, not yet even partially immunised against disease by scientific breeding, was singularly liable to failure.

Twenty-four failures of the potato crop were listed by the Census of Ireland Commissioners of 1851. In 1728 there had been "such a scarcity that on the 26th of February there was a great rising of the populace of Cork"; in 1739 the crop was "entirely destroyed"; in 1740 "entire failure" was reported; in 1770 the crop largely failed owing to curl; 1800 brought another "general" failure; in 1807 half the crop was lost through frost. In 1821 and 1822 the potato failed completely in Munster and Connaught; distress, "horrible beyond description," was reported in and near Skibbereen, and sub-

scriptions were raised for relief, £115,000 in London and
£18,000 in Dublin. 1830 and 1831 were years of failure in
Mayo, Donegal and Galway; in 1832, 1833, 1834 and 1836 a
large number of districts suffered serious loss from dry rot and
the curl; in 1835 the potato failed in Ulster, and 1836 and
1837 brought "extensive" failures throughout Ireland.

In 1839 failure was again universal throughout Ireland,
from Bantry Bay to Lough Swilly; famine conditions followed,
Government relief works were started and a Treasury grant
made. In 1841 the potato crop failed in many districts, and in
1844 the early crop was widely lost.

Thus the unreliability of the potato was an accepted fact in
Ireland, ranking with the vagaries of the weather, and in
1845 the possibility of yet another failure caused no particular alarm.

However, at the beginning of July of that year, the potato
crop promised remarkably well—the weather was then dry
and hot. The abrupt change which followed, extraordinary
even for the fickle climate of Ireland, brought for upwards of
three weeks "one continued gloom," with low temperatures
and "a succession of most chilling rains and some fog."
Nevertheless, at the end of July the crop was still exceptionally heavy, and on July 23 the *Freeman's Journal* reported
that "the poor man's property, the potato crop, was never
before so large and at the same time so abundant." There
was every sign of a year of plenty; old potatoes of excellent
quality were, "even at this advanced season," being sent in to
market, showing that ample stocks were still in hand, new
potatoes were already "coming in freely," and on July 25,
1845, *The Times,* printing favourable reports from all four
provinces of Ireland, announced that "an early and productive
harvest was everywhere expected."

The first disquieting news came from an unexpected quarter. At the beginning of August, Sir Robert Peel, the British
Prime Minister, received a letter from the Isle of Wight, as
famous for its market gardens as anywhere in the South of
England, reporting that disease had appeared in the potato
crop there.

Though the significance of the news was not realized, this
was the first recorded evidence that the "blight" which had
recently ravaged the potato crop in North America had
crossed the Atlantic.

The British Government was anxious not only for Ireland

but for England. During the previous fifty years potatoes had
assumed a dangerous importance in the diet of the English
labouring classes. Hard times, the blockade during the Napoleonic wars, the unemployment and wage-cutting, which
followed the declaration of peace after Waterloo, had been
gradually forcing the English labourer to eat potatoes in place
of bread, and on September 30, 1845, *The Times* reported
that in England the two main meals of a working man's day
now consisted of potatoes. Indeed, but for the intervention of
the blight, it is almost certain that the English labourer, however unwillingly, would have been driven to greater and greater dependence on the potato, and in due course suffered the
insecurity a potato diet brings.

Sir James Graham, the Home Secretary, circulated a letter
of inquiry about the crop, and on August 11 Mr. Parker, a
large grower and salesman, reported severe blight in Kent. The
previous Tuesday he had driven round Sandwich, Ash and
Wingham, to find the whole of the crop, early and late, including potatoes in the cottage gardens, "entirely destroyed."
On Thursday, at Maidstone and Gravesend, he found "fearful
destruction"; that evening he had found blight just appearing at East and West Ham, and next day he had seen it at
Leytonstone. It was understood, he added, that the situation
was the same in Holland and France. If the failure should
become general it would be "a shocking calamity for the
poor."

A failure would be serious enough for England, but for
Ireland it would be disaster, and Ireland loomed in every
mind, wretched, rebellious and utterly dependent on the potato. "Ireland, Ireland that cloud in the West, that coming
storm," wrote Gladstone to his wife that summer. As yet,
however, no disease was reported from Ireland, though the
weather had again become wet.

The leading horticultural paper in Great Britain was the
Gardeners' Chronicle and Horticultural Gazette, which owed
its influence and authority to the distinction of its editor, Dr.
John Lindley, the first professor of botany to be appointed in
the University of London and the man responsible for the
establishment of Kew Gardens as the headquarters of botanical science for the British Empire. On August 16 he printed,
without undue alarm, a report which described "a blight of
unusual character" in the Isle of Wight, and invited advice
from subscribers. Potato disease was familiar in England: it

had occurred, for instance, in East Kent in the previous autumn, and the news from the Isle of Wight caused no great apprehension. But a week later, on August 23, Dr. Lindley was telling his readers, in consternation: "A fearful malady has broken out among the potato crop. On all sides we hear of the destruction. In Belgium the fields are said to be completely desolated. There is hardly a sound sample in Covent Garden market . . . As for cure for this distemper, there is none . . . We are visited by a great calamity which we must bear."

It was now only a question of time before the blight spread to Ireland, and on September 13 Dr. Lindley held up publication of the *Gardeners' Chronicle* to make a dramatic announcement. "We stop the Press with very great regret to announce that the potato Murrain has unequivocally declared itself in Ireland. The crops about Dublin are suddenly perishing . . . where will Ireland be in the event of a universal potato rot?"

Nevertheless, through the next few weeks the British Government was optimistic. Very likely the failure would be local, as had often happened in the past; and the Home Secretary, who "repeatedly" requested information from Ireland, was receiving many favourable reports. These were explained later by the sporadic nature of the failure of 1845—"the country is like a checker-board," wrote a Government official, "black and white next door. Hence the contradictory reports." It was, too, the habitual policy of British governments to discount the veracity of news from Ireland: "there is such a tendency to exaggeration and inaccuracy in Irish reports that delay in acting on them is always desirable," wrote Sir Robert Peel on October 13, 1845. For the credit of British administration it was perhaps better not to admit that Ireland was as poverty-stricken and wretched as reports persistently affirmed.

However, the potato disease devastating Europe had undeniably appeared in Ireland. Now the question was, how far would it spread?

For the next week or two it was possible to hope. On September 25, 1845, Mr. Robert Murray, of the Provincial Bank of Ireland, in Dublin, wrote to Mr. Henry Goulburn, the Chancellor of the Exchequer, that the "alleged failure of the potato crop was very greatly exaggerated." A week before this a circular had been sent to all officers of the Irish Constabulary, directing that weekly reports be submitted on the state of the crop in their districts, and on the 28th Sir

James Graham, the Home Secretary, received "more satisfactory accounts of the potato crop in Ireland" and was
"willing now to hope that the failure, though extensive, is by
no means general." On October 6 he wrote again that the
accounts of the potato crops were more favourable than he
had ventured to expect, though "the recent terrible rains"
would do harm; and two days later he was still "sanguine in
my belief that the potato crop, tho' damaged, is not so much
below the average as some of the exaggerated reports from
Ireland have led us to apprehend."

A week later it was time for the potatoes to be taken out of
the ground. As soon as digging began disastrous reports
poured in.

Sir James Graham wrote to Sir Robert Peel, the Prime
Minister, in the utmost agitation. He had received information
of the most serious nature from the Lord-Lieutenant of Ireland, Lord Heytesbury, and it required the immediate attention of the Government. Alarming reports on the state of
the potato crop were being received in Dublin, and Lord
Heytesbury had warned the Government to be prepared for
the worst. Though, Graham added, he himself was still willing
to hope that present fears might be exaggerated, nevertheless,
"our Lord-Lieutenant . . . does not readily give credit to false
alarms." It was necessary to be prepared for famine in Ireland. And what substitute could be found for the potato,
the cheapest of all foods? Perhaps Indian corn [maize], but
that was an acquired taste. Should the ports be opened to free
trade in food? Should the duties be lifted on flour and oatmeal? What should be done? ·

On the same day Sir Robert Peel wrote to Graham that he,
too, had heard from Lord Heytesbury and that he found the
accounts "very alarming," though he again reminded Graham
that there was always a tendency to exaggeration in Irish
news. However, at an early period the Cabinet would have
"imposed" on them the necessity for adopting measures for
relief. It had been suggested that the export of food from
Ireland should be prohibited and that the distillation of spirits
from grain be made illegal, but he had no confidence in the
efficacy of these measures—"the removal of impediments to
import is the only effectual remedy."

The implications of that phrase were very nearly as alarming to Graham as the prospect of famine in Ireland. Removal
of impediments to import meant the removal of the duties on

foreign grain, the famous Corn Laws, which protected the price of United Kingdom home-grown grain. No issue was so violently controversial and so dangerous, politically, as the repeal of the Corn Laws.

Graham hastened to procrastinate and to soothe the Prime Minister. No steps need be taken yet, he wrote on October 15, since the truth about the potato crop could not fully be ascertained until digging was completed. He agreed, however, that to prohibit the export of food from Ireland would be an inadequate measure to meet the crisis.

Sir Robert Peel, on whom as Prime Minister the responsibility for Ireland would fall during the coming crisis, was a man of outstanding talents with considerable experience of Ireland—he had been Chief Secretary for six years.

During that period he had shown no liking for the Irish character, no sympathy with Irish aspirations; "cordially detested" Irish life, and had identified himself with the extreme Protestant party. Year after year he had opposed the motions for Catholic emancipation and for enquiry into the state of Ireland; he had also been largely responsible for a severe Coercion Act and had supported the revival of punishing clauses from the repealed Insurrection Act. The Duke of Leinster, premier nobleman of Ireland and head of the great Norman-Irish family of FitzGerald (called the "good family" in Ireland), recalled that Peel, when Chief Secretary for Ireland, frequently rose after dinner and, assuming the traditional attitude, "standing on his chair with one foot on the table," drank the Orange toast to "the pious, glorious and immortal memory of William III." These and similar activities led O'Connell to give him the nickname, by which he is still remembered in Ireland, of "Orange Peel."

Deliberate in manner, carefully and cautiously weighing his words and possessing a singularly chilly smile, "like the silver plate on a coffin," Peel did not readily inspire liking; he had, wrote Greville, "no popular or ingratiating qualities." But though Peel might be a man whom it was difficult to like, he was also a man whom it was impossible not to respect. His family and his friends loved him, he possessed consummate political skill, vigour and power in debate, and a supreme capacity for administration. Extreme conscientiousness and a sense of justice were his leading characteristics, and however little liking Peel might feel for the Irish people he could be relied upon never to allow his feelings to influence what he considered to be his duty towards Ireland.

The passage of time had somewhat softened Peel's attitude on Irish questions; it was nearly thirty years since he had drunk the Orange toast, and recently he had been responsible for measures of conciliation; he had appointed the Devon Commission in 1843, he trebled the annual grant to the Catholic seminary of Maynooth, and he established non-sectarian "Queen's Colleges" in three Irish towns.

Sir James Graham, the Home Secretary, was already distrusted in Ireland for his part in the eleventh-hour suppression of the monster meeting at Clontarf and for the subsequent arrest and trial of Daniel O'Connell. Head of an old north-country family, tall, handsome and supercilious, he also possessed personal integrity and a capacity for business, and showed an invaluable attention to detail. He was Peel's closest colleague and had been in office as Secretary of State for Home Affairs, and consequently responsible for the administration of Ireland, since 1841.

❧

As digging of the potato crop progressed the news from Ireland grew steadily worse, and the Constabulary Reports of October 15 were the gloomiest yet forwarded. In Antrim, the failure was more serious than at first supposed; Armagh had hardly a sound potato; in the South, Bantry and Clonakilty reported great failure; in Bandon and Kinsale disease was extending, while in the fertile midlands and Kildare blight had appeared. In Wicklow potatoes grown between the sea and the mountains, where the clouds broke on the mountains in rain, were diseased to an alarming extent. In Monaghan, Tyrone and several other counties it was reported that "potatoes bought a few days ago, seemingly remarkably good, have rotted."

The soundness of the potato when first dug was responsible for bewildering contradictions. Optimists, delighted to witness the digging of what seemed a splendid crop, hastened to send off glowing accounts. Lord Heytesbury received one such report, on October 17, from the Dean of Ossory, though in forwarding it he wrote he "must observe that the Dean tho' a sensible is a somewhat sanguine man."

In almost every case, hope was short-lived. Within a few days the fine-looking tubers had become a stinking mass of corruption, and growers began to flood the market with potatoes, anxious to get rid of them before the rot set in.

For some years Peel had been on friendly terms with Dr. Lyon Playfair, a scientist and chemist of considerable reputation, and on October 18 he was staying at Peel's country house. Dr. Playfair had studied chemistry under the great Liebig, but was perhaps more successful as a courtier than as a scientist. He had conducted scientific experiments before Queen Victoria and was a noted sitter on Parliamentary enquiries and Royal Commissions. Subsequently he became a gentleman usher in Prince Albert's household and was, finally, elevated to the peerage as the first Baron Playfair of St. Andrews.

He now advanced a theory that potatoes which were apparently sound, or almost sound, when dug could be given a chemical treatment to prevent them from rotting: "it might be possible to mitigate the evil of the potato disease by some chemical application and by the issue of plain, practical instructions for the treatment of those potatoes which are not at all, or only partially, affected by the disease."

Peel decided to set up a Scientific Commission in Ireland to investigate what science could do to save the potato. Dr. Lindley agreed to serve with Playfair, and they crossed immediately to Dublin. By October 24 the Lord-Lieutenant, Lord Heytesbury, was reporting that "the two professors" were already "earnestly employed." Indeed, that very day, as a proof of "unremitting attention," the first of six long documents was addressed to Lord Heytesbury. In addition, Peel arranged for the co-operation and assistance of an Irish Catholic scientist of eminence, Professor Robert Kane, knighted in 1846, who was already making an investigation of the potato disease on behalf of the Royal Agricultural Improvement Society for Ireland and had recently published an important book, *The Industrial Resources of Ireland*. Kane was to supply local knowledge and information, and it was hoped that, since neither Lindley nor Playfair had any previous connection with Ireland, they would be able to form "a dispassionate judgment as to the real character and extent of the evil to be apprehended."

No deliberation was necessary. The briefest possible enquiry was sufficient for the professors to become alarmed, and after two days Playfair wrote to Peel that "the account is melancholy and it cannot be looked upon in other than a most serious light. We are confident that the accounts are under-rated rather than exaggerated. . .I am sorry to give you so desponding a letter, but we cannot conceal from ourselves that the case is much worse than the public supposes."

All too soon the Scientific Commissioners were estimating that half the potato crop of Ireland had either been already destroyed or would shortly perish; thus to find a method of preventing potatoes sound when dug from rotting was of over-whelming importance. A number of suggestions were now put forward by the Commissioners. Advanced in all good faith, these recommendations were the first evidence of that fatal ignorance of conditions in Ireland which was to be responsible for a large part of the suffering in the famine years.

The traditional Irish method was to store potatoes in a pit; to dig a pit was simple, and in it the tubers were to some extent protected from frost and rain. In the Commissioners' "Advice concerning the Potato crop to the Farmers and Peasantry of Ireland" the peasant was instructed to dry his potatoes in the sun, then to "mark out on the ground a space six feet wide and as long as you please. Dig a shallow trench two feet wide all round, and throw the mould upon the space, then level it and cover it with a floor of turf sods set on their edges." On this was to be sifted "packing stuff," made by "mixing a barrel of freshly burnt unslacked lime, broken into pieces as large as marbles, with two barrels of sand or earth, or by mixing equal parts of burnt turf and dry sawdust."

There followed instructions so complicated that the "in-defatigable trio of potato Commissioners," as the *The Times* called them, appear to have had some doubts as to their in-telligibility, for they concluded, "If you do not understand this, ask your landlord or clergyman to explain its meaning."

To deal with diseased potatoes, the Irish peasant was to provide himself with a rasp or grater, a linen cloth, a hair sieve or a cloth strainer, a pail or tub or two for water, and a griddle. He was then to rasp the bad potatoes, very finely, into one of the tubs, wash the pulp, strain, repeat the pro-cess, then dry the pulp on the griddle, over a slack fire. In the water used for washing the pulp would be found a milky substance, which was starch. Good, wholesome bread could be made by mixing the starch with dried potato pulp, peas-meal, bean-meal, oatmeal or flour. "There will be of course," wrote the Commissioners, "a good deal of trouble in doing all we have recommended, and perhaps you will not succeed very well at first; but we are confident all true Irishmen will exert themselves, and never let it be said that in Ireland the inhabitants wanted courage to meet difficulties against which other nations are successfully struggling."

Seventy thousand copies of these well-meant suggestions were printed by the Government and circulated to local agricultural committees, to newspapers, and to parish priests, who received thirty copies each.

This was only a beginning. For between October 26 and November 12 the "untiring industry" of the Commissioners produced, in rapid succession, what *The Times* called "four monster reports," as well as two statements dated from the Royal Dublin Society and addressed to the Lord-Lieutenant. Of these Graham wrote to Peel, on November 8, that it was "difficult to extract much that is useful from Playfair's letters."

Four days later, having been in Ireland something less than three weeks, the men of science returned to London.

Meanwhile, in Ireland, the possibility of making use of diseased potatoes was being anxiously explored, and confusion arose about starch. In the *Nation* a correspondent stated that as much as twenty to twenty-one pounds of starch might be extracted from every hundred pounds of diseased potatoes, and this could be used, mixed with flour, for pies, puddings and "farinaceous spoon meat"; at the same time the *Freeman's Journal* urged that a machine for extracting starch on a large scale be installed in every workhouse.

Unhappily, the Commissioners were obliged to point out that "starch is not the material which serves for the support of the human frame, and an animal fed merely on starch dies of starvation nearly, if not quite as soon, as if totally deprived of food."

Perhaps, then, the good and bad parts of a partially blighted potato could be used separately? Sir John Murray, at any rate, printed in the *Nation* a recipe he claimed to have tested: "cut off diseased parts and steam or boil into a mash with bran and salt. When warm [it] is nourishing for pigs and cattle but tainted potatoes cold are apt to disagree." Other correspondents' proposals directed that the potatoes should be cut up in slices and soaked in bog water, or dried out in ovens, or spread with lime and salt, or treated with chlorine gas, which was to be manufactured by the Irish cottiers themselves mixing vitriol, manganese dioxide and salt, thus embarking on the domestic manufacture of poison gas.

Common sense was forgotten. One suggestion called for the baking of diseased potatoes, presumably in primitive Irish cabins, for 18 to 22 minutes at a temperature of 180 degrees Fahrenheit. When "blackish matter" with a foul smell oozed out, the potatoes would, it was claimed, then turn white, and could be peeled.

All specifics, all nostrums were useless. Whether ventilated, desiccated, salted, or gassed, the potatoes melted into a slimy, decaying mass; and pits, on being opened, were found to be filled with diseased potatoes—"six months' provisions a mass of rottenness." Alarm turned to terror.

Where did the rot come from, people asked fearfully? Did it fall from the sky in rain, did it drop from the clouds, did it rise from the ground? Had the soil itself become infected?

Wild suggestions were advanced. Had the potatoes become blighted by "static electricity," generated in the atmosphere by the puffs of smoke and steam issuing from the hundreds of locomotives that had just come into use? Or was the disease caused by "mortiferous vapours" rising from "blind volcanoes" in the interior of the earth? Another school of thought blamed guano manure, consisting of the droppings of sea fowl, which had recently become fashionable. From County Clare came a new theory: a field was partly covered with clothes laid out to dry, and the covered portion escaped the blight—"this," reported the *Nation,* "proves that the blow came from the air."

The opinion of Dr. Lindley himself was that the potatoes had contracted a kind of dropsy. Through the extraordinary dampness of the weather they had become laden with water they could not absorb, and "wet putrefaction" had set in. Torrential rain was commonly blamed. It is the "general opinion," wrote Lord Heytesbury, that "the season had been so ungenial and the absence of sunshine so remarkable during the last two months that the potatoes have imperfectly ripened."

At the end of October urgent warnings began to reach the Government. Lord Monteagle, one of the most enlightened Irish landowners and a man of importance—he had been Chancellor of the Exchequer from 1835 to 1839—told Sir Robert Peel on October 24 that he did not "recollect any former example of a calamitous failure being anything near so great and alarming as the present. . . I know not how the peasantry will get through the winter in very many cases."

Another ominous warning came from Coleraine. The condition of the potato crop throughout the whole country was "deplorable," wrote the medical officer to the Coleraine workhouse on October 15. "Nothing else is heard of, nothing else is spoken of. . .Famine must be looked forward to and there will follow, as a natural consequence, as in former years, typhus fever, or some other malignant pestilence."

On November 5 the Under-Secretary at Dublin Castle was warned by Lord Clare that he would not "answer for the consequences" if a famine occurred. "The farmers with a good supply of corn and high prices will struggle through the year; but what will you do with the unemployed multitude whose store of provisions for the next ten months is gone and who have not a shilling to purchase food. . .the thousands of the occupiers of conacre land in wild and remote districts, how are they to exist until August 1846?"

Suggestions for adding to the available food supply included one for reducing the amount of corn given daily to Government horses: if the 12,000 police and army horses in Ireland were given five instead of ten pounds of corn daily, an extra 60,000 pounds a day would be available to feed the people. More far-reaching was a suggestion made by the Duke of Norfolk, that in place of the potato the Irish should learn to consume curry powder, on which, mixed with water, he appeared to believe the population of India was nourished.

Meanwhile, apart from the appointment of the "men of science," the Government had taken no steps, and on October 28 a meeting was called by a committee of the Dublin Corporation, under the chairmanship of the Lord Mayor. Three days later a meeting of citizens was called, which appointed a committee presided over by the Duke of Leinster. As a result on Novermber 3 a deputation of the highest respectability waited on the Lord-Lieutenant, Lord Heytesbury, to urge him to adopt measures "to avert calamity." The deputation included the Duke of Leinster, Daniel O'Connell, Lord Cloncurry, the Lord Mayor of Dublin, Henry Grattan, son of the famous patriot, Sir J. Murray, John Augustus O'Neill and some twenty others. The proposals, drawn up by O'Connell, called for the immediate stoppage of the export of corn and provisions and for the prohibition of distilling and brewing from grain; the ports should be thrown open for the free import of food and rice and Indian corn imported from the colonies; relief machinery must be set up in every county, stores of food established, and employment provided on works of public utility. It was proposed that the cost be met by a tax of ten per cent. on the rental of resident landlords and from twenty to fifty per cent. on that of absentees. In addition, a loan of £1,500,000 should be raised on the security of the proceeds of Irish woods and forests.

The Lord-Lieutenant received the deputation "very coldly" and read aloud a prepared reply. Reports on the potato crop varied and at times contradicted each other, and it was impossible to form an accurate opinion of the extent of the failure until digging was completed. The proposals submitted by the deputation would at once be placed before the Government, but the greater part of them required new legislation, and all must be "maturely weighed." As soon as Lord Heytesbury "had concluded reading he began bowing the deputation out."

Next day the *Freeman's Journal* denounced the Government in a furious leading article: "They may starve! Such in spirit, if not in words, was the reply given yesterday by the English Viceroy to . . . the deputation which . . . prayed that the food of this kingdom be preserved, lest the people thereof perish."

In fact, Peel had arrived at a momentous decision. To compensate for the failure the millions of Irish who had lived on potatoes must be fed on grain; to accomplish this, grain must be freely imported, and therefore the Corn Laws must be repealed.

The decision was not sudden but the result of long deliberation. Though famine in Ireland provided the immediate cause, Peel had been painfully moving for more than four years towards the conviction that he no longer believed in protection for British agriculture, and that the Corn Laws must be removed. He was well aware that to advocate Corn Law repeal meant almost certain political ruin—his old friend and supporter, the Duke of Buckingham, had gone to the length of resigning from the Cabinet in 1842 on a mild modification of the Corn Laws being proposed. Now, as the news from Ireland grew steadily worse, Peel suffered mental torture. "I never witnessed in any case such agony," wrote the Duke of Wellington. By October 15 Peel's decision had been made. "The remedy," he wrote, "is the removal of all impediments to the import of all kinds of human food—that is, the total and absolute repeal for ever of all duties on all articles of subsistence." And to inform the Cabinet of this most serious decision he summoned an emergency meeting for October 31.

∾

The entanglement of the Irish famine with the repeal of the Corn Laws was a major misfortune for Ireland. Short of civil war, no issue in English history has provoked such passion as Corn Law repeal. As a consequence of Peel's decision the country was split in two, and the controversy was conducted with frightful acrimony and party bitterness. The potato failure was eclipsed by the burning domestic issue of Corn Law repeal. The Irish famine slipped into the background.

In the simplest terms the purpose of the Corn Laws was to keep up the price of home-grown grain. Duties on imported grain guaranteed English farmers a minimum and profitable price, and the burden of a higher price for bread was borne by the labouring classes, in particular by the millions of factory workers and operatives toiling in the great new industrial cities.

It was asserted that if the Corn Laws were repealed all classes connected with the land would be ruined and the traditional social structure of the country destroyed, and in "the rising wrath of Tories and landlords" all interest in Ireland was submerged.

More unfortunate still, because the potato failure in Ireland provided an urgent reason for pressing forward with Corn Law repeal, the opponents of repeal denied that any failure had taken place, "except to a very partial extent," and famine in Ireland became a Party question. The Tory Mayor of Liverpool refused to call a meeting for the relief of Irish distress, the Mansion House Committee in Dublin was accused of "deluding the public with a false alarm," and the blight itself "was represented as the invention of agitators on the other side of the water." "To profess belief in the fact of the existence of a formidable potato blight," wrote Mr. Isaac Butt, Q.C., "was as sure a method of being branded as a radical as to propose to destroy the Church."

Peel's position was painful. He was leader of the Conservative Party, the Protectionist party, and he was aware that for him to propose repeal would be considered gross and shameful treachery.

The emergency meeting of the Cabinet summoned by him took place on October 31, and immediately it began "very serious differences of opinion" became evident. The first day was occupied in reading aloud memoranda and reports from Ireland on the potato failure; next day the Prime Minister proposed that a relief commission should be set up in Ireland, employment on drainage increased, and a sum of money advanced to the Lord-Lieutenant to buy food for destitute districts. These proposals were readily approved; indeed, they were standard measures which had already been adopted in previous periods of famine in Ireland.

But, as Peel went on to point out, these measures required an advance of public money, and the first sum voted for the purchase of food to be issued to destitute districts must unavoidably open the whole question of the Corn Laws. "Can we vote public money for the sustenance of any considerable portion of the people on account of actual or apprehended scarcity and maintain in full operation the existing restrictions on the free import of grain? . . . I am bound to say," declared Peel, "my impression is we cannot."

The crucial point had been reached, the issue of Corn Law repeal was out in the open, and the Cabinet split, with an overwhelming majority against Peel. To reach a decision proved impossible, and the Cabinet adjourned until November 6.

On that day Peel laid proposals before the Cabinet for the immediate relaxation of the Corn Law duties and the modification of the Corn Laws themselves in a bill to be brought forward after Christmas. He was once more defeated, being supported by only three of his fourteen Cabinet Ministers. Nevertheless, he determined not to resign on the spot: time should be allowed for reflection. The Cabinet was once more adjourned.

On November 15 Dr. Lindley and Dr. Playfair issued their official report. They had visited Louth, Meath, Westmeath, part of Kildare, and the districts round Dublin and Drogheda, some of the most fertile country in Ireland, and had examined official reports and returns at Dublin Castle. "Judging from the evidence thus collected . . . we can come to no other conclusion than that one half of the actual potato crop of Ireland is either destroyed or . . . unfit for the food

of man. We, moreover, feel it our duty to apprise you that
we fear this to be a low estimate . . . We would now add,
melancholy as this picture is . . . that in all probability the
late rainy weather has rendered the mischief yet greater."

When the Cabinet met again, on November 25, its attitude
had modified, and after a further meeting, on December 2,
Peel was "not without hopes that there will be general con-
currence."

His hopes were not realized. After further discussion at
Cabinets held on December 4 and 5, twelve out of his four-
teen Cabinet Ministers, including the Duke of Wellington,
were "reluctantly" persuaded to agree with him, but two
Ministers of immense influence and importance stood out.
Neither Lord Stanley nor the Duke of Buccleuch would sup-
port "a measure involving the ultimate repeal of the Corn
Laws."

Peel decided he must resign. Without the support of Lord
Stanley and the Duke of Buccleuch he thought it "very doubtful" whether he could carry Corn Law repeal "to a successful
issue," and on December 5 he "repaired to Osborne in the
Isle of Wight" and tendered his resignation to Queen Victoria.

According to custom, the Queen then sent for the Leader
of the Opposition, and requested him to form a government.
The Party in opposition, the Whig Party, was led by Lord
John Russell, who was pledged to Corn Law repeal; but after
ten days' suspense, negotiation and intense excitement, known
as "the famous ten days," Lord John, on December 20, wrote
to the Queen, to state that he had found it impossible to
form an administration. Great political difficulties, he wrote,
lay before a government "prepared to attempt the settlement
of the Corn Laws," and the formation of a Cabinet had
proved impossible because Lord Grey refused to take office
if the headstrong and high-handed Lord Palmerston were
made Foreign Secretary.

What Disraeli described as "the poisoned chalice" was now
handed back to Peel, who was summoned again by the Queen.
"On entering the room," wrote Peel, "Her Majesty said to
me very graciously, 'So far from taking leave of you, Sir
Robert, I must require you to withdraw your resignation
and remain in my service'."

So Peel was Prime Minister once more, but in a situation
of unexampled difficulty and complexity. Leader of the Tories,

he was now to carry Corn Law repeal against a majority of his Party and in the midst of "such a storm of rage and hatred as no other Minister was ever exposed to." He was accused of apostasy, of turning his coat for his own ends; his conduct was christened the "Great Betrayal," and Lord Alvanley declared he should not be allowed to die a natural death.

His support must come from the Opposition, but that support would be unwilling and resentful, since the Whigs considered Corn Law repeal their measure, and Peel had filched it from them. It was a further complication that between Peel and Lord John Russell the Whig leader a "mutual antipathy" existed.

Nevertheless, Peel took up office again, with feelings of satisfaction. "I resume power," he wrote to Princess Lieven on December 26, 1845. ". . . I feel like a man restored to life after his funeral service has been preached."

In common with the rest of the Conservatives, however, the Duke of Wellington, Peel's intimate friend and the pillar of the Tories, found the situation unpalatable. "Rotten potatoes have done it all," he grumbled to Greville, "they put Peel in his d—d fright."

Chapter III

SOME WEEKS before these dramatic events Peel had taken a bold step. On November 9 or 10—"some days after the Cabinet meeting November 6"—he had ordered, acting on his own responsibility and without waiting for Treasury sanction, £100,000 to be spent on Indian corn (maize), to be purchased in the United States and shipped to Ireland.

It was a step which could only have been taken by a Minister exercising Peel's authority. With the single exception of Corn Law repeal, his "mastery" over his cabinet was said to be complete; he had "got them as obedient and well trained as the crew of a man of war." His purchase of Indian corn proved the decisive factor in relieving the distress of 1845-46, but the subsequent value to Ireland of Peel's boldness, independence and strength of mind was unfortunately outweighed by his belief in an economic theory which almost every politician of the day, Whig or Tory, held with religious fervour.

This theory, usually termed *laissez faire*, let people do as they think best, insisted that in the economic sphere individuals should be allowed to pursue their own interests and asserted that the Government should interfere as little as possible. Not only were the rights of property sacred; private enterprise was revered and respected and given almost complete liberty, and on this theory, which incidentally gave the employer and the landlord freedom to exploit his fellow men, the prosperity of nineteenth-century England had unquestionably been based.

The influence of *laissez faire* on the treatment of Ireland during the famine is impossible to exaggerate. Almost without exception the high officials and politicians responsible for Ireland were fervent believers in non-interference by Government, and the behaviour of the British authorities only becomes explicable when their fanatical belief in private enterprise and their suspicions of any action which might be considered Government intervention are borne in mind.

The loss of the potato crop was therefore to be made good, without Government interference, by the operations of private enterprise and private firms, using the normal channels of commerce. The Government was not to appear in food markets as a buyer, there was to be "no disturbance of the ordinary course of trade" and "no complaints from private traders" on account of Government competition.

The flaw in the plan was the undeveloped state of the food and provision trade in a great part of Ireland. Large numbers of people, especially in the west and south-west, hardly purchased food at all; they grew potatoes and lived on them. Shops and organizations for importing foodstuffs and distributing them on the English model were generally found only in more prosperous districts in north-east Ulster, Dublin, some places in Eastern Ireland, and the larger towns, like Cork. Where relief would be most needed, the means by which it was to be supplied seldom existed.

Peel's plan, nevertheless, was far-seeing and ingenious. He intended to use the Indian corn he had bought as a weapon to keep prices down. It was to be held in reserve, controlled by Government, and a supply "thrown in" whenever prices rose unreasonably. At no time did he contemplate attempting to feed on Indian corn all those who had lost their potatoes; that loss has been estimated by a modern authori y at a value in money of £3,500,000, and £100,000 of Indian corn could not conceivably replace it.

Indian corn was purchased because doing so did not interfere with private enterprise. No trade in Indian corn existed: it was virtually unknown as a food in Ireland or any other part of the United Kingdom and was neither imported nor bought and sold. No complaints of Government interference could therefore be made "in a trade which did not exist, nor could prices be raised . . . on an article of which no stock was to be found in the home market." Moreover, it had the immense advantage of being cheap, one of the cheapest foods on which a human being could keep alive.

The possibility that a situation would arise in which no food of any kind was offered, at prices extortionate or otherwise, and that the Government's Indian corn would become the only food available was not foreseen, even by Peel.

Placing the order caused some misgiving. How was the purchase to be made? Would not "doubts and apprehensions" arise in the minds of merchants if the Government appeared "as a purchaser in a new field of operations?" Would not prices rise instantly if the Government were known to be the buyer?

At this date the only Government department which had experience of buying food on a large scale was the Commissariat department, which supplied food for the British Army; and Sir Randolph Routh, senior officer in that department, was consulted. He had served in Canada and married there, and since the purchases were to be made in the United States he suggested that his brother-in-law, a merchant in Quebec, should be employed and, to "avoid all appearance of interference by Government," buy in his own name. But the Commissariat department was not highly regarded, and Sir Randolph was snubbed. The Chancellor of the Exchequer wrote, on November 11, that Routh's brother-in-law, though "doubtless respectable," was "hardly likely to be a first-class merchant," and suggested that the great mercantile house of Baring Brothers, with its international organization, should be employed.

For its part the Treasury pressed for official purchasing: a representative should be sent to New York, "to buy under Treasury rules. Any increase in price would be counterbalanced by the advantage of adhering to official rules."

Treasury advice, however, was not followed. Mr. Thomas
Baring was consulted, and on November 15 he submitted a
plan. Baring Brothers had a confidential agent in Boston, Mr.
Thomas Ward, "in whose discretion and management we have
the greatest confidence." Mr. Ward would distribute orders
throughout the United States, so that no unnecessary rise in
prices would result and it would not be known "who are the
real buyers and for what purpose the purchase is being made."
The scheme was accepted and the choice proved admirable.
A complicated series of transactions was carried through
without any leakage of information; "Economy is desirable
but secrecy is essential," wrote Mr. Ward to Baring Brothers'
representative in New Orleans; and on December 30 Mr.
Thomas Baring assured the Treasury, "No one in our counting
house has been entrusted with any particulars, except my
partner and myself, and, what is perhaps of more importance,
no one in the United States, except those to whom the
execution of the order has been confided."

So well was the secret kept that when the first cargoes
from America arrived "they had been more than a fortnight
in Cork Harbour before it became generally known that such
a measure was in progress."

Baring Brothers were not only efficient but public-spirited.
Regarding the execution of the transactions as the fulfilment
of a duty, they declined any commission on purchases which
had employed their organization for more than six months.

While this operation was being carried out the Relief Commission for Ireland, approved before the Cabinet split on Corn
Law repeal, had been appointed, and it held its first meeting
on November 20. The members mainly consisted of the senior
members of those departments of the Irish Government concerned, Sir James Dombrain, Inspector-General of the Coastguard service, who had already served on Irish famine relief
in 1836-39; Colonel Harry Jones, a distinguished English
officer of the Royal Engineers, who had been appointed
Chairman of the Board of Works, Ireland, a few weeks before,
and knew Ireland well; Mr. Twisleton, the resident Irish
Poor Law Commissioner, and Colonel McGregor, Inspector-
General of the Constabulary. The Chairman, Mr. Edward
Lucas, had been Under-Secretary at Dublin Casde, and the

Secretary was the able and enlightened John Pitt Kennedy, who had successfully managed properties in Donegal and Tyrone and been Secretary of the Devon Commission. At Peel's request, Professor later Sir Robert Kane was added. "He is an Irishman, a Roman Catholic, and we have not one on the Commission," wrote Peel to Graham on November 9. "He has gained some practical knowledge from having served on other Commissions . . . he has written on the industrial resources of Ireland. But, mainly, he is a Roman Catholic."

The leading member of the Commission was Sir Randolph Routh, of the Commissariat department of the British Army, whose brother-in-law had been rejected as Government buyer in North America; it was Sir Randolph Routh's duty to distribute the Indian corn.

There was much to be said in favour of putting Routh in charge, for he possessed "more extensive experience than any other person . . . of feeding large bodies of people in sudden emergencies." He had served throughout the Peninsular campaign and been senior Commissariat officer at Waterloo. Transferred to Canada, he had achieved unusual success, been appointed a member of the executive council and, finally, knighted for his services in the Canadian rebellion of 1837-38. He was, moreover, recommended as being "remarkable for the invariable quality of acting cheerfully and cordially with those with whom it is his duty to act."

Yet his appointment had drawbacks. During the period of severe military economy which followed Waterloo, the Commissariat had been cut to the bone, and the efficiency of the department impaired; within nine years it would be largely responsible for the disaster which destroyed the British Army in the Crimea. It was another drawback that Commissariat officers were regarded as inferior by other officers of the army. Though their work was with the army, it was administered by the Treasury; supply was considered to be merely a business of accounts and bills, which could be performed by any clerk. The Commissariat was thus a civilian department of clerks, responsible to the Treasury, and not of soldiers, responsible to the War Office. Every Commissariat officer received a commission from the War Office and what was termed a "constitution" from the Treasury; this inconsistency was not corrected until 1855.

Routh, in fact, had been trained to cheesepare, to save a

farthing wherever a farthing could be saved; nor in dealing
with his superiors was he likely to make a stand for any
opinion of his own, especially as he was answerable to the
rigid and all-powerful department of the Treasury.

All expenditure required Treasury sanction: the money to
be spent on famine relief, the expenses of the Relief Commission, the grants for Poor Law, for public works, for
medical services; and at the Treasury, standing guard over
the British nations' money-bags, was the formidable figure of
Charles Edward Trevelyan.

The official title of Trevelyan was Assistant Secretary, but
he was in fact the permanent head of the Treasury, and
owing to his remarkable abilities and the structure of British
administration, which results in a capable, permanent official
exercising a high degree of power, he was able to influence
policy to a remarkable extent.

Trevelyan was by far the ablest man concerned with Irish
relief and, unaffected by changes of government and policy,
he remained a dominant figure throughout the famine years.
He had been brought up in what was known as the "Clapham
Sect," not a religious body but a number of highly-cultivated
families (including the Wilberforces and the Thorntons of
Battersea Rise) who lived round Clapham Common and were
distinguished for their philanthropic and evangelical views.
Trevelyan, who was of rigid integrity, delighted in reading
chapters of the Bible aloud in a "deep sonorous voice."
At the outset of his career, when he was no more than
twenty-one, in India, he risked his future by publicly denouncing his superior, a very powerful and popular man, for taking
bribes. "A perfect storm was raised against the accuser,"
wrote Macaulay, who was in India at the time and knew
Trevelyan well. "He was almost everywhere abused and very
generally cut. But, with a firmness and ability scarcely ever
seen in a man so young, he brought his proofs forward, and,
after an inquiry of some weeks, fully made out his case." His
superior was dismissed with ignominy and Trevelyan himself
applauded "in the highest terms," though Lord William Bentinck, Governor-General of India, remarked, "That man is
almost always on the right side in every question; and it is
well that he is so, for he gives a most confounded deal of
trouble when he happens to take the wrong one."

Seven years later Trevelyan married Macaulay's idolized
sister, Hannah, in India. At the time of the marriage Macau-

lay, who was greatly attached to Trevelyan, wrote: "He has no small talk. His mind is full of schemes of moral and political improvement, and his zeal boils over in his talk. His topics, even in courtship, are steam navigation, the education of the natives, the equalization of the sugar duties, the substitution of the Roman for the Arabic alphabet in Oriental languages." His temper was pronounced "very sweet," his religious feelings ardent, but he was rash and uncompromising in public affairs, and his manner was blunt, almost to roughness, and at other times awkward.

Trevelyan was proud of being a man of family, "one of the best and oldest families in England"; the Trevelyans originated in Cornwall, a few miles from Fowey, and the name of the family is recorded as far back as the reign of Henry III. He described himself as being a Celt, "belonging to the class of Reformed Cornish Celts, who by long habits of intercourse with the Anglo-Saxons have learned at last to be practical men."

At the time of the famine Trevelyan was thirty-eight, at the height of his powers, immensely conscientious, and with an obsession for work. Though his integrity was absolute and he had a strong sense of justice, yet he was not the right man to undertake Ireland. He disapproved of the Irish; the cast of his mind, his good qualities, were such as to make him impatient with the Irish character, and some slight family difficulties may have intensified his feelings. His cousin, Alfred Trevelyan, married the daughter of Mr. Boyse, "a respectable solicitor of Limerick," and soon she was left a widow, with an infant son in whose welfare Trevelyan took, in his own words, a great interest. The boy was brought up in Limerick, but not, Trevelyan thought, suitably: he was not sent to a public school, and members of the Trevelyan family went over to Limerick to try to induce his mother to send him to Cambridge, "under a Church of England tutor." Trevelyan even appealed for help to Lord Monteagle, an important figure in Limerick, but with what result does not appear.

The episode was characteristic of a weakness in Trevelyan; conscientious, acting from a genuine conviction of doing right, he found it impossible to refrain from interference, official as well as private, when he considered matters were going wrong, and irritated complaints came from other departments of the meddling ways of the Treasury. Trevelyan's mind was powerful, his character admirably scrupulous and upright, his

devotion to duty praiseworthy, but he had a remarkable in-
sensitiveness. Since he took action only after conscientiously
satisfying himself that what he proposed to do was ethical
and justified, he went forward impervious to other considerations, sustained, but also blinded, by his conviction of doing
right. As a result, Trevelyan, the strict adherent to Treasury
rules, the terror of the departments, could sometimes be
indiscreet.

A remarkable episode occurred at the height of the repeal
agitation, the period of the monster meetings, in 1843. Trevelyan went to Ireland, probably in connection with young
Alfred Trevelyan's affairs, and on his return, in an interview
with Sir Robert Peel and Sir James Graham, made a confidential report on the state of Ireland. Immediately afterwards he published two long letters in the *Morning Chronicle*,
on October 11 and 14, signed Philalethes (lover of truth),
in which he predicted an early rebellion, described warlike
preparations, accused the Catholic priests of fomenting a
rising, abused O'Connell as being actuated by "the vulgar but
nevertheless very powerful motive of saving himself from
pecuniary ruin," and related a number of conversations with
Irish peasants so hair-raising that it is probable he had been
a victim of the favourite Irish sport of "codding" a stranger.

Peel identified Philalethes and was furious. "How a man
after his confidential interview with us could think it consistent
with common decency to reveal to the Editor of the *Morning
Chronicle*, and to the world, all he told us, is passing strange.
He must be a consummate fool. Surely he might have asked
us what we thought of his intended proceedings?" he wrote
to Graham. Trevelyan was unmoved, and after being rebuked
for publishing the first article told Sir James Graham that,
though he might have made a mistake in writing to the
Morning Chronicle, "I think there cannot be a doubt that
now the first portion of the letter has been published it will
be better than the second portion should be also," and
published it was.

Trevelyan's qualities of rectitude, industry and complacency
were not calculated to win popularity, and the Treasury is
not in any case a much-loved department. In 1846 Lord
Lincoln, Chief Secretary for Ireland under Peel, called Trevelyan "our old incubus," and added that he "knew as much
about Ireland as his baby, if he has one." Trevelyan at the
time did in fact have a baby, who was destined to become

the historian Sir George Otto Trevelyan, Bt., Chief Secretary
for Ireland, 1882-84.

❧

When the first Relief Commission started work in November, 1845, the influence of Trevelyan was limited; his relations with Peel on Ireland were not good. Peel himself laid down the policy for the Relief Commission, and the instructions for putting it into effect were drawn up by Sir James Graham. Within a few months, however, Trevelyan had become director and virtually dictator of Irish relief.

The consequences of a potato failure are not immediate: "The first effect of the disease is not scarcity, but plenty, owing to the people's anxiety to dispose of their potatoes before they become useless." It was not until five or six months after a failure that famine began, after every scrap of food, every partially-diseased potato, every fragment that was conceivably edible by human beings, had disappeared. On October 27, 1845, Sir James Graham, the Home Secretary, wrote to Peel: "The extreme pressure from want will not take place until the month of April or May. It was then in 1822 that distress became extreme."

Until April or May, then, the Commissioners had an interval to prepare. They were to "ascertain the extent of the deficiency and watch approaching famine, even in the most remote localities" and to "assist in devising the necessary measures for the employment of the people and their relief."

The relief plan devised by Peel fell into four parts. The first and most important was the organization of local efforts: the Relief Commissioners were instructed to form committees of local landowners, or their agents, magistrates, clergy and residents of importance. These committees would raise subscriptions, out of which food was to be bought for resale to distressed persons, or in urgent cases given free. Local employment schemes were to be started and landlords persuaded to give increased employment on their estates. The Government pinned its faith on the landlords; "Our main reliance," said Peel, "must be placed on the co-operation of the landed interest with local aid."

The second part of the plan depended on the Irish Board of Works; it was to create extra employment by making new roads, a traditional undertaking for the provision of famine relief.

The third part was concerned with "destitute poor persons affected by fever"; in previous famines the British Government had learned that fever always followed scarcity in Ireland. Fever patients might be maintained in a fever hospital, or a house could be hired for their reception; or they could be put in a separate building in the grounds of the local workhouse but not in the workhouse itself. A circular containing these directions was sent to the Clerk of the Board of Guardians in every Union, and the Poor Law Commissioners directed that a separate fever hospital was to be got ready as soon as possible in connection with each workhouse.

Finally, the sale of the Government Indian corn would keep down food prices: as soon as they rose unreasonably a sufficient quantity of the Indian corn was to be thrown on the market to bring them down.

～✅

The scheme was on a larger scale than had ever before been undertaken by a British government for the relief of an Irish famine; and Peel was later accused of having embarked on plans which were too costly and too large. There was, however, an important restriction—a distinction was to be made and relief to be given only to those who were in distress solely on account of the recent failure of the potato.

On January 1, 1846, as soon as he arrived in Dublin, Routh wrote to Trevelyan: "Claims will be made on account of the distress of the people, rather than from their want of food proceeding from losses of the potato crop. There must be a distinction clearly kept."

It was at once evident, however, that to make such a distinction was all but impossible. Distress was the normal condition of a great mass of the Irish people, and the Poor Inquiry Commission had stated that 2,385,000 persons in Ireland were in a state of semi-starvation every year, whether the potato failed or not. It was easy to issue an order in London that no relief was to be given to what was termed "ordinary distress." But starvation carries no certificate of origin, and imposition on a large scale did undoubtedly take place; yet it was imposition which, in the words of a relief official, was "difficult to detect and cruel to expose."

Meanwhile, the Relief Commissioners were finding their other instructions equally difficult to put into practice. Peel had stated that the "main reliance" of the relief scheme must be placed on local landowners; and now, presumably to assist the Relief Commissioners, Trevelyan sent each of them a memorandum containing copies of correspondence describing what had been done for relief in six previous famines. It was not an encouraging document, since on previous occasions local aid had entirely failed to materialize. In the famine of 1839, for instance, Captain Chads, the officer in charge of relief, had written to the Chancellor of the Exchequer that "after having visited the most distressed districts from Bantry to Lough Swilly . . . there had hardly been a single instance in which adequate relief might not have been afforded to the poor without calling for aid from Government" but the landlords were "looking to their future rents only and setting aside the calls of justice, duty and humanity."

The fact was that a large number of Irish landlords were hopelessly insolvent. The extravagance of their predecessors, the building of over-large mansions, reckless expenditure on horses, hounds and conviviality, followed by equally reckless borrowing, had brought very many landowners to a point where, however desperate the needs of their tenantry, they were powerless to give any help.

On the subject of road-making, Colonel Harry Jones, Chairman of the Board of Works, was discouraging. In his opinion road-making offered no solution. The districts where distress would be greatest were poor, uncultivated and boggy; the important lines of communication had already been made through them, in earlier famines, and the only roads left to be made were farm roads, which would unduly profit the owner of the land through which they passed and would not provide a large amount of employment.

Moreover, before public works of any description could be satisfactorily established a great deal of preliminary work must be done. He suggested that a meeting of gentlemen should be called in each neighbourhood where distress was expected, with a representative of the Board of Works in attendance; it would then be possible to ascertain what help could be given by local proprietors and how many persons would need employment. Proposals for possible works could be examined and estimates prepared.

On January 10, 1846, the first local meeting was held at Kilkee, County Clare, but it was a failure. "The room was so filled with people that very few of the proprietors could gain access to it." A committee elected without official authority occupied itself in passing resolutions, complimenting the local Catholic clergy on their "untiring and unremitting zeal in the cause of the people," and returning "warmest thanks" to the chairman for the "dignified manner" in which he conducted the proceedings.

That afternoon the principal landlords in the district assembled at the hotel in Kilkee and drew up a statement: "Under their present difficulties and in the apprehension of those which may come on them in the spring, they neither can advance funds now, nor can they offer any sufficient security for the payment by instalments hereafter."

Next, unexpected difficulties arose with regard to the Indian corn. On January 5, 1846, the United States Chargé d'Affaires at Brussels wrote to warn Barings that Indian corn could not be treated as an ordinary grain: it was very hard and was called "flint corn." In fact, "hominy," a staple food in the southern states of America, was not ground at all but "chopped" in a steel-mill. Ordinary millstones might not answer.

Indian corn was also very liable to sweating and overheating; and having regard to the long voyage from the United States, it was essential that, immediately ships arrived, cargoes should be taken out of the holds and ground at once. It was impossible. The Irish ate potatoes, not bread. Mills were not to be found, as in England, and Routh wrote that by the middle of May only 30,000 bushels would be ground, "and we shall have arriving 350,000 bushels." Even in Cork, the centre of import trade into Ireland, only 2,400 bushels could be ground weekly, even supposing that ordinary millstones could be used.

The solution was highly complicated. The Indian corn, having arrived at Cork, was to be unloaded at once, and, to prevent heating, dried in kilns for eight hours, being turned twice, to avoid parching; next it was to be cooled for 70 hours, dressed, and cooled again for 24 hours, before sacking. Ordinary millstones would have to be used, but to produce a reasonably fine and digestible meal the corn was to be ground twice—which to Trevelyan seemed an unnecessary piece of refinement. "We must not aim at giving more than wholesome food," he wrote to Routh. "I cannot believe it will be necessary to grind the Indian corn twice . . . dependence on charity is not to be made an agreeable mode of life."

Even with the help of these arrangements only a limited quantity of meal could be produced, and Trevelyan wrote to Barings, on January 2, 1846, asking that the order should be cut down, for the moment, by fifty per cent. and that in future, whenever possible, Indian corn-meal should be sent instead of Indian corn in the grain.

❧

The Relief Commissioners became discouraged, and on January 20 drew up "conclusions" which breathed despair. They "entertained the greatest doubt whether any adjustment of public works can be made," and were of opinion that "there was a widespread failure in the potato crop but there was no legislation, either in existence or contemplated by Government, which could relieve it."

As a result, in February, the Relief Commission was re-organized. Routh became chairman; new "formal and detailed" instructions were drawn up, and this time by Trevelyan; a Treasury accountant was sent over, and to expedite decisions an executive committee was formed within the Commission. "Our Commission is to be remodelled, thank God," wrote Routh, on February 19, 1846. The committee met daily at 11 a.m., and though Mr. Twisleton, the Poor Law Commissioner, was included, Colonel Harry Jones, chairman of the Board of Works, was not. The third member was Robert Kane.

Trevelyan was now exercising great authority over Irish relief. The administration would be carried out according to his ideas and decisions on points of detail or of policy made by him.

The supply and distribution of food was to be in the hands of the Commissariat; two main depots were established at Cork and at Limerick, each under the charge of a senior Commissariat officer. At Cork, Deputy Commissary General Hewetson was responsible for receiving, unloading, drying, milling and dispatching cargoes of Indian corn; at Limerick Deputy Commissary General Edward Pine Coffin, of the well-known Devon family of Pine Coffin, a man of marked ability and of higher social rank than the majority of Commissariat officers, was to arrange for the supply of the remote and impoverished districts of the west and south, where distress would be most severe.

Out-depots varying in size were to be in charge of Com-

missariat officers and Commissariat clerks, and every member
of the Commissariat was under Treasury control, that is the
control of Trevelyan. They were dependent on him for their
future careers, they made applications for employment to
him, and he decided the appointments, issued the instructions,
meted out praise or blame. It was with a distinct note of
command that Trevelyan told Routh on February 20, "The
time has come for the authoritative promulgation of the
plans of the Government."

Routh, however, was struggling with difficulties; every aspect of the Government plans, laid down in Whitehall, bristled
with problems. He had been instructed to establish depots of
food against the coming shortage, but how was he to fill them,
since the purchase of any food in ordinary use was forbidden
in order to avoid competition with private enterprise and
private traders? On January 25 Trevelyan had sent Routh a
list of food in Government hands, and the total was far from
encouraging. The principal item was the Indian corn, in
process of being imported; to this, wrote Trevelyan, might
be added certain supplies of biscuit and oatmeal which had
been in store at different military stations since the troubles
of 1843, and some quantity of similar supplies in naval
establishments. However, Mr. Hewetson, the Commissariat
officer in charge at Cork, wrote that oatmeal which had been
in store since 1843 was not fit for human food. It seemed
that Routh would have to depend on the Indian corn and
little else.

More difficulties arose over transport. The plan was to send
supplies from Cork to the west coast by sea, but the west
coast of Ireland is notoriously dangerous, and on February
25, 1846, Barings wrote to warn Trevelyan that all charters
were for the east coast of Ireland, or Cork; if cargoes were
to be sent to the west coast, freights would be much higher.

It was decided to use Admiralty steamers; but the Admiralty
detached only two, *Alban* and *Dee,* and *Dee* was "proverbially
slow." Routh protested vehemently; two steamers were "entirely insufficient"; three, at least, were needed for the west,
and there should also be a large steamer to supply the depots
on the east coast. Two more steamers were then detached,
one of which was immediately condemned as unseaworthy,
while the other, wrote Routh, "only moves at four miles an
hour."

When supplies did reach the west coast of Ireland it came

as a surprise to find that no satisfactory harbours existed. To Routh this was yet another proof of Irish inadequacy: and he wrote to Hewetson, "It is annoying that all these harbours are so insignificant. It shows Providence never intended Ireland to be a great nation."

It had been realized that there would be great difficulty in setting up the organization to distribute relief, because the class of responsible person suitable to undertake such work hardly existed in Ireland; Routh expected, however, that the officials of the Irish Poor Law would assist: Boards of Guardians would work with Commissariat officers, help in distribution, take charge of supplies, and supervise accounts. He was flatly refused. Under the Irish Poor Law Act, outdoor relief, that is, relief to persons outside the workhouse, was illegal, and Mr. Twisleton, the resident Irish Poor Law Commissioner, interpreted the Act as forbidding any participation by Poor Law officials in the relief scheme because the relief was to be distributed outside the workhouse.

Routh was dismayed. "Mr. Twisleton's declaration seems . . . as I understand it, to throw on me a mass of detail worthy of much thought and apprehension," he told Trevelyan on February 9, 1846, and he warned Coffin at Limerick that no help of any kind must be expected. "We are thrown back on Commissariat resources."

Meanwhile the filling of the depots proceeded very slowly, and in addition to previous difficulties a series of violent storms delayed February cargoes for nearly a month. "Time is gaining on us," wrote Routh to Trevelyan on February 18. "We are driven into a corner for assistance." By March "scarcely any" of the depots had been formed, and Routh feared they could not be full before the first of May, "even if they are then."

Urgent appeals for relief were already coming in. The Relief Commission set up an intelligence service, one of their best measures, with £5,000 granted by the Treasury to cover the cost, and as early as January 10, 1846, it reported complete destitution in Killarty, a village near Limerick. Hewetson sent an officer from Cork to investigate; destitution of the most appalling nature proved to exist, and £15 was sent immediately from a private charitable fund.

But, Routh told Trevelyan, such cases were continually being reported. Within the last few weeks he had investigated complaints of distress from Bantry, Skull, Baltimore, Crookhaven and Castletown Berehaven, all of which proved genuine. This district, not far from Skibbereen, was particularly wretched, though, as Routh observed, £50,000 of rents were collected there annually, and he attached to his letter a list of the landlords and the amounts they received yearly.

By February 20, 1846, Routh had reports of more than ninety cases of extreme distress. In the far West, at Belmullet, in Erris, the Commissariat officer had already been forced to distribute food, and by March 6 his supplies were exhausted.

Much, perhaps even most, of this starvation and destitution could be attributed to "ordinary" distress, and residents in Ireland refused to admit a crisis. "It is always so at this time of year," an Irish landowner told the Commissariat officer in charge of the depot at Banagher; and on February 17 Frederick Shaw, Member for Dublin University, reminded the House of Commons that distress in Ireland was a "usual occurrence." Though he did not doubt that, owing to the failure, there would be an aggravation of distress during the coming season, at the same time when Drs. Playfair and Lindley reported that at a low estimate one half of the potato crop was destroyed, "there was no practical man in Ireland who did not believe they had been imposed upon."

With Irish residents denying the existence of a crisis, subscriptions were not coming in, and on March 17 Routh wrote that he had only one subscription from the whole of County Clare. Trevelyan directed that lists of landlords who failed to subscribe were to be sent to the Lord-Lieutenant, with their reasons for refusing; but relief committees were unwilling to provoke local magnates, and few lists were ever forthcoming.

The local relief committees, generally speaking, were proving a failure, largely because unsuitable persons contrived to become members, especially in poor and remote districts. This problem had at once become evident when the first disorderly relief meeting was held at Kilkee, County Clare, and the Government tried to ensure that relief committee members possessed some education and standing by issuing additional instructions laying down that members must be chosen from the semi-official or professional classes. The respectability of relief committees was in fact of immense importance because not only did they handle subscriptions but the Government proposed to add a substantial contribution to sums raised locally, varying from one-third to one-half. The instructions were circulated at the end of February, 1846, but a large number of districts either never received them or ignored them, and elected relief committees without reference to the Government's directions.

As a result, a number of responsible landlords were unwilling to subscribe money to be spent by committees in whom they had no confidence, and instead did what they themselves considered necessary for their tenants. Many were unable to subscribe on account of financial embarrassment, while absentees frequently denied all responsibility: if the land had been leased to a middleman they declared it had long ago passed out of their control. Whatever the cause, it was noticed that when a landowner refused to subscribe unrest and bad feeling followed throughout the neighbourhood.

In many parts of the country signs of disaffection appeared, threatening letters were sent, arms stolen. In one week in November, 1845, notices were posted on church doors and gates in Clare, Limerick, Louth and Cavan telling the people to pay no rent and thrash no corn on account of the potato failure. In the neighbourhood of Ennis "resident aristocracy and absentee noblemen" were threatened if they did not "come forward with plans to help"; and in Tipperary bands of men visited tenants and instructed them to refuse payment for rent.

Landowners in Ireland, whose feelings of security were never great, at once became alarmed, and in a letter to the Military Secretary at Kilmainham one of them, Sir Charles O'Donnell, demanded "fixed patrolling of the country with a mixed force of military and police at unexpected times during the day and night," with "concentrations of military at fixed points"; he stated that "attempts to assassinate, assaults, way layings and nightly visitations for the purpose of . . . intimidation" were taking place.

On February 12, in the House of Lords, another Irish landowner, the Marquess of Clanricarde, declared that a great part of Ireland was already in a state of insurrection. He demanded instant action by the Government—a Bill for the Protection of Life in Ireland must be brought in at once, and such a Bill, known as a Coercion Bill, was introduced into the Lords on February 23, 1846. A Coercion Bill enabled the Lord-Lieutenant, by issuing a proclamation, to place any district under what amounted to martial law; a strict curfew was imposed between sunset and sunrise, magistrates were given exceptional powers—for instance, they could sentence to transportation for seven years—arrests could be made on suspicion, and the possession of any description of firearms was a criminal offence. Seventeen previous Coercion Acts had been in operation at various times during the forty-six years since the Union; the new Bill, however, as Lord Brougham remarked, "possessed a superior degree of severity."

No objection was made to the Bill in the House of Lords, but in the Commons William Smith O'Brien, a member of perhaps the leading family of the ancient Irish aristocracy—he was descended from Brian Boru—fiercely attacked the Government. Famine was menacing Ireland, and the Government sent not food but soldiers—Ireland was to starve, and be coerced.

⁓

Nevertheless, in the spring of 1846, a wave of hopefulness swept over the Irish people; the establishment of the Relief Commission had become known, food was being brought into the country; and as the people knew nothing of the strict limitations of relief they believed the Government was going to "do something" for Ireland at last. Faith in the power of England was absolute—"people have unlimited confidence in the Government," wrote a Commissariat officer. Routh's own experience was that "there was a general impression that Government was about to issue free food to the whole population."

It was now six months since the blight had struck the potato, and in many districts the people had begun to starve: they were eating anything that could conceivably be devoured, food that stank, diseased potatoes that brought sickness and caused death in pigs and cattle.

In Limerick, Smith O'Brien saw families eating potatoes which no Englishman would give his hogs; in Clare, people were eating food "from which," said Lord Monteagle, "so putrid and offensive an effluvia issued that in consuming it they were obliged to leave the doors and windows of their cabins open"; and illness, including "fever from eating diseased potatoes," was widespread.

The Government decided that the expected epidemic of fever, following famine, was about to break out, and on

C

March 13, Sir James Graham, after telling the House of
Commons, "In all the provinces, almost in every county . . .
dysentery has made its appearance attended by fever in many
instances," announced that a Board of Health was to be
established in Dublin by the Lord-Lieutenant. Five honorary
commissioners, of whom Routh was one, were given powers
to require Boards of Guardians to set up fever hospitals and
to provide medical assistance, nursing and comforts in every
Union where there was an "appearance of fever in a formidable shape." The measure was not permanent; it was designed
to meet the coming crisis only and would expire in September.

ربی

Throughout these months, as famine, in Routh's words, was
"steadily and gradually approaching," evictions were reported
weekly. The potato failure endangered the payment of rents,
a swarming population was likely to become unprofitable, and
landlords were eager to clear their property of non-paying
tenants.

Evictions, however, were not confined to populations of
paupers and squatters living in mud huts. The most notorious
instance, was the eviction of 300 tenants by Mrs. Gerrard
from the village of Ballinglass, County Galway, on March
13, 1846. A population reasonably prosperous, according to
Irish standards, was evicted with the assistance of police and
troops, in order that the holdings might be turned into a
grazing farm.

The village of Ballinglass consisted of 61 houses, solidly
built and well-kept, with thick plastered walls. The inhabitants
were not in arrear with their rent, and had, by their industry,
reclaimed an area of about four hundred acres from a neighbouring bog. On the morning of the eviction a "large detachment of the 49th Infantry commanded by Captain Brown"
and numerous police appeared with the Sheriff and his men.
Taking part in evictions was disliked by troops; a little later,
on April 9, at an eviction of nine families at Guitmore,
County Tipperary, a detachment of the 72nd Highlanders
"openly said they detested this duty and gave the people
money."

At Ballinglass, the people were officially called on to give
up possession, and the houses were then demolished—roofs
torn off, walls thrown down. The scene was frightful; women

running wailing with pieces of their property and clinging
to door-posts from which they had to be forcibly torn; men
cursing, children screaming with fright. That night the people
slept in the ruins; next day they were driven out, the founda-
tions of the houses were torn up and razed, and no neighbour
was allowed to take them in.

Turned from every door, it was common for the evicted
to seek refuge in what was called a "scalp." A hole was dug
in the earth, two to three feet deep, roofed over with sticks
and pieces of turf, and in this burrow a family existed. Slightly
superior was a "scalpeen," a rather larger hole often made
within the ruins of a "tumbled" house. Both from "scalps"
and "scalpeens" the evicted when discovered were remorsely
hunted out.

The Ballinglass eviction caused a scandal and was "personally investigated" by Lord Londonderry, a great Ulster landlord and a staunch Tory. On March 30 he made a statement
in the House of Lords. He was "deeply grieved," but there
was no doubt the statements with regard to the eviction at
Ballinglass were true: "76 families, comprising 300 individuals,
had not only been turned out of their houses but had even—
the unfortunate wretches—been mercilessly driven from the
ditches to which they had betaken themselves for shelter and
where they were attempting to get up a covering of some
kind by means of sticks and mud . . . these unfortunate
people had their rents actually ready . . . If scenes like this
occurred," finished Lord Londonderry, " . . . was it to be
wondered at . . . that deeds of outrage and violence should
occasionally be attempted?"

Lord Brougham, however, a staunch supporter of *laissez
faire,* held a different view. He said on March 23 in the
House of Lords: "Undoubtedly it was the landlord's right to
do as he pleased, and if he abstained he conferred a favour
and was doing an act of kindness. If on the other hand he
chose to stand on his right, the tenants must be taught by
the strong arm of the law that they had no power to oppose
or resist . . . property would be valueless and capital would
no longer be invested in cultivation of land if it were not
acknowledged that it was the landlord's undoubted, indefeasi-
ble and most sacred right to deal with his property as he
list. . . ."

It happened that at the time Britain was celebrating a
great feat of arms in India, where General Gough, against

enormous odds, had won the two battles of Aliwal and
Sobraon. When the lists of the killed came in Daniel O'Connell
observed, "On looking over the returns from the two glorious
battles lately fought in India . . . I find a great number of
names in the list exactly resembling the names of the cottagers
dispossessed by Mrs. Gerrard."

Ominous reports came in. From the beginning of April
Constabulary reports recorded that in Kerry, Galway and
Kilkenny men were gathering in crowds, declaring they were
starving; a provision ship was plundered on the river Fergus;
at Mitchelstown, a mob of about a hundred women and
children held up carts going to the Commissariat store, cut
the meal-bags and took about two tons. Similar incidents
were repeated in the western and southwestern half of Ireland,
and in some districts in the east—nothing was taken but
food.

A new difficulty now arose; at first the Government's Indian
corn-meal had been loathed—it was called "Peel's brimstone"
from its bright yellow colour. "Never was anything so calum-
niated as our corn meal," wrote Routh to Trevelyan on March
19. Attempts to introduce it into workhouses to replace potatoes caused riots; the inmates at Limerick refused to touch
it; at Waterford it was declared that persons who ate it had
been poisoned and died, and its appearance was greeted by
weeping and wailing. This prejudice was founded on the fact
that in the famine of 1831 a quantity of very bad quality
meal had been distributed as an experiment. It had been
damped by the millers to increase weight, was sour and unfit
for human food and the people became ill when, driven by
hunger, they ate it.

However, as the season advanced and food grew scarce
Indian meal began to be eaten. "Gradually the bolder and
more hungry tried it," Trevelyan was informed on March
30, and it became immensely popular. Trevelyan conducted
"Indian corn experiments" on himself, eating the meal as
stirabout (porridge) and in cakes, and he arranged for a halfpenny pamphlet to be prepared, with simple instructions for
cooking.

On March 28 "the Relief Committee of the Gentlemen of
Cork" announced that, as an experiment, Indian meal would
be on sale that day at cost price, 1d. a pound. The result,
reported The Times, was alarming: a huge crowd gathered,
there was a "tremendous rush" for the meal, and a disturbance

that was almost a riot took place. It was all instantly bought up, and more was demanded; but the senior Commissariat officer in charge at Cork refused a second issue, saying he had no further instructions. At this, many hundreds of persons who were still waiting for a share became "angry and threatening," and the demonstrations subsided only when the Mayor issued a notice saying that further supplies were expected daily. This was not true; in fact, the Relief Commissioners, frightened by the revelation of mass hunger, and dreading a "rush upon the Commission," would allow no further issue. On April 9 John Pitt Kennedy, secretary of the Relief Commission, wrote to the Relief Committee of the Gentlemen of Cork that "it was intended to reserve issues from the depots for the more heavy pressure of the summer months . . . until then landholders and Relief Committees were expected to exert themselves to meet the existing distress."

By April 2 the demand for the pamphlet of cooking instructions "exceeded all credibility"; two weeks later Routh told Trevelyan he "could not have believed Indian Corn meal would become so popular" and officially informed the Lords of the Treasury that the demand continued to increase "beyond my anticipations."

The *Freeman's Journal* now printed a furious denunciation of the Government's policy: holding over the Indian cornmeal was "positive cruelty," the poor were left to the mercy of speculators and would be destroyed before the Government interfered. Routh insisted that "we must hold out with a little firmness in spite of the wretchedness and bad character of the people"; the habitual want of the country was not to be thrown on to the potato failure.

There was, however, a fact of which relief committees and newspapers appeared to be unaware—Government supplies were only a drop in the ocean compared with the needs of Ireland. Potatoes worth £3,500,000 had been lost, and to make good that deficiency, in Trevelyan's words "to fill the vacuum," the Commission had at their disposal £100,000 of Indian corn and an uncertain quantity of biscuit. It was indeed, as Trevelyan put it, a "delicate and anxious . . . operation," and Coffin at Limerick, the most intelligent of the Commissariat officers, estimated that four million people would have to be fed during May, June and July before the new crop of potatoes was fit to eat. The task was clearly impossible.

Peel made a statement in the House of Commons on April 17: he had received "an entreaty that for God's sake the Government should send out to America for more Indian corn," and the pressure was no doubt very severe. But "if it were known that we undertook the task of supplying the Irish with food we should to a great extent lose the support of the Irish gentry, the Irish clergy and the Irish farmer. It is quite impossible for Government to support 4,000,000 people. It is utterly impossible for us to adopt means of preventing cases of individual misery in the wilds of Galway or Donegal or Mayo. In such localities the people must look to the local proprietors, resident and non-resident." Sir James Graham added, "We never said this foreign supply would be sufficient for the whole population of Ireland; but we believed that under the judicious management of this supply the markets could be so regulated as to prevent an exorbitant price for native produce."

Yet throughout these months and throughout the famine years the "native produce" of Ireland was leaving her shores in a "torrent of food."

❧

In the long and troubled history of England and Ireland no issue has provoked so much anger or so embittered relations between the two countries as the indisputable fact that huge quantities of food were exported from Ireland to England throughout the period when the people of Ireland were dying of starvation. "During all the famine years," wrote John Mitchel, the Irish revolutionary, "Ireland was actually producing sufficient food, wool and flax, to feed and clothe not nine but eighteen millions of people"; yet, he asserted, a ship sailing into an Irish port during the famine years with a cargo of grain was "sure to meet six ships sailing out with a similar cargo."

Figures were produced in the House of Commons giving the amounts of grain and cereals exported from Ireland to England for a period of, roughly, three months from the date when the potato failure was established up to February 5, 1846. 258,000 quarters of wheat and 701,000 hundredweight of barley, worth about a million pounds, had left Ireland with, in addition, 1,000,000 quarters of oats and oatmeal; and since February 5 export had been continuing at the same rate.

Coffin wrote to Routh from Limerick pointing out "the

inconsistency of importing supplies into a country which is at the same time exporting its own resources." Limerick was an export centre, and no doubt Coffin had seen ship after ship laden with wheat, oats, cattle, pigs, eggs and butter, sailing away down the Shannon from a country which was on the verge of starvation. He urged that the Government should buy and store all the grain, which would otherwise be exported, and sell it when the time of extreme scarcity came. He did not succeed.

At first sight the inhumanity of exporting food from a country stricken by famine seems impossible to justify or condone. Modern Irish historians, however, have treated the subject with generosity and restraint. They have pointed out that the corn grown in Ireland before the famine was not sufficient to feed the people if they had depended on it alone, that imports must be examined as well as exports: in fact, when the famine was at its worst four times as much wheat came into Ireland as was exported, and in addition almost 3,000,000 quarters of Indian corn and 1,000,000 cwts. of Indian meal.

Suppose, however, the grain and other produce had been kept in the country, it is doubtful if the starving would have benefited substantially. The districts where distress was most severe, Donegal, Mayo, Clare, west Cork, produced little but potatoes. Food from other districts would have had to be brought in and distributed. Grain would have had to be milled which, as the British government had discovered, was a difficult problem.

Moreover in the backward areas where famine struck hardest, cooking any food other than the potato had become a lost art. "There is," wrote Trevelyan, "scarcely a woman of the peasant class in the West of Ireland whose culinary art exceeds the boiling of a potato. Bread is scarcely ever seen, and an oven is unknown"; and Father Mathew, the celebrated apostle of temperance, whose crusade against drinking had for a time almost suppressed the national vice and whose knowledge of Ireland was unmatched, wrote, "The potato deluge during the past twenty years has swept away all other food from our cottagers and sunk into oblivion their knowledge of cookery." There was no means of distributing home-grown food, no knowledge of how to use it and in addition the small Irish farmer was compelled by economic necessity to sell what he grew. He dared not eat it. Routh writing to Trevelyan on January 1, 1846, told him that the Irish people did not regard wheat, oats and barley as food—they were grown to pay the rent and to pay the rent was the first necessity of life in Ireland. It would be a desperate man who ate up his rent, with the certainty before him of eviction and "death by slow torture." Therefore the Irish peasant sold his little produce, even when his children were crying with hunger, to save them from a worse fate.

Nevertheless the harsh truth that the poverty of the Irish peasant, the backward state of his country and the power of his landlord prevented him from benefiting from home-grown food did not mitigate his burning sense of injustice. Forced by economic necessity to sell his produce he was furiously resentful when food left the market towns under the eyes of the hungry populace, protected by a military escort of overwhelming strength. From Waterford, the Commissariat officer wrote to Trevelyan, on April 24, 1846, "The barges leave Clonmel once a week for this place, with the export supplies under convoy which, last Tuesday, consisted of 2 guns, 50 cavalry and 80 infantry escorting them on the banks of the Suir as far as Carrick."

It was a sight which the Irish people found impossible to understand and impossible to forget.

Chapter IV

SIR ROBERT PEEL, having completed his arrangements for controlling the price of food, went on to attempt some solution of the unemployment which, as the Devon Commission had reported, was responsible for the unhappy condition of the peasantry in most parts of Ireland and "the privations which they and their families patiently endure."

He now introduced four Bills to increase employment in Ireland, and on March 5, 1846, they received the Royal Assent. The first, and most important, was intended to provide for the rapid establishment of public works. Five persons of respectability, two magistrates and three county taxpayers, could meet in any barony—a barony being a county division, used in Irish local government—and send to the Lord-Lieutenant proposals for local works; if approved, the works were to be executed with Government funds, half being a loan, repayable to the Treasury, and half a grant.

A second Act provided for the execution of specified works by contractors, such as road repairing, levelling, drainage and sewerage. It was found to be "ill adapted": the procedure was slow, contractors proved unreliable, and in addition the whole sum, instead of only half, advanced out of public funds had to be repaid by the barony that obtained the loan.

The two other Acts, of less importance, dealt with the construction of piers and fishing harbours and the encouragement of large projects of drainage, water power and improvement of navigation. The sum set aside for piers and harbours, £5,000 a year, for ten years, was too small to be effective, and for large projects, a preliminary survey had to be carried out, at the applicant's expense; consequently, only one important work, the drainage of the river Fergus, in County Clare, was undertaken under the Act.

These Acts were to be put into operation and administered by the Irish Board of Works, and it was a heavy and difficult task. Businesslike habits and technical knowledge were rare in backward Ireland. Moreover, the Irish Board of Works, established in 1831, was lamentably under-staffed and already charged with extensive duties: thanks to a "rage for economy" it consisted of only three members and a "niggardly office establishment." At one point, a fourth member had been added, to deal with fisheries and drainage, but he was never to be found, because he happened to be a Parliamentary draftsman, and was kept busy at Dublin Castle, preparing Bills for Parliament which were in no way connected with the Board of Works. Nevertheless, only two or three persons were added to the staff in preparation for administering the four new Acts.

Though its duties were exclusively Irish, the Board was under the control of the Treasury. "The Board of Works," stated Trevelyan, "is a subordinate Board to the Treasury; they are under their orders and the Treasury have full power to give them any directions they think proper."

The authority which Trevelyan exercised over the distribution of food for relief, through the Commissariat, would now cover the establishment and administration of public works; thus, item by item, Irish relief plans came under Treasury control, and Treasury control was strict and jealous. The procedure following the initial meeting of five persons, as directed in the first of the new Acts, bristled with safeguards and was immensely complicated. Estimates and plans had to be prepared, a difficult task in primitive Ireland, and submitted in turn to three sets of officials, the County Surveyor, the Lord-Lieutenant and the Relief Commissioners; if all three approved, then an official of the Board of Works visited the site and made a detailed report; if this, too, was satisfactory, the papers were posted to the Treasury, in Whitehall, for final sanction. Further, the type of works which might be undertaken as public works was restricted. They were to be, wrote Trevelyan, "of such a nature as will not benefit individuals in a greater degree than the rest of the community and therefore are not likely to be called for from any motive but the professed one of giving employment." In other words, all works were to be useful to the community in which they were carried out and not simply of benefit to individuals.

The length and intricacy of the procedure bewildered officials in Ireland. "I really do not see my way clear with the Board of Works," wrote Routh to Trevelyan, on March 18. "Something more direct, more immediate is necessary. The forms of office and the course of law, so invaluable at other times, must give way to a system more rapid in its erection and more powerful in its application."

Difficulties were now enormously increased by the arrival of a deluge of applications, overwhelming the inadequate organization of the Board of Works. The fact was that the Government had failed to realize the financial attraction to landowners of the first of the new Acts. Half the money to be expended was a free grant, twenty years were allowed for repaying the remaining half, and making the application was simple—the only simple step, in fact, in the entire procedure.

Landlords hurried to secure a share of government money, innumerable meetings of two magistrates and three county ratepayers were held, and before the end of May applications for works to cost no less than £800,000 had been received. Baronies sent in applications not for one or two but for dozens of works—one barony applied for ninety-nine, another for one hundred and thirteen. The consequent burden thrown on the Board of Works was crushing. Though some fifty surveyors were detached from the Ordnance Survey and six officers seconded from the Royal Engineers the technical staff remained totally inadequate, while the three or four members of the Board in Dublin had piled on them the impossible task of sifting and making a decision on a mass of proposals from all over Ireland. Applications piled up unanswered, undertakings were not inspected, employment did not begin, and the country became rebellious.

On March 23, 1846, a deputation from Limerick, headed by the Mayor, came to Dublin to urge the Relief Commission to hurry on with the works: if employment were not instantly provided there would be an outbreak in Limerick. On April 6, a riot took place in Carrick-on-Suir—a mob marched through the town, demanding work, and troops were called out; the rioters, however, quietened down on being given some temporary employment. In the course of similar riots disappointed unruly mobs invaded the Petty Sessions, declaring that "all they sought for was employment and wages"; and Routh anxiously urged Trevelyan to hurry schemes through: "employment is the only way of restraining the people."

But hurrying on proved impossible; and as late as July 31, 1846, Lord Monteagle declared that though both he and Lord Kenmare had, months since, put in applications for works they had been quite unable to get the Board to do the preliminary survey.

Usually well over 60,000 men migrated from Ireland to England for the harvest, but this year few went. As there was hope of employment at home, on the public works, men were unwilling to leave their families at a time of crisis; and very few had a stock of potatoes to feed their families while they were away.

The numbers who applied for employment were frightening. Tens of thousands appeared, the relief committee rooms were "besieged with unfortunate people," and, in a panic, committees issued tickets broadcast. In answer to criticism from Trevelyan, Routh pointed out that it might seem easy to adhere to rules in Whitehall, but for the relief committees it was a very different matter. Faults of "looseness and irregularity" were readily committed when one was "surrounded by an immense population clamorous for food and employment." "Work at any cost," wrote the Board of Works, "was prayed for as the only means of saving the people from famine and property from pillage," and the meetings of magistrates and ratepayers, which should have deliberated what could best be done in the neighbourhood, "through haste and pressure became useless."

With a strong sense of grievance, the Board of Works complained of the position into which they had been forced and the useless works they had been compelled to undertake. A "rush" had taken place and pressure was so great that "the Commissioners of Public Works . . . felt themselves under the necessity of recommending . . . works which were not really wanted . . . and to authorise the commencement of works sooner than was required"; distress had swept away caution and magistrates and ratepayers had undertaken to re-pay sums far beyond the means of the barony. Meanwhile, the impossibility of finding suitable staff in Ireland made supervision of the works impossible; labourers were to be seen "in groups, talking or smoking tobacco," and Board of Works' officers were assaulted and ill-treated by groups of idlers who had failed to get employment. In the opinion of an intelligent observer, Mr. John Ball, a Catholic Irishman who inspected 219 relief districts as Assistant Poor Law Commissioner and, later, entered politics and rose to ministerial rank, this unsatisfactory state of affairs was largely due to the relief committees; members were unsuitable persons and too close-ly connected with the distressed population, as neighbours or even relations, though he observed that many of their actions, for instance the broadcast distribution of tickets, were due to genuine, if mistaken, benevolence. They were also usually at daggers drawn with the officials of the Board of Works, who accused them of interference with the Board's officials and instructions.

Difficulties with relief committees were, however, of minor importance compared with the supreme cause of the confusion —the ignorance of the British Government about conditions existing all over Ireland, with the exception of north-east Ulster and large towns in the east—conditions which made providing relief through employment an almost impossibly difficult task. In Whitehall, providing relief through employ-ment appeared simple. Everyone knew that the number of applications would depend on the rate of wages offered—this was an economic law. Therefore all that was necessary was to fix the rate of wages, on the public works, below what was usually offered locally: "a lower rate of wages acts as a test of destitution." The British Government, however, now discovered that in Ireland "there is no such thing literally as wages."

The potato, not money, was the basic factor by which the value of labour was determined. Farmers and landlords gave their labourers a cabin and a piece of potato ground, or permitted them to put up a cabin and allowed them a portion of conacre. Rent, in each case, was worked off in days of labour, at wages varying from 4d. to 8d. a day, with frequently two meals on each working day. These wages were not given in money into the labourer's hand, but set off against his rent, and they did not represent the real reward for his labour. The real reward was the patch of potato ground. Customarily the only dealing in money was the receipt of a few shillings from the sale of a pig, and this provided such clothing as the family possessed. The poorest labourers could not afford a pig, and coins of small value only were involved: unfamiliarity with money was so great that coins and notes of value were not recognized.

When *The Times* Commissioner, Mr. Campbell Foster, for example, visited Galway in 1846 he found "so little do the people know of the commercial value of money that they are constantly in the habit of pawning it." A pawnbroker in Galway city had shown him a drawer full of coins and notes of substantial value which had been pawned; they included a ten-pound Bank of Ireland note, pawned six months previously for 10s., and a gold guinea, pawned two months previously for 15s. It was not unusual for owners to fail in redeeming their pledges.

But ignorance of values did not mean that money in the shape of those coins which the people understood was not prized; it was prized inordinately. Money meant ability to purchase land, and land was life itself in Ireland. However wretched a family, if they had a little money they would not use it to improve their living conditions but jealously hoarded it. In a graphic phrase a witness said that money was never used or even put out at interest—it was "stuck in the thatch." Consequently, as soon as silver coins were paid out on the public works they vanished.

For instance, on August 8 the Board of Works told the Lords of the Treasury that at Kilrush, in County Clare, £11,360 had been issued in silver but only £4,760 had come back through the banks. So extra coin, in boxes containing

£500 to £1,000, had to be sent down in charge of confidential clerks, "a risky proceeding."

Whether wages were at a low rate or a high rate made no difference. In many districts only 6d. or 8d. a day was offered; nevertheless, whatever the rate, the prospect of wages paid into the labourers' hand in coin was irresistible, and holdings were left uncultivated and farming operations abandoned as eager crowds besieged the relief committee rooms for employment. Moreover, the British Government had failed to take into consideration how, without potatoes, a man and his family were to keep alive while cultivating the ground for next year's crop; and landlords were already proceeding against the luckless hirers of conacre—150 in Fermoy alone. It was an added inducement that wages on the public works were paid by the day; there was no "task" or piece-work, which Irish labourers detested because so much power was given to stewards; and workers on the Shannon Navigation scheme earning 1s. 6d. a day by task-work walked out, to apply for employment on the public works at 9d. a day.

While the Board of Works, struggling with these difficulties and hopelessly under-staffed, was being overwhelmed, the month of May arrived, the period when, as Sir James Graham, the Home Secretary, had stated, the effects of the potato failure would be severely felt, and when, every year, a kind of famine more or less intense occurs in Ireland between the going out of the old and the coming in of the new crops. Applications became even more numerous, crowds began to get out of hand, threatening language was used by labourers with destitute families, and "larger numbers than could be employed forced themselves on the works." The height of the season of "normal distress," enormously intensified by the potato failure, was approaching.

Trevelyan now judged the time had come to call in the Commissariat, and he fixed May 15 as the date when the depots in Ireland would open for the sale of Indian corn. The two senior officers of the Commissariat, Routh in Dublin and Coffin in Limerick, were dismayed—the depots were not filled. Eight thousand tons of Indian corn and meal was the quantity, by no means excessive, ultimately imported by the British Government into Ireland, but this total was reached only on July 31. On May 15 there was much less, and on the

13th Coffin had written urging that opening should be postponed until further supplies had come in.

Nevertheless, the opening took place. Routh directed
Coffin to restrict issues as far as possible, to make no "regular
supply daily or monthly," to consider each issue as "single
in itself and dependent on the merits and truth of each
separate representation," and to instruct all officers to "distinguish between the usual scarcity of the season and the
present extraordinary dearth."

A rush followed; at about 1*d.* a pound the Government
Indian corn was by far the cheapest food available, and
depots everywhere were besieged. At Limerick, Coffin was
writing two or three letters a day to relief committees to
explain why demands could not be met; "I am instructed not
to promise any specific supply"; "the aim of the depots is
to maintain an equilibrium of prices, they are not intended
to feed the whole population and are not adequate to do so";
"Meal is not sold as the sole or even the principal resource
for the period of want. . . ." These and similar letters were
received by the committees throughout Ireland with angry
indignation. "They universally thought," Coffin told Trevelyan, on June 4, "all their demands would be filled and they
had only to send a carter to the depot with money in his hand
as to an ordinary shop."

Trevelyan's intentions were very different. Irish relief was to
be restricted to a single operation; the government Indian
corn, purchased at the orders of Sir Robert Peel, was to be
placed in depots by the Commissariat, sold to the people—
and that was the end. There was to be no replenishment, even
if there was a sum of money in hand from sales; once
supplies had been disposed of relief was over. In several
letters, written with unusual boldness, Routh begged Trevelyan to allow further purchases. The demand on the depots
was "immense," far heavier than anything that had been
anticipated, and it was increasing every day; surely the
depots should remain open until September. The new potato
crop would not provide any food whatsoever for the people
before the middle of September at the earliest, while "lump-
ers," the huge, coarse potato called the "horse" potato, on
which the people mainly depended, would not be ready until
the end of that month. Trevelyan refused; relief was to be
brought to a close; possibly some depots might shut down a
little later than others, but issues must shortly cease. By the

end of June, 1846, government supplies were all but exhausted; on the 24th of that month, 5,000 bushels of Indian
corn were all that remained in Cork and, at that, were unground, while in remote districts the people were starving.
The revenue cutter, *Eliza,* making a visit of inspection, on
June 22, to the Killeries, a wild district of mountain and deep
ocean inlets in the far west, was implored for food by a boat-
load of skeletons. The Commissariat officer at Westport,
supply centre for the Killeries, had been instructed to send no
more meal to the region because the depot was becoming
empty.

One man, stated the officer in command, was lying on the
bottom of the boat, unable to stand and already half dead,
the others, with emaciated faces and prominent, staring eye-
balls, were evidently in an advanced state of starvation. The
officer reported to Sir James Dombrain, Inspector-General of
the Coastguard Service, who had served on relief during the
famine of 1839, and Sir James Dombrain, "very inconven-
iently," wrote Routh, "interfered." He "prevailed" on an officer at the Westport depot to issue meal, which he gave
away free; he also "prevailed" on the captain of the Government steamship, *Rhadamanthus,* to take 100 tons of meal,
intended for Westport, to the Coastguard Station at the
Killeries. "The Coast Guard with all their zeal and activity
are too lavish," wrote Routh to Trevelyan.

Almost on the same date Coffin at Limerick wrote Trevelyan an urgent letter. He could not answer for the consequence if the depots were closed. "Only issues of food," he
declared, "keep the country peaceful . . . Only for the
Government meal thousands would be now dying by the
road side." In a private letter to Routh, Coffin confessed himself bewildered and depressed. Intelligent, well-intentioned and
widely experienced though he was, the state of Ireland
baffled him. "I sincerely hope August will see us out of our
troubles," he wrote; ". . . the most anxious and unsatisfactory
task I ever undertook, working in the dark . . . I have often
felt I could not go on any longer."

Nevertheless, on June 25, Routh received directions to carry
out "the closing measures of our present service"; supplies
were to be transferred from less destitute to more destitute
districts, demand cut down by raising prices, and the relief
scheme wound up. In a private letter to Routh, Trevelyan
attributed the enormous demand on the depots to the low

price at which the meal was sold; above all, to the fact that it was sold to persons suffering from distress, normal at the time of year, and not solely to persons whose distress was caused by the potato failure. Indiscriminate sales had "brought the whole country on the depots, and without denying the existence of real and extensive distress," the numbers were beyond the power of the depots to cope with; they must therefore be closed down as soon as possible.

Meanwhile, across the Channel, in London, dramatic events were taking place, and a change of Government was imminent.

Repeal of the Corn Laws was proving Peel's downfall. He was regarded with detestation by the Protectionists, who formed a large part of his own Party, and the Whigs, forced into the mortifying position of supporting their chief enemy, who had, they considered, stolen their principal measure, were consumed with vindictive fury. The ingenious mind of Benjamin Disraeli devised a way to bring Peel down. Whigs and Protectionist Tories must combine. Nothing could be done, as far as the Bill to repeal the Corn Laws was concerned, since the Whigs could hardly vote against a measure with which they had been identified; but if the second reading of the Irish Coercion Bill, introduced by Peel in February, was opposed by a combination of Whigs and Protectionist Tories, the defeat of Peel was assured. There were difficulties, since both Lord George Bentinck, leader of the Protectionists, and Lord John Russell, the leader of the Whigs, had previously voted in favour of the Irish Coercion Bill; but scruples were overcome "with boldness and dexterity."

The momentous night was June 25, and by a curious coincidence, as the debate on Irish Coercion was in progress, messengers entered the House of Commons, returning with the Bill repealing the Corn Laws, which had just received the assent of the Lords. The debate was interrupted while "Mr. Speaker, amidst profound silence, announced that the Lords had agreed to the . . . Bill . . . without any amendment."

A few hours later the House divided on Irish Coercion; Disraeli's scheme succeeded, and Sir Robert Peel fell, defeated by a majority of 73 votes. His resignation was officially announced on June 29, 1846.

The majority which defeated Peel had no connection whatsoever with the real situation in Ireland. Indeed, the apathy of the House of Commons with regard to Irish affairs

was seldom more marked than during the discussions on the
Coercion Bill. During the debate on the first reading Mr.
Fitzgerald, Member for Tipperary, noted there were "not half
a dozen gentlemen on the benches opposite"; and when the
Bill was debated for the second time there were not twenty-
five Members present, and the number never rose to more
than forty. As was said at the time, the majority which defeated Peel had "as much to do with Ireland as Kamschatka."

The new Whig Government, under Lord John Russell, was
more to Trevelyan's taste than Peel's administration. As a
government servant he had no politics, but in private life he
was a Whig, and his relations with Sir Robert Peel had not
been happy. On July 6 he wrote in a private letter to Routh,
"The members of the new Government began to come today
to the Treasury. I think we shall have much reason to be
satisfied with our new masters," and he added, on the 13th,
"Nothing can be more gratifying to our feelings than the
manner in which the new Chancellor of the Exchequer has
appreciated our exertions."

The new Chancellor of the Exchequer, Charles Wood, who
succeeded as Sir Charles Wood, Bt., in December 1846 and
was later created first Viscount Halifax, was congenial to
Trevelyan. To a solid mind, he united a fixed dislike both of
new expenditure and new taxes, and was a firm believer in
laissez faire, preferring to let matters take their course and
allow problems to be solved by "natural means." Head of an
ancient Yorkshire family, he united love of liberty with
reverence for property, a strong sense of public duty, lack
of imagination and stubborn conservatism. Humanitarianism
was not among his undoubted virtues. Charles Wood remained
in office, as Chancellor of the Exchequer, for six years, and
came increasingly under Trevelyan's influence. The two men
were alike in outlook, conscientiousness and industry, and
Charles Wood brought Trevelyan a further access of power
in the administration of Irish relief.

Winding up relief was now pushed on vigorously, and on
July 8 Trevelyan rejected a shipload of Indian corn. "The
cargo of the *Sorcière* is not wanted," he wrote to Mr. Thomas
Baring; "her owners must dispose of it as they think proper."
Mr. Baring sent congratulations "on the termination of your
feeding operations." But Routh, in Ireland, was depressed.
He sincerely hoped that congratulations might not prove

premature; the pressure on the depots was still increasing. "This is a worse month than June," he wrote.

Trevelyan, however, had an urgent reason for wishing to get Sir Robert Peel's relief scheme for the 1845 failure cleared up and out of the way. He disagreed with it in several important respects, and during the last few weeks a new and alarming probability had become evident—there were unmistakable signs that the potato was about to fail again.

As early as February 16, 1846, new potatoes had been shown at meetings of the Horticultural Society in London "in which the disease had manifested itself in a manner not to be mistaken," and on February 20, a question had been asked in the House of Commons. In reply Sir Robert Peel admitted that the potatoes "exhibited the disease of last autumn," but added that they had been grown from sets of potatoes which were themselves slightly diseased.

Whether blight reappeared or not, however, the outlook for the potato crop was poor. Distributing seed potatoes had proved impracticable. Immense quantities would have been needed, "nearly a ton an acre," wrote Trevelyan, and there was neither an organization to buy such huge amounts nor means of conveying and distributing them.

In April, Mr. E. B. Roche, Member for Cork, had warned the House of Commons that thousands of people were eating seed potatoes as a result of the refusal of the Government to open the depots; and on July 10 Routh reminded Trevelyan, "You must remember we kept back all issues during the winter making the people consume their potatoes." Routh estimated that the acreage of potatoes planted in 1846 was about one-third less than in 1845, and since the quantity of potatoes grown was never sufficient, except in a very good year, scarcity in the coming season was inevitable, unless the crop was overwhelmingly good.

An overwhelmingly good crop, however, was what the people of Ireland persisted in expecting. There was a belief that plenty followed scarcity; the Irish temperament is naturally optimistic, and hope ran high. During May and June the weather was warm and the plants grew strong; on June 10 the Commissariat officer at Clonmel reported that the crop of early potatoes "looks most abundant. It is generally supposed here that the crops have never looked better at this season." On the 26th the *Freeman's Journal* confirmed

that there was "every appearance of an abundant harvest"
—crops were "most luxuriant." In the spring there had been
"icy continuous drenching rain," but now the weather was
"most propitious for growing crops."

True, on July 3 the *Freeman's Journal* noted reports of
"a few cases of potato disease," but "not enough to cause
any excitement" and, later, "exaggeration" was rebuked: "Every spot and blemish" was being "magnified" into incipient
disease.

Routh, however, who was receiving daily reports from
every part of the country, could not be optimistic, and on
July 14 he told Trevelyan, "Disease is reappearing." Three
days later he wrote a letter of solemn warning: "The reports
of the new potato crop are very unfavourable. All letters
and sources of information declare disease to be more
prevalent this year than last in the early crop." It was too
soon to speak of the main crop, the "people's crop," but
he judged that most of the early crop had already been
lost.

Trevelyan considered these ominous facts as the strongest
possible argument for winding up the present relief scheme
with all possible haste. If Government relief was still available
when the people became aware that another failure had
occurred they would expect to be fed. "The only way to
prevent the people from becoming habitually dependent on
Government," he told Routh, on July 17, "is to bring the
operations to a close. The uncertainty about the new crop only
makes it more necessary." In a second letter he wrote,
"Whatever may be done hereafter, these things should be
stopped now, or you run the risk of paralysing all private
enterprise and having this country on you for an indefinite
number of years. The Chancellor of the Exchequer supports
this strongly." Routh received instructions to close the Commissariat depots on August 15.

Had the decision rested with Routh he would not have closed
the depots in the face of a second failure. However, he shrank
from opposing Trevelyan; the training of a lifetime forbade
it, and his admiration for Trevelyan's capacities was great.
He tried therefore to convince himself that Trevelyan's
policy was just and wise. "The apprehensions for the new
crop make it all the more necessary that we should close our
present labours on August 15," he wrote to some of his
senior officers on July 20, ". . . so as to allow the Government

time to make up their opinion as to the future, for if we were to remain at our stations and depots until the end of September when the fate of the late crop will be determined, it might be difficult to relieve us, and the authorities might be forced into a continuance of the same measures without a fair opportunity of consideration."

Trevelyan next turned his attention to the Board of Works. Of the bodies concerned with relief, the Board of Works had been the least satisfactory; not only Trevelyan, but Routh, declared "the Board of Works has been a failure"; and on July 20, Trevelyan wrote, privately and peremptorily, to the chairman of the Board, Colonel Jones, telling him that the Board was to be reorganized. The reconstruction had been already drafted in a Treasury minute, and was, wrote Trevelyan firmly, "as good as settled."

The minute, dated July 21, 1846, directed the closing of all public works, save in exceptional circumstances, on August 15, and also directed the reconstruction of the Board and the augmentation of its staff "to meet the increased magnitude of the coming exigency." Proper plans and estimates for works under the recent Acts were to be prepared now, in anticipation of the new emergency, in order that the confusion of the previous season might be avoided.

The Board of Works received the Treasury minute with indignation. It was not possible or reasonable to stop works, without warning, at only three weeks' notice. How could works be left in their present state? Many roads were actually dangerous to the public; was this to be ignored? Local distress was already more urgent than ever, and immense new destitution was known to be impending.

The Government gave way. An attempt was made to limit expenditure, but in fact what amounted to a general renewal of relief works took place. Trevelyan became exasperated, and so much annoyance was evident in his letters that Routh ventured to remonstrate. The Board of Works, admittedly, had been a failure, but he was not sure, he wrote, on August 3, that the relief committees had been unsatisfactory: "Pray if you put forth any public documents on the subject speak carefully of the Committees whose assistance you will certainly require next year. Praise if you like, but do not find fault, at least publicly; they are very sensitive and so are all the Irish." Whatever their shortcomings, the relief committees had collected £98,003 by July 31, 1846, the largest sum ever raised in Ireland for the relief of distress; to this, £65,914 10s. 0d. was added by the Lord-Lieutenant out of public funds, as the Government contribution.

The Government had now accepted the fact that a second failure of the potato was about to occur, and Trevelyan was preparing plans. He was determined to pursue a new policy, a policy which all but reversed that of Peel.

Trevelyan and Charles Wood, the Chancellor of the Exchequer, had decided that, in the second failure, there was to be no Government importation of food from abroad and no interference whatsoever with the laws of supply and demand; whatever might be done by starting public works and paying wages, the provision of food for Ireland was to be left entirely to private enterprise and private traders.

The new policy was received by officials in Ireland with dismay, and on August 4 Routh pressed Trevelyan to import food, now and at once. "You cannot answer the cry of want by a quotation from political economy. You ought to have 16,000 tons of Indian corn . . . you ought to have half of the supply which you require in the country before Christmas." How great a quantity would be needed, wrote Routh, would be determined this month, when the main crop began to be dug.

No preparations, however, even if preparations had been made on double the scale urged, could, in fact, have saved the Irish people from the fate which lay before them. Before the depots could be closed or the public works shut down, almost in a night, every potato in Ireland was lost. "On the 27th of last month," wrote Father Mathew to Trevelyan, on August 7, "I passed from Cork to Dublin and this doomed plant bloomed in all the luxuriance of an abundant harvest. Returning on the third instant I beheld with sorrow one wide waste of putrefying vegetation. In many places the wretched people were seated on the fences of their decaying gardens, wringing their hands and wailing bitterly the destruction that had left them foodless."

"I shall never forget," wrote Captain Mann, a Coastguard officer employed in relief service, "the change in one week in August. On the first occasion, on an official visit of inspection, I had passed over thirty-two miles thickly studded with potato fields in full bloom. The next time the face of the whole country was changed, the stalk remained bright green, but the leaves were all scorched black. It was the work of a night."

Sir James Dombrain reported that, in a tour of eight hundred miles during the first week in August, "all is lost and gone"; the horrible stench from the diseased potatoes was "perceptible as you travel along the road"; in Cork, on August 3, the stench from rotting potatoes was "intolerable." On August 7 Colonel Knox Gore, Lieutenant of County Sligo, found "from Mullingar to Maynooth every field was black," and on August 8 the steward of the Ventry estates wrote that "the fields in Kerry look as if fire had passed over them." Failure was "universal" in Ulster by August 7, and in Longford, Galway, King's County, Westmeath and Co. Dublin every potato was completely blighted.

Disaster was universal. The failure of 1845 had, to some degree, been partial; the loss, though serious, had been unequally distributed, and the blighted areas "isolated and detached." The country, in Routh's words, had been "like a checker board, black and white next door," and Trevelyan, summing up the first failure, was able to describe it as "a probationary season of distress."

The difficulties experienced in administering Sir Robert Peel's relief scheme were due to the state of Ireland, the poverty, the unemployment, the annual semi-starvation which millions customarily endured. It was these unfortunate wretches, "the old habitual mass of want in Ireland," the "fixed tide of distress which never ebbs" who, besieging the relief committee rooms and surging on to the public works in tens of thousands, had broken down the administrative machinery.

In the first failure, with the exception of the potatoes, the harvest had been above the average, and though distress was greatly intensified, yet thanks to the relief scheme the people in many districts had been better off than usual. Trevelyan, with whom John Ball agreed, wrote, "In the first failure the people suffered less than in ordinary years, owing to the pains taken to prevent them from feeling want."

In the summer of 1846 the situation was very different. The harvest generally, was poor, and the people were at the end of their resources. Every rag had been already pawned to buy food, every edible scrap had gone. The people were weakened and despairing. "A stranger," wrote a sub-inspector of police from County Cork, on August 4, "would wonder how these wretched beings find food . . . Clothes being in pawn there is nothing to change. They sleep in their rags and have pawned their bedding."

The whole face of the country was changed. "From the Giants Causeway to Cape Clear, from Limerick to Dublin, not a green field is to be seen." Violent thunderstorms occurred: "electricity"—lightning—was seen playing over the blackened fields, torrential rain fell, the country round Dublin was flooded, and an "extraordinary dense fog" was seen by Routh on August 6 to descend over blighted areas, "cold and damp and close without any wind."

It is, declared a leader-writer in *The Times* on September 2, "total annihilation."

Chapter V

IT IS now known that blight is caused by a fungus named *Phytophthora infestans*.* It was not a sickness of the plants themselves which turned the potato fields of Ireland black almost overnight. Invasion by a microscopic living organism took place, an organism able to reproduce itself with lightning speed and "an addition to the known flora of Europe and a part of the creation which had never been catalogued before."

Blight is with us still. Every year since 1845, in potato fields throughout the northern hemisphere, the blight fungus has been present, waiting only for the right weather conditions to multiply with fearful rapidity, as again happened, with exceptional severity, in 1958.

Up to 1939 blight is estimated to have cost the United Kingdom an average of five million pounds a year. In a bad year—1879 for instance—potatoes worth six million pounds were destroyed in Ireland alone. In the United States during

* For the material in this chapter I am indebted to the kindness and patience of Mr. Geoffrey Samuel, late of the Agricultural Research Council, and for the historical aspects to Mr. E. C. Large of the Plant Pathology Laboratory, who has generously allowed me to make a free use of the facts in his remarkable book *The Advance of the Fungi*. I should also like to thank Dr. N. Robertson of the University of Hull for his valuable suggestions.

the severe attack of 1928 a single state, the State of New York, lost thirteen million bushels.

Where the potato blight originated and how it came to Europe is a mystery. Early botanists and natural historians do not mention any disease resembling blight, and potatoes had been grown in most European countries for nearly two hundred years before blight appeared. A potato disease identical with blight was found in North Germany near Hanover about 1830, but the first fully-recorded outbreak took place in the New World in 1842, when potatoes along the Atlantic coast of North America, from Nova Scotia to Boston, were destroyed. This attack was followed, in Europe, by the serious outbreak of 1845 and the total loss of 1846.

It has been proved that the organism of the blight fungus is so sensitive to heat and drought that its spread, for any considerable distance, by air currents is impossible, and the blight fungus almost certainly reached Europe in a diseased tuber, carried in a ship from North America. When this took place is not known, but the description of blight in Germany about 1830 disposes of a pleasing theory, that blight had to wait for the coming of steam to cross the Atlantic. It had been argued that potatoes stored in the hold of a sailing-ship became so warm during the slow passage through the Doldrums that the fungus was killed, whereas the shorter passage, by steam, allowed it to survive. But the first crossing of the Atlantic by a steamship was not accomplished until 1838, eight years after blight was observed in Germany; and early steamships, owing to their extravagant consumption of fuel, were not used to any extent as cargo vessels for more than fifteen years after the initial crossing.

Blight is now treated by spraying with copper compounds, such as Bordeaux mixture, the compound of copper sulphate and quicklime first used in the vineyards of France against *Peronospora*, the deadly fungus of the vines. Potato crops attacked or threatened by blight are nowadays sprayed on a large scale, frequently from aeroplanes and helicopters, and though blight remains the most serious plant pestilence in the northern hemisphere complete destruction of a crop no longer takes place.

In 1846, however, there was no notion of treating or protecting potato plants, nor any comprehension of the nature of blight. More than fifteen years were to pass before blight was acknowledged to be the work of a fungus and nearly forty before, in 1885, Bordeaux mixture was first used.

Yet almost as soon as blight appeared the truth was discerned; what was lacking was proof.

In the summer of 1845 the Reverend M. J. Berkeley, a country clergyman, perpetual curate of the parishes of Wood Newton and Apethorpe, in Northamptonshire, observed that whenever the mysterious new disease attacked the potato plants in his parish a tiny growth, a minute fungus, was invariably to be found on the blighted parts of leaves and tubers. Mr. Berkeley was no ordinary country parson. A gentleman "eminent in his knowledge of the habits of fungi," he had done valuable work on molluscs, seaweeds and algae when a curate at Margate, and been responsible for the volume on fungi in Smith's famous *English Flora,* published in 1836.

Mr. Berkeley was in the habit of corresponding with a French botanist of eminence, Dr. Montagne, originally a surgeon in the Napoleonic army who had become an authority on mosses and lichens. When blight appeared in France, Dr. Montagne also observed the tiny growth, and communicated with Mr. Berkeley; drawings and descriptions were exchanged, and the growth in England and the growth in France proved identical. On August 30, 1845, at a meeting of the Société Philomatique, in Paris, Dr. Montagne described the growth and claimed the discovery of a new species of fungus. The claim was recognized and accepted.

Mr. Berkeley now went further. In January, 1846, after the first failure, he published an article in the *Journal of the Horticultural Society* of London, entitled "Observations, Botanical and Physiological, on the Potato Murrain," in which, after describing the new fungus, he asserted that it, and it alone, was the cause of the recent potato pestilence. The disease known as blight, he declared, was caused by the growth of the fungus, as a parasite, on the potato plant, and by nothing else.

Vehement controversy followed. Mr. Berkeley's theory, the "fungal theory," as it was called, contradicted the doctrines generally held at that time, and many scientists, including Dr. Lindley, the well-known editor of the *Gardeners' Chronicle,* disagreed. A prolonged altercation followed, and Dr. Lindley and Mr. Berkeley argued hotly, week after week, in the columns of the *Horticultural Journal* and the *Gardeners' Chronicle.*

It was generally believed then that fungi were the consequence, not the cause, of decay. Because they were usually to
be found on rotting matter it was argued that fungi appeared
as a result of the heat and fermentation which accompany
the processes of decompostion; and there was also a lingering belief that the fermentation and heat of decomposition
could somehow generate life, that overripe cheese could
generate mites and bad meat blowflies. An earlier generation
had believed that old rags and stale cheese, shut up together
in a box, could produce mice, and though scientists had
discarded these fables more than a century ago, they still
believed that such rudimentary forms of life as fungi could
be produced by the processes of decomposition.

Therefore, though Dr. Lindley, too, had observed the
invariable presence of the tiny fungus on blighted plants, he
had passed it over as being a normal consequence of decay,
or of the "wet putrefaction" and "dropsy" which, in his
opinion, were the cause of blight.

Moreover, Mr. Berkeley was now asked some very awkward
questions. Mr Berkeley's theory, the "fungal theory," must
depend on the order in which the fungus and the blight
appeared, and if the fungus caused blight, it must come first;
could Mr. Berkeley prove this? Could he demonstrate that
healthy plants were attacked by the fungus and then developed blight? It was admitted that the fungus was invariably
to be found on the blighted parts of leaves and tubers, but
that fact proved nothing, except its close association with
decay, which was already known.

There was another important question. If a fungus was
responsible, how was it that potatoes not yet dug and still
in the ground were found to be blighted? True, certain
species of fungi had airborne spores, and might spread from
leaf to leaf of the potato plants, but how could tubers, which
were underground, be affected?

To these and other questions Mr. Berkeley could give no
satisfactory answer; though with a flash of genius he had
divined the truth, he had little evidence to support his theory,
and the "Observations," now regarded as a landmark in
botanical history, which he published in the *Journal of the
Horticultural Society* were almost universally rejected.

Unfortunately Mr. Berkeley never did produce proof, and
the truth of the fungal theory was established very slowly, over
more than three-quarters of a century. While mycology, the

science of the fungi, made notable advances in the fifty years
following 1845, and the life cycles of *Rust,* the fungus of
wheat, and *Oidum,* the fungus of vines, were traced and a
remedy brought within sight; the life cycle of the potato
fungus remained a mystery. It was not until well into the
twentieth century that, after "one of the longest games of
hide-and-seek in natural history," the enigma was solved and
the habits, the method of functioning and the manner in
which *Phytophthora infestans* survives and propagates itself
became known.

By a stroke of poetic justice it was in Ireland that much
of the final research was carried out, by Professor Paul
Murphy, a Kilkenny man, at the Albert Agricultural College,
Glasnevin, Dublin.

&

Phytophthora infestans first makes its appearance as a minute,
whitish growth, resembling a fringe, just visible to the naked
eye, surrounding the blighted and decaying parts on the
leaves of infested potato plants. Under the microscope, this
"down" is seen to be made up of countless long, slender,
branching filaments, each carrying at its tip a minute pear-
shaped swelling. The filaments are, in fact, fungus-tubes, and
the pear-shaped swelling each carries is a container, like a
capsule, which contains the spore of the fungus. The blight
fungus consists of these fungus-tubes; they form a vegetable
organism of great destructive power; without roots, without
flowers, without any differentiation between stem and leaves,
which grows and develops within the plant, and, by means of
the spore container, is able to propagate itself with frightening rapidity. The spores formed on a single potato plant
which has been invaded by the blight fungus can, if weather
conditions are favourable, infect many thousands of other
plants in a few days.

The spore containers grow at the ends of the fungus-tubes,
like fruits on a branch, until they are mature, when they
become separated. The lightest breeze detaches them; the
gentlest rain or dew washes them off. Countless thousands
then fall to the ground; other myriads become airborne, and
drift.

When an airborne spore container drifts on to the leaf of
a potato plant it settles and, given one necessary condition,
germinates at once. The necessary condition is moisture. The

spore of the blight fungus is water-borne; when it moves it swims and, therefore, to germinate effectively it needs a drop of moisture. The scientists of 1846 who attributed blight to the wetness of the summer were very nearly right. Though rain and damp are not the cause of blight, without them the fungus does not multiply rapidly. Consequently, in a dry summer there is little blight, and the fungus, though present, is more or less dormant; while during a damp season blight is at its most vigorous. Violent driving rain does not provide the conditions most favourable to the spread of blight; in gales of rain the down-like fringe, consisting of thousands upon thousands of fungus-tubes, is washed off. It is when the atmosphere is moist and muggy that spore production reaches its height, and the blight fungus spreads with such rapidity that potato fields seem to be ruined overnight. The soft, warm climate of Ireland, particularly in the west, with its perpetual light rains and mild breezes, provides ideal conditions for the spread of the fungus, and has been truly described as a forcing-house for blight.

Given adequate moisture, the container proceeds surprisingly to germinate in two different ways. Sometimes it germinates as one unit, sending a single germ-tube instantly into the potato leaf, sometimes its contents split up within the container and become from six to sixteen smaller spores, which are then released in a swarm. Under the microscope these spores can be seen, at the moment of release, jostling each other, "much more like little uni-cellular animals let out of a bag than anything one might expect to find in the vegetable kingdom." The tiny spores are called zoospores, meaning that they are able to move; after liberation they swim away and, settling on a fresh part of the leaf, each sends out a minute germ-tube to invade the leaf, but at six to sixteen points instead of one.

In a short time the leaf is overrun by a system of radiating fungus-tubes, pushing their way through, to emerge in due course, each bearing at its tip the pear-shaped containers which, in a very few hours, will release fresh hordes of spores. In this process the potato plant is destroyed. As the fungus-tubes, whether originating from large or small spores, work their way through the leaf, lengthening and branching, they leave ruin behind, the juices of the leaf are drained and the tissues exhausted; a change takes place in the matter of which the leaf is composed, fermentations appear, followed by discoloration and mortification; finally, the entire foliage of the potato plant turns black, withers and dies. Yet this process is not purely destructive; it is from the fermentation and decay of the leaf that the fungus extracts its nourishment, the "protoplasm," or vital substance, which enables the fungus-tubes to live.

The unfortunate potato plant is now not only being devoured but choked as well. "If a man," writes Mr. E. C. Large, "could imagine his own plight, with growths of some weird and colourless seaweed issuing from his mouth and nostrils, from roots which were destroying and choking both his digestive system and his lungs, he would then have a very crude and fabulous, but perhaps an instructive, idea of the condition of the potato plant. . . ."

Meanwhile, beneath the ground, the blight fungus is attacking the potatoes themselves. How this happens was for many years one of the major mysteries of blight. It used to be thought that the disease travelled down the stem of the plant to the tubers, and one of the earliest treatments for blight, still occasionally practised today, was to cut off the stems and foliage of infected plants, close to the ground. But this operation by no means invariably prevents infection, and if done too early it may prove as ruinous as blight itself. Once stems and foliage are amputated, none of the food material which the plant derives from the green chlorophyll in the leaves can pass down to the tubers, growth stops, and the result is a useless crop of wizened, dwarfed potatoes the size of walnuts.

It has now been established that blight penetrates the soil to the tubers. Moisture is, once more, the deciding factor; if rain is sufficiently heavy and continuous, some of the myriads of spore containers which fall to the ground are washed down, through the soil, on to the potatoes. The process of destruction which took place on the leaf is now repeated: the spore container germinates, each spore, whether entire or the result of splitting up, sends a germ-tube into the tuber and the fungus then works its way from cell to cell. Blackened and decomposing patches appear on the skin of the potato and in its flesh, and eventually the exhausted tissues collapse into pulp.

As a rule, however, blight fungus remains inactive for a considerable period when it has entered the potato; only a discoloration of the skin betrays the presence of the fungus within, and such infected tubers are the means by which

blight is most commonly spread. If tubers containing the
dormant blight fungus are planted either accidentally or because the importance of the partial infection is not realized, as
happened in Ireland in 1845-46, a small number will throw up
shoots early in the season; these are infected with blight
when they appear. A fungus-tube from within the potato has
grown up inside the stem of the shoot, and thus, at the
beginning of the season, a nucleus of infection is established,
ready to develop with lightning rapidity when the weather
becomes warm and moist in July, August, or September.

The Ministry of Agriculture in London forecasts the onset
of blight each year from a study of the weather records. As
soon as conditions favouring blight occur, warnings are issued
recommending potato growers to spray their crops.

The blight fungus also infects potatoes after digging, a
source of despair and bewilderment in 1845. The top and
foliage of a plant can be destroyed by blight while the
potatoes in the ground beneath may be sound: either the
potatoes were too well-covered with earth for the blight
spore to reach them or, as was frequently the case in Ireland,
rain was light and did not wash the spore containers down
through the soil. But, even so, danger of infection is not over;
countless thousands of live spore containers are on the leaves
of surrounding plants, and as the potatoes are dug they are
showered with spores. If the weather is dry no harm is done,
but if it is moist the spore containers find the drop of water
they must have to germinate, and within a few hours the
fungus is active, growing rapidly through the tubers. In a few
weeks the potatoes which were sound when dug are a mass
of rottenness.

In 1845 much of the infection occurred after the potatoes
were dug. In 1846 rain was exceptionally heavy, the spore
containers were washed down on to the tubers, which were
then devoured by the fungus and became rotten in the ground.

The life of the blight fungus is short. If the air is dry the
spore containers carried at the end of each fungus-tube live
for only a few hours; if the weather is damp, and the spore
germinates, the new germ-tube must penetrate a leaf quickly,
or it dies. When cold weather comes, the work of destruction
being completed, the fungus dies.

For long it remained a mystery how the fungus survives
the winter and starts its work of destruction again the following year. It has never been proved that the spore of the

blight fungus can survive the winter in European soil, but it appears that the fungus survives from season to season, lying dormant in the slightly diseased potatoes which are occasionally planted, through ignorance or accident, with healthy tubers. The fungus grows up within the stem, diseased shoots develop, and as soon as conditions of weather and temperature are favourable the fungus begins to form its spores again. Once spore production has started the blight fungus can spread with astonishing rapidity. In moist, warm conditions one diseased plant within a day or two releases several million spores, each one of which is capable of dividing within itself and producing a swarm of smaller spores. If a number of slightly diseased seed potatoes have been planted in different places, and diseased shoots appear in any quantity, blight can become general in a few weeks. Countless millions of spore containers germinate hourly; germ-tubes work their way into leaf and tuber, reducing green and healthy plants to decay; fields are seen to turn black, tubers, hastily dug, collapse into stinking masses, and the fearful stench of decomposition hangs over the land.

In Ireland in 1846 conditions favoured the spread of the blight fungus to an extent which has not been recorded before or since. There had been an outbreak of blight the previous year, and very many slightly diseased potatoes had been planted in the fields, sending up diseased shoots. The weather of 1846 was wet—"continual rain" yet warm; on June 6 *The Times* recorded a heat wave. Ignorance was complete; blight was not known to be a fungus; treatment with Bordeaux mixture was not attempted for nearly forty years.

The great Irish failure of 1846 is the classic example of an outbreak of blight, and the people of Ireland, gazing over their blackened fields, despaired. They were already exhausted. What resources they possessed had been used up, and death from starvation was not a possible but an immediate fate.

Once more, the question so frequently asked in the past was on every lip—what would the British Government do to save Ireland?

Chapter VI

THE GOVERNMENT in power was the Whig Government which had defeated the Tories under Sir Robert Peel at the end of June, and at first glance it seemed as if the Whigs were more likely to be sympathetic to Ireland than the Tories.

Civil and religious liberty was the Whig watchword, and the Whig leader, Lord John Russell, had an impressively liberal record. He had moved the first reading of the famous Reform Bill on March 31, 1831; he had brought forward a resolution, in 1834, to inquire into the expenditure of the immense revenues of the Established Protestant Church of Ireland; after the Repeal crisis, he had moved for an inquiry into the state of Ireland, which resulted in the great Irish debate of February, 1844. William IV had called him "a dangerous little Radical."

His radicalism was, however, qualified by the circumstances of his birth. John Russell was the son of the sixth Duke of Bedford, and with liberal principles he combined a strong, at times an overweening, sense of rank. His manners were arrogant; his brother, the Marquess of Tavistock, warned him in 1838 that he was giving great offence to his followers in the House of Commons by not being courteous to them, by treating them superciliously and *"de haut en bas"*; while the diarist Greville complained of being received in John's "coldest and most offensive manner, nothing could be more ungracious and I mentally resolved never to go near him again. . . ."

He had had to contend, however, with disabilities which would have crushed a less determined man. To begin with, he was so small as to be little more than a dwarf. The savage wit of the period caricatured him as a large-headed midget, a puny little girl, an elderly child seated on Melbourne's lap; and when he married, as his first wife, the widow of Lord Ribblesdale, he was nicknamed "The Widow's Mite."

John Russell had some connections with Ireland: his father had been Lord-Lieutenant between 1806 and 1807,

and Lord John had spent three months of the summer of
1806 at the Vice-Regal Lodge in Phoenix Park; there was also
a family property, Ardsallagh Castle, in County Meath.

He was now to be in control of the fate of Ireland throughout the coming crisis. He held office from June, 1846, until
February, 1852, the worst of the famine years, and during
that period the Irish policy of the British Government was
his responsibility. When he ceased to be Prime Minister, in
1852, the famine, officially at least, was over.

❦

One of the first acts of Lord John Russell's administration
was to appoint a new Lord-Lieutenant of Ireland; the office
was political, and when the Tories went out their Lord
Lieutenant, Lord Heytesbury, automatically resigned. Lord
Bessborough was selected, an admirable and popular choice.
He was head of the respected family of Ponsonby; his estates
at Bessborough were well administered, and he was not only
a good but a resident landlord, the first resident landlord to be
appointed Lord-Lieutenant since the Union. His temper was
"remarkably calm and unruffled," and he had distinguished
himself as a minister during two successful terms of office.
Most important of all, he had been "during almost the whole
of his life on terms of warm friendship" with O'Connell and
had introduced him to the House of Commons when no one
else would do so, on O'Connell's first taking his seat, after
Catholic emancipation was passed. It was hoped that, through
Lord Bessborough, the enormous power O'Connell wielded in
Ireland would be used for, and not against, the Government
during the coming crisis.

But in the summer of 1846 O'Connell's power was no
longer absolute. The Liberator was seventy-one years of age,
his health was beginning to fail; within the Repeal Association
there was discontent, and a group of intelligent, ardent young
Repealers had formed themselves into a new party, which
they called "Young Ireland." The Young Irelanders were
extremists; their language was violent, and they declared that
O'Connell's policy of moral force, his insistence on "the
carrying the Repeal by peaceable, legal and constitutional
means and by *none other*," had failed, and must be discarded.

In July, 1846, on the eve of the total failure of the potato,
and the month when Bessborough took office, differences
between Young Ireland and Old Ireland came to a head, on

the question of resorting to physical force to win freedom, and the leaders of Young Ireland, now labelled the "physical force men," walked out of Conciliation Hall, Burgh Quay, Dublin, the Repeal Association's headquarters.

O'Connell's power and prestige were shaken, armed rebellion appeared a possibility, very violent language had been used. Bessborough became alarmed. In spite of his Irish sympathies, he asked for a Coercion Bill declaring that Ireland could not be governed without emergency powers amounting to martial law. The Coercion Bill was, in fact, withdrawn; for no reason connected with Ireland, but because members of Parliament, having turned out the Tory Government on a vote against Irish Coercion, refused to vote in favour of it a few weeks later; nevertheless, irreparable damage had been done. Young Ireland, the physical force men, had presented a fatal image of Ireland when the time of her greatest need was just at hand.

English newspapers represented the Irish, not as helpless famine victims, but as cunning and bloodthirsty desperadoes. *Punch,* for instance, published cartoons week after week depicting the Irishman as a filthy, brutal creature, an assassin and a murderer, begging for money, under a pretence of buying food, to spend on weapons. "With the money they get from our relief funds, they buy arms," wrote Greville.

Ireland was a disturbing thought, and it was therefore a comfort to be able to believe that the Irish were not starving or, if some of them were, the depravity of the Irish was such that they deserved to starve; and to treat Ireland's desperate appeals, as famine approached, as merely another whine from a professional beggar. "It is possible to have heard the tale of sorrow too often," observed *The Times* lead-writer, on August 3, 1846.

∽

Yet no doubts of the gravity of the impending catastrophe were felt by Lord John Russell and his Government; reports of the universal failure of the potato were being confirmed by every mail, and new measures for Irish relief had been in course of preparation for some weeks.

The new plans were the work of Trevelyan. He prepared a memorandum, dated on August 1, 1846, in which he detailed last season's relief plans, set out the respects in which they had failed, and outlined a plan to meet the coming crisis. This memorandum formed the basis of the new scheme, and Trevelyan, who possessed the administrative abilities which Lord John Russell's colleagues on the whole lacked, now became virtually dictator of relief for Ireland.

～

On August 17, 1846, Lord John Russell rose in the Commons to acquaint the House, "with great pain," that "the prospect of the potato crop is even more distressing than last year— that the disease has appeared earlier, and its ravages are far more extensive"; it was "imperative on the Government and Parliament to take extraordinary measures for relief."

The new relief scheme, briefly, fell under two main heads. First, though public works were again to be undertaken, and on a large scale, the British Government would no longer, as last year, bear half their cost. The whole expense was to be paid by the district in which the works were carried out. "Presentment sessions," meetings of ratepayers at which works were proposed, would be held as before, but instead of being voluntary meetings they were to be summoned by the Lord-Lieutenant, at his discretion. Works were to be approved and executed by the Board of Works. The cost was to be met by advances from the Treasury, repayable in their entirety in ten years, at 3½ per cent. interest, and the money for repayment was to be raised by a rate levied on all poor-rate payers in the locality, a momentous and contro-versial innovation. The expense was designed to "fall entirely on persons possessed of property in the distressed district," who were, after all, responsible for the poor on their estates. This part of the new procedure was embodied in an Act, "to facilitate the employment of the Labouring Poor for a limited period in distressed districts in Ireland," popularly called the Labour Rate Act. This measure was the most im-portant section of the new scheme, and proved a source of difficulty, confusion, discontent and ruin. In addition, the modest sum of £50,000 was to be spent in free grants to those districts in Ireland too poor to bear the whole cost of public works.

Second, the Government would not import or supply any food. There were to be no Government depots to sell meal at a low cost or, in urgent cases, to make free issues, as had been done during last season's failure. No orders were to be sent abroad, nor would any purchases be made by Government in local markets. It was held that the reason why dealers and import merchants had so signally failed to provide food to replace the potato last season had been the Government's purchases. Trade, said Trevelyan, had been "paralysed" on account of these purchases, which interfered with private enterprise and the legitimate profits of private enterprise; and how, he asked, could dealers be expected to invest in the very large stocks necessary to meet this year's total failure of the potato if at any moment Government might step in with supplies—sold at low cost—which would deprive dealers of their profit and "make their outlay so much loss?"

This section of the scheme was received with consternation, and Routh, with unaccustomed boldness, wrote from Dublin, "As for the great question of leaving the country to the corn dealers they are a very different class of men from our London, Liverpool and Bristol merchants. I do not believe there is a man among them who would import direct a single cargo from abroad."

On August 7, 1846, Father Mathew, the "apostle of Temperance," wrote in agitation to Trevelyan: he had heard rumours that "the capitalists in the corn and flour trade are endeavouring to induce government not to protect the people from famine but to leave them at their mercy," and he implored Trevelyan to take some action to feed the people.

The merchants however declared "they would not import food at all if it were the intention of government to do so"; they required an official assurance that no Government importation was contemplated, and Charles Wood, Chancellor of the Exchequer, told the House of Commons on August 17, 1846, that the assurance had been given. The Government was pledged "not to interfere with the regular mode by which Indian corn and other grains were brought into the country," but "to leave that trade as much liberty as possible." Trevelyan and Charles Wood were convinced that, once wages were being paid on the new large-scale public works, and the people had money to spend on food, then food would be attracted to Ireland. The field was to be left strictly to private enterprise.

The west of Ireland, however, was to receive special treatment. In Kerry, Donegal, the country west of the Shannon, and that part of west Cork which included Skibbereen, and the Dingle Peninsula, the population lived so exclusively on the

potato that no trade in any other description of food
existed; and here, and here only, Government food depots
were to be established. Each depot was to be in charge of a
Commissariat officer; officers stationed in Canada, the West
Indies and the Mediterranean, had already been instructed to
proceed home "without delay," and gaps were to be filled
by temporary appointments of military officers. But even in
these districts depots were to be opened only as a last resort,
when private traders had failed to provide supplies of food;
and the Government gave a pledge that the eastern part of
Ireland was to be left wholly to private enterprise. Members
of local relief committees were no longer to be elected,
but nominated by the Lieutenant of the county, and instead of
issuing employment tickets would "furnish lists of distressed
persons eligible for employment." Nominations must be of
persons holding official or semi-official positions, magistrates
and resident magistrates, senior constabulary and coastguard
officers, chairmen of Poor Law unions, and the principal
clergymen of each denomination, Protestant, Roman Catholic
and Nonconformist. The regulation specifying only principal
clergymen had the effect of excluding Catholic curates; and
through it was true that during the previous year some
Catholic curates had found difficulty in working smoothly with
persons not of their religious persuasion, they undoubtedly
possessed an intimate and invaluable knowledge of the inhabitants of their parishes. "You must not exclude R.C.
curates," wrote Lord Monteagle, a Protestant, to Lord
Bessborough; "without them we could not do a stroke and
here they are labouring like tigers for us, working day and
night."

Lieutenants of counties had power to add members to
committees, but whether or not this power was ever exercised
in favour of Catholic curates does not appear to be recorded.

Subscriptions were still to be collected locally in aid of
relief, but the Government donation was limited to half the
total amount collected, at the most. Finally, officials employed by the Commissariat and the Board of Works would
be paid by the British Government.

Such, very broadly, were the outlines of the scheme devised by Trevelyan for the Government of Lord John Russell
to meet the total failure of the potato. In the course of
relieving last season's failure some very painful lessons had
been learned. Then the whole labouring population of Ireland,

wherever they had the chance, had rushed to throw themselves on the Government works; the scheme had, to a large extent, been swamped; there had been confusion and waste, and very large sums of public money had melted away. Yet last year's failure had been only partial; the prospect of relieving a total failure by the same methods was impossible to contemplate—Trevelyan declared that the Exchequer itself would not be equal to the occasion.

Therefore, the first object of the new plans was to "check the exorbitant demands of last season"; they were, in fact, designed not to save Ireland but to protect England. The scheme was to be in force for a year, and no longer; writing to Mr. Labouchere, appointed Chief Secretary for Ireland by the Whigs, Trevelyan spoke of "the year of relief," and laid down, in a Treasury minute, "No advances . . . will in any circumstances be made for carrying on . . . works after the 15th August 1847."

It has to be admitted, wrote a Whig historian, "that the Government in the summer of 1846 did not realize the full consequences of the loss of the potato."

Trevelyan anticipated that there would be what he called a "breathing time" about the second week in August, when the potatoes from the new crop became fit to eat. Last year there had been such a pause: while the crop was hurriedly dug and every potato conceivably edible eaten before it rotted. He intended to use this "breathing time" to overhaul the relief organization, so that the departments would be ready "to put our whole machinery in motion at an early date"; in particular, he was determined that the Board of Works should be set out "to re-organize to meet the increased magnitude of the coming exigency." At the beginning of the scheme he lost one of his ablest colleagues: Edward Pine Coffin, who had been in charge of the depot at Limerick, was knighted in recognition of his services and sent to report on distress in the highlands of Scotland.

Throughout August, 1846, Trevelyan worked very hard indeed. He speaks of being at the Treasury until 3 a.m., "dead beat," and of working weekdays and Sundays alike. An official of the Board of Works, summoned over to London, was told "to come on Sunday and knock at the private entrance in Downing Street below the Treasury." Every detail of the new relief scheme was controlled by Trevelyan, and all Commissariat and Board of Works, Ireland, letters, as well as all private letters, were, by his instructions, sent up to him unopened. Commissariat officers recalled from Canada and the West Indies each received a personal letter from Trevelyan, with "blue books" to study during the voyage. It was, he wrote, "the most difficult and responsible task that has ever fallen to my lot."

Great exertions were expected of his subordinates; Mrs. Perceval, wife of a Commissariat officer, wrote to Trevelyan complaining that her husband was being worked so hard that he was losing his health, and was told, shortly, by Trevelyan, on July 9, that he had "never known a person injured by hard work."

All these exertions were in vain. It was too late for preparation. Disaster was upon Ireland now.

No "breathing time" occurred; the "influx of early potatoes," wrote Routh, on August 13, 1846, "due to the desire to realize something before that something shall be wholly lost . . . failed on account of the rapid progress of the disease"; and the notification that the Government depots were to close brought frantic protests. Already, in the west, the Government meal was all that stood between a swarming population and starvation. From Swineford, the secretary of the Relief Committee wrote on August 5, 1846, that closing the depot there would produce "the extremest misery"; all the new potatoes had failed and the price of meal was already more than doubled. At Ballyhaunis the people were "not far off starvation": if the Government depot shut down there would be violence. At Ballina Mr. Vaughan Jackson, a well-known resident landlord, considered the situation critical; if the depot closed peace would be endangered.

Outside Government circles, closing the food depots at the moment of total failure appeared inexplicable. *The Times,* no advocate of relief for Ireland, found it impossible to understand why "the authorities cut off supplies with the undisputed fact of an extensive failure of this year's potato crop staring them in the face," and the Catholic Archbishop John MacHale, known as "the Lion of St. Jarlath's," told Lord John Russell, "You might as well issue an edict of general starvation as stop the supplies. . . ."

But Trevelyan and the British Government were not to be shaken in their determination. A quantity of meal, rather under 3,000 tons in all, the residue of Sir Robert Peel's scheme, remained in the depots, and permission was given to distribute this to starving districts, but in the smallest possible quantities, and then only after a relief committee had been formed and a subscription raised to pay for it. No free issues whatever were to be made. Nevertheless, Commissariat officers in Ireland did give food away; a Major Wainwright, for instance, was detected in giving a quantity of meal to starving persons in Oughterard, County Galway, early in August, and was reprimanded from Whitehall.

Closing the public works was even more difficult. The Treasury minute of July 21, 1846, directing all works to be closed, except in certain unusual cases, had had little effect; on the excuse that works were not finished, or that extraordinary distress existed in the neighbourhood, a large number continued. The Chancellor of the Exchequer now ordered that all undertakings must be shut down on August 8, irrespective of whether or not they were completed and of the distress in the district.

Angry demonstrations followed. In Limerick, on August 5, on being told their employment was to end, labourers tore up the stretch of road they had just laid; in Cork, about August 18, a mob of 400 labourers, declaring they were starving, marched into the town carrying their spades and demanding work; however, they dispersed "quietly," on being addressed by the Sub-Inspector of Police, who added a note to his report that "employment is very much needed." Bodies of starving, workless labourers marched into Dungarvan, Clogher and Macroom, and the Poor Law Guardians of Bandon, "expecting a visit from a mob demanding employment," asked for Government protection.

Suffering was so painful and widespread that by order of the Lord-Lieutenant, Lord Bessborough, all uncompleted works were re-started on September 6. The unfortunate Board of Works thus received a double task, to get the works of last season going again and to set up an organization capable of meeting the demands which would follow the first presentment sessions to be held under the new Act, in September. Staff was wanting, office space in Dublin was wanting, the interval for reorganization did not occur, and even before the new scheme began the Board of Works was in confusion.

Mr. Richard Griffith and Mr. Thomas Larcom were appointed, by Act of Parliament, special Commissioners, to supervise relief works, and two better men could not have been found; Mr. Griffith had pushed through a scheme which

fixed the value of land throughout Ireland; Captain Larcom
had played a large part in the Ordnance Survey and had
been a Census Commissioner in 1841. The *Freeman's Journal*,
however, remarked that, whatever their attainments and
aptitudes, they could not possibly get through "all that was
heaped upon them."

Extra office accommodation for the new Commissioners
was not provided, and the offices of the Board in Dublin
were crammed to bursting point. Desks stood in corridors,
"in every available place where there was light for a clerk to
see," and corridors and passages were further "blocked with
deputations and expectants for office." Trevelyan was asked,
on September 17, to sanction the addition of an extra storey
to the Board of Works' building, at a cost of £905 4s.,
and refused.

"A stranger can form no idea!" wrote Colonel Jones. "Instead of the quiet of a well regulated London office, ours
resembles a great bazaar."

Meanwhile, from London, Trevelyan, toiling to produce
order and method, sent directions and requests for information which must have arrived in the "great bazaar" of the
Board of Works' office like messages from another world.
On August 26, for instance, he directed Colonel Jones to
submit "a sketch map of Ireland showing the number of
separate works and the total . . . *in each Barony,* and distin-
guishing *improvements of roads, etc., and their cost* from
new roads and their cost, and also stating the number and
amount of works of each of the two above descriptions which
have been discontinued, that is the *number sanctioned and not
commenced,* the number *commenced and stopped,* and the
amount which has been saved by each of these proceedings."

No answer appears to have been received, and in any
case a few days later the information would have been useless.
The Labour Rate Act received the Royal Assent on August
28. Presentment Sessions, under the Act, began on September
4, and applications immediately poured into the Board of
Works in numbers exceeding the worst expectations. Last
year's history repeated itself on an immensely larger scale,
and the Board of Works was again swamped.

The object of the Labour Rate Act was to force Irish
landlords to pay for the relief of their distressed tenantry.
Since they had failed to do their duty voluntarily, they were
to be compelled: under the new Act, there could be no

evading payment of the rate to be levied. "The backwardness
of the landlords had made compulsory measures inevitable,"
Trevelyan wrote to Stephen Spring Rice, Lord Monteagle's
son, on September 2.

Trevelyan was further convinced that because, under the
Labour Rate Act, the whole of the money advanced had to
be repaid by the district in which it was spent, the scramble
of last year would not take place and property owners would
think twice before sending distressed labourers in droves to the
works, when the result would be that they incurred a mountain of debt.

Yet there was a possibility which the Government had not
considered. How would the Labour Rate Act operate if the
landlords did not possess sufficient funds to pay the rate for
relief works assessed on them? Trevelyan, however, chose to
believe as firmly in the financial resources of Irish landlords
as in the capacity of Irish private enterprise; and the only
direct contribution Government proposed to make was the
£50,000 advanced, under the Labour Rate Act, to districts so
poor that it was impossible advances should ever be repaid.

Fifty thousand pounds to save a starving people! exclaimed
Archbishop MacHale, and he reminded Lord John Russell
that although twenty million pounds of public money were
spent by England to emancipate the Negroes of the West
Indies, £50,000 was all that was to be allotted to save Ireland
from death.

Irish landlords considered they had been disgracefully
treated by the British Government over the Labour Rate Act
—it was pushed through and became law before they realized
what was taking place. Stephen Spring Rice, Lord Monteagle's
son, wrote that "the Irish gentry were taken by surprise."
The Act "was not introduced until the middle of August
1846, and was hurried through in ten days, after almost all
the Irish Members had left London." "It is enough to make a
man turn Repealer," he told Trevelyan angrily, "to have
such a measure hurried through Parliament . . . without giving
us an opportunity to be heard"; while Lord Palmerston, then
Foreign Secretary and an Irish landlord, observed that if the
Act was to remain in force for any length of time "the landlords will in the end be as well qualified as their cottiers to
demand admission into a Union [Work] House."

The Labour Rate Act, however, contained a fatal and
most alluring provision—no money had to be found imme-

diately. In 1845, landlords who assumed half the cost of a
work undertook a considerable personal responsibility, even
though the other half was a free grant. This year, under the
Labour Rate Act, personal responsibility was removed and
the liability spread over all ratepayers in a district. No man
felt the debt would fall on him; if he could not pay, someone
else would, and repayment was in any case ten years away.
The result of the Act was the direct opposite to Trevelyan's
expectation, and there was an orgy of wild extravagance.
"Large sums are voted at baronial sessions, as if there were
no such thing as repayment in the memory of the ratepayers,"
reported *The Times,* on September 22, 1846.

Presentment Sessions were held in public, to prevent property owners from evading their obligations; any person might
attend and any person might put forward proposals for works.
From these the most suitable were selected by what, in effect,
was a committee of ratepayers and submitted to the Board
of Works; and to make certain that adequate relief works
were provided the Act required the ratepayers to select works
large enough to employ all the distressed in the district.

The consequence, however, of admitting the public was
chaos. "All persons," wrote Mr. Stephen Spring Rice, "had a
right to attend and make proposals without stint, mobs beset
and crowded the session-houses until there was scarcely
space to sit or air to breathe. Hundreds of proposals, drawn
up by illiterate and interested persons—labourers, petty farmers or whiskey sellers—were thrust before the persons appointed to preside, and supported by threats within doors and sometimes by violence without."

At a typical session, held at Kilfinan, Coshlea, County
Limerick, Lieutenant Inglis, of the Board of Works, reported
on September 20 that "all was riot and confusion. Sums were
named without any regard whatever to the nature and extent
of the work. . . Everything was approved. No one dared oppose
. . . During this, the riot both inside and outside the court
became more and more violent, and the confusion on the
Bench became more and more confused. At length we left
and passed with difficulty through the crowd to a neighbouring hotel." At a township named Hospital, near Ennis, on
September 30, a Board of Works' officer, Mr. Kearney, was
"hunted like a mad dog by the whole country population."
It was believed by the people that Mr. Kearney was preventing works being started in the district, and they were,

he wrote, "in a fury." Police had to interfere, "with loaded carbines," before he could drive off in his gig, "under awful groaning and pelting of stones. . . Several hundred disencumbering themselves of their coats, shoes and stockings. . . followed me for 4 miles, but thanks to a good horse I got off with my life."

Even at Shanagolden, County Limerick, where the landlord, Lord Monteagle, was one of the best in Ireland, the Sessions were, wrote Monteagle to Charles Wood, on October 4, "tumultuous." On the one hand, some ratepayers were "prepared to pass anything up to the Board of Works for the sake of peace and quietness. . . others were encouraging a lavish expenditure in the hope that repayment will be rendered improbable if not impossible." On October 7 he described to Trevelyan a "presentment session in the midst of a crowd of hungry peasants and eager farmers to give consideration to no less than 200 projects." Deliberation and discussion were impossible, and on the advice of the Board of Works' Inspector the whole 200 proposals were sent up to the Board of Works in Dublin. Though the rates collected, annually, for all purposes in the district amounted only to £34,303, the proposed works would cost £53,000.

What the *Dublin Evening Mail* described as a "delirium of presentments," and *The Times* as "presentment mania," took place. Poverty-stricken Mayo, with a total annual rateable value of only £293,282, presented, within a month, works to cost £403,466; in about the same period the County of Cork, containing some of the poorest and most distressed districts in Ireland, asked for £600,000, while turbulent, half-starving Clare in six Presentment Sessions demanded £300,000. A total of more than a million and a half pounds' worth of works was sent forward in the first month.

Panic had seized the country, and the people clutched wildly at public works as their only hope of staying alive. On September 5, the day after the Presentment Sessions began, Colonel Jones told Trevelyan that "dismay appears to have taken possession of men's minds"; those who were "optimistic in 1845 are despairing now," and Trevelyan himself wrote, "The general failure of the potato spread despondency and alarm from one end of Ireland to the other."

Presentments, however, enormous though they might be, did not produce wages; and while the Board of Works, on receiving proposals, was very ready to send forms and requisitions for further information, the operation of the Act then stopped dead.

It was impossible for a staff which, up to September 30, consisted of only 24 county surveyors, 15 engineers in charge, 39 assistant engineers and 36 inspecting officers to examine, sift and establish works out of a total of a million and a half pounds' worth of applications.

"The utter inadequacy of the Government measures," wrote a resident of Skibbereen, was "impossible to describe." All the Government had done was to send a printed circular, requiring names of all families, number in each family, whether large families or small families, and the names of all persons requiring employment on the public works. How was this information to be obtained? It would not be worth while to collect it. What use were a few relief committees "in a corner here and there" to deal with the sufferings of "hundreds, thousands, nay millions of starving people. . .I defy anyone to exaggerate the misery of the people. . .it is impossible. . . Whatever is done by Government or Public Works will be too late, after people have been driven to desperation by hunger. The whole country is nothing but a slumbering volcano. It will soon burst."

On September 5, Sir James Dombrain, Inspector-General of the Coastguard Service, informed Routh that his officers had found it necessary to make free issues of meal. The coastguards and Sir James Dombrain were not popular in Whitehall, and Trevelyan had directed that this year they were to be employed only for transporting supplies in their cutters. However, coastguard officers, making tours of inspection in the Killeries, Clifden and Ballinakill, remote districts in the far west, had found the people apparently dying, owing, said the local dispensary doctor, to a "total absence of food." Upon this, Sir James Dombrain decided that "people must not be allowed to starve," and in the circumstances "Her Majesty's Government would justify the issue of small quantities of food on certificates of the Dispensary Surgeon," and free issues were then made. He was, he admitted, "quite unprepared for the quantity thus issued, though in every case on doctor's certificate"—it amounted to as much as 11,663 lb.

For this action Sir James received a public and severe rebuke, in a Treasury minute. He had no authority, he was informed, to give meal away free. His proper course would

have been to call upon the leading persons in each distressed
locality to form themselves into a relief committee, and raise
a fund by private contribution, which might possibly be increased later by a Government donation. On September 18
Sir James replied, shortly, "No Committee could have been
formed. There was no one within many miles who could
have contributed one shilling. . . The people were actually
dying."

At Lochrus, near Adara, the people had been starving from
August 25 onwards; the district was mountainous, no grain
was ever grown and the only food was potatoes, which were
entirely lost. Mr. Moore, a coastguard officer, managed to
obtain some meal from Sligo, but only enough for one-third
of the people. "I never saw anything like it," he wrote,
"and I hope I never will. People came 18 miles for a little
meal, which I could not give. 14 tons, all but one bag, went
in a day." Unless the Government sent a supply of food the
people must inevitably die of starvation.

In Longford, on August 20, not "a loaf of bread or half
a cwt. of meal" was to be obtained, even from a meal-
merchant; and on September 5 *The Times* reported "people
hunting up and down Longford with money in their pockets
looking for food." In neighbouring Roscommon the people
were getting out of hand; Lord de Freyne, a large landowner,
had been hanged in effigy opposite the hall door of his
mansion, Frenchpark; and the O'Conor Don wrote urgently
to Routh, on September 7, telling him that destitution in
Roscommon was fearful and that supplies of food must be
sent at once. The letter was sent on to Trevelyan, who saw a
chance to get rid of some of the unwanted biscuit, which had
been in store since 1843. He wrote by return, pointing out
to Routh that the destitution in Roscommon was the right
kind of opportunity to transfer the broken biscuit from military stores; his letter contained no other comment or suggestion.

The British Government was not prepared to supply food
but very ready to call out troops. On August 28, for instance,
the people of starving Longford were "made angry" by two
troops of Dragoons galloping through the town, to "repel a
hunger movement of the people" in Roscommon. The hunger
movement consisted of 200 to 300 starving men, marching to
make a protest at Lord Crofton's seat, Mote Park.

Protests, however, were few and violence rare; the general

feeling was despair. Fear of famine was in the Irish people's
blood; only too clearly they realized that they were helpless
before the fate overtaking them, and turned blindly to those in
authority for salvation.

"The subjection of the masses," wrote Captain Perceval,
the Commissariat officer at Westport, County Mayo, was
"extraordinary." On August 31 a "large and orderly body of
people," including "many respectable persons," marched, in
fours, through Westport to Westport House and asked to see
Lord Sligo. When Lord Sligo came out, someone cried
"Kneel, kneel!" and the crowd dropped on its knees before
him. The state of Westport, Captain Perceval had already
reported to be "indescribable"; it was "a nest of fever and
vermin."

Nothing was done; nothing could be done. An unforeseen
situation was upsetting the plans of the Government; 1846
was a year of general shortage in Europe, and not only were
the expected imports of food into Ireland not arriving, but the
British Government was experiencing difficulty in securing
any supplies at all.

Chapter VII

ALL OVER Europe the harvest of 1846 was wholly or partially
a failure. The wheat crop was scanty, oats and barley "decidedly deficient," rye and potatoes a total loss, and "general famine" followed. European countries outbid Britain for
supplies. Ships bringing cargoes were diverted from British to
European ports, and Trevelyan complained that France and
Belgium, by paying high prices, secured "more than their
share in the Mediterranean market, besides placing large
orders in the United States."

The British Government could not have foreseen the general
failure of the harvest in Europe, but it might have led them
to modify their Irish relief plans. No modification was attempted, the scheme stood as drafted. No orders for food were to
be placed abroad; no Government food depots were to be

established, except in the west; all importing was to be left
to private enterprise.

Routh was uneasy and apprehensive. He did not agree
that private enterprise would bring in sufficient imports of
food, and towards the end of August he came over to London
and saw Trevelyan and Charles Wood at the Treasury. He
failed to obtain permission to place any large orders. All
he could get was a promise that Barings should be asked to
purchase the moderate amount of 2,000 tons of Indian corn,
and in the United Kingdom only. Trevelyan was insistent
that purchases made in foreign markets would raise prices
against British buyers, and pointed out that the British people
were also suffering from the European shortage. An exception
to the rule of buying only in the United Kingdom was made
in favour of "floating cargoes," that is, cargoes already at sea
and on their way to European ports. Trevelyan frequently
referred to "floating cargoes" as if they constituted a substantial resource.

This year, however, Barings declined to act. The request,
officially made on August 25, 1846, in a highly complimen-
tary Treasury minute, was declined by Mr. Thomas Baring,
who wrote that in view of the new policy, which "excludes
from its operations all purchases in foreign countries. . . Government does not need the co-operation of a mercantile house
of general business, but of a reliable corn-factor," and he
recommended Mr. Erichsen, of 110 Fenchurch Street, in the
City of London.

Mr. Erichsen's appointment was announced on August
28, and on the same day he broke the news to Trevelyan
that to buy 2,000 tons of Indian corn in the United Kingdom was all but impossible: supplies of Indian corn on the
Liverpool and London markets were already short, he wrote,
and as for floating cargoes, "there are two or three buyers
for every seller." On September 2 prices were still rising,
and on September 7 there was yet another "considerable
rise" on the Liverpool market.

Private enterprise was operating briskly. "Everything that
offers is being bought up with the greatest eagerness for
Ireland," wrote Erichsen, but by a very different class of
trader from the respectable corn-merchants and provision
dealers of Trevelyan's imagination—it was the Irish meal-
dealer and petty money-lender who was active, the dreaded
"gombeen man," the merciless and rapacious ogre of the

Irish village. By September 15 meal, except at enormous cost, was unobtainable by relief committees and philanthropic private persons. Dealers "hungry for money," wrote Captain Pole, Commissariat officer at Banagher, "buy up whatever comes to market and offer it again in small quantities at a great price which a poor man cannot pay and live."

Sales of a pound or two at a time, at exorbitant prices, produced large profits, and Irish dealers in the west paid high figures for meal; 50s. a quarter was being paid in Sligo when Trevelyan was instructing Erichsen to buy for Government at 40s. Even so, price was not the real difficulty, as Erichsen warned Trevelyan, on September 14; the real difficulty was to find anything to buy at all. When purchasing for his own account, Erichsen had been "obliged to give 46s. for the *only* good lot of Indian corn in London, and then it was only 500-600 quarters I could get." Trevelyan, however, ignoring Erichsen's warnings, instructed him, on September 17, to purchase "5,000 quarters of Indian corn to be delivered on the West coast of Ireland in November and December at 40s. to 41s. ." That day Erichsen wrote an alarming letter. Any supply wanted before the end of November would be extremely difficult to obtain, at any price, and as for talking in figures of thousands of quarters, "what I have actually secured amounts only to 900-1,000 quarters."

A quantity of 1,000 quarters to feed the starving millions of the west of Ireland was so evidently inadequate that Trevelyan agreed to allow Erichsen some latitude in price. It was too late; the season for importing Indian corn was coming to an end, famine conditions in Europe had produced a demand previously unknown, and it had vanished from British markets. On September 23 Erichsen wrote from London, that "not one single cargo offers here"; on the Liverpool market on October 13, Indian corn reached 54s., and even at that price was virtually unobtainable.

Trevelyan was forced to give up his plan of buying only in the United Kingdom. British markets, he wrote, were "so bare that we have had to have recourse to the plan of purchasing supplies of Indian corn already exported to Continental ports." Nevertheless, prices were still too high, and in a typical instance Erichsen reported being "outbid for 3,000-4,000 quarters at Antwerp after venturing as high as 47s. before retiring."

Trevelyan for his part was able to consider the rise in

prices a "great blessing." He pointed out to Routh that high prices, by limiting consumption, exercised a "regulating influence" in time of shortage; they were also "indispensably necessary to attract from abroad the supplies necessary to fill up the void occasioned by the destruction of the potato crop." "Nothing," he wrote, "was more calculated to attract supplies, and especially from America," than high prices, and he drew a picture of what would happen in the United States when high prices made themselves felt—"then down from Cincinnati and Ohio would come quantities of Indian corn, formerly used to keep pigs."

He appeared to be unaware of the conditions governing the export of Indian corn from the United States. It was not fit for export until several months after it was harvested, and the Indian corn sold for export in the summer of 1846 was the harvest of 1845. True, the harvest of 1846 had been particularly abundant, but the produce would not be exportable until 1847. Moreover, the period during which Indian corn was shipped to Europe was limited; at that time crossing the Atlantic in late autumn and winter was a dangerous proceeding—ships were sailing-ships, and few left for Europe after September. The clearance of the 1845 harvest of Indian corn had been early and complete; the hungry nations of Europe had acted promptly and paid high prices, the crop was shipped and gone. Those large supplies which Trevelyan imagined could be diverted from the pigs of Cincinnati and Ohio to the starving Irish were non-existent.

In Ireland, Routh was in a state of "painful anxiety." Nothing whatever, he wrote, on September 19, had arrived at either Westport or Sligo, the two centres of supply for the most remote and poverty-stricken western districts. He had seen Erichsen's bills of lading, and the quantities secured were much too small; when they did eventually come in they would be "eaten up within 24 hours or less of arrival." He needed "at least" 1,000 tons each for Westport, Sligo, Killibegs, Limerick and Galway, and this would make only a "temporary impression."

The quantity Erichsen had managed to buy by the end of September amounted only to 35,500 quarters of Indian corn and 500 quarters of Indian corn-meal; about 7,200 tons in all. He had attempted to purchase barley, but owing to the European demand had secured only 1,085 quarters. On September 21 Routh wrote again, this time almost in dis-

traction, privately to Trevelyan and officially to the Lords
Commissioners of the Treasury. He feared that the Government, by purchasing solely in the United Kingdom and
European ports, would not be able to secure the quantity
of Indian corn required to fulfil their pledge to feed the west;
and he begged the Lords Commissioners of the Treasury to
authorise "importation from the U.S.A."—sixty to eighty
thousand quarters should be ordered immediately. And he told
Trevelyan that in his judgment a further contract should be
made for 125,000 quarters at least.

Trevelyan now renounced a basic principle of his scheme:
orders for Indian corn were sent to the United States by the
September packets. It was too late. The next arrivals of
Indian corn from the United States could not reach the
United Kingdom until the spring of 1847. "We have relied
too much on the resources of the American market," Trevelyan wrote privately to Routh. "The produce of the present
harvest will only begin to be fit for exportation in December
or January . . . and then it will be subject to serious obstruc-
tion from the closing of the rivers by ice."

On the same day, however, in a Treasury minute, Routh
was officially rebuked: he was asking too much for Ireland.
Scarcity of food, he was reminded, extended over the whole
of western Europe and the United Kingdom, and nothing
ought to be done for the west of Ireland which might send
prices, already high, still higher for people "who, unlike the
inhabitants of the west coast of Ireland, have to depend on
their own exertions."

The views of the Treasury were shared by *The Times*.
In a "Sermon for Ireland," on September 8, *The Times*
leader-writer declared that this year "the Irishman is destitute,
so is the Scotchman, and so is the Englishman . . . It appears
to us to be of the very first importance to all classes of Irish
society to impress on them that there is nothing so peculiar,
so exceptional, in the condition which they look on as the
pit of utter despair . . . Why is that so terrible in Ireland which
in England does not create perplexity and hardly moves compassion?"

❧

Commissariat officers serving in Irish relief declared that
the English knew as little of Ireland as of West Africa: in
fact, they knew less. The distant parts of the Empire which

Britain then ruled, in Africa, India, China, were more carefully studied than Ireland and their economic structure better understood.

For instance, Routh wrote from Sligo, on September 14, that harvest was in progress, and he could not understand why distress in Sligo was so acute that 200 tons of meal had to be issued weekly at a time when "the fields were teeming with crops," or why frantic appeals for food were coming in from Bantry, Valencia, Cahirciveen and Gweedore in the last twenty-four hours. "It is impossible there can be this total want, this extinction of every supply in the midst of harvest."

British high officials, in spite of the previous season's experience, failed to grasp the place of the grain harvest in Irish life. Grain and oats were not grown to eat but to pay the rent. "If the people are forced to consume their oats and other grain, where is the rent to come from?" wrote the Commissariat officer at Westport.

Trevelyan, in Whitehall, however, doubted if any real want yet existed. In his opinion "the scramble for our supplies is indicative, not so much of a general destitution, as of a perfectly natural desire to get food where it can be had at the cheapest rate." Rejecting an appeal from Roscommon he wrote, "I cannot believe there is no store of food in Roscommon from the oat harvest."

It was notorious that, for the Irish peasant, failure to pay his rent meant eviction. Yet even in the present emergency no protection, no period of grace, was given the small tenant; he was left to the mercy of his landlord, and as a Commissariat officer wrote to Trevelyan from Sligo, "The first object of landlords will be to collect rents."

A letter survives written on September 20, 1846, by Simon Dunane, a small farmer at Gurtnahaller, County Limerick. He tells his landlord that he can pay his rent only by thrashing and selling his oats, and since all his potatoes are lost this means death by starvation for himself, his wife and his six children. Nevertheless, since fear of eviction was in the very blood of the Irish peasant, grain was sold, rents were paid, and Simon Dunane, with his fellows, flocked, starving, to the depots.

A number of landlords did reduce their rents, or agreed to forgo them altogether, among them Lord Rossmore, the Earl Erne and the Marquess of Ormonde; Sir George Staunton, owner of Clydagh, County Galway, though an absentee, renounced his rents entirely, as did Mr. Henry O'Neill of Derrymacloughlin Castle, whose tenants lighted bonfires and danced in his honour; and near Tuam, Mr. Charles Cromie, of Annefield House, instructed his steward to arrange for all oats and grain grown on his property to be ground and made into meal and flour for distribution to tenants. In October the Duke of Devonshire gave rent reductions varying from 33 per cent. to 50 per cent.; Lord Fortescue followed, and by the middle of November, 1846, the *Nation* was publishing lists of landlords who were reducing or forgoing rents.

Feelings of humanity were not, however, universal. "Every day there has been some notice of sale for rent," wrote the Dublin *Evening Mail* on September 18. Troops and bodies of police were called in to enforce the law; and in a notorious case at Ahascragh, County Galway, forty-seven persons were evicted by being thrown bodily out of their houses by a numerous force of constabulary.

The Irish peasant was told to replace the potato by eating his grain, but Trevelyan once again refused to take any steps to curb the export of food from Ireland. "Do not encourage the idea of prohibiting exports," he wrote, on September 3, "perfect Free Trade is the right course."

Routh disagreed, a rare occurrence. He considered exports to be a "serious evil" and estimated, on September 29, that by the end of the harvest, of oats alone, apart from other produce, "60,000 tons" would have left the country. Trevelyan would not be moved; according to Free Trade doctrines the sale, by export outside Ireland, of grain and other produce which commanded a high price should provide Irish merchants with money to purchase and import low-priced foods, to replace the loss of the potato. However, the undeveloped commercial system of Ireland made any such operations highly improbable. Merchants engaged in the import business, of the type common in England, were very few—a handful of firms only, operating in ports such as Cork and Belfast. The dealers in the backward west knew nothing whatever of importing. "Their operations," wrote the Commissariat officer at Sligo, "are restricted to exportation." The dealers bought produce and sent it out of the country, but they never imported anything. Even had they wished to do so, wrote the officer, they were quite unable to reverse their businesses at short notice and, he added, there had been "no

importation whatever since my arrival in the district of any
Indian corn or cheap food on private account."

So the enormous void left by the loss of the potato
remained unfilled, and the grip of hunger tightened on Ireland.

On market-day, September 12, 1846, in Skibbereen, County
Cork, an agricultural centre, there was not a single loaf of
bread or pound of meal to be had in the town. The Relief
Committee applied to Mr. Hughes, the Commissariat officer,
asking him to sell or lend some meal from the Government
depot. He refused, saying "his instructions prevented him,"
and an angry scene followed. Two days later, members of the
Committee again came to see him, followed by a starving
crowd, imploring food. The sight was too much for Mr.
Hughes. The misery in Skibbereen, he assured Routh on
September 20, had not been exaggerated, and he issued two
and a half tons of meal, instantly distributed in small lots.
Upon this, the Catholic curate of Trellagh, a neighbouring
village, came and asked for two tons, telling Mr. Hughes
his people were starving and he dared not return empty-
handed. Again Mr. Hughes gave way. The curate of Trellagh
was followed by the Relief Committee of the village of Leap,
who asked for ten tons; Mr. Hughes refused, and a most
painful scene took place. In the presence of Captain Dyer,
the Board of Works' inspecting officer, and Mr. Pinchen,
sub-inspector of Police, the spokesman for the Relief Committee of Leap said, "Mr. Deputy Commissary, do you refuse
to give out food to starving people who are ready to pay
for it? If so, in the event of an outbreak tonight the
responsibility will be yours." What, Mr. Hughes asked Routh,
was the right course for him to pursue? Routh, in reply,
instructed Mr. Hughes to "represent to applicants for Government supplies of food the necessity for private enterprise
and importation . . . Towns should combine and import from
Cork or Liverpool . . . Now is the time to use home produce."

By September 25 the people at Clashmore, County Waterford, were living on blackberries, and at Rathcormack,
County Cork, on cabbage leaves. In Leitrim, where there were
few shops, the parish of Cloone, with 22,000 inhabitants, had
no provision dealer or baker or any kind, and people were
starving "by hundreds." Even in prosperous Leinster food became unobtainable. In Maryborough (Port Laoighise), on
September 30, there had not been a grain of oatmeal in the

town for three weeks, and the bakers had no flour to make bread.

To people desperate with hunger the sight of food streaming out of the country was once more unbearable, and serious riots took place—more serious than any riots of the previous years. At Youghal, near Cork, a small port much used for export, an outbreak took place on September 25. A large crowd of country people, described by the police as "enraged," attempted to hold up a boat laden with export oats—the police sent for troops, and the crowd was checked, with difficulty, at Youghal bridge. The disturbance was sufficiently important for Mr. T. N. Redington, the Under-Secretary at Dublin Castle, to be sent over to London by the next boat to explain to the Government.

A riot, with loss of life, occurred at Dungarvan, County Waterford, on September 29. A crowd of starving unemployed entered the town, threatened merchants and shopkeepers, ordering them not to export grain, and plundered shops. The Resident Magistrate had the ringleaders arrested and put in the lock-up, upon which the crowd declared they would not go home until the prisoners were released.

After the police had tried, in vain, to clear the streets, the 1st Royal Dragoons were called out; the crowd began to pelt them with stones and the Riot Act was read. But as stone-throwing continued the officer commanding the Dragoons, Captain Sibthorp, gave the order to fire, and twenty-six shots were fired into the crowd, which then retreated. Several men were wounded and two were left lying on the ground, dead.

Four companies of the 47th Foot were then sent to keep order in Dungarvan; nevertheless, on October 1 vessels in Dungarvan harbour could not be loaded with grain for export because the labourers, hired to load, were afraid of the crowds.

The British Government now took strong steps to defeat anti-export disturbances, and Trevelyan arranged for the provisioning, with beef, pork and biscuit, of 2,000 troops, formed into mobile columns "to be directed on particular points at very short notice." Provisions for six weeks were sufficient, wrote Trevelyan, because "food riots are quite different from organized rebellion and are not likely to be of long duration."

In addition, all vessels loaded with grain or meal passing up the river Fergus were to have a naval escort, and the

Admiral at Cork, Sir H. Pigot, suggested that a "vessel of war," with a detachment of marines on board, should be sent to lie off Bantry and Berehaven. Government food depots and sub-depots were guarded by police and troops; and Mr. Hewetson reported from Limerick, on October 10, that troops were sent out daily into the harvest fields to "protect" the corn, because the people were cutting the traces of the horses which drew carts and wagons to prevent grain being taken away.

Yet had all food been kept in the country, and home-grown grain and provisions been on sale, had private enterprise succeeded in functioning and supplies of cheap food been freely available, the Irish people would have been little better off. They were penniless; even if food had been abundant, they could not have bought it. The Government scheme was relief through employment—wages were to be paid on the public works so that food could be bought. But, once again, public works failed to get started.

The deluge of applications for works, sent forward, wholesale, by the Presentment Sessions, combined with the strictness of Treasury control, created interminable delays. Every application forwarded to the Treasury was personally examined and pronounced upon by Trevelyan, entailing so much work that he left his wife and family and went to live by himself in lodgings, in order, as he wrote, on September 28, and underlined, "to give up the *whole of my time to the public.*"

Districts which had sent forward proposals for works at the beginning of September expected employment to begin almost at once. In disturbed districts, angry mobs dispersed on hearing that proposals had been submitted, expecting speedy employment. Weeks passed, nothing happened, and desperate appeals began to pour in. The inhabitants of Athy, County Kildare, had "pawned everything and cannot bear it much longer"; in Waterford, "the privation had reached its utmost limit and the promised works must be started at once"; at Castleisland, County Kerry, on October 18, a notice was posted that work must be started or there would be plunder—the men of Castleisland could not "bear the cries of hungry children any longer." Lord Devon, chairman of the celebrated Devon Commission, estimated, on October 2, 1846, that four thousand men in his neighbourhood required employment and "could not be pacified by words"; his house was daily surrounded by men whom he knew to be starving. Delays, however, dragged on, in some places until the end of November; in Rosbercon Ross, County Kilkenny, the starving were still waiting for works to begin on November 25 and being driven "frantic by repeated delays."

When works did begin immense difficulties arose. In consequence of the idling of last season, all works were "to be executed by task," that is, payment was to be by results, in proportion to the amount of work done; and as had been demonstrated in the previous year Irish labourers detested task-work; they alleged that stewards showed favouritism and that the Board of Works was so short of staff that it was impossible to get work measured promptly for payment.

In Limerick opposition was so strong that, rather than introduce task-work, the County Surveyor "thought it wiser to retire," and his successor warned the constabulary on October 21 that task-work was so "furiously disliked" that he "dreaded an outbreak." An outbreak did take place, at Ballingarry, on October 27, when a mob of two thousand unemployed compelled men working by task to down tools; a riot followed, and troops were called out.

In a number of places the introduction of task-work was held up because the Board of Works had no staff available to plan and measure, and when wages were paid by the day the rate was universally declared to be too low. The Commissariat officer at Banagher, Captain Pole, warned Trevelyan that, with rising prices, the wages proposed by the Board of Works "will not prove enough to buy food"; and Father Mathew wrote, from Cork, that "a shilling a day or even one and sixpence is nothing to a poor man with a large family if he has to pay 2d. a lb. for Indian meal." Rates of pay were, nevertheless, fixed at 6d., 7d. and, at the most, 8d. a day. Hostile demonstrations followed. At Mallow, County Cork, for instance, when 7d. was fixed a body of 218 labourers marched to the Poor House and forced their way in, demanding to be admitted as paupers rather than be abandoned to die slowly from hunger on 7d. a day. When the rate was raised to 8d. the Mallow Relief Committee described it, in a memorial to the Lord-Lieutenant, as "arbitrary cruelty" and declared that "the men on the works are starving."

Moreover, the payment of wages was irregular. The shortage of silver coin, which had been felt last season, became acute, and on September 5 the Board of Works complained to the Treasury that difficulty in collecting coin was causing serious delay in the payment of wages. The Government steamship *Comet* was then sent round the coast of Ireland by the Treasury with about "£80,000 of small silver," and Trevelyan arranged with the Deputy Master of the Mint and the Governor of the Bank of England for "all silver coin any part of Ireland may require being immediately furnished through the Bank of England."

Even so, wages continued to be irregularly paid because of the crippling dearth of staff, the cause of almost all the confusions and difficulties in which the Board of Works became daily more entangled.

Men were not paid because there were no pay clerks to pay them; works were not started because there were no engineers to lay them out; task-work was not measured up because there were no stewards who could be entrusted with the calculation. The impossibility of securing suitable staff in Ireland had been demonstrated last season, yet Trevelyan and the British Government expected difficulties which had proved fatal on a small scale to solve themselves when the scale was enormously enlarged.

On October 29 Lord Monteagle described to Lord Bessborough his difficulties with the Board of Works' staff. On his estate at Shanagolden, County Limerick, a Captain Kennedy had first been appointed; he resigned and was succeeded by a Mr. Owens, "who walked out in the midst of our troubles, with works to be laid out on which human lives depended." Mr. Owens had "gone off without telling anyone and not even leaving the documents which were needed to enable the labourers to be paid"—Monteagle had "paid the men out of his own pocket." "Today," he went on, "two sets of labourers holding Government tickets have been turned away by the Board of Works' officer and sent home." The people were distracted, and Monteagle did not know what to say to them. The County Surveyor was "utterly incompetent to undertake executive duties," and "a mass of discontent [is being] created . . . the refusal to pay men working under your Engineers tickets for work" and "the disappearance of Mr. Owens were enough to throw the most tranquil country into confusion."

"You must have mercy and pity us," wrote Richard Griffith, the new Commissioner for Relief Works, to Lord Monteagle. "We are perfectly unable to meet the requirements for . . . engineers." Only fifteen men capable of acting as engineers in charge had been found by the end of September. "The Inspecting Officers," continued Mr. Griffith, "are all failing us. Two in Clare have resigned, one in Cork, one in Waterford, and we are threatened with resignations in Fermanagh and Leitrim."

Board of Works' employment was not attractive. Officials were hard-worked—"up until 2 and 3 a.m. and up again at 7 a.m.," wrote Colonel Jones. At Presentment Sessions the officials, "day after day" met with "opposition, difficulties and insults" from a "yelling mob" and had to travel long distances from one work to another, in all weathers, and were frequently subjected to "severe wettings." "Some," wrote the Commissioners of the Board of Works to the Lords of the Treasury, "resign from inability to support the strain, some from intimidation, some have resigned the moment they joined and found the prospect that lay before them."

As under the 1845 scheme, no works were to be undertaken from which one person in the district would profit more than another. The drainage works, of which Ireland stood so greatly in need, could not be undertaken, since owners of lands bordering on a drainage scheme would have their property improved and increased in value, while owners whose property was further away would receive little or no benefit. The same objection was found to apply to every kind of undertaking proposed, with the exception of roadmaking, and once again the public works executed under the Labour Rate Act were, almost without exception, new roads. But as a legacy from previous famines Ireland already had an unusually large number of roads. From Limerick, for instance, Stephen Spring Rice wrote "our roads were nearly perfect. We had already the roads we wanted and they were as good as we wanted," and in a graphic phrase an inspecting officer of the Board of Works reported that Limerick was "regularly riddled with roads."

Lord Monteagle protested vehemently against useless works undertaken under "this wretched Act of Parliament," and supported by Lord Devon he succeeded in convincing Lord Bessborough that the present policy must be modified. Works termed "reproductive" or "profitable," that is, which might confer some benefit on some individual, above all drainage works, must be allowed, or millions of pounds, which property owners would ultimately have to find, would be wasted: "Expending a sum which . . . may exceed three millions on unprofitable labour is a fatal mistake."

Lord Bessborough then told Monteagle to write personally to Trevelyan—nothing could be done with the Chancellor of the Exchequer without Trevelyan's support. Monteagle's representations succeeded, and on October 5, 1846, an official letter, written by the Chief Secretary for Ireland, Mr. Labouchere, announced that "reproductive" works, including drainage, might be carried out under the Labour Rate Act provided certain conditions were complied with.

Lord Monteagle was delighted: he believed that the "Labouchere letter," as it was called, would in effect replace the Labour Rate Act: it was, he wrote on October 16, "not merely an amendment . . . but a new and greatly preferable law." Unhappily, the benefits anticipated did not follow, because the terms of the Labouchere letter were "so guarded as to be not clearly intelligible." One stipulation required that all landed proprietors without exception, in the district where works were to be executed, must sign an undertaking making themselves personally responsible for repaying the whole expense; and to get such an undertaking proved all but impossible. Further, districts which had already submitted proposals for roads, at a time when they could submit nothing else, were not allowed to send in revised schemes; and though it had been hoped that large scale drainage schemes would be undertaken, in fact the expenditure on them under the letter represented only about five per cent. of the total expended under the Labour Rate Act. On November 14 Trevelyan told Mr. Labouchere: "The scheme laid down in your letter is practically inefficient, both as a measure of relief and as a measure of improvement."

❧

During a bad year in Ireland the condition of the people invariably took a sharp turn for the worse after October 1; vegetables and gleanings were finished, and in normal years this was the moment at which the people became dependent on the potato—and if the crop was poor this was when they began to starve. And now there were no potatoes at all.

October came, and food prices rose to such heights that on the 6th the magistrates of the City and Borough of Cork asked for the Government food store to be opened: the

people, even those with wages, were starving because they
could not pay the exorbitant prices. The Cork magistrates
were refused. Government supplies were only for the west,
and even in the west there was no intention of opening the
depots while any produce remained from the harvest—and
it was considered produce did remain. Requests from all over
Ireland were refused in the same terms.

The Government's attitude appeared unreasonable, tempers
began to rise, and Irish landowners wrote angry letters to
Routh in Dublin.

Viscount Bernard "firmly protested against the course
pursued by Government": Bandon was refused a depot because it was not in the west, but he wished to know how
Sir Randolph Routh expected a relief committee, in a district
which was already destitute, to raise enough money to supply
a large population with food? Sir Richard Musgrave, one of
the best landlords in Ireland, went further and wrote, on
October 19 that "many magistrates will resign, and probably
lieutenants of counties also, if ministers adhere to the line
they have chalked out." The people, he pointed out, were
"only asking for necessities," and in his opinion the Government ought to purchase Indian corn and sell it cheaply.

On October 10 the Board of Works wrote an official letter
informing the Lords of the Treasury that their officers were
"pressing" for depots to be opened immediately in remote
districts: some places—Inniskeel, in County Donegal, for
instance—were forty-five miles away from the nearest market. The Board of Works was refused. Nothing would be
issued, even in the west, while produce was considered to
remain from the harvest.

Routh could hardly tell the truth—the depots could not
be opened because they did not contain sufficient supplies;
they were, in fact, not very far from empty.

As Lord Monteagle wrote, he "doubted very much if the
magnitude of the existing calamity and its dangers are appreciated in Downing Street." However, by an Order in Council the Dearth and Scarcity Prayer was directed to be used
in Protestant churches throughout the United Kingdom, on
Sunday, October 11, and following Sundays, immediately after
the third collect at both morning and evening service.

❧

Applications now began to flood in by the hundreds; relief

committees, alleging that their districts were starving, begged
and implored Government to establish and open depots where
the people might buy food at a low price. Contrary to expectation, the great majority of these, fifty-one in the three
days October 5-7, came from the eastern division of Ireland,
from such counties as Meath, Waterford and Kilkenny, which,
according to the Government plan, should have been supplied
by private enterprise.

To deal with these applications Trevelyan, on October 7,
drew up "Heads of Answer," which Routh was instructed to
use. Applicants were to be informed, first, that it was not
the intention of Government to open depots, except in the
west, and that, even there, they would be opened
only when food was not provided in sufficient quantities by
private traders; second, that from the deficiency of foreign
grain, supplies would not be available in sufficient quantities
before December or January; and, third, that it was therefore
"advisable for gentlemen of local influence to unite in exertions for having the Home harvest produce brought extensively
into use."

Even applications from the west, where the Government
was pledged to provide food, were refused. Mr. Garvey, of
Murrisk Abbey, for instance, chairman of the Kilgeever Relief Committee, asked for the establishment of a depot at
Louisburgh, County Mayo, one of the few towns in that wild
and poverty-stricken district. Mr. Garvey was told, bluntly,
"there will be no depot in Louisburgh." No offer of assistance
was made, but the relief committee of Kilgeever was instructed to raise a fund "to be employed in the purchase of
supplies of food," which might then be sold by the committee.
On no account, however, were supplies to be given away
or sold cheaply; sales must always be "at prices sufficient to
repay the first cost with all charges, and a commission allowance of £5 per cent."

In the official view, the famine in Ireland offered traders
an opportunity to make profits, of which it would be unjust
to deprive them; and on October 18, 1846, Routh circularized
relief committees in the west, telling them not to expect that
Government food would be sold cheaply. In no circumstances,
he wrote, were traders to be undersold, and therefore no
prices were to be fixed which "would not enable traders
selling at the same rates to realize their profits." Captain
Nugent, of the Royal Navy, for instance, who appealed on

behalf of the starving inhabitants of Newport, County Mayo, was told, "even if it were practicable at the moment to open our depots . . . it would obviously be extremely prejudicial to owners of grain, inasmuch as at present extraordinary prices can be realized."

Trevelyan gave his blessing on economic grounds to profits being made by traders out of the scarcity of food. "If dealers," he wrote, "were to confine themselves to what in ordinary circumstances might be considered fair profits, the scarcity would be aggravated in a fearful degree." When the Marquess of Sligo complained, on October 12, that the Commissariat officer at Westport was "creating fury" by refusing to open the depot for sales of food, though the people were starving, because they could not pay the exorbitant prices asked by dealers, Routh told him, "We must bear in mind that if an article is scarce . . . a smaller quantity must be made to last for a longer time, and that high price is the only criterion by which consumption can be economized."

Routh did not, however, go on to explain to Lord Sligo that there was a practical and conclusive reason why the depots could not be opened—they were all but empty. On October 17 the official return of "provisions at Commissariat depots in Ireland," which included not only Indian corn, in grain and meal, but also oatmeal and biscuit, in sacks and bags, amounted, approximately, to 3,102 tons only. Routh's estimate, on August 3, had been for 16,000 tons immediately, and on September 21 he had asked for a further 25,000 tons to be ordered from the United States of America. At Westport, when angry demands were being made for instant opening, the depot contained only 150 tons of Indian corn, and this was unground. Limerick, a central store depot, had received no new supplies whatsoever, and the stock "consisted entirely of the remains of last season"; at Cork, the most important reserve depot, Hewetson declared himself "helpless without supplies from abroad." "I tremble," wrote Routh to Trevelyan, "when I think of the number of empty depots we have to fill"; and not only were the Government depots un-filled, they were likely to remain unfilled for a considerable time; the promises of the Government that "ample supplies" would arrive in December or January had no foundation in fact.

On October 14 the American packet had brought a dis-couraging report to Liverpool. Orders for the new crop of

Indian corn, to be exported in the spring, were ten times the quantity obtainable; the French Government, in particular, was buying very largely. As for rye, the Prussian Government had bought up all available supplies in August and September. Nevertheless, the British Government continued to take refuge behind the promise that ample supplies would arrive in December or January, and Routh repeated it—once again, to Lord Monteagle, on October 22. Behind the scenes, however, Routh was painfully anxious and urging Trevelyan to buy something, anything. "I care not what Erichsen sends," he wrote, on October 28, "whether barley, wheat or Indian corn, so we obtain the article."

Barley had already proved unobtainable, wheat had risen to an immoderate price, and Prussia had all the rye; why not, Routh suggested, try importing yams, the root called the sweet potato, which was a staple food in the Caribbean and the southern states of America? Trevelyan doubted whether yams would be "a practical import in quantity," and tropical yams would, unquestionably, have proved a difficult crop to cultivate in the west of Ireland. Trevelyan did not dismiss the idea, and he consulted a Commissariat officer with West Indian experience. "What do you think of the yam as an article of import?" he inquired; and yams continued to be considered, from time to time, as a possible food for Ireland.

If, however, by a miracle, the promised "ample supplies" of Indian corn had arrived in Ireland, the Commissariat would have been quite unable to deal with them.

Milling continued an insoluble difficulty; either there were no mills or, as in Westport and other places, the mills were occupied by merchants milling grain for their own account and for export, protected by the Government's tenderness for private enterprise, while the Indian corn for the starving remained unground. In September an additional misfortune occurred; during a spell of exceptionally hot weather, streams all over Ireland went dry, and small country mills were unable to grind. "How is grain to be ground for a population that has existed on the potato?" Trevelyan wrote to Routh.

Eventually, the Government Indian corn was milled in the Admiralty mills at Deptford, Portsmouth and Plymouth, the naval mills at Malta, and in hired mills at Rotherhithe and Maldon, Essex, and taken by Admiralty steamer to Ireland. A scheme for using mills in Jersey had to be discarded, because

E

the difficulty of milling the iron-hard grain was too great.

Trevelyan was then struck by the idea of handmills—why should not the people grind the Indian corn themselves, he asked? True, the grain of Indian corn was so hard that, in the southern states of America, it was milled more than once; but Trevelyan borrowed a hand-mill from the museum at India House, a quern, a celtic handmill, from the west of Ireland, and another from Wick, in the Shetlands, and "by putting all three into the hands of skilful workmen" hoped "to produce something." A "manufactory of handmills" was actually established by Captain Mann at Kilkee, County Clare, early in November; each hand-mill cost the impossibly large sum, for the Irish destitute, of 15s., but a number were bought out of charitable funds and distributed free.

Yet there was a simpler solution; why should not the people eat Indian corn, unground? On October 9 a memorandum was sent out to relief committees, informing them that "Indian corn in its unground state affords an equally wholesome and nutritious food" as when ground into meal. It could be used in two ways: the grain could be crushed between two good-sized stones and then boiled in water, with a little grease or fat, "if at hand." Or it could be used without crushing, simply by soaking all night in warm water, changing this, in the morning, for clear, cold water, bringing to the boil, and boiling the corn for an hour and a half—it could then be eaten with milk, with salt, or plain. Boiling without crushing was the method particularly recommended. "Ten pounds of the corn so prepared is ample food for a labouring man for seven days . . . Corn so used," continued the memorandum, blandly, "will be considerably cheaper to the Committee and the people than meal, and will be well adapted to meet the deficiency of mill power. . . ."

Unground Indian corn is not only hard but sharp and irritating—it even pierces the intestines—and is all but impossible to digest. Boiling for an hour and a half did not soften the flint-hard grain, and Indian corn in this state, eaten by half-starving people, produced agonizing pains, especially in children.

Another difficulty lay in getting it to the people. The harbours of the west of Ireland had not improved in twelve months, and it was as difficult for ships to get over the bar, into harbour, at Sligo and Westport in 1846 as it had been in 1845. A promising plan, outlined in a Treasury minute at the end of August, provided for two store-ships to be stationed in Clew Bay, County Mayo, and two off the bar of Sligo harbour, each with three powerful steamers attached, to convey supplies promptly round the coast to distressed areas. It had, however, been overlooked that neither in Clew Bay nor off the bar of Sligo harbour was there sufficient water, either for a storeship or a powerful steamer. The weather in the autumn of 1846 was stormy, and when Routh obtained, with difficulty, the loan of the excise steamer *Warrior* to take fifteen tons of meal to destitute districts in Donegal, she took more than a month to make the delivery, spending most of that time taking refuge from the weather in Mulroy Lough. And ships ran aground; in less than a month *Princess Royal* at Killibegs, *Dolphin* at Gurney Island, and *Andromeda* in Valentia harbour.

When cargoes were successfully landed, distribution was difficult. Towns in the west were few, immense tracts of country were wild, and small settlements isolated. Though Government authorities considered that "thirty miles is no bar to traffic in food," the inhabitants of remote hamlets starved. Petty difficulties held up supplies. In North Mayo, for instance, piracy was not infrequent: thirty-four men, in eleven curraghs (Irish canoes), from Blacksod Bay, plundered a ship ten miles out at sea. Boats sent with meal to islands off the coast were then ordered to be accompanied by naval escorts, but the escorts failed to appear punctually or did not appear at all. Trevelyan arranged for stores and depots to be guarded by troops, but adequate guards could not always be spared, and the commanding officer at Limerick complained that his troops were "harassed off their legs by daily calls for the military."

The major difficulty, however, as always, was that responsible persons who would have undertaken relief work in England were not to be found. However excellent the schemes, they came to grief in execution. "The machinery for the new state of things," wrote Mr. Nicholas Cummins, a magistrate in Cork, to Trevelyan, *"does not exist."* The general feeling, he added, was "gloomy foreboding at the rapid increase of distress."

At the end of October relief committees sent in fresh and piteous appeals—the people were living on nettles and weeds. In two days, October 24 and 25, three such reports came in from the more prosperous north, from Fermanagh, Blacklyon

and Enniskillen. In Roscommon, the constabulary report of
October 12, 1846, stated that 7,500 people were existing on
boiled cabbage leaves once in forty-eight hours. In Kilmoe
and Crookhaven, County Cork, on November 9, 7,000 persons
were completely without food; here, everything directed by
the Government had been done—a relief committee formed
and a subscription raised. But the money was now spent; the
people were penniless, and no mill or bakery existed within
thirty miles. The Tralee Relief Committee sent a piteous
memorial: the district was starving, private enterprise had
failed to provide food, and they implored the Government
to act.

The Government responded by sending additional troops
to distressed districts. "Would to God the Government would
send us food instead of soldiers," a starving inhabitant of
Ballinrobe, County Mayo, was heard to lament as the 7th
Hussars entered the town.

Official statements now took a new line. No more was
heard of ample supplies arriving shortly: it was alleged that
to send food to Ireland would be unjust to the rest of the
United Kingdom—it was useless, wrote Trevelyan, "to transfer famine from one country to another." If food was bought
for Ireland in the present scarcity, prices must be sent up,
and the English and Scots working-classes would pay more
for their food. Large sums of public money had already been
spent on Irish relief, and "you cannot expect the English and
Scotch labourers to support Ireland and pay famine prices
as well." Everything that could be done had been done: "My
purchases are carried to the utmost point short of transferring
the famine from Ireland to England."

The utmost point, however, still stopped short of filling the
depots. In the west, although the depots had not officially
been declared open, issues were being made in badly distressed
districts—most depots, though they had received no fresh
supplies, had some "remains" from last season. Orders were
now sent to Commissariat officers that all issues, whatever
the circumstances, must cease, and high officials in Whitehall
and at Dublin Castle managed to persuade themselves that
the Irish people could live on the produce of their own
country if they chose. It was some perversity, some dis-
honesty, which caused the Irish to turn their backs on their
own home-grown wheat, barley, bacon, eggs, butter and meat,
and besiege the depots for Indian corn. Routh, sending to

Mr. Lister, the Commissariat officer in charge at Westport, the order to cease sales, told him, "You will find there is no spot so bad that there is not some supply and we must force the people to consume that." The time had come, continued Routh, "to subject the people to a little pressure." Mr. Lister passed on the order to Mr. Parker, the Commissariat clerk in charge of the sub-depot at Clifden, and Mr. Parker was extremely angry. Clifden, on the coast of Galway, served wild and poverty-stricken districts, including Connemara, where frightful misery was being endured, and he wrote a furious personal letter to Mr. Lister: far from closing down, more supplies must be sent at once.

It was a pity, Mr. Lister replied, that Mr. Parker had not written "officially," and he hoped that the "representations were too strongly worded." If things were really as bad at Clifden as Mr. Parker alleged a few sales, of the smallest quantities only, might be made, say twice a week; but Mr. Lister could do very little to help. Some biscuit had just arrived, and he would send seven or eight tons by boat, but that was all. He had no Indian corn-meal at all in store at Westport, and did not know when he would be able to send a further supply of biscuit; and, once again, he repeated the standard instructions, to "arouse the rich, respectable and influential, form a Relief Committee and raise a fund."

Three weeks later, at the end of October, Mr. Parker wrote another angry letter. The people living in the Killeries were in frightful distress—this was the district which had been reported as starving by Sir James Dombrain as long ago as the beginning of August. And Mr. Parker now urged that he should be allowed to send four to five tons of Indian corn from Clifden. Mr. Lister found this request unpractical and irritating: let Mr. Parker examine the contents of his depot —was it "prudent" to part with four to five tons of Indian corn? Where did Mr. Parker propose to obtain further supplies? Mr. Lister could not hold out any hope whatsoever from Westport. "Should we not countenance a little pressure to induce, or even to compel them to avail themselves of their own supplies?" he wrote. Sir Randolph Routh "had information" that the people in the Killeries had potatoes enough to last until Christmas. "We are not prepared to open our depots and this you must state in strong and unequivocal language," Mr. Lister concluded.

Hunger in the west, however, had now reached a pitch

which made withdrawing all supplies impossible. On October 30 Mr. Dobree, a seasoned and unsentimental Commissariat officer, wrote from Sligo that, in spite of the order, it had been "quite out of his power . . . to shut his stores altogether against a little relief for the poor people," and he did not intend to do so "without a positive order to that effect." Told that he must reduce his sales further, he wrote, on November 3, that, "in spite of the most harassing applications," he had "screwed them down" to twenty-three tons for his whole enormous district last week. He had exacted a "solemn pledge" from relief committees to distribute only to those who had absolutely no food of any kind. Sligo was not a grain-growing country, and it was useless to tell the people to consume their own supplies.

Again a peremptory order was sent to Achill Island, off the coast of Mayo, "cease sales, it can be done"; and the result, wrote Mr. Wood, Commissariat Clerk at Dugort, in an indignant letter was that people were actually dying of starvation. Mr. Wood then received permission to make a few sales, "but only to the point which is absolutely necessary for the preservation of human life."

On the whole, Commissariat officers, working in distressed districts, took the part of the people.

The sufferings of the people had become so great that Routh was alarmed. Starvation was producing desperation; there was "a spirit of revolution abroad, and the only way to check it," he told Trevelyan on November 3, "is to have a supply of food." Two hundred tons each of some kinds of food should be sent immediately to two danger spots, Belmullet, in Erris, and Mr. Parker's depot, Clifden, in Galway. Trevelyan refused, and a promise of 3,000 barrels of barley-meal, sometime in the future, was all Routh could obtain.

❧

Trevelyan wrote a long explanatory letter to Routh on November 12. It appeared that the Government had reconsidered their past undertakings, and the pledge to feed the west had faded away. True, Trevelyan wrote, "our object ought to be to take care . . . that no part of the districts in the west of Ireland for which we are responsible shall be destitute of the means of subsistence," but he now added a qualification, "as far as we are able," which effectually released the Government from responsibility. Further, he denied that the Government's duty was to bring in cheap food to replace the potato and prevent famine prices: "all we can safely aim at is to accomplish such a just distribution and equalization of the existing stock of food that the people in every part of Ireland may have the opportunity of purchasing food at current prices"; he added, however, "if they have the means to do so." Those who had not the means to buy "must be placed on a footing of charity," but how this was to be accomplished, for several million people, he did not specify.

Famine in Ireland had now reached a point where general disorganization was setting in. Bands of starving men roamed the country, begging for food, "more like famishing wolves than men"; on being given bread they "went away quietly"; and the employment lists for the public works, which should have been carefully prepared by the local relief committees, became a farce, through fear of the starving mobs. From Nenagh, the Board of Works' Inspecting Officer reported on October 31, "Gentlemen from Relief Committees are constantly pouring into this office with lists of names in such numbers that if half of them were put on the Public Works they would not have room to work . . . Some of the gentlemen assure me that neither their lives nor their properties are secure if they return to their houses without promises of employment." The relief committee at Carlingford, "very much afraid of the people, put on the name of every person old enough to walk."

Those who failed to get employment tickets forced themselves on; at Tulla, in Clare, "men and boys crowd in upon the works that are in progress and *insist* upon working"; and in one among several similar episodes, a Mayo priest marched "a large body of destitute" from his parish and put them on the works, without any reference to the Board of Works' officer. At Castlebar men were driven off the works by a band, who asserted that they had a better right and that the poorest had not been given tickets.

In County Clare the distress was so overwhelming that engineers began the works the instant they were laid out and employed all who came, without waiting for the issue of tickets. Destitution was so universal, however, wrote Captain O'Brien, the Board of Works' Inspecting Officer, on November 8, that only a very small number of men were unjustifiably employed. In many places the masses of starving and discontented labourers began to gain the upper hand—

"No Engineer or Gangsman can or *dare* do his duty," a Limerick magistrate told the Lord-Lieutenant on October 29. The men "defied all regulations and attempts to restrain them . . . these armed masses of hungry people with spades and pickaxes in their hands are perfectly unmanageable."

As a result, delays in paying wages increased; on November 2 the pay clerks for the district of East Carbery, County Cork, threw up their posts rather than venture among the turbulent inhabitants; at Clonakilty the pay clerk was attacked and beaten. The recruiting of pay clerks became more difficult than ever, and Captain Kennedy, the Board of Works' officer for County Meath, reported that the pay department was so understaffed that one clerk was expected to pay 5,000 men in three different baronies, which was clearly impossible. At Kells the men had not been paid for more than two weeks, and only the action of the Savings Bank manager, who advanced £150, prevented an outbreak. In several places it was not even known how many men were employed.

When a man named Denis McKennedy died on October 24 while working on road No. 1, in the western division of West Carbery, County Cork, it was alleged he had not been paid since October 10. A post-mortem examination was carried out by Dr. Daniel Donovan and Dr. Patrick Due, and death was pronounced to be the result of starvation. There was no food in the stomach or in the small intestines, but in the large intestine was "a portion of undigested raw cabbage, mixed with excrement." At the coroner's inquest a verdict was returned that the deceased "died of starvation caused by the gross neglect of the Board of Works."

At Bandon, where three weeks' wages were owing on October 31, deaths were alleged to have occurred; and on November 3 the Lord-Lieutenant called for a report of the number of persons who had died from starvation on the works, because their wages were delayed.

❧

Autumn was now passing into winter. The nettles and black-berries, the edible roots and cabbage leaves on which hundreds of people had been eking out an existence disappeared; flocks of wretched beings, resembling human scarecrows, had combed the blighted potato fields over and over again until not a fragment of a potato that was conceivably edible remained.

Children began to die. In Skibbereen workhouse more than fifty per cent. of the children admitted after October 1, 1846, died; the deaths, said the workhouse physician, were due to "diarrhoea acting on an exhausted constitution."

Lord Monteagle now made a personal appeal to Routh, begging him, in view of the sufferings of the people, to open the depots. Routh refused. "We can obtain no effort until the parties are subjected to a little pressure," he wrote, on November 21. He did, however, suggest to Trevelyan that the Government might "begin to consider the question in December," and possibly some of the depots in the far west, Clifden, Belmullet, Achill, might be opened one or two days a week. Trevelyan wrote back in alarm. Once the depots were opened they could not be closed, and since the depots did not contain a sufficient quantity to meet the demands of the people "the greatest discontent will be caused and danger of outrage." The Chancellor of the Exchequer, wrote Trevelyan, had said that the longer the opening of the depots could be put off, the better, "provided there is no real danger of starvation." Trevelyan was writing on November 24; and so the deaths which had already occurred, and were occurring, were apparently not considered to indicate any "real danger" of starvation.

At this moment of suffering unprecedented weather added greatly to the misery of the people. The climate of Ireland is famous for its mildness; years pass without a fall of snow; in the gardens of the south and west semi-tropical plants flourish, and tubers of the genus Dahlia can be left to winter in the ground without damage from frost. In 1846, at the end of October, it became cold, and in November snow began to fall. Six inches of snow and drifts were reported at the early date of November 12 from Tyrone.

It seemed that Nature herself was now enrolled among the enemies of unhappy Ireland.

Chapter VIII

THE WINTER in Ireland of 1846-47 was "the most severe in living memory," and the longest. Snow fell early in November;

frost was continuous; icy gales blew "perfect hurricanes of snow, hail and sleet," with a force unknown since the famous "great wind" of 1839; roads were impassable and transport was brought to a standstill.

The prevailing wind in Ireland is a west wind, and though the approach of winter is usually heralded by a gale blowing up out of the Atlantic, it is mild in spite of its force. But in the autumn and winter of 1846-47 the wind came from the north-east—it had blown across Russia, and it was icy. The whole continent of Europe that winter was gripped by bitter cold, and in England, by the middle of December, the Thames was a mass of floating ice.

To the Irish people the abnormal severity of the winter brought disaster. One of the compensations of the nineteenth-century Irish peasant's life was warmth. The climate was normally mild and the possession of a supply of turf, that is peat, almost universal; a turf fire burned in the Irish cabin night and day, and in normal times did not go out perhaps for a century. Since potatoes do not require cultivation during the winter the Irish peasant was not forced to go out in bad weather; he spent the cold, wet days indoors, and though he was dressed in rags and his children were naked, except for a single garment, they endured little hardship.

Now he must go out in his rags to labour on the public works, be drenched with rain and driving snow and cut by icy gales; and, more often than not, he was already starving. Labourers began to "faint with exhaustion," and a Board of Works' engineer told Trevelyan that "as an engineer he was ashamed of allotting so little task-work for a day's wages, while as a man he was ashamed of requiring so much." After the end of November Routh's reports contained a rapidly-increasing number of cases of deaths on the works from starvation, aggravated by exposure to cold, snow and drenching rain.

The people became bewildered. They had taken in very little of what was happening; at this period Irish was spoken in rural districts and English barely understood, while in the west English was not understood at all. No attempt was made to explain the catastrophe to the people; on the contrary, Government officials and relief committee members treated the destitute with impatience and contempt; the wretched, ragged crowds provoked irritation, heightened by the traditional English distrust and dislike of the native Irish.

"Everything has been tried but a little sympathy and kindness," declared an eye-witness on December 2, 1846; and Trevelyan reproved Routh for the "unnecessary harshness of manner" reported to be used by Government officials towards the poor.

Bewilderment was succeeded by panic, the unreasoning terror which makes animals stampede and which, a little later, brought about headlong flight from Ireland in the famine emigration.

The first to succumb were the poorest of all, the "squatters," who had put up a hut of sods in a bog, or on the seashore, for the sake of seaweed for potato manure. These unfortunate creatures had never had any other means of existence but their small crop of potatoes, and with the potatoes lost they abandoned their hovels and descended on the towns in droves. Five thousand beggars roamed the streets of Cork; Oranmore, in Galway, had "hundreds of poor creatures wandering about"; complaints from Thurles in Tipperary reached the Lord-Lieutenant that a "vast population" had "poured in from the surrounding country, half are starving." These unhappy beings slept in ditches and in doorways, begged, and were driven away and, wrote Father Mathew on December 16, in Cork alone died at the rate of one hundred a week.

Fear hung over Ireland like a cloud. "There is an undefined notion that something very terrible is going to take place soon," wrote Colonel Jones to Trevelyan.

Meanwhile, the numbers employed on the public works leapt upwards with frightening rapidity; 30,135 in September, 150,259 in October, 285,817 in November; and the Board of Works, hopelessly understaffed, was utterly unable to deal with such numbers. Only 4,021 overseers and stewards had been found to arrange and supervise the work of nearly 286,000 labourers on works all over Ireland, and they were, frequently, men of low intelligence, quite incapable of assessing piece-work. In Leitrim, one case out of dozens, 150 men were without work for three weeks because no one could be found capable of measuring tasks, and as well as being stupid many of these men were untrustworthy. "It is universally reported" that the officials "are dishonest and unfair to the poor people," wrote a Board of Works' inspector from Roscommon.

By the end of November task-work as originally planned had been abandoned. "The incompetency of the Board of

Works' subordinate officials makes task-work impossible"; and the only tasks allotted were breaking a certain quantity of stones. "It requires a certain talent to measure out work of a higher class," wrote Routh. The struggle to establish that system which, Trevelyan said, "nearly led to a dissolution of society in some districts," had been in vain.

Far more serious than the abandonment of task-work was a change which had taken place in the type of labour employed. The original plan, laid down in Whitehall, was to employ able-bodied men and to exact a fair day's work for a day's wage; but because destitution was the qualification for employment it proved impossible to refuse destitute women, especially destitute widows with families. Thus by the end of October Routh was allowing relief committees to employ women on the works, mainly "breaking stones at 4d. a day"; on the same grounds destitute "old, feeble and very young persons were engaged." Board of Works' officers complained that "Relief Committees place women and children on the roads, with spades and shovels, completely unfit for work," and it was "impossible to keep within estimates" if such labour was employed.

The presence of hordes of wretched, half-starved women and children, totally unfit for manual labour, ended any hope of discipline; on the works the mobs of labourers began to get out of hand, and irregularities became common. For instance, the lowest kinds of drinking-dens, in wooden sheds, were hastily erected, the magistrates, Father Mathew told Trevelyan, "with culpable facility," granting licences for the sale of liquor whenever works were begun.

Overseers and pay clerks paid out wages in these "pestiferous erections," and even had a financial interest in them. In one case the local publican was a member of the relief committee, and would recommend a man for the works only on condition that he spent part of what he earned in the drinking-shop. Owing to the shortage of silver coin, gangs were paid jointly with a single note. They then had the choice of taking the note to the nearest town to be changed, and losing a day's work, or of going for change to the drinking-shop and, too frequently, remaining. Through the intervention of Father Mathew, who appealed to Trevelyan, the erection of drinking-shops was, to some extent, at least, forbidden.

In obtaining tickets for employment all the frauds and impositions of the previous year were repeated on an enlarged scale. Prosperous farmers got themselves put on the works, tickets were bought and sold, sometimes several times over. "Landlords competed with each other in getting their tenants on the lists . . . clergy insisted on the claims of their respective congregations." Collusion between labourers and overseers was "habitual," and false returns gave men task-work rates of pay without the labour. Meanwhile, free from supervision, the enormous and rapidly-increasing multitudes idled on the works, "doing literally nothing but what they please," wrote Captain Wynne from Ennis, County Clare, on December 5.

Because farming work was neglected the prospects for next year's harvest were disastrous. On November 14 Colonel Jones of the Board of Works reported that, in the course of a journey of fifty miles, he saw "only one plough and one man sowing"; holdings in Sligo were reported "choked with weeds"; near Oughterard a Commissariat officer found three hundred farmers working on the public works while only two men were tilling the soil.

For this deplorable state of affairs the British Government blamed the Irish people: as Irish cottiers were notoriously idle, they preferred to do nothing on the works rather than labour on their farms. The Irish were hopelessly improvident, therefore they closed their eyes to the terrible fate which must await them if next year's harvest were lost.

The British Government did not suggest how people who were without food of any kind were to keep alive until next year's harvest while they tilled their ground. "The people are driven to the Public Works," wrote a Commissariat officer, "by the utter impossibility of cultivating their own small-holdings unless assisted in doing so by a loan . . . to keep them from starving in the meanwhile." Moreover, though labourers were accused of criminally deserting the farms, the truth was that farmers were turning their labourers adrift. Hired labourers in Ireland customarily received one or two meals a day as part of their remuneration, and farmers who had paid their labourers mainly in potatoes were quite unable to produce money instead. "The small farmer," wrote a Commissariat officer, "says . . . owing to the total loss of his potato crop he . . . has no means to feed and pay the servants he once kept." It was true, wrote an inspector, that a "large part of the men on the works have left the land . . .

the greater number however have been discharged and are bitter."

The lack of demand for labourers was proved when, on October 29, the Board of Works issued a circular for distribution to farmers directing them to apply to the stewards on the public works for the number of labourers they required—any man refusing to return to farm-work would be instantly discharged. No applications were received. "Every opportunity is given to farmers of taking men from the public works but they never demand them," reported a Board of Works' inspecting officer on November 15.

While the hired farm labourer could find no employment, the occupier of a piece of land, the small farmer, had nothing to put in it. In the extremity of hunger as the terrible winter dragged on, farmers were reported to be "actually consuming the seed which should be sown for next year's crop." From Tipperary, Colonel Douglas, the Board of Works' Relief Department Inspector, wrote to Routh on December 8, "I think it incumbent on me, under a solemn sense of the truth of what I now write, to state my conviction that *nobody* who has not personally seen the state of matters in this country can form to himself any idea of the inevitable result of the present system . . . Farmers have been grinding and consuming their own corn . . . the supply of seed will be eaten for food and this is the most productive wheat country in Ireland."

A few days later he wrote again: seed oats as well as seed corn were being consumed and "farmers were asking, what is the good of preparing the ground when there was going to be no seed?"; he implored the Government to arrange a scheme to supply seed. Throughout November and December urgent and, indeed, abject petitions to the Government for seed of any kind were forwarded to Trevelyan from all over Ireland. All were refused. " . . . the conclusion," wrote Trevelyan, "inevitably arrived at was, that the moment it came to be understood that the Government had taken upon itself the responsibility of this delicate and peculiar branch of rural economy, the painful exertions made by private individuals . . . to reserve a stock of seed would be relaxed. . . ."

At the express desire of Lord Bessborough an attempt was made to buy seed rye, but it was too late; and though Erichsen was instructed to buy 5,000 quarters, 600 quarters was all he could secure, "with the utmost exertion." On his advice seed rye was given up, "as the season is so far advanced," he wrote on November 3. Some landlords, including the Duke of Manchester at Tandragee Castle, had bought seed rye privately and distributed it to their tenants, but apart from private philanthropy virtually nothing was done.

Shortage of seed, however, was not the sole reason why holdings lay uncultivated. The Irish small farmer knew that the landlord would have no scruple in taking possession of his harvest, even at such a time, if he owed rent.

"The land," wrote Mr. Lowe, a Board of Works' inspector, on December 5, "is neglected . . . partly from the inability to get seed and partly from the feeling that if they do sow it the landlord will seize the crop." The people were in anxiety over their rent; they had "nothing left to give the landlord" and "naturally concluded," wrote Mr. Lowe, that when they did have something he would take it.

Various schemes to end the alarming neglect of agriculture were pressed on the Government. A deputation from a "large and respectable meeting" at Fermoy urged that small-holders, while cultivating their land, should be paid the same wage as on the public works; another, put forward by Stephen Spring Rice, proposed that labourers should be "drafted" off the works and "assigned" to farmers, being paid by Government at the same rate as on the works.

Trevelyan rejected all these proposals. The "social evils which beset us on every side," he wrote to Stephen Spring Rice, were due to Government interference; for Government now to provide "the funds required by farmers for carrying on the ordinary cultivation of the land" was to extend Government interference to a fatal extent.

The appalling results which must follow a shortage in the following year's harvest were better appreciated in Dublin than in Whitehall, and Richard Griffith, one of the two Commissioners in charge of the Board of Works' Relief Department, worked out a scheme, termed "family task work," which would give small farmers something to live on while they cultivated their plots; and on December 9, 1846, a circular, No. 38, announcing the scheme was issued by the Relief Department of the Board of Works. The Treasury was not consulted.

Under the plan drainage and sub-soiling (improvement of the soil), the two great necessities in Ireland, were to be

executed by spade labour, thus employing the poorest class.
Each man was to have a task allotted to him, estimated to
require fourteen or twenty-one days; he was to dig a certain
length of drain and break stones with which to construct
it. His wife and family might assist him, and if he chose
to work hard and finish his task in six to eight days he
could collect his wages and spend the rest of the allotted
time cultivating his own ground.

Circular No. 38, with its details of the plan, burst on the
Treasury like a bombshell, and on behalf of the Lords of
the Treasury Trevelyan wrote the Commissioners of the Board
of Works a letter of majestic indignation. The circular had
been issued without Treasury sanction; it had been read with
great surprise by the Lords of the Treasury. "My lords are
in hopes that its circulation may hitherto have been confined
to officers acting under orders of the Commissioners and
that there may yet be time to withdraw it without its being
publicly known . . . it is quite impossible for my lords to
give their sanction to parties being paid from public funds
for the cultivation of their own land. . . ." The circular was
suppressed.

Meanwhile, snow had continued to fall throughout November—"an appalling aggravation of the frightful misery round
me," wrote a Board of Works' relief inspector. Small farmers
who had been struggling to attempt some cultivation were
now "forced on the relief works by the severity of the
weather," and an even more general rush to get tickets began.
"The whole labouring population seems to be seeking employment on the Public Works," wrote a Board of Works'
officer on November 28. That night snow was falling thickly,
in the west inspections were held up and mountain roads
blocked. "From morning till night" hundreds of labourers
and small farmers thronged the doors of houses where Board
of Works' officials lodged, a sight "painful in the extreme."
In Westmeath, in the once-prosperous midlands, the Board
of Works' officer, Captain Maxwell, reported on December
5 that he had "poor wretched half-clad wretches howling at
the door for food." Six hundred persons waited outside the
door of Mr. Millet, the engineer, at Ennistymon, County
Clare, and "handled him roughly" when he came out. From
Monaghan the Board of Works' Inspector wrote that he did
not think the public works could possibly cope with the
enormous numbers. He was beset morning, noon and night

by hundreds of applicants and "besieged" by clergy imploring employment for their flocks.

Yet wages on the works were only a few shillings a week; 10*d*. a day was about the average earned, and 10*d*. a day, wrote an inspecting officer on November 28, "will only give one meal a day to a family of six." In the bitter weather crowds of starving, half-clothed men, women and children huddled on the works. Could not some kind of rough shelter be made of furze and stones, or screens made of old sails, asked the Board of Works' Inspector for Wicklow? For some months, if bad weather made work impossible, a day's pay was lost; however, on December 14 a circular was issued directing that half a day's wages, about 4*d*. or 5*d*., be paid when weather stopped work; but even so early morning roll-call, which frequently involved a walk, in snow and sleet, of several miles, must be attended.

Yet so immense was the number of applicants that though the total of employed rose with dangerous rapidity only a fraction of the destitute, in badly distressed districts, could be given work. In Mayo, in November, 13,000 were employed, but 400,000 were estimated to be destitute; in Galway 3,000 out of 9,000 received tickets; in Roscrea, Tipperary, 75 per cent. of the applicants were rejected.

Even so, Colonel Jones complained that the paper-work involved was so great that inspecting officers could do nothing else, and instead of being on the works, supervising and inspecting, they were forced to spend their days in an office. "Filling up tickets" repeatedly appears in inspecting officers' diaries as the whole of a day's activities. "The ticket system is such a bore an I.O. can do nothing else," wrote Captain Stirling, the Inspecting Officer for Mayo, on December 5. When a new work was opened in Galway, on December 6, it took the Inspecting Officer and two clerks from morning until 11 p.m. to make out the tickets.

Bodies of sullen, emaciated men with spades looking for work, marching on the roads, inspired fear, and rumours began to spread that people were arming. Firearms were reported to be selling, "to an alarming extent," in King's County; in Clare it was declared that "every man in the country is armed"; in Tipperary even the "lowest class now carry firearms." A private letter written from Liverpool on December 15, and forwarded to the police, asserted that

10,000 stand of arms* were known to have been purchased recently in Birmingham for Ireland, and 20,000 more had been ordered; "What can be the cause of this frightful arming of the people?"

In a manuscript dated January 4, 1847, James Hack Tuke, a Quaker philanthropist who had just returned from the West, wrote, "The subject of the "arming of the peasantry" having been . . . the means of steeling so many hearts to the sufferings of the Irish; it may be well just to state that to the many questions we put upon this question we received but one answer, viz. the poor starving people are not those who buy arms, it is quite impossible that people dying with hunger or earning only 8d. and 10d. a day . . . could buy them. It is the sons of our large farmers and apprentice boys and young men in the towns who are induced to buy a few fowling-pieces and pistols for amusement, it being a novelty here to possess arms, owing to the Irish Arms Bill having just expired." The fairly well-to-do, went on Mr. Tuke, bought arms for the protection of property; the starving, even if weapons were put into their hands, had not, in his opinion, the physical power left to use them.

On the public works themselves, however, where tens of thousands of starving discontented men were brought together, mutinies and acts of violence were common. Men in women's clothes, and with blackened faces, were reported to be "appearing everywhere and threatening the stewards, overseers and officers." Employees of the Board of Works were assaulted on the works, while the labourers looked on without attempting to interfere, and gangs in disguise broke into the houses of officials, dragged them from bed, and beat them. A rule was then made that works on which an "outrage" had occurred were to be closed down until the person or persons committing the outrage was in the hands of the authorities.

"Any officer of the Board of Works who does his duty properly incurs considerable personal danger," reported a Board of Works' inspector; and from the turbulent district of west Clare Captain Wynne, an exceptional officer of the Board, wrote that when unpopular orders were issued "the

---

* A 'stand' of arms is an Anglo-Irish term denoting a single rifle or musket complete with bayonet.

employees of the Board of Works resign rather than carry them into effect."

Relief committees became intimidated. "Such is the state of alarm in which they live" that they "dare not do their duty for fear," wrote an inspecting officer, and the gentry were terrorized. The Inspecting Officer in Thurles wrote on December 10 that very frequently, at the same time as he received a *"strong recommendation"* of a man from one of the gentry, he was also sent a private message not to attend to the recommendation, for the writer had "dared not refuse" to give it.

Under the relief scheme of 1846 the Lieutenant of the county was to nominate relief committee members, but in practice relief committees were self-constituted; ". . . any persons who on moderately plausible grounds made application to the Lieutenant of the County for permission to form themselves into a committee received his sanction . . . all have the same end in view, viz. to gain popularity at the expense of the Public purse," wrote an inspecting officer, on December 12.

Lists from such committees, Colonel Jones told Trevelyan, were "prepared with a desire to impose"; persons "with stacks of corn, with stores of meal, with cows and houses" were recommended, while "the poorest are passed over in every district." The highly unpopular task of examining applicants and striking those who were not, in fact, destitute off the lists fell on the Board of Works' Inspector; and instead of assisting him dishonest committees violently opposed revision, sometimes refused to allow an examination at all, and implanted the idea that the Board of Works' Inspector was the enemy of the destitute.

The resentment formerly felt by the people of Ireland against the landlords was now, wrote Trevelyan, transferred to the officers of the Board of Works. "This is the man who is starving you," shouted the parish priest of Islandeady, pointing his finger at Captain Carey, the Board of Works' Inspector for County Mayo; all those present, he went on, should tell their friends that Captain Carey was the cause of their sufferings. It was a fact that in Islandeady distress was very great, but Captain Carey's instructions allowed him to employ only a limited number.

One of the most turbulent districts was west Clare; "these people are dangerous," wrote the County Surveyor. A vast poverty-stricken population was further increased by unknown thousands of destitute "squatters," who lived in huts on the seashore. "All the money in the Treasury cannot meet the wants of this *frightful* population," wrote the Inspecting Officer, Captain Wynne. Relief lists were dishonest, terrorization prevalent, and outrages common; "Strong nerves are needed in the present state of west Clare society," wrote Captain Wynne to Trevelyan. Captain Wynne, however, did possess strong nerves, and he proceeded to go through the lists name by name, striking off those who were not destitute. The reductions were made in public, accompanied by shouts and threats from an angry crowd. At Ennistymon, for instance, "two hours were occupied in attack and defence . . . with the sole purpose of holding us up to the assassin, and hallooing on a mob of about a thousand of the worst possible types." Eventually, wrote Captain Wynne, "I have displaced upwards of 9,400 persons, chosen and placed upon the works by the several committees in my seven baronies, and I have placed upon the lists the poor starving labourers who had been neglected because nobody had a direct interest in their welfare, and I have not refused employment in any instance to real destitution."

The result was a typical outrage. On Saturday, December 5, 1846, at about 5:30 p.m., a man named Hennessy, Captain Wynne's principal overseer of works at a place named Clare Abbey, was walking home, accompanied by a clerk, named McMahon, and a boy; just in front of them three soldiers of the 73rd Regiment were walking abreast on the road, while two others were on the footpath. A man appeared out of the ditch at the side of the road, within six feet of Hennessy, and fired a blunderbuss at him, point-blank. Hennessy was wearing a thick coat, which saved his life, but 120 shots penetrated it, 85 entering his body and the remainder wounding him on the thigh. His assailant paused to explain that he did not intend to shoot anyone but Hennessy, and then "walked quietly away," no one, including the five soldiers, making any attempt to stop him. Hennessy meanwhile fell on the fence, in "great agony and torture," while the clerk, McMahon, exclaimed, rather surprisingly, "Boys, what have we done? Mr. Hennessy is dead." Hennessy managed to stagger to his house in Clare village, about three-quarters of a mile away, upon which the inhabitants gathered in a mob outside, "laughing, joking, refusing to go for a doctor," and "signifying their complete approval of the outrage."

The people of Clare village paid dearly for their revenge. On Monday, December 7, in accordance with regulations, the works at Clare Abbey were closed down until Hennessy's assailant should be in the hands of the authorities: "900 persons are turned adrift," wrote Captain Wynne, ". . . I do not like to think what the consequences will be." Distress in west Clare was desperate; more than 25,000 people were on the lists for employment on the works and, even so, "a vast amount of destitution goes unrelieved."

Snow continued to fall: reports from inspecting officers for the weeks ending December 12 and December 19 recorded snow and gales throughout Ireland from Donegal to Wicklow; snowfalls were reported in Dublin, mountain roads blocked, works "everywhere" stopped; in Mayo the snow was so deep that the works could not even be seen; and from Cork the Inspecting Officer reported that "people were dying fast." Since no information leading to the arrest of Hennessy's assailant came in, the works at Clare Abbey remained closed, and on December 19 Captain Wynne reported that the people of Clare Abbey were starving, "but as yet peaceably."

However, on December 24, in bitter weather, Captain Wynne paid a visit to Clare Abbey, and that evening he wrote two urgent, personal letters, substantially the same; one to Colonel Jones of the Board of Works, the other to Trevelyan, to the effect that the works at Clare Abbey must be started again, whether Hennessy's assailant was brought to justice or not. "I ventured through the parish this day," he wrote, "to ascertain the condition of the inhabitants, and, altho' a man not easily moved, I confess myself unmanned by the intensity and extent of the suffering I witnessed more especially among the women and little children, crowds of whom were to be seen scattered over the turnip fields like a flock of famishing crows, devouring the raw turnips, mothers half naked, shivering in the snow and sleet, uttering exclamations of despair while their children were screaming with hunger. I am a match for anything else I may meet with here, but this I cannot stand. When may we expect to resume the works? Nothing but dire necessity would make me advocate this step, feeling as I do that I thereby throw away the only armour we possess against the bullet of the assassin, but it cannot be helped."

The works at Clare Abbey were reopened on December 28. The arrest of Hennessy's assailant does not appear to be recorded.

≈≈

On December 8 the Board of Works' returns showed that 300,000 persons were employed on the works, at a monthly cost of £500,000; while in Dublin the Board itself had become, in Trevelyan's words, "the centre of a colossal organization; 5,000 separate works had to be reported upon; 12,000 subordinate officers had to be superintended." The correspondence was immense; on November 30 2,000 letters were received and on December 12 2,500. A member of the Board wrote that the period, ". . . . looking back on it . . . appears to me not a succession of weeks and days, but one long continuous day, with occasional intervals of nightmare sleep. Rest one could never have, night nor day, when one felt that every minute lost a score of men might die."

It is not easy to understand why the British Government did not foresee what would happen; the relief scheme so recently brought to a close had already demonstrated both the extent of destitution in Ireland and the difficulty of administering a scheme of public works; and now, after the total failure of the potato, with additional hundreds of thousands made destitute, the public works became impossible to control. Trevelyan, however, was still undaunted, and on December 8 he wrote to Routh, "we have reached an important crisis in our operations." Future prospects were, he wrote, "appealing," and owing to the "neglect of all the most ordinary farming operations" the Government was shortly going to be faced with the alternative of letting the Irish starve or of feeding them out of the public purse. The numbers employed on the works must not be allowed to rise, and his solution was to tighten official control. "We must at this stage throw all our strength into our inspecting machinery," he wrote. Yet before the letter even reached Routh the numbers had jumped again; on December 9 they were 310,-000, an increase of 10,000; next day Colonel Jones reported a further jump to 319,000. The final total for December proved to be between 450,000 and 500,000.

These complications confirmed Trevelyan in his low opinion of the Irish. "The great evil with which we have to contend," he wrote to Colonel Jones, on December 2, is "not

the physical evil of the famine, but the moral evil of the
selfish, perverse and turbulent character of the people."
These feelings—held not only by Trevelyan—exercised a
momentous influence on the Government's policy towards
Ireland during the period of the famine now about to open.

∽

By this time assistance for Ireland was being organized by
bodies other than the British Government, and in England,
Ireland and elsewhere philanthropists and humanitarians
formed committees and raised subscriptions for Irish relief.
The first sum was subscribed as early as April, 1846, thousands
of miles away, in Calcutta, where £14,000 was collected as
soon as news of the distress, arising from the first failure of
1845, reached India. A high proportion of the Queen's troops
in India was Irish, and many younger sons of Irish families
served in the East India Company. Next, on September 2,
1846, an organization called the Irish Relief Association, originally formed to provide relief in the famine of 1831, was
revived, ultimately collecting more than £42,000; another
Irish committee, the General Central Relief Committee, was
set up in Dublin on December 29, 1846, under the presidency
of the Marquess of Kildare, eldest son of the Duke of Leinster,
and it collected more than £63,000. "Ladies' Work Associations" were formed in England and Ireland to make clothes
and knit jerseys for the destitute poor. "It was common practice," wrote Trevelyan, "for ladies in England to have parishes
assigned to them in Ireland, and each lady raised all she
could, and made periodical remittances to the clergyman of
her adopted parish, receiving accounts from him . . . The
self-denial necessary to support this charitable drain was
carried to such an extent at Brighton and elsewhere, that
the confectionery and other trades-people suffered severely in
their business." Government officials, especially in the Commissariat, wrote home to friends in England and raised small
funds.

On November 13, 1846, an organization of historical importance was formed: the Society of Friends, the Quakers,
set up the Central Relief Committee of the Society of Friends,
in Dublin, supported by a sister-committee in London.

One of the first objects of the Central Committee was to
obtain "trustworthy information respecting the real state of
the more remote districts," and the members of the Society

of Friends are witnesses whose integrity it is difficult to challenge. The sufferings endured by the people of Ireland during the famine, the ghastly happenings in the bogs of Erris, the mud huts of Mayo, the lanes of Skibbereen, might be dismissed as exaggeration if it were not for the calm and sober evidence of the Quakers.

The membership of the Society of Friends extended all over Ireland, and "corresponding members," in addition to the central Committee, were appointed in various districts such men as Mr. Marcus Goodbody, owner of the well-known mills at Clara, King's County. In Munster, which included the badly-distressed districts of the south-west, four sub-committees of local residents were formed, but in Connaught, the most distressed province in Ireland, including Mayo, Connemara and Sligo, an effective organization was impossible, on account of the backward state of the country, the want of respectable residents and of the "machinery" of civilized life. No organization was necessary in north-east Ulster.

Mr. William Forster, a minister in Norwich and one of the most respected members of the Quaker community in England, had been intending to visit Ireland on his own account, and he undertook the first investigation, starting on November 30, 1846. He was accompanied by James Hack Tuke, who was to be the ardent champion of Ireland for forty years, and another well-known Quaker, Joseph Crosfield, and was later joined by his son, W. E. Forster, a brilliant young man of twenty-eight. Time transformed the young man into the hated Chief Secretary, "Buckshot" Forster, so-called because, it was alleged, he had ordered the constabulary—though for humanitarian reasons—to load with buckshot when firing into a crowd; but in 1846, he was heart and soul in sympathy with Ireland.

The Central Committee had decided to finance the establishment of soup kitchens—Quakers, and Mr. Forster in particular, had experience in managing soup kitchens for the English poor. Only persons who received no relief or inadequate relief from Government were to be helped, and the "strictest instructions were given . . . that no preference should be made in the distribution of relief on the ground of religious persuasion."

From the first Mr. Forster's investigation "disclosed a state of destitution and suffering far exceeding that which had been

at first supposed." The public works were not saving the
people from starvation, on account of the enormous rise in
food prices. In Westmeath, on December 1, 1846, a typical
family, consisting of seven persons, was found to be living
on 10*d*. a day; only a single member of the family had
obtained employment, and to earn 10*d*. he had to walk 3½
miles to work and 3½ miles back. The sole meal that day was
to be "a small ration of oatmeal"; the day before they had had
a turnip. At Carrick-on-Shannon well over a hundred persons
waited outside the workhouse to apply for thirty vacancies,
and a "painful and heart-rending" scene took place, mothers
imploring that two or three of their six or seven children be
taken in, since it was impossible to feed them on 8*d*. or
10*d*. a day. Mr. Forster particularly noticed the children,
"like skeletons, their features sharpened with hunger and
their limbs wasted, so that there was little left but bones,
their hands and arms, in particular, being much emaciated,
and the happy expression of infancy gone from their faces,
leaving the anxious look of premature old age." A member of
the Board of Guardians remarked callously to him that the
poor "were dying like rotten sheep"; and two clergymen said
that, while they were at their meals "poor famishing wretches
appear before the windows and groan in the most pitiable
manner." Throughout the country, he noted, pigs and poultry
had "entirely disappeared."

At Stranorlar, in County Donegal, on December 12, Mr.
Forster found that no public works had yet been started—
many of the inhabitants were "scarcely able to crawl." They
were existing on a little Indian meal on some days, on a little
cabbage on others, and sometimes on nothing at all.

His next stop was at Dunfanaghy, and the jouney was
made in "deep snow" and with "constant storms of snow and
hail." The two younger men walked up all the hills, and finally
the luggage had to be temporarily abandoned because the
horse could not pull the loaded car through the snowdrifts.
Dunfanaghy was without public works or any employment
whatsoever; fishing was the local occupation, but the severity
of the weather made it impossible for the "wretched boats"
to go out. James Hack Tuke found as many as seventeen
persons living in a single hut not six feet high; the children
lying on the ground on a little straw, and there was "nothing
whatever" in the hut in the shape of money or food.

Worse still was the condition of what Mr. Forster described

as "the miserable and neglected tenantry of the Marquis of Conyngham, an absentee proprietor who holds an immense tract of land here." No Sessions had been held to propose public works, and no relief of any kind was given.

At each place he visited Mr. Forster offered to provide a boiler and give a donation to get a soup kitchen started, and with the exception of Castlerea the offers were gratefully accepted. At Castlerea the Catholic priest refused, because the result would be to bring the poor from the surrounding country into the town, "by which they would be overwhelmed."

In January 1847 W. E. Forster joined his father for about ten days, and they visited Mayo, where conditions were very bad. Westport was "a strange and fearful sight, like what we read of in beleaguered cities, the streets crowded with gaunt wanderers . . ." Across the harbour, at Bundorragha, in Galway, the population "were like walking skeletons, the men stamped with the livid mark of hunger, the children crying with pain, the women, in some of the cabins, too weak to stand . . . all the sheep were gone, all the cows, all the poultry killed; only one pig left, the very dogs . . . had disappeared." At Clifden W. E. Forster was "quickly surrounded by a mob of men and women, more like famished dogs than fellow creatures, whose figures, looks and cries all showed they were suffering the ravening agony of hunger."

"When we entered a village," wrote W. E., "our first question was, how many deaths? 'The hunger is upon us' was everywhere the cry, and, involuntarily, we found ourselves regarding this hunger as we should an epidemic, looking upon starvation as a disease." There was an idea in England, he wrote, that the accounts of the state of Ireland given in the newspapers were exaggerated, "but no colouring can deepen the blackness of truth."

As the winter continued with unrelenting severity, frantic appeals for food poured into Whitehall from all over Ireland. Money was becoming useless in Limerick, reported Mr. Hewetson, the senior Commissariat officer—even if people had money they could find nothing to buy. From Cork on December 12 Mr. Nicholas Cummins, J.P., wrote, "The alarming prospect cannot be exaggerated . . ." In the whole of the city and port of Cork there were only 4,000 tons of "bread stuffs." "Unless great amounts reach us from other quarters, the prospect is appalling." "I assure you that unless

something is immediately done the people must die . . ." the
Board of Works' Relief Inspector at Sligo told Trevelyan;
"Pray do something for them. Let me beg of you to attend
to this. *I cannot express their condition.*" Appeals were not
only from the west. In Wicklow on December 16 there were
already 25,000 paupers and no food; in Monaghan public
works alone could not solve the problem, there must be food.

"The distress of the wretched people is heart-rending,"
wrote the Commissariat officer at Burtonport, County Donegal; "something ought to be done for them . . . there is
absolutely nothing in the place for food . . . It strikes the
people as very unfeeling to keep corn in the stores without
using it"; and Colonel Jones told Trevelyan "a panic appears
to have come over the people's minds; they are apprehensive
there is not enough food in the country . . . The applications
to Sir Randolph Routh to open his stores, when refused, give
rise to a feeling of discontent."

Routh meanwhile, miserably conscious that his stores did
not contain sufficient to make opening possible, was pressing
Trevelyan, without success, for adequate supplies. "I wish
you would consider that little important word *'quantity,'*"
he wrote on December 15 and 16; "with 4,800 tons in
store, I am really afraid of the result. Pray do not think me
importunate or troublesome, if I repeat to you my anxiety to
see a further reserve of as much more. . . ." Trevelyan
answered, irritably, "Our purchases, as I have more than once
informed you, have been carried to the utmost limit short
of seriously raising the price in the London market." Routh's
anxiety was so acute that he persisted, reminding Trevelyan
of the Government's pledge to feed the west. Why not
purchase eight, ten or fifteen thousand tons "to keep the
pledge to the west and secure the tranquillity of the country?"
he asked.

But Trevelyan had reached the conclusion that everything
that could and should be done for Ireland had been done,
and that any further step could only be taken at the expense
of the rest of the United Kingdom. "I deeply regret the
primary and appalling evil of the insufficiency of the supplies
of food in this country," he wrote on December 22, "but the
stores we are able to procure for the western division of
Ireland are insufficient even for that purpose, and how can
we undertake more?" In a private letter to Routh he wrote,
". . . if we were to purchase for Irish use faster than we are

now doing, we should commit a crying injustice to the rest of the country."

The outcome of this policy was such a tragedy as overtook the district of Skibbereen. Starvation in Skibbereen had been reported as early as September, and on December 3 two Protestant clergymen from the district, Mr. Caulfield and Mr. Townsend, crossed to London and saw Trevelyan at the Treasury. They told him the Government relief scheme was failing in Skibbereen; "practical and influential persons of property and respectability" had not come forward to serve on the relief committee; no subscription had been raised; the committee was now in a "state of suspension," and useless. The sole employment in Skibbereen was on the public works, but only 8*d*. a day was paid, which was not sufficient to feed a family; sixty to seventy persons who would otherwise die of hunger were fed daily with soup at Mr. Caulfield's house. The two clergymen implored the Government to send food. No food was sent.

On December 15 the Commissioners of the Board of Works wrote an official letter drawing the attention of the government to the extreme destitution existing in Skibbereen, upon which, on December 18, Trevelyan wrote a letter to Routh "with reference to what is now going on in Skibbereen." He was afraid that Routh would be persuaded to send Government supplies—because a relief committee was not operating in Skibbereen the town was not eligible for relief under the Government plan. Trevelyan reminded Routh that there were "principles to be kept in view." The relief committee system must be adhered to, in order to prevent a run on Government supplies and "to draw out the resources of the country before we make our own issues." There was, moreover, the unpleasant truth, which Trevelyan admitted by forbidding issues, but never stated, that the Government depots did not contain sufficient supplies to meet the demand if an attempt was made to feed the starving. Routh was ordered to "act with firmness and be prepared to incur much obloquy, but it will be as nothing compared with the just reprehension you would rightly incur from Government and public if you were to allow your depots to become exhausted." Finally, to protect private enterprise, Trevelyan concluded: "We attach the highest public importance to the strict observance of our pledge not to send orders abroad, which would come into

competition with our merchants and upset all their calculations."

However, on December 15 Mr. Nicholas Cummins, the
well-known magistrate of Cork, had paid a visit to Skibbereen
and the surrounding district, and had been horrified by what
he saw. He appears to have written to the authorities, but
without result, because on December 22 he addressed a letter
to the Duke of Wellington, who was an Irishman, and also
sent a copy to *The Times*. It was published on December 24,
1846.

"My Lord Duke," wrote Mr. Cummins, "Without apology
or preface, I presume so far to trespass on your Grace as to
state to you, and by the use of your illustrious name, to present
to the British public the following statement of what I have
myself seen within the last three days. Having for many years
been intimately connected with the western portion of the
County of Cork, and possessing some small property there,
I thought it right personally to investigate the truth of several
lamentable accounts which had reached me, of the appalling
state of misery to which that part of the country was reduced.
I accordingly went on the 15th instant to Skibbereen, and to
give the instance of one townland which I visited, as an
example of the state of the entire coast district, I shall state
simply what I there saw . . . Being aware that I should have
to witness scenes of frightful hunger, I provided myself with
as much bread as five men could carry, and on reaching the
spot I was surprised to find the wretched hamlet apparently
deserted. I entered some of the hovels to ascertain the cause,
and the scenes which presented themselves were such as no
tongue or pen can convey the slightest idea of. In the first,
six famished and ghastly skeletons, to all appearances dead,
were huddled in a corner on some filthy straw, their sole
covering what seemed a ragged horsecloth, their wretched legs
hanging about, naked above the knees. I approached with
horror, and found by a low moaning they were alive—they
were in fever, four children, a woman and what had once
been a man. It is impossible to go through the detail. Suffice
it to say, that in a few minutes I was surrounded by at least
200 such phantoms, such frightful spectres as no words can
describe, either from famine or from fever. Their demoniac
yells are still ringing in my ears, and their horrible images
are fixed upon my brain. My heart sickens at the recital, but
I must go on.

"In another case, decency would forbid what follows, but it must be told. My clothes were nearly torn off in my endeavour to escape from the throng of pestilence around, when my neckcloth was seized from behind by a grip which compelled me to turn, I found myself grasped by a woman with an infant just born in her arms and the remains of a filthy sack across her loins—the sole covering of herself and baby. The same morning the police opened a house on the adjoining lands, which was observed shut for many days, and two frozen corpses were found, lying upon the mud floor, half devoured by rats.

"A mother, herself in a fever, was seen the same day to drag out the corpse of her child, a girl about twelve, perfectly naked, and leave it half covered with stones. In another house, within 500 yards of the cavalry station at Skibbereen, the dispensary doctor found seven wretches lying unable to move, under the same cloak. One had been dead many hours, but the others were unable to move either themselves or the corpse."

These facts were confirmed by Government witnesses. Mr. Richard Inglis, a Commissariat officer, was ordered to Skibbereen on about December 17, and horrified by what he saw he sent a statement to Mr. Hewetson, the senior Commissariat officer at Limerick, who forwarded a certified copy to Trevelyan on December 21. As Mr. Inglis arrived in Skibbereen he saw three dead bodies lying in the street, and he buried them with the help of the constabulary. Deaths were occurring daily; 197 persons had died in the workhouse since November 5, and nearly 100 bodies had been found dead in the lanes or in derelict cabins, half-eaten by rats. Mr. Inglis brought with him £85, which he had collected privately, and started two soup kitchens. Major Parker, Relief Inspector of the Board of Works, estimated that about 200 people had died in Skibbereen during the last few weeks. "A woman with a dead child in her arms was begging in the street yesterday," he wrote on December 21, "and the Guard of the Mail told me he saw a man and three dead children lying by the roadside . . . nothing can exceed the deplorable state of this place."

Routh blamed the landlords. The proprietors of the Skibbereen district, he told Trevelyan, "draw an annual income of £50,000." There were twelve landowners, of whom the largest was Lord Carbery, who, Routh declared, drew £15,000 in rent; next was Sir William Wrixon-Becher, on whose estate the

town of Skibbereen stood; Sir William, alleged Routh, drew
£10,000, while the Reverend Stephen Townsend, a Protestant
clergyman, drew £8,000. "Ought such destitution to prevail
with such resources?" Routh inquired, but suggested no action,
and, officially, the appeals for Skibbereen were answered by
a Treasury minute, written on behalf of the Lords of the
Treasury by Trevelyan on January 8, 1847. "It is their Lord-
ships' desire," ran the minute, "that effectual relief should
be given to the inhabitants of the district in the neighbourhood
of Skibbereen . . . the local Relief Committees should be
stimulated to the utmost possible exertion; soup kitchens
should be established under the management of these Committees at such distances as will render them accessible to all
the destitute inhabitants and . . . liberal donations should be
made by Government in aid of funds raised by local subscriptions."

These counsels of perfection closed the discussion. Trevelyan wrote privately to Routh suggesting that Mr. Bishop, the
senior Commissariat officer in west Cork, should address
letters to landlords in the Skibbereen district pointing out the
urgent distress existing on their estates, and urging them to
contribute to relief; but no emergency supplies of food were
sent to Skibbereen.

Chapter IX

ONE OF the reasons why the British Government did not
feel bound to send food to Skibbereen was that ample
food was to be found there already. "On Saturday, notwithstanding all this distress," wrote Major Parker, the Board of
Works' Relief Inspector, on December 21, "there was a
market plentifully supplied with meat, bread, fish, in short
everything." This extraordinary contradiction occurred all
over Ireland during the famine years, and was not understood
by the British Government. Trevelyan insisted that the "resources" of the country should be "drawn out," failing to
realize that those resources were so utterly inaccessible to
the unfortunate wretches dying in the streets and by the

roadsides that they might as well never have existed. The
starving in such places as Skibbereen perished not because
there was no food but because they had no money with
which to buy it.

The British Government had started Irish relief with a
millstone round its neck—the 2,385,000 persons who, as the
Poor Inquiry Commission reported, starved, more or less,
every year in Ireland, whether the potato failed or not. This
hopeless, wretched, multitude, already starving, already diseased, unemployed beggars, dispossessed squatters, evicted
persons, penniless widows, starving children, snatched at every
offer or relief, swamped every scheme, and formed a hard
core of destitution whose numbers could be reduced only by
death. In every town and village, large or small, there were
noisome alleys and filthy mud-choked lanes where such people
took refuge, sheltering in derelict rat-infested cabins and, if
they died, lying undiscovered for days. In the county of Cork
alone the state of Skibbereen was reported to be paralleled in
Skull, Bantry, Bandon, Baltimore, Crookhaven and Castle-
haven; and however rapidly numbers employed on the public
works increased, a mass of destitution remained untouched,
starving and miserably dying.

Yet the total of labourers employed on the public works
was rising alarmingly. Trevelyan had feared that numbers
might total 500,000 in January, but on January 16, the total
was already 570,000. The daily expenditure was now almost
£30,000, the weekly cost more than £172,000, the staff of
the Board of Works amounted to 11,587 persons. And the results of this expenditure were not merely useless, they were
disastrous. The roads of Ireland were ruined—the Board of
Works was described as "wholesale destroyers of Her Majesty's
highways." Distances which were formerly driven in about an
hour and a half, for instance the fifteen miles between Roscommon and Athlone, now took four hours, and accidents
were frequent: Lord Farnham had been upset in the Enniskillen mailcoach, Lord Sligo in the Ballina mail, and the
Dublin mail had upset close to Limerick. "Roads were laid out
which led from nowhere to nowhere; canals were dug into
which no drop of water has ever flowed; piers were constructed which the Atlantic storms at once began to wash
away."

Under severe pressure the local organization of the Board
of Works began to fall apart. At the end of December

Captain Wynne reported from west Clare, "I greatly fear our staff will not hold together much longer, they appear to me to be only waiting a decent excuse to be off. Mr. Webb is *gone*, his successor, Mr. McBride, going (having received threatening notices this week), Mr. Pratt has resigned. Mr. Gamble (the engineer in charge) thinks Mr. Millet's life is in danger and is going to remove him." Money to pay wages ran out because the numbers employed were infinitely larger than had been expected, and labourers were left with employment tickets and no work.

In County Clare, for instance, at Moyarta and Kilbally, £8,000 was granted in September, but because by January 12, 13,555 persons were employed the money was spent. In some places, Shanagolden, for instance, the money allowed was exhausted before all applicants for employment had been examined; in others, the large numbers employed resulted in works being so quickly completed that the labourers were left without work to do.

Before new works were started or fresh funds provided another Presentment Session had to be held, and applications again submitted, scrutinized and approved. During this interval labourers had to wait unemployed; at Clonakilty six men were reported to have died of starvation before they could be taken on again; and Colonel Jones told Trevelyan on January 6, 1847, that several other deaths had been reported from the same cause.

Meanwhile, in spite of all efforts, the numbers employed on the works still increased; in February, a total of more than 700,000 was reached, and Trevelyan began to feel dubious of the possibility of continuing. "The tide of Irish distress has been for some time steadily rising," he told Colonel Jones, "and appears now to have completely overflowed the barriers we opposed to it."

At the same time as the public works were being overwhelmed the relief committees were sliding into insolvency. The Government's rule that relief committees should sell at the current market price, plus five per cent. for selling and storage costs, was intended to keep the sum each committee had raised "undiminished"; it was to be used "constantly through the period of distress in purchasing successive supplies of food," and at that point it seemed that the Treasury did not despair of making famine in Ireland a going concern. Conscientious relief committees, however, had expected their activities to be largely charitable; they would sell food cheaply to the starving or, in urgent cases, give it away; and by December 7, 1846, the Relief Commission office in Dublin was receiving more than twenty-five letters daily, asking permission to sell food under cost. Permission was invariably refused, and committees breaking the rule were not given a Government grant to add to their funds. A large number of relief committees, "feeling imperatively called on to provide assistance for the people," sold at a loss, making good the deficit out of their funds, and being refused a Government donation rapidly became insolvent.

However, Mr. Marcus Goodbody, the miller, told the Board of Works' Inspector that, in his experience, purchases made by relief committees and sold at reduced prices had no injurious effect on either wholesale merchants or retail dealers, and as far as he and his firm were concerned he felt it an "imperative necessity" to issue to the destitute "on any terms." He went on to give a warning that the demand for food was going to be much larger than the probable supplies, and Government had better "pay close attention to this fact."

Throughout December, 1846, prices rocketed, and speculators made fortunes out of Indian corn. Mr. Hewetson, at Cork, wrote on December 30 that "£40,000 and £80,000 were spoken of as having been made by merchants" in Cork, and he wished Government would do "something to check the extortionate prices," but supposed they were "according to the spirit of trade and therefore legitimate."

By the end of December funds in the hands of relief committees had, generally, been used up. "Almost all the Committees have spent their money," reported a Commissariat officer on December 20. "Wherever I go I find their money gone, the price of food having risen beyond their most liberal expectations." From Ennis, Captain Wynne wrote, "The Relief Committees have not a shilling, they cannot pay even for stationery and postage. The Poor House is full, and police are stationed at the door to keep the numerous applicants out. What is to be done?"

∽

The moment at last arrived when official permission was given to open the depots in the west. On December 28, 1846, Trevelyan wrote to Routh, "The depots in the western district are to be henceforth opened for the sale of food as far as may be prudent and necessary." Also, the amount raised locally by subscriptions would be doubled by the Lord-Lieutenant. The rule of selling at market price plus five per cent. was, however, to be observed. On January 9 Routh begged that prices at the depots should be reduced. "The people cannot purchase at our prices to the extent they require," he told Trevelyan, who replied, angrily, "If we make prices lower, I repeat, for the *hundredth time* that the whole country will come on us." On January 21 he administered a snub to Colonel Jones: "It is useless to say to us again and again 'Command these stones that they be made bread' "; and on January 22 told Routh, "However serious and painful it may be, it is indispensable that the prices at our depots should keep pace with the Cork prices . . . else mercantile supplies will cease to be sent to at least one half of Ireland."

It now began to be evident that although the depots were opened the people in the west were dying of hunger. "You would be horrified," wrote Police Sub-Inspector Hunt from Swineford, County Mayo, on January 7, 1847, "to see the multitude of starving men, women and children, who daily swarm the town soliciting with prayers just one meal of food." There was not enough of the coarsest food in his district to last one month. From Sligo, on January 17, Mr. Dobree wrote that the pauper population was "fast extending," artisans and small shopkeepers were being reduced to beggary and must die of starvation, since no cheap food was available, meal was "touching £23 a ton," and otherwise there was only seaweed—"the distress and destitution seems almost beyond the reach of human relief."

The celebrated author, Miss Maria Edgeworth, in reply to an application form sent out by the Society of Friends, gave a picture of the district round Edgeworthstown, County Longford, her father's property. The population, she wrote, was about 5,000, and 3,000 were in need of relief; even in the "ordinary way" employment was scarce, and only about 100 found work at 8*d*. to 10*d*. a day. Now 400 persons were on the public works, but at the present price of food wages were not sufficient to support a family. There were no factories or indoor employment, no cultivation was being done, no stock of seed existed, and there was no expectation that any considerable quantity of potatoes would be planted in the coming season. More than 500 persons were incapable of work, and Longford workhouse, seven miles away, was full. There was a great deal of sickness and some fever. In a private letter to Dr. Harvey, a member of the Society of Friends, Miss Edgeworth wrote, "Our poor must come to starvation in the course of the next four months, if they are not assisted."

There was, however, a new and powerful organization which was beginning to bring help to Ireland. On January 1, 1847, at a meeting held at Messrs. Rothschild's offices in St. Swithin's Lane, in the City of London, "The British Association for the relief of the extreme distress in the remote parishes of Ireland and Scotland," known as "The British Association," was formed. It was described as "Rothschild, Kinnaird and some dozen other merchant princes meeting every day and working hard." Baron Lionel de Rothschild and Mr. Abel Smith were founder-members, and Mr. Thomas Baring was the first chairman. Mr. Pim, of Dublin, who was secretary to the Central Relief Committee of the Society of Friends, and Mr. J. J. Cummins, of the well-known Cork family, attended meetings and advised. The aim of the Association was to relieve the "very numerous class of the sufferers . . . who are beyond the reach of the Government"; assistance was to be "afforded by the distribution of Food, Clothing and Fuel; but in no case shall money be given to the parties relieved."

When Trevelyan was first approached at the end of December, 1846, he did not believe the scheme would succeed. "Feeling in London is so strong against the Irish," he wrote, "that I doubt if much progress will be made in subscription until further horrifying accounts are received." However, he sent Stephen Spring Rice, who was largely responsible for founding the British Association, twenty-five pounds, and in fact, over £470,000 was collected, one-sixth being devoted to distress caused by the failure of the potato in Scotland.

The records of the Association disprove a legend, widely believed in Ireland, to the discredit of Queen Victoria. It is said in Ireland to this day that when the Queen was asked to subscribe to the relief of her starving Irish subjects she gave a mere five pounds. Her subscription, in fact, was £2,000; this figure appears not only in the official report of the British Association but in the original subscription list, preserved in the National Library, Dublin, and written in Stephen Spring Rice's own hand. On the list are the words, also in his hand, "taken from a notebook in which I kept the promises as they were made." The first name is "H.M. The Queen, £2,000," followed by "Rothschild's, £1,000," "Duke of Devonshire, £1,000," "Charles Wood, £200."

The British Association did not set up its own organization but worked through the relief committees, which numbered "upwards of 1,000," and the Commissariat. "Assist the committee by taking charge of their stores and holding them at the disposal of the committee and their officers," Trevelyan instructed his officials, and the British Government also undertook to pay all expenses, freight, insurance, and shipping charges on Association supplies. The main store in Dublin was under the "entire care and management" of Routh, and local stores were in charge of Commissariat officers. Application forms for Association supplies were distributed in destitute districts by Commissariat officers, and were scrutinized and authorized by them. For instance, on January 22, 1847, the minute book of the Association records a grant of £25 in provisions for Arranmore, County Donegal, "authorized" by Routh.

On January 1 the British Association Committee made an important appointment: Count Strzelecki, a member of a noble Polish family who had become anglicized and distinguished himself as an explorer in Australia, was engaged as agent for the counties of Donegal, Mayo and Sligo, the committee judging that Count Strzelecki would be more welcome to the Irish than an Englishman. He left immediately for Westport, and wrote on his arrival, "No pen can describe the distress by which I am surrounded . . . You may now believe anything which you hear and read, because what I actually see surpasses what I ever read of past and present calamities."

Even Trevelyan no longer attempted to minimize the seriousness of reports from Ireland. "This is a real famine, in which thousands and thousands of people are likely to die," he told Henry Kingscote, one of the "Clapham Sect" and a member of the British Association Committee. But Trevelyan was still determined to be cautious in giving help: "if the Irish once find out there are any circumstances in which they can get free government grants . . . we shall have a system of mendicancy such as the world never saw," he wrote.

❧

The Government now decided on a radical change of policy. The attempt to feed starving Ireland through the agency of the relief committees, with meal at market prices, was to be given up; there was to be a "new scheme for feeding the people," and they were to be given soup. Soup kitchens were a favourite philanthropic activity of the period in England, and now in Ireland soup kitchens were already being run successfully by, among others, Father Mathew in Cork, Mr. Inglis in Skibbereen, and the Society of Friends in the west, while many of the Irish resident gentry were making soup privately and distributing it from their own kitchens. Soup would also save money; as Routh wrote to Trevelyan, soup "will have the double effect of feeding the people at a lower price and economizing our meal."

During the first week of January, 1847, Commissariat officials visited relief committees, urging them to raise a new subscription to establish soup kitchens; the response was good and by January 9, 930 committees were in communication with Routh. The Government was prepared to give substantial financial help, and Routh was allowed to double and, in urgent cases, treble the new subscriptions. On January 20 relief committees were notified that free issues of food were now permitted, always provided the workhouse was full, to "infirm, poor widows, orphans and children . . . The food best suited for free relief is soup. Soup should also be sold, wherever possible, to economize meal."

The British Government, however, had come to a further decision far more important than setting up soup kitchens—the scheme of relief by employment was to be abandoned. The public works had failed. The expenditure had been enormous, the work hopelessly inefficient, the right persons had not been employed, there had been violence, corruption, scandals. Now the works were to stop and Irish relief administered on an entirely different principle.

Lord John Russell presented the new scheme to the House of Commons on January 25. It was divided into two parts, and the first, concerned with soup kitchens, passed into law as the Temporary Relief Destitute Persons (Ireland) Act, popularly called the Soup Kitchen Act. For the third time since the first failure of the potato new relief committees were to be nominated by the Lord-Lieutenant, and they were charged with the duty of establishing soup kitchens from which soup would be distributed without any work being required in return. With a startling reversal of previous policy, Lord John announced that the object of the free distribution

of soup was "so that labouring men should be allowed to
work on their own plots of ground, or for the farmers, and
thus tend to produce food for the next harvest and procure
perhaps some small wages to enable them to support their
families." Meanwhile, as the distribution of soup became general, the public works were gradually to be closed. "There
will be no rude dismissal of the people at once," Lord John
told the House of Commons, ". . . but when arrangements
have been made for carrying the scheme I have described
into effect, it will be provided that no further presentment
should be made and no Public Works undertaken." A sum
of £50,000, to be repaid before December 31, 1847, was to be
lent to landlords, enabling them to buy seed for distribution
to their tenants, and an important concession was made with
regard to payment for the public works, on which an enormous debt had accumulated. The public works had been
financed by advances from the Treasury, repayable by instalments over a period of ten years; Lord John now announced
that when the first half of the debt was paid off the second half
would be remitted.

He again gave an assurance that the Government would
not import food from other countries: "we think it far better,"
he said, "to leave the supplying of the people to private
enterprise and to the ordinary trade."

Such, briefly, were the proposals advanced in the first part
of the new scheme, but they were of minor importance
compared with the proposal advanced in the second. Distressed persons were to be classed as paupers, placed under
the Irish Poor Law and, when strictly necessary, be given
outdoor relief paid for out of the local rates. To carry out
this proposal a drastic change was to be made in the existing
law. It was a fundamental principle of the Irish Poor Law
that outdoor relief was not given—destitution in Ireland
was so great that allowing relief to persons not inmates of a
workhouse would spell ruin. This rule had been very strictly
enforced. In December, 1846, at Cashel, where the workhouse was in a state of "frightful overcrowding," 550 destitute,
everyone of whom was eligible for admission into the workhouse had it not been full, were given a daily meal inside the
building; and other places did the same when the workhouse
was full. Local authorities pleaded that because the food was
eaten within the workhouse the relief was within the spirit
of the Poor Law Act; but the Poor Law authorities ordered

the meals to stop at once. A month later, however, this principle was abandoned; in his speech Lord John Russell announced that the Government had become convinced that in Ireland "the poor law ought to be more extensive than it is," and that a Bill permitting outdoor relief was being prepared. Lord John did not, however, propose to introduce the Bill until later in the session, as much consideration was required. But the first part of the new relief scheme, the Soup Kitchen Act, was to be put into operation immediately.

Once again a Relief Commission was set up in Dublin, this time with Major-General Sir John Burgoyne as chairman. Sir John Burgoyne was a soldier of distinction and an experienced man of affairs. He had served as commanding Royal Engineer, under Wellington, had sat on innumerable Royal Commissions, "from one on the penny post to one on the proposed site of Waterloo Bridge," and had been chairman of the Irish Board of Works for fourteen years—from 1831-45. At the moment he was Inspector-General of Fortifications in Great Britain, but he was given three months' leave of absence at the personal request of Lord John Russell. Sir Randolph Routh also sat on the new Commission, but he was no longer chairman. In a long and flattering letter to Routh, dated February 2, Trevelyan wrote that while Sir John Burgoyne was expecting to be advised by Routh "on everything," Routh's "official footing" would be to take charge of relief correspondence and letters to relief committees, "under the Commission of which you will be a member"; his importance was, in fact, diminished. Routh was not always easy to work with. Mr. Labouchere, the Chief Secretary, wrote that "he provokes one a little now and then," and by an "oversight" this letter was sent on to Routh, who was much offended, though Trevelyan endeavoured to pass off the comment as "playfulness." Routh had not Trevelyan's devotion to work; he had wanted, for instance, to take leave at Christmas, 1846, and Trevelyan told him he could not go away "at this critical stage"; he wished to attend drawing-rooms and levees at Dublin Castle, where the Lord-Lieutenant, as the Sovereign's deputy, kept semi-regal state; and for this Trevelyan rebuked him, pointing out the "impropriety of appearing in Public when the lives of such multitudes of persons depend on your unremitting exertions."

The Soup Kitchen Act was preliminary to the transfer of the distressed to the Poor Law, and it was to be carried out mainly through the Irish Poor Law organization. Though subscriptions were to be collected wherever possible, and increased by Government donations, the money spent on the soup kitchens was to come out of the rates. "The expense," wrote Trevelyan, "was to be defrayed by payments made by the Guardians out of the produce of the rates."

The Government was anxious to hasten the establishment of soup kitchens. About six weeks, it was estimated, would be needed to draft the new outdoor relief Bill and get it passed through Parliament, and in that time it was intended that soup kitchens should be generally established and public works closed down. Once the people were living on distributions of soup, the transfer to relief, under the Poor Law, would be simple. The Treasury was therefore prepared to make immediate advances of money against the security of rates to be collected in the future. An agreed sum, sufficient to start a soup kitchen, would be lent, but the Poor Law Guardians were required, simultaneously, to cover the sum advanced by "striking" a rate, that is, agreeing on the amount of rate in the pound to be levied, and issuing an order for collection. In each Poor Law Union finance committees, nominated by the Lord-Lieutenant, were to control expenditure, while inspecting officers, chosen for their ability from the Commissariat and the Board of Works, were to certify all payments and form the "medium of communication" with Sir John Burgoyne in Dublin. Yet these arrangements, however admirable on paper, ignored the fact that while both the Soup Kitchen Act and the far more drastic outdoor relief Bill which was to follow depended on the collection of rates, to collect rates in Ireland was not merely difficult—in a large number of districts it was practically impossible.

Before the failure of the potato, in March, 1844, seven hundred troops, besides police, had been required to collect poor rate in Galway; in Mayo, the warship, *Stromboli*, and two revenue cruisers, *Dee* and *Comet*, stood by in Clew Bay, and in addition the Mayo rate collectors had the assistance of two companies of the 69th Regiment, a troop of the 10th Hussars, fifty police, two police inspectors and two stipendiary magistrates. When a question on these proceedings was asked in the House of Commons the Government admitted that "one or two warships" were used for their "moral effect" in the collection of poor rate in Ireland.

However, these combined operations of Navy and Army brought in only a quarter of the rate, and Dean Kirwan, the Catholic Dean of Mayo, calculated that each shilling had cost a pound or more to collect.

Yet the British Government now assumed that, when Ireland was famine-stricken and disorganized, a poor rate could be collected which would almost certainly be ten to fifty times larger than ever before. Further, the workhouses themselves were not in a condition to become centres for relief; in the parts of Ireland which were now most distressed the workhouses, from the day they opened, had been insolvent, dirty and disorganized, and at this moment when the transfer of the destitute to the Poor Law was proposed, several were on the point of closing their doors.

The history of the workhouse at Westport, County Mayo, was typical. Under the Irish Poor Law Act of 1838 Ireland had been divided into 130 Poor Law Unions and the building of workhouses was to be financed by advances from the Treasury.

The Westport Board of Guardians under the Chairmanship of the Marquess of Sligo held its first meeting in August, 1840, and borrowed £9,800. Two years later, the building was completed and in November, 1842, the Poor Law Commissioners declared it to be "fit for the reception of the destitute poor."

But the cost of the workhouse and its running expenses were to be paid for out of the poor rate, and this it was impossible to collect. Westport Union was primitive and poverty stricken; no funds came in and the workhouse remained shut.

For the next two years the Guardians struggled to collect the rate; troops and police were freely used, additional magistrates appointed, extra pay and an escort for protection given to collectors. Even so next to nothing came in and the workhouse did not open.

In October, 1844, nearly two years since it had been declared fit for occupation, the workhouse was still shut and it had accumulated debts which would absorb the whole of the outstanding rate and a fresh rate as well, supposing these could be collected. The Board of Guardians resigned.

A new Board of Guardians was elected and proved no more

successful, almost nothing came in and, for "remote and wild" districts, such as Kilgeever and Clare Island, no one bold enough even to attempt collection could be found. The matter was now taken out of the Guardians' hands. In June, 1845, a writ of mandamus compelled Westport workhouse to be opened and unwillingly on November 5, six months after the issuing of the writ and three years after the completion of the building, Westport workhouse opened. Tuam and Castlerea amongst others had also to be compelled to open by a writ of mandamus, they too were in debt and could collect no rate.

On August 5, 1846, the week in which the potato failed completely, £800 was owed by Westport, in addition to instalments due for repayment on the erection loan totalling over £1,000, and no rate at all had been collected. By December 5, when the famine was raging, only a little over £62 had been collected, 600 destitute paupers were in the workhouse but it had no funds to feed them and one of the Guardians, Mr. George Hildebrand, then advanced £60 out of his own pocket to save the unfortunate inmates from starvation.

The Westport Guardians wrote a desperate appeal to the Lord-Lieutenant on January 13, 1847: how could they relieve "the starving population of this impoverished district without the means of purchasing even the food necessary for one day's consumption? . . .were it not for the generous, humane and charitable conduct of George Hildebrand Esquire, one of the Guardians, we should have closed this house and expelled the paupers."

By the 20th, Mr. Hildebrand's £60 was spent and the 600 wretched paupers were about to be turned out into the bitter winter when Lord Sligo came forward and, "rather than that the unhappy occupants should be expelled," offered to support the house at his own expense for three weeks.

This was the state of Westport only a week before Lord John Russell announced to the House of Commons that the Government intended to turn the Irish distressed over to the Irish Poor Law. Westport was not an isolated case; at Ballina in January, 1847, more than £2,000 was owed to provision merchants—the Treasurer had not a penny in hand to buy food for the coming week, and collecting the rate was "totally impossible." At Castlebar, at this time, more than £3,000 was owed, and the Guardians declared themselves without funds. Scariff, in Clare, was about to shut, and at Clifden in Galway the workhouse had actually been closed and the destitute expelled.

On this tottering structure the British Government planned to place an enormous load, resolutely refusing to admit that the immense rates required could not be collected. Unions, begging for a loan, were told by Sir George Grey, the Home Secretary, that "the non-payment of the Poor rate must be dealt with in the same way as that of any other rate or tax, and the alleged impossibility of collecting it does not appear to afford any ground for making a loan to the Union."

The new scheme was warmly welcomed by Trevelyan; he had performed almost superhuman exertions in the administration of the previous scheme, and it had been an ungrateful task. The Government would now be relieved from "feeding the people through its officers," and the responsibility of finding a supply of food for use in the soup kitchens would be placed on the relief committees; "They must buy it wherever they can. . . ."

He felt he had done his best and could do no more. "We deeply sympathise with you and other officers," he wrote to the Relief Inspector, Colonel Douglas, on February 1, 1847, "who daily have to witness scenes of heart-rending misery without being able to give effectual relief but, as justly observed by you, *we must do all we can and leave the rest to God.*" The thought that famine was the will of God was a consolation to him, and he hoped that the Catholic priests were making this clear. "It is hard upon the poor people that they should be deprived of knowing that they are suffering from an affliction of God's providence," he wrote.

The introduction of soup was greeted at first with enthusiasm. "Of all the remedies to avert the horors of starvation, none has equalled the establishment of soup kitchens," wrote a Commissariat officer at the end of January; and Colonel Jones told Lord John Russell that "the small amount of nourishment has a very great effect on the famished individuals whose stamina are thus partially revived," adding that soup kitchens "have the advantage of bringing to our aid the active assistance and benevolence of the other sex."

Good soup, if accompanied by a piece of bread or a meal-cake, was of value, and private persons, often of moderate means, kept hundreds of people alive by distributing it.

Much of the soup, however, was not so much soup for the poor as poor soup. At Vicarstown, Queen's County, the estate of the Right Hon. James Grattan, son of the great Henry Grattan, 30 gallons, or 120 quarts, of soup were made for well under 1*d*. a quart on January 18. The ingredients were one oxhead, without the tongue, 28 lb. turnips, 3½ lb. onion, 7 lb. carrots, 21 lb. pea-meal, 14 lb. Indian corn-meal, and the rest water. The local schoolmaster described the mixture as a "vile compound," and the people, after one trial, refused to accept it, declaring it gave them "bowel complaints."

Equally economical was the soup made by Mrs. Neale, wife of Sir Richard Bourke's bailiff, at Castleconnel, County Limerick. On January 23 she used 30 lb. beef, 8 lb. barley, 8 lb. steeped peas, 2 stone turnips, 5*d*. worth of "leeks and other vegetables," and 190 quarts of water.

Alexis Soyer, the famous French chef of the Reform Club, had created a sensation in London by composing recipes for soup costing three farthings a quart, and distributing it, daily, to two or three hundred of the London poor. His recipes were alarmingly economical. Recipe No. 1, which, Soyer asserted, "has been tasted by numerous noblemen, members of Parliament and several ladies. . .who have considered it very good and nourishing," used ¼ lb. of leg of beef, costing 1*d*., to 2 gallons of water, the other ingredients being 2 oz. of dripping: ½*d*.; 2 onions and other vegetables: 2*d*.; ½ lb. of flour, seconds: ¼*d*.; ½ lb. pearl barley: 1½*d*.; 3 oz. salt and ½ oz. brown sugar; total cost: 1*s* 4*d*. Recipe No. 2 was even cheaper—100 gallons could be made for under £1, including an allowance for fuel.

"Medico," however, writing to the Press from the Athenaeum, described Soyer's recipes as "preposterous." "The debilitating effects of a liquid diet are so well known to the medical officers of our hospitals, prisons and other public establishments that it is unnecessary to dwell on the subject." Any person "in the slightest degree acquainted with the elements of organic chemistry" could see, at a glance, that the soup was "utterly deficient in the due supply of those materials from which the human frame can elaborate bones, tendon, blood, muscle, nervous substance, etc."

This was confirmed in Ireland; Mr. Bishop, Commissariat

officer in west Cork, complained in a letter that soup "runs through them without affording any nourishment," while a doctor in the starving town of Skibbereen had told him it was "actually injurious" to the very large number of people who were suffering from dysentery.

Soup, wrote Mr. Dobree, from Sligo, was "no working food for people accustomed to 14 lb. of potatoes daily"; and the appearance of the people soon betrayed the disastrous effects of a soup diet. Nevertheless, Soyer's claim that a meal of his soup once a day, together with a biscuit, was sufficient to sustain the strength of a strong and healthy man, was too tempting for the British Government to ignore. After all, Soyer enjoyed immense prestige; he was perhaps the most famous chef in Europe, and at the request of the Lord-Lieutenant he was invited to come to Dublin, install boilers, and superintend his scheme for the mass distribution of soup. "Soyer is on his way," wrote Routh to Trevelyan on February 22.

Soyer's new model soup kitchen was constructed in front of the Royal Barracks in Dublin and opened on April 5. It was a wooden building, about 40 feet long and 30 feet wide, with a door at each end; in the centre was a 300-gallon soup boiler, and a hundred bowls, to which spoons were attached by chains, were let into long tables. The people assembled outside the building, and were first admitted to a narrow passage, a hundred at a time; a bell rang, they were let in, drank their soup, received a portion of bread, and left by the other door. The bowls were rinsed, the bell rang again, and another hundred were admitted. Sir John Burgoyne disapproved—it was a mistake, he wrote, to feed the destitute like wild animals.

But the people of Dublin were starving, and they crowded to the kitchen; 5,000 rations had been considered the probable maximum, but 8,750 were supplied daily. Soyer's model kitchen was finally bought by Government and handed over to the Relief Committee of the South Dublin Union.

Food had now risen so high in price that reports from Commissariat officers in February described "women and children returning home sobbing with grief at the insufficient food they have been able to procure with the wages of their husband and father"; the officers, wrote Trevelyan, told him they could "bear anything but the ceaseless misery of the children."

The demand for soup became impossible to satisfy. In west Cork, for instance, towards the end of January, 17,000 pints of soup were being distributed daily under the Soup Kitchen Act, and about 14,000 daily by the Cork Auxiliary Committee of the Society of Friends. But, wrote Mr. Bishop, of the Commissariat, not a tenth of the destitute population could be supplied—it was "a mere drop in the ocean." Crowds waited, hour after hour, at the distributing centres, sometimes all night, and savage struggles took place when distribution began. Colonel Douglas, the Relief Inspector, reporting on the Clonmel soup kitchen, broke off to write *"I have witnessed such scenes. . . ."*

February was the worst month of the terrible winter. Board of Works' inspectors reported heavier falls of snow and fiercer gales; roads became impassable, carts could not travel, horses sank in drifts and had to be dug out, the streets of towns and villages became "full of starving paupers." Not only in Connaught and Munster but in Ulster destitution increased daily. "Mobs of men and women imploring employment assail you on the road," wrote Captain Glascock, an inspector from Armagh. Families without food or fuel took to their beds, and "very many perished unknown." "People sink," wrote Mr. Bishop; "they have no stamina left, they say 'It is the will of God' and die."

The period during which the public works were to begin closing down started in February, but the severity of the weather sent fresh masses of destitute surging on the works, and applications for employment rapidly increased. In Galway, on February 6, applications "exceeded by many hundreds any previous demand." In Meath, one of the more prosperous midland counties, lists were increasing "by 100 names a day." In Leitrim, 600 new names were brought forward in 24 hours.

On February 4, in the House of Commons, Lord George Bentinck, an extreme Tory, proposed a Bill to spend sixteen million pounds on building railways in Ireland. There were at the moment, said Lord George, "500,000 able-bodied persons in Ireland living upon the funds of the state . . . commanded by a staff of 11,587 persons, employed upon works which have been variously described as 'works worse than idleness' . . . as 'public follies' and as 'works which will answer no other purpose than that of obstructing the public conveyances'." Yet, as he pointed out, there were in Ireland only 123 miles of railway and 164 miles only under construction. He proposed that the destitute should be employed on a scheme which would be financed by Government loans up to £16,000,000, advanced at 3½ per cent., the loan to be repaid with interest in 37 years, and the railways taken as security.

Trevelyan had already considered railway construction as a means of relief, and on October 6, 1846, in a long letter to Mr. Labouchere, he had pointed out the objections. The only item of railway construction requiring unskilled manual labour was earthworks, and that expenditure was only one-third of the whole. The most distressed of the population would not be reached, because railway lines were not constructed through impoverished districts, and far from giving employment to the helpless and destitute "the object of railway companies is to select the ablest labourers who will give the best return for their wages." Finally, railways were not permitted, under their Acts, to borrow until half the amount of their shares was paid up; as Irish railways were in a bad financial state, only two railways in Ireland would be eligible.

Lord George Bentinck's Bill was defeated. But, later, Parliament voted a sum of £620,000 for loans to Irish railways which were able to establish that half their capital was paid up and were also able to spend a sum from their own resources equal to the loan. Only one line qualified, the South Western, running between Dublin and Cork, and railway construction therefore played a negligible part in relief during the famine.

☙

When about two weeks of the six allowed for the establishment of soup kitchens had passed, the Treasury sent a minute to the Board of Works, reminding them that the public works should be closed "as soon as the means of subsistence have been provided for the destitute in each neighbourhood"; to establish sufficient soup kitchens to feed the armies of the destitute had, however, proved impossible. By February 20, for instance, in Killarney there was only one soup kitchen for 10,000 persons, and Tarbert had two "small establishments" for 18,000. The workhouses were full; on January 23 there were already 108,487 persons in institutions built to take 100,480, and those who had no money, no employment and no soup kitchen within reach, were doomed to starve.

In Leitrim there was a "fearful measure of distress," wrote Captain Layard, the Board of Works' Inspector. "Two cart loads of orphans, whose parents had died of starvation, were turned away from the workhouse yesterday." Something must be done; and he dashed off a list of suggestions. Why not a soup shop at every police barracks throughout the country? Why not the immediate establishment of a provision depot at Mohill? Why not put small stores of meal in schoolhouses, to be guarded by police or military? *"Something must be done,"* he repeated, urgently underlining his words, *"and that without delay."*

Horrors were reported; at a farm in Caheragh, County Cork, a woman and her two children were found dead and half-eaten by dogs; in a neighbouring cottage five more corpses, which had been dead several days, were lying; and Father John O'Sullivan, parish priest of Kenmare, found "a room full of dead people"; a man, still living, was lying in bed with a dead wife and two dead children, while a starving cat was eating another dead infant.

Commander Caffyn, of H. M. Steam Sloop *Scourge*, "a man of undoubted honour and veracity," wrote a letter on February 15 which Trevelyan described as "awful." He had been discharging a cargo of meal for the Society of Friends at Skull, where a population of 18,000 inhabited a parish 21 miles in extent; and three-quarters of that population were skeletons, with swelling of the limbs and diarrhoea universal. In one cabin four adults and three children were crouched, silent, over a fire, while in another room a man and woman lay in bed, mere skeletons, the woman shrieking for food, the man past speech. The son of these people had been on the public works, and earned 8*d.* a day, which was not enough to keep the family from starvation, and he himself was now ill from hunger. These had been prosperous people.

In a second cabin a mother and daughter, reduced to skins stretched over bones, lay in bed. "Both must be dead by this time."

The third cabin contained an old woman and her daughter, whose husband had deserted her, with three little children. The grandmother had already died and was lying in the room, but her daughter was too exhausted to move her body.

The fourth cabin also contained a corpse which had been lying there for four days—no one could be found with sufficient strength to take it away.

Commander Caffyn saw a mass of bodies buried without coffins, "simply a few inches below the soil; when warm weather comes and they decompose there must be a pestilence." Bodies half-eaten by rats were an ordinary sight; "two dogs were shot while tearing a body to pieces." "Never in my life," wrote Commander Caffyn, "have I seen such wholesale misery."

Numbers of landlords and middlemen now cleared subdivided estates of their swarming population. High rents had made sub-division tolerable, but this year rents had not been paid, and without the potato they would never be paid again. Wheat was to be substituted for the potato, and the minute holdings resulting from sub-division were a hopeless obstacle to wheat culture. "It is evident," wrote Mr. Todhunter, a member of the Central Relief Committee of the Society of Friends on January 23, "that some landlords, forgetful of the claims of humanity and regardless of the Public Welfare, are availing themselves of the present calamity to effect a wholesale clearance of their estates."

All the same, the Government was determined to bring the public works to an end, and on February 22 the Board of Works sent out a circular to all inspecting officers instructing them to strike every possible name from the lists, as "the Public Works are drawing to a close."

Inspecting officers, however, were powerless; the vast crowds of wretched, starving and, in the Government's own phrase, "half-dying" wretches were beyond control. A hundred names might be struck off in a week, wrote Captain Kennedy, Inspector for Meath, but 150 new names come on every day. In Galway "lists after lists" were pouring into the Board of Works' Inspector's office, "containing hundreds of names representing people stated to be literally starving." Meanwhile, the relief committees had "almost ceased to act." In some places a committee of hopelessly unsuitable persons had been sanctioned; in Glenties, County Donegal, the chairman was a "tinker," as the gipsies of the Irish countryside were called, and two of the Guardians had got tickets for the public works; in others, committees refused to take the risk of discharging starving, desperate men. In Carlow the Inspecting Officer had to give the order to turn off 140 men himself, and in public, because the relief committee "could not be got to do it."

On March 2, 1847, Trevelyan wrote Colonel Jones a stern

official letter. The public works were now costing £40,000 a day, in addition to what was being spent on Commissariat operations and Sir John Burgoyne's new Relief Commission to operate the Soup Kitchen Act, and Colonel Jones had better confer with Sir John Burgoyne and see what could be done. At the same time Trevelyan wrote Colonel Jones a private letter in threatening terms: "The exceptional rate at which Relief expenditure is proceeding and the lack of any effectual steps to bring it under control have attracted the attention of the Chancellor of the Exchequer and other members of the government . . . It is impossible for me to describe in too strong terms the degree in which the public credit and safety are considered to be involved with you." Forty-eight hours later, in another private letter, Trevelyan wrote, "I entreat of you to give your earnest attention to my recent official and other letters." The rate at which expenditure was proceeding was "fearful." "If we continue we shall add national bankruptcy to famine."

Colonel Jones was aggrieved; Trevelyan had no conception of the difficulties he was contending with: "Nearly all the Relief Committees have abandoned the duties they were supposed to perform, turning loose on our officers every man, woman and child who applied for relief. If the officer refuse them employment then he is told that their deaths will be laid at his door, and the deaths are rapidly increasing. . . ; we see no chance of abating the evil until the new Acts are brought fully into play."

Prospects for the Soup Kitchen Act coming into full play were not encouraging. On March 10 Routh told Trevelyan that only one hundred committees would be actually operating soup kitchens by March 26, and as late as April 10 it had to be admitted that the new system was still "getting on very slow indeed," largely because there was a marked disinclination on the part of the ratepayers to add a fresh burden to the rates.

Meanwhile, an extraordinary situation was developing. From the end of the first week in February supplies of food began to arrive in Ireland. "Considerable importations of Indian corn, Indian meal and other supplies are now fast coming up the Shannon with every westerly wind," wrote Mr. Hewetson, from Limerick. Arrivals at Cork, wrote Mr. Nicholas Cummins to Trevelyan, on February 24, were "very large, heavy importations of maize continue almost daily to arrive

. . ." On February 26 there were 250 sail in Cork harbour, bringing 50,000 tons of foodstuffs.

Private enterprise was functioning at last, and the "ample supplies" promised by Government were actually arriving; but they were useless to the people. Destitution and disorganization had gone too far; Ireland was ruined, and high prices and lack of money placed the long-expected food out of reach of the starving.

In a letter to Trevelyan, dated February 24, Mr. Nicholas Cummins wrote that these "splendid efforts" were in vain—prices were too high for the people to pay, and stocks of food were actually accumulating; while Colonel Jones reported that, in spite of the new supplies, not a piece of seaweed existed west of Skibbereen; it had all been picked for food.

At this juncture the Government gave a trial to the scheme of growing yams, sweet potatoes, in Ireland. A barrel of seed was sent from the West Indies and Dr. Lindley was instructed to supply "cultural directions." Enclosing them, he wrote, on February 26, that he could not feel "optimistic" about the prospect of the yam succeeding in Ireland, since it was a native of the tropics and would not grow either in France or Spain. Nevertheless, packets of seed, with directions, were distributed all over Ireland, with what result is not recorded.

Meanwhile, at the end of the first week in March the total number employed on the public works stood at 734,000, while the daily expenditure had risen to more than £43,000. The Treasury now took decisive action; after stating, in a minute of March 10, that "all instructions to reduce the works . . .are quite ineffectual," it issued "positive instructions on the direct responsibility of Her Majesty's government" to begin closing down the works at once. By Saturday, March 20, the number of persons employed was to be reduced by not less than twenty per cent.—"the remainder will be further diminished by successive reductions, in the proportions and at the times to be hereafter fixed by the Board of Works until the new system of operation under 10 Vic. C.7 [the Soup Kitchen Act], shall be brought into operation." Persons holding ten acres of land and over were to be discharged on March 20, even if they exceeded the requisite twenty per cent. Otherwise those discharged were to be the persons on each work who held the largest amount of land or any other property. If soup could be supplied to the destitute in the district, either under the Soup Kitchen Act or from any other source, the works were to be completely closed down at once.

This ultimatum produced terror. Hundreds of desperate appeals poured in, addressed to the Lord-Lieutenant, to the Board of Works, to the Relief Commissioners, to Lord John Russell, begging for no dismissals until the soup kitchens were in operation, or suggesting that a grant should be made to bridge the gap until soup kitchens were general or that temporary works should be started, and imploring, over and over again, that dismissals should not start so soon, when the people were utterly destitute and before the new system was functioning.

The Government, nevertheless, went steadily forward and the works began to close down in earnest.

After the date of the Treasury minute, March 10, permission to hold Presentment Sessions, at which proposals for new works were considered and sent on to the Board of Works, was refused; then on March 13 a circular from the Board of Works directed that all the infirm were to be discharged from the works—only the able-bodied were to remain. At this, from Ballinakill, as from many other places, the relief committee wrote that deaths, already between 100 and 150 a week, would be "wholesale," and the committee implored that the order should at least be temporarily countermanded. Able-bodied men, the relief committee declared, had ceased to exist; and it was true that reports of Board of Works' engineers described labourers as "too feeble to perform tasks, however willing," "falling down dead from exhaustion," "numbers fainting on every work," "feeble, cannot do road making and cutting," "too weak to work." From Cork the Engineer reported, "We have not an able-bodied man on the works"; and in King's County, even if the men had been given seed, they were too weak to prepare the ground. All appeals received the same answer. "The Relief Commissioners can do nothing in this matter."

Sir Lucius O'Brien, of Dromoland Castle, County Clare, later 13th Baron Inchiquin, had already written a number of letters urgently asking the Lord-Lieutenant not to close down the works in Clare, and on the eve of the reduction, March 19, he wrote again. If the reduction of twenty per cent. did take place, he asserted, there would be 1,200 men starving in Ennis and Newmarket on Fergus. He begged for another

Presentment Session and for the works to be continued; but if the reduction was carried through, then a grant must be given, to bridge the gap until the new Act was in operation. He was given an evasive answer, upon which he lost his temper—"I am going out to meet hungry and excited mobs . . . What am I to say to them? Is the population to be left to starve? Are you going to abandon us?"

The only satisfaction Sir Lucius received was an official note: "H.E. the Lord Lieutenant can only renew the expression of his anxiety that the Relief Act, 10 Vic. C.7," the Soup Kitchen Act, "should be brought into operation without delay in the County of Clare."

Pinned to letters, often dirty and ill-written, to desperate and illiterate appeals, to official minutes and reasoned arguments, official endorsements survive. "Government arrangements must stand"; "New Relief and Finance Committees must hurry"; "Government having determined that employment on the Public Works shall cease as soon as possible, all depends on the exertions of the Committees"; "H. E. does not anticipate that any great delay will take place in bringing the Act 10 Vic. C.7, into operation if Committees proceed with the discharge of their duties."

For those who were to be turned off the works there was, as one of the discharged wrote, "nothing to do but bar the door, lie down and die." On March 20, despite everything, the reduction did take place.

And now, as if starvation were not enough, a new terror assailed the Irish people. The Government had been warned, in the autumn of 1846, that after famine "there will follow, as a natural consequence, as in former years, typhus fever or some other malignant pestilence," and fever, on a gigantic scale, was now beginning to ravage Ireland.

Chapter X

THE IRISH people spoke of "famine fever," but in fact two separate diseases were present, typhus and relapsing fever, both conveyed by the common louse and both already familiar in Ireland. Typhus is caused by microscopic organisms resembling infinitesimally minute rods entering the blood. These organisms are now called Rickettsia, after the American scientist Ricketts, who however did not discover them until April, 1910. Ricketts was not then ready to claim that he had discovered the organism causing typhus, and, while doing further experimental work, in Mexico City, caught typhus himself, and died in May, 1910, at the age of thirty-nine. The transmission of typhus by lice was proved by Charles Nicolle, director of the Pasteur Institute in Tunis, who received the Nobel Prize in 1928 and died in 1936. Thus more than sixty years passed after the black year of 1847 before the nature of the epidemic which struck Ireland began to be understood.*

The louse conveys typhus by becoming infected itself and then transmitting Rickettsia to the human beings it preys upon. The food of the louse is human blood, and in feeding on a person suffering from typhus the louse swallows Rickettsia and contracts typhus. The disease is often as fatal to the louse as to the human being. Professor Hans Zinsser, a friend of Charles Nicolle, thus describes the fate of a typhus-stricken louse: "In eight days he sickens, in ten days he is in extremis, on the eleventh or twelfth day his tiny body turns red with blood extravasated [forced out] from his bowel and he gives up his little ghost." Until this final stage is reached Rickettsia multiply in the intestine of the louse and are passed out with its excrement, which under a microscope is seen to swarm with organisms. Rickettsia make their way into the human blood-stream through the skin; the bite of the louse is intensely irritating, the victim scratches, the skin is broken, Rickettsia enter and infection takes place. If the infected louse is damaged or crushed by a slap from its victim, Rickettsia are released from the damaged intestine and enter through the slightest scratch or injury on the skin. So infectious is the excrement of the typhus-stricken louse that its mere deposit on the skin permits invasion, without a bite, through any minute abrasion; and even when the excrement has dried to a fine dust Rickettsia remain active and can enter through the eyes, and even be inhaled. Thus, benevolent per-

* In writing this chapter I have been most generously assisted by Lieut-Gen. Sir William MacArthur, K.C.B., D.S.O., who is the leading authority on the subject, an Irishman and a fluent speaker of the Irish language.

sons who gave aid to the victims of the great Irish epidemic of 1847, clergy, nuns, doctors, resident landlords and Government officials, contracted typhus and died, though they themselves may never have harboured a louse.

Typhus is a horrifying disease and was regarded by the Irish people with terror. Rickettsia attack the small blood-vessels of the body, especially those of the skin and brain, and the patient becomes all but unrecognizable; the circulation of his blood is impeded, his face swells, and he turns the dark congested hue which has given typhus its Irish name of "black fever." The patient's temperature rises, in a severe case his limbs twitch violently; he raves in delirium, throws himself about; as the fever becomes intense and his body burns he is apt to jump out of the window, or plunge into a river in search of coolness; the rash appears from which typhus derived its former name of "spotted fever." Meanwhile, the patient is in acute pain—he vomits, develops agonizing sores and sometimes gangrene, followed by the loss of fingers, toes and feet. A loathsome symptom is the odour from the typhus patient, described by William Bennett, of the Society of Friends, as "an almost intolerable stench"; when occupants of a cabin were in fever, he wrote, "the smell was sufficiently perceptible from without." Dr. Crumpe, medical officer of Tralee Gaol, where typhus was rampant, records that when the door was opened he was "always seized with most violent retching," and was "forcibly driven back by the smell."

Relapsing fever, the second disease generally included at this period under the term "fever," is transmitted, like typhus, by a louse which has swallowed blood containing the micro-organisms of the disease. These, which are completely different from the Rickettsia of typhus, were discovered in 1873, many years before Ricketts's discovery, by a German scientist, Otto Obermeier, who died of cholera in the same year. They belong to the group called "Spirochaetes," and are some forty times longer than Rickettsia, resembling not minute rods but threads. They multiply in the body and limbs of the louse, not its intestine, and are released if the louse is even slightly damaged, but do not pass out in the excrement. Like Rickettsia, the organisms of relapsing fever enter the human blood-stream through the skin, and once infection has taken place the progress of the disease is rapid; within a few hours high fever and vomiting begin, continuing for several days. A crisis, with profuse sweating, follows, succeeded by extreme exhaustion. At this point, examination under a microscope of a drop of the patient's blood shows the number of Spirochaetes present to be sharply reduced. One crisis, however, does not indicate the end of the attack; six to seven days later there is a relapse, microscopic examination shows Spirochaetes to be swarming in the blood once more, high fever and vomiting are again followed by a crisis, and should the patient survive the pattern may be repeated three or four times before the attack finally comes to an end.

Relapsing fever is often accompanied by jaundice; observers in 1847 noted the yellow colour of the people's skins, "all gaunt, yellow, hideous," wrote Mr. Maguire, M.P., of a crowd of destitute in Cork, and the name for the disease, in the Irish language is the "yellow fever."

What proportion of "fever" cases were typhus and what relapsing fever is difficult to determine. Dr. Robert Graves, editor of the *Dublin Quarterly Journal of Medical Science*, sent a questionnaire on the famine epidemics to every doctor in Ireland, and in 1849 published selections from their replies. In most of these the symptoms and course of relapsing fever are faithfully described, but there is a tendency to consider both relapsing fever and typhus as variations of "fever." In Roscrea, for instance, "the disease was characterized by frequent relapses"; in Limerick the difference between "fever" in this and previous epidemics was "the tendency to relapse"; and in Cork, a particularly black spot, relapses were considered "a peculiar feature of the epidemic, taking place in at least one-sixth of the cases."

Infestation with lice does not necessarily mean an epidemic of typhus and relapsing fever. Sir William MacArthur, the eminent medical historian, writes, "In the early part of the First World War in France . . . the speed with which louse infestation ran through the occupants of crowded dug-outs and billets came as a revelation to all who witnessed it. Fortunately, there was no existing focus of infection to spark off an epidemic." In nineteenth-century Ireland, however, cases of typhus and relapsing fever ordinarily occurred. The towns and villages were devoid of sanitation, streets were not cleansed, disgusting nuisances were permitted, drainage was unknown. Dublin, "dear dirty Dublin," for all its beauty was renowned for filth; and the pestilent lanes of such small towns as Skibbereen were common throughout Ireland. In rural areas conditions were hardly better. Mud cabins were inhabited under conditions which made cleanliness hardly possible, and dwellings customarily had trickling manure heaps immediately before the entry. The swarming population of pre-famine Ireland produced universal overcrowding—"families were more numerous than houses"—and the poorer classes were, very frequently, infested with lice. The Report of the Select Committee on the state of the Poor in Ireland of 1830 states that 60,000 persons passed annually through the fever hospitals of Dublin, and medical officers and doctors accepted typhus as an ordinary feature of Irish life. For instance, Dr. Lynch, of Loughrea, County Galway, writes, before the epidemic of 1847, that there was "nothing remarkable in the sanitary condition of this district. During the preceding five years maculated typhus . . . was more or less prevalent, and varied remarkably in severity in different years." Dr. Lalor, of Kilkenny, refers familiarly to "our old endemic fourteen-day maculated typhus"; and a report from County Down refers to "the ordinary average of fever cases."

Thus that "focus of infection" which, fortunately for the British Army, was missing from the dug-outs and billets of World War I was dramatically present in Ireland, and never had conditions been so fatally favourable to the rapid spread of lice as in the famine winter of 1846-47. The people were filthy. They had sold every stitch that would fetch the fraction of a penny, and they were wearing the same rags, day after day and night and day. Their bedding had been sold, and they slept covered with rags and old coats; to heat water to wash themselves or their clothes was out of the question; they were eating their food half, or wholly, raw, because they had no money to buy fuel; indeed, after months of starvation, even the strength to fetch water had disappeared.

The abnormal severity of the winter drove the people to huddle together for warmth; a fire or even a light in a cabin attracted neighbours and passers-by; the traditional hospitality of the Irish poor provided a welcome, and all lay down to sleep in the warmth, side by side, on the cabin floor.

Hosts of beggars and homeless paupers tramped the roads, drifting from place to place without a fixed destination, filthy, starving and louse-infested, often with fever actually on them. "Whole families were to be seen lying in fever by the roadside"; the contemporary name for the epidemic was road fever. Yet the poor Irish, however distressed themselves, never refused admission to the poorest and most abject mendicant. The Irishman, wrote the Central Board of Health, "thinks himself accursed if he refuses admission to a begging stranger."

Once infection had been brought into a district it spread with lightning rapidity among the crowds brought together for relief. On the public works, in close proximity, were thousands of destitute, unwashed persons; some had left members of their family in fever at home; some came with the fever on them, hardly able to stand. Closely packed together, they waited for hours for their wages, and waited again, sometimes all night, at the soup kitchens. A brush in passing was enough to transfer the fever-transmitting louse or its dustlike excrement to a new victim, and one fever-stricken person could pass on infection to a hundred others in the course of a day. A crowd of destitute was something to be shunned, and early in 1847 George Hancock, a member of the Society of Friends, and supercargo of the relief steamer, *Albert,* was warned, at Rutland, County Donegal, that he was endangering himself by standing in a crowd of "about 200 wretched looking objects" who were waiting for a distribution of food. The people were in such a state that the odour from a crowd of starving destitute was intolerable; and a well-known and humane doctor, Dr. Phelan, found himself unable to support the smell of a crowd at Clifden, Galway, "although in the exercise of his profession he was accustomed to exhalations."

The courage of those who came to the help of the people during the epidemic is beyond praise. Among doctors in 1847, and the losses can be equalled among clergy, especially Catholic priests, the deaths were formidably high. Seven doctors died in Cavan in twelve months; in Connemara, where for thirty miles small villages and isolated cabins along the coast were nearly depopulated, two out of three doctors died; four died between Clifden and Galway, three between Oranmore and Athenry, and four between Anadown and Kilmaine. The French Government sent two physicians to study the epidemic, and a Dublin professor of medicine conducted them round; two died, one of them the professor. In the province of Munster as a whole forty-eight medical men died, "the great majority of fever." Dr. Traill died, the Protestant Rector of Skull who had interceded with Trevelyan for the Skibbereen district and been one of the first private persons to establish a soup kitchen.

The main epidemic in 1847 was of typhus and relapsing fever, but at the same time other diseases afflicted starving Ireland. On January 18, 1847, W. E. Forster wrote that "the most usual form of the famine plague," in Westport, was dysentery, which was "sweeping off the people by ten and twenty a day."

Two types of dysentery occurred in Ireland during the famine, and the two were confused. Some degree of dysentery, producing diarrhoea, must have been universal among people who had been existing for months on a diet of old cabbage leaves, raw turnips, seaweed and Indian meal, half cooked or raw. But though painful and exhausting it was not usually fatal, except to children; its danger lay in the fact that it paved the way for infection with the terrible disease, bacillary dysentery; and bacillary dysentery became epidemic in Ireland.

Bacillary dysentery is the "bloody flux" which devastated armies in the past; it accompanies famine; it ravages the besieged city, attacks the army operating in a country laid waste or in occupation of conquered, famine-stricken territory. The disease is caused solely by a group of bacilli conveyed in excrement from infected human beings, in contaminated food and in the excrement of flies. The bacilli are swallowed with infected food or inhaled from excrement, and multiply in the stomach and bowels. Inflammation, ulcers and, finally, gangrene follow, with intense pain, diarrhoea, violent straining and the passing of clots of blood, resulting, in a high percentage of cases, in death. During the famine it was frequently recorded that cases of dysentery, "in a very severe form," and "exceedingly fatal," that is, bacillary dysentery, had become epidemic. In the fever hospital at Ennis a severe dysentery was common, within a few hours twelve to twenty intestinal evacuations "consisting of a serous bloody fluid." In Skull, agonizing dysentery was "attended . . . with a great amount of suffering" and "excessive abdominal pains," and the matter passed was "pure blood and mucus. . ." "It was easily known if any of the inmates in the cabins of the poor were suffering from this disease, as the ground in such places was marked with clots of blood."

Another appalling condition, not infectious, was called "famine dropsy." William Bennett, of the Society of Friends, described it, in March, 1847, as "that horrid disease—the

results of long continued famine and low living—in which the
limbs and then the body swell most frightfully and finally
burst." He noted that children in Belmullet, Erris, who had
previously been emaciated, now exhibited "frightful swelling,"
though most of them were too weak to stand. "Famine dropsy"
has no connection with the condition normally termed dropsy;
it is produced by starvation in its last stages, and is medically
known as hunger oedema. So little was the condition understood in 1847 that it was diagnosed as a symptom of fever;
and Dr. Taylor, of the Kenmare workhouse, cites diarrhoea,
dysentery and anascara, dropsical affection of the limbs, as
symptoms of "fever," and "highly contagious."

Hunger oedema was distressingly prevalent in starving
Ireland. Commander Caffyn, in his report on Skull, written
on February 15, 1847, wrote that though three-quarters of
the population were "skeletons" nevertheless "swelling of
limbs" was universal; in Killala the people "swell up and are
carried off at once"; and Elihu Burritt, a self-taught American
scholar and philanthropist, visiting Skibbereen, in February,
1847, saw men whose bodies were swollen to twice their
natural size at work on the public works. He was shown
a boy of twelve whose body had swollen to three times its
normal size and actually burst the garment he wore; and the
body of a baby of two was swollen to the size of an adult,
though the arms, he noted, were "like pipe stems."

Scurvy, in an advanced stage, was also general. Scurvy is a
non-infectious condition, produced by a diet lacking in Vitamin
C, the vitamin mainly supplied by fresh vegetables and fruit.
Scurvy had, hitherto, been unknown in Ireland because the
enormous quantities of potatoes eaten, normally 14 lb. daily,
supplied the necessary quantities of Vitamin C even for an
able-bodied man; but when the potato was lost and Indian
corn (maize), which contains no Vitamin C, became the staple
food, scurvy became general. The progress of scurvy is painful and revolting; gums become spongy, teeth fall out, joints
are enlarged and cause acute sufferings. Blood-vessels burst
under the skin, especially on the legs, producing dark, disfiguring blotches; in its advanced stages the legs turn black
up to the middle of the thigh—the colloquial name for scurvy,
in the Irish language, is "black leg."

By the spring of 1847 starvation had so reduced the people
that they seemed "too attenuated to live." At Templecrone,
Donegal, the population was "walking skeletons," at Skull,

"when dead bodies were found lying on their backs the stomach falls in and the articulations of the spine can be counted." Sidney Godolphin Osborne, later one of Florence Nightingale's helpers in the Crimea, wrote that, in distressed persons, "attenuation seems to have absorbed all appearance of flesh or muscle." The bones of the frame were covered with something which was skin but had a peculiar appearance, rough and dry like parchment, and hung in folds; eyes had sunk back into the head, the shoulder-bones were so high that the neck seemed to have sunk into the chest; face and neck were so wasted as to look like a skull; hair was thin, and there was an extraordinary pallor such as he had never seen before. The worst sufferers were the children; starving children were skeletons, many too far gone to be able to walk. The skin over the chest-bones and upper part of the stomach was stretched so tight that every curve of the breast-bone and ribs stood out in relief. "No words," wrote Sidney Godolphin Osborne, "can describe the appearance of the arms, from below the elbow the two bones seem to be stripped of every atom of flesh. If you take hold of the loose skin within the elbow joint, and lift the arm by it, it comes away in a long, thin fold as if you had lifted one side of a long narrow bag in which some bones had been placed." Starvation had affected the children's bones; the jaw-bone was so fragile and thin that a very slight pressure would force the tongue into the roof of the mouth. In Skibbereen, Elihu Burritt met children with jaws so distended that they could not speak; in Mayo the starving children had lost their voices. Many were in the stupor characteristic of death by starvation. Sidney Godolphin Osborne visited workhouses, infirmaries and hospitals and never heard a single child utter a cry or moan of pain—"in the very act of death still not a tear nor a cry. I have scarcely ever seen one try to change his or her position . . . two, three or four in a bed, there they lie and die, if suffering still ever silent, unmoved . . ." James Hack Tuke noticed the children's "unmeaning vacant stare" and the extraordinary thinness and pallor of their skins, "like muslin." By April, 1847, children were looking like little old men and women of eighty years of age, wrinkled and bent—every trace of childish gaiety had disappeared and even the babies were "aged."

A curious phenomenon was the growth of hair on starving children's faces. The hair on the head fell out and hair grew on the face. Children in County Clare had hair on their heads only in patches, but over their foreheads and temples "a thick sort of downy hair grows." Elihu Burritt wrote that in Skibbereen the hair on the children's faces was as long as on their heads, and R. D. Webb, of the Society of Friends, commented that starving Irish children, presumably owing to hair on the face, "look like monkeys."

～

In 1847 it was universally believed that "fever" was caused by starvation. Since every famine in Ireland was followed by a fever epidemic, "with the regularity of clockwork," it was not unreasonable to deduce that "fever owed its origin to want of food."

A fever epidemic had been expected to follow the first failure of the potato in 1845, and in March of the following year Sir Robert Peel's Government passed an Act ". . . to make temporary provision for the Relief of destitute poor persons afflicted with fever in Ireland." Under the Act, which expired on August 31, 1846, a Central Board of Health was set up, with authority to require Boards of Guardians to provide hospitals and dispensaries, while the Lord-Lieutenant could appoint extra medical officers, to be paid by the Treasury. The Central Board of Health, however, did not consider a fever epidemic imminent in the summer of 1846, one reason being that, though applications for admission to fever hospitals had increased, they came mainly from women, whereas experience showed that when an epidemic was imminent the majority of applications came from men. The Board, moreover, had made themselves unpopular, there were "multitudinous complaints forwarded from every part of the country," and, it was said, the Board was responsible for a "useless expenditure of so much money." And so on August 31 the Act was allowed to expire, the Central Board of Health ceased to function, and the extra medical officers who had been engaged were dismissed.

When the second, and total, failure of the potato declared itself the Central Board of Health was not re-established. Indeed, on January 25, 1847, Mr. Labouchere, the Chief Secretary, assured the House of Commons that there was no need to call for additional powers—it was "better to depend on the ordinary law." In fact, the "ordinary law" concerned with fever in Ireland did not contain provisions which were in any way adequate to meet a fever epidemic. Under the Irish Poor Law, Boards of Guardians were instructed to provide for fever-stricken persons by building permanent or temporary fever wards, on sites separate from the workhouse itself, by hiring buildings for use as fever hospitals, or by arranging for fever cases to be received in county fever hospitals. Less than half the unions, however, only fifty in all, had made any such arrangements by the date of the first failure of the potato, in 1845, and if an epidemic did occur, fever patients would have to depend on the county fever hospitals. These had been founded before the introduction of the Irish Poor Law, in 1838, and were supported partly by subscriptions and partly by grants voted at Assizes. But the scheme had not been successful, because sufficient subscriptions were not forthcoming. "The county fever hospitals were small and poorly equipped," writes Sir William MacArthur, "and their funds inadequate for the expansion necessary to meet a sudden emergency." Over the whole of Ireland only twenty-eight hospitals had been established, and in the more remote and impoverished parts of the country, the district round French-park, Roscommon, for instance, with a population of 30,000 persons, inhabiting an area of more than 135 square miles, there was none. Dispensaries in Ireland now amounted to about 450, with about 42 more attached to fever hospitals, and these dispensaries did valuable work, but they were, as the Poor Law Commissioners themselves wrote, very unequally distributed. "In the county of Dublin, containing, exclusive of the city, about 176,000 inhabitants and about 375 square miles there are 24 dispensaries, about one to every 7,333 inhabitants. In the county of Meath, containing about 176,800 inhabitants, and about 886 square miles, there are 19 dispensaries, or one for every 9,305 inhabitants. In the county of Mayo containing 366,328 inhabitants and about 2,100 square miles, there is only one dispensary supported at the public expense." George Nicholls, the Poor Law authority, wrote, "Such . . . are the necessary consequences of a law which renders the establishment of a dispensary contingent upon voluntary contributions. In districts abounding in rich resident proprietors, a medical charity is least wanted, but subscriptions are there most easily obtained; whilst in districts where there are few, or possibly no, resident proprietors, the aid is most wanted but there are no subscribers, and consequently there is no medical charity."

With this amount of medical assistance and accommodation for fever patients, Ireland had now to face a fever epidemic of immense size.

The British Government, however, was unwilling to admit that any epidemic was likely to occur; and Mr. Labouchere declared in the House of Commons, on January 25, 1847, that though "some cases" of fever had accompanied hunger, yet at the moment Ireland was free from the fever which follows famine. "The accounts given to the contrary were, to a very great extent, undoubtedly inaccurate." Yet in reports from doctors in a wide range of districts, a fever epidemic was stated to have been already raging for several months. In Mitchelstown, County Cork, the epidemic began in November, 1846; in Waterford, in October, 1846; in Carrick-on-Shannon, in June, 1846; in Galway, as early as April; and, only two days after Mr. Labouchere had made his statement in the House of Commons, Captain Fishbourne, Inspecting Officer at Scariff, wrote urgently to Routh for help. Two hundred and fifty persons were ill with fever in the Scariff Union workhouse, and the institution was so much in debt that it was on the point of closing. It was impossible to turn loose 250 persons actually in fever, to spread infection throughout the country; something must be done. On the same day fever was reported, by Mr. Bishop, to be raging in west Cork, in and round Skibbereen, Skull and Ballydehob. The precise extent was difficult to assess because the people were so terrified of fever that they would not help those who were stricken and consequently did not know when they died. The members of the Ladies' Association at Ballydehob, with "great courage and self-sacrifice," were visiting even the worst cases in the district and distributing food and clothes.

Within a few days, alarming reports were coming in from all over the country. On February 6 fever was reported to be rapidly on the increase in Kerry and prevalent, "to a fearful extent," in Leitrim; on the 7th fever had "a firm hold" in Cork: the hordes of starving, wretched fugitives who were inundating the city had brought the infection with them; and throughout the rest of the month reports grew steadily worse—fever was "making havoc" in Kenmare, spreading rapidly in Bantry, increasing in Mayo. In King's County, once one of the more prosperous districts, the people were "dying fast . . . if something is not done the summer will be awful."

G

The Central Board of Health was now reappointed, and remained in existence until August, 1850, opening 373 temporary fever hospitals and engaging 473 additional doctors for fever duty.

By March, 1847, the existence of a fever epidemic was undeniable. In Skibbereen there was "scarcely a house that has not fever." The Sub-Inspector of Police was very ill with it, as well as the manager of the local branch of the Provincial Bank of Ireland, the wife of the Protestant clergyman, and one of the local doctors. On the morning of March 4 two persons died of fever in the street. Major Parker, the Inspecting Officer, caught fever and died, and his successor, after spending twenty-four hours in Skibbereen, resigned and fled. In Bantry and in Kilrush, large numbers were dying, and a rapid increase was reported from County Louth. On March 9 fever was raging in the west, at Westport, Foxford, Newport, in the town of Castlebar, and in every parish within thirteen miles of it, dead and dying were lying together and there was great want of medical aid. Eight out of sixteen patients in the Castlebar prison had typhus, and by April an epidemic raged, cases were "heaped together," and the Catholic chaplain, the deputy governor, the deputy matron and the turnkey died.

The want of hospital accommodation for fever patients was disastrous. The workhouses were overcrowded; and in the extremity of distress to which the people were now reduced, almost every person admitted was suffering from some complaint, diarrhoea, or extreme exhaustion, or the first stages of fever. The workhouse hospitals were far too small to deal with the numbers, or to separate the sick from the healthy; even medical examination of applicants, to detect infection, became impossible, and "the whole workhouse was changed into one large hospital without the appliances necessary for rendering it efficient as such," through which fever spread with terrible rapidity. The Central Board of Health laid down that temporary wooden fever wards, "fever sheds," were to be erected, and that each patient was to have a separate bed and fresh bedding, with a clean night-shirt weekly or more frequently if soiled. But for unions in the distressed districts the expenditure required was out of the question. Ballina accepted a tender for erecting "fever sheds" on March 3, but could do nothing further; the Union was all but bankrupt and the guardians were considering closing the workhouse. Between March 13 and March 22 fever cases jumped from 140 to 430, and these cases had all to remain in Ballina workhouse.

In March, 1847, the Central Board of Health sent doctors to inspect and report on the state of the workhouses of Cork, Bantry and Lurgan. Their report was horrifying. In Cork the state of those admitted was "utterly wretched and deplorable . . . many in a dying state, or a state surely leading to death," and a death was taking place every hour. The workhouse was overcrowded, ventilation was lacking, drainage and drains were deficient, and the stench almost insupportable, even in cold weather. At Bandon, visited on the way to Bantry, "all appeared in a state of confusion, no order, completely chaotic state." One hundred and two boys had slept the previous night in a ward 45 by 30 feet in 24 beds, in some cases six to a bed; and in the hall 700 persons slept and ate every day. One hundred and twenty persons were occupying 45 beds in the convalescent ward, and all had been in fever. The drains were "revolting" and a "disgusting stench lasts all day."

Conditions in Bantry workhouse were better; the wards were clean and orderly, but Bantry had a fever hospital and, in the words of the inspecting doctor, Dr. Stephens, "Language would fail to give an adequate idea of its state, it was appalling, awful, heart sickening." He "did not think it possible to exist in a civilized and Christian community." Fever patients were lying naked on straw, the living and the dead together. The doctor was ill and no one had been near the hospital for two days. There was no medicine, no drink, no fire; wretched beings were crying out "Water, water!" but there was no one to give it to them; the sole attendant was one pauper nurse, "utterly unfit."

In Lurgan, the inspecting doctor, Dr. Smith, reported equally horrible conditions, with the addition that the dead were buried not four yards away from the fever hospital, and that in the centre of the burial ground was the well, from which the fever hospital drew its water. The Master had died, the Matron was ill; two of the doctors were down with typhus; everything had fallen into confusion, and the Board of Guardians did not seem to know anything, except that the workhouse was overcrowded.

The Government now ceased to assert that no fever epidemic was taking place in Ireland, and a new Irish Fever

Bill, to operate until August, 1850, was introduced; it became law on April 27, 1847. The epidemic had then been raging for three months. "The object . . . in view," declared Mr. Labouchere, in contradiction to his former statements, "was paramount to every consideration of money, namely to prevent the spread of disease and pestilence in Ireland, which, under the circumstances, he thought there was but too much reason to apprehend." The new Act placed the responsibility of providing for fever patients in the hands of the relief committees; they had authority to go over the heads of Boards of Guardians and erect temporary fever hospitals, hire and equip houses for fever patients, and attend to the proper burial of the dead; and the cost of these operations was to be met, not by the Poor rate, but out of the general relief fund. "It had been found by experience," Mr. Labouchere told the House of Commons, "that it was necessary to have a more summary mode of proceeding than was applicable with the machinery of the Poor Law."

The new Fever Act was slow in coming into operation; in the very large impoverished unions resident gentry were few or nonexistent and relief committees weak or indifferent. Often, members of relief committees were also guardians and, not understanding that expenditure on fever patients would not fall on the rates, hesitated to incur further debts. Ballina, for example, never erected wooden fever wards; lean-to sheds, built against the walls of the workhouse, remained the only accommodation, and on July 5, 1847, fever patients in the lean-to sheds were lying on the ground, without beds. In Cavan, when the guardians were ordered to provide a fever hospital, they refused to spend the money; and, on June 10, people in fever were reported to be lying at night in the streets of Kanturk, County Cork, because no accommodation for them had yet been provided. On the report Trevelyan has scribbled "Why?"

In Sligo, on August 1, outside the hospital, "three wretched creatures were groaning on mats on the other side of the road because they could not be taken in," and Mr. Gildea, the Protestant rector of Newport, County Mayo, protested, on August 6, that "very many cases are in the open fields without shelter or covering, some by the wayside."

One solution was to use tents. Given an adequate supply of cots and weather not too cold or windy, tents have advantages for fever patients; the air is purer and fewer patients are in proximity to each other. Towards the end of May the Lord-Lieutenant asked for tents, and on May 31, 35 tents and 96 marquees, the "hospital marquees," used by the British Army, were dispatched by the Board of Ordnance. A large number of urgent applications followed from all over Ireland, amongst others from Cork, Dublin, Queen's County and Tyrone; Roscommon was especially pressing because no fever hospital of any kind existed, and it was impossible to wait while one was erected; and further requests for tents were received from the Lord-Lieutenant on June 17 and June 21. Tents appear to have been satisfactory—most had boarded floors—and were approved by Irish doctors.

The new Irish Fever Act was, on the whole, a success. It led to piles of filth, such as lay in the streets of Skibbereen and Tullamore, being removed, cabins cleansed, corpses decently interred, and the provision of additional hospitals and dispensaries, with accommodation for 23,000 patients, and staffed with doctors, nurses and scrubbers. The expenditure, £119,055, was eventually made a free gift to the unions by the British Government.

In workhouses and fever hospitals the epidemic seems to have reached its height in April when, during a single week, April 3-10, 2,613 inmates of workhouses were officially reported to have died. In the Ballinrobe workhouse, for example, fever was so universal that Mr. Kirwan, a member of the Finance Committee, refused to attend there; at Castlerea, County Roscommon, both the Master and Matron died, the doctor resigned, and out of 990 inmates 830 had fever; in Cork workhouse 757 persons died during March; the Government was approached to draw a *cordon sanitaire* round the city, and a protective guard was formed by the medical officers of health.

The situation in Dublin was still critical in May, and Sir John Burgoyne told Trevelyan on May 17 that at the principal fever hospital, "every corner, including the cellars and a number of tents, were filled . . . all insufficient, and a number of applicants sent away to spread disaster through the city." The epidemic in Dublin reached its height in June, 1847, and did not slacken until the following February. Figures of deaths returned by union and workhouse officials were almost certainly on the low side, especially in those unions which were financially and administratively in confusion. For instance, in the minute book of the Westport

Board of Guardians, on July 3, 1847, the number of sick
recorded is 106, yet there was an angry dispute over the
erection of a "fever shed," on August 18; and on August 23,
the Catholic chaplain consecrated a quarry, near the workhouse, for use as a mass grave.

The moment when the epidemic broke out in any locality
depended when infection was brought there, usually by one
of the unfortunate homeless who tramped the roads. Ballinrobe, for instance, escaped infection until the end of February, but then a "strolling mendicant" was admitted to the
workhouse, and died of fever a few days later. The Warrenpoint-Rostrevor area, in County Down, appears to be the
only district recorded as having escaped fever entirely, and
the local doctor wrote that very little fever was prevalent
there at any time. The explanation, in all probability, is that
the Warrenpoint-Rostrevor area lay off any main route to a
large town and was therefore not inundated by wandering
paupers who brought fever with them. Inishbofin and Inish-
ark, remote islands off the West coast, starved, but had no
fever until infection reached them as late as the summer of
1848.

About September, 1847, the epidemic began to subside.
An epidemic begins to subside when the number of people
who can be infected begins to decrease, either because they
have taken the infection, recovered and gained some immunity, or have died. In many districts, however, the epidemic
continued, even into the following year. From Ennis, Dr.
Cullinan reported fever as still continuing in November, 1848;
he had 400 patients in the County Clare fever hospital, and "I
fear the epidemic is far from exhausted"; and in Belfast, where
about 17,000 cases were treated, in hospital and at home,
the epidemic continued until October, 1848.

Deaths which took place in workhouses and hospitals were
only part of the total: "Many people died without having
applied for medical relief at all," wrote Dr. Turner, from
Tuam, County Galway. "Of those who did, many never applied a second time, or were totally lost sight of." In Dublin,
though 2,500 beds were provided, 1,000 more than in any
previous epidemic, as many as 12,000 cases of "fever" applied to the Cork Street Hospital in ten months. Two doctors,
Dr. Cusack and Dr. Stokes, who worked in the city through
the epidemic, wrote, "Still, it may safely be stated that all
this would give a very imperfect idea of the real amount;

for all who had to go amongst the poor at their own houses
were well aware that vast numbers remained there who could
not be accommodated in hospital or who never thought of
applying. It was quite common to find 3, 4 or even 5 ill in
a house when application had been made only for one."

The Irish poor hated and dreaded the workhouse and the
fever hospital, "because so many had died there," and they
were justified. In Ennis, deaths were far fewer among those
not in hospital, while in Tralee "Persons who would go to
hospital *contrary to all advice* were quickly attacked by
fever." Thousands preferred to die in their own houses, and
in the country districts the instinct of the Irish peasant to
shrink from the British Government official and conceal his
misfortunes kept an unknown number of cases secret. Many
deaths were unrecorded because the Irish horror of "fever"
even conquered the bond of family affection, which is the
strongest bond in Ireland: for in an extremity of fear, wrote
Mr. Bishop, Commissariat officer in west Cork, parents deserted their children, and children their parents; neighbours,
usually kindly and generous in Ireland, would not cross the
threshold of a cabin where fever was known to exist, and in
lonely districts fever-stricken persons died in their cabins,
without anyone coming near them, and their bodies were left
to rot. Often families buried the bodies of their relatives in
fields and on hill-sides; the people in west Cork told Mr.
Bishop, "Better times will come and then we will get church
rites for the bones." In Clifden, County Galway, corpses were
burned, in other districts they were buried under the cabin
floor; the family then fled and pulled down the roof over
the dead. In Leitrim, many died of fever and were buried in
ditches, unknown to anyone.

The total of those who died during the fever epidemic
and of famine diseases will never be known, but probably
about ten times more died of disease than of starvation.
Among the upper classes the percentage of those who caught
fever and died was high; in Cavan, upper-class mortality was
estimated at sixty-six per cent.; round Ballinrobe, seventy per
cent. who took the fever perished, and in Sligo, Roscommon,
Newry, Tuam, Leitrim, Tyrone, Lowtherstown, and almost
every district in Ireland mortality among the upper-classes
was reported to be proportionately much higher than among
the poor. The reason probably was that the constant occurrence of fever cases in their midst had brought the poor

Irish some degree of immunity. No legal register of deaths existed at the period, and though the Government asked repeatedly for estimates of the number of deaths they were told an estimate was impossible. "There are no records, even round figures," wrote Mr. Dobree to Trevelyan. "Thousands have disappeared." Major Halliday, Inspecting Officer for Leitrim, thought the population there had recently been reduced by about a quarter, but Commander Brown, R.N., after inspecting Kenmare in the company of both the Protestant and Catholic clergymen reported that the number of dead "cannot be ascertained." Too many had died, the clergymen told him, for a funeral service to be said over the bodies, and corpses had been burned at night, leaving no trace.

❧

But the horrors taking place in Ireland were only one aspect of the fever epidemic. As the terrible months of the autumn and winter of 1846-47 went by, and the total failure of the potato brought starvation, and to starvation was added pestilence, the minds of the Irish people turned in an unprecedented direction. Before the potato failure, to leave Ireland had been regarded as the most terrible of all fates, and transportation was the most dreaded of sentences. But now the people, terrified and desperate, began to flee a land which seemed accursed. In a great mass movement they made their way, by tens of thousands, out of Ireland, across the ocean, to America, or across the sea to Britain. Yet they did not leave fever behind; fever went with them, and the path to a new life became a path of horror.

Chapter XI

THE FAMINE emigration, the exodus from Ireland, in which hundreds of thousands of Irish, with fever on the one hand and starvation on the other, fled from their country because to remain was death, is historically the most important event of the famine.

It was the famine emigrants—leaving their country with hatred in their hearts for the British and the British Government—who built up communities across the ocean, above all in the United States, where the name of Britain was accursed and whose descendants continued to be Britain's powerful and bitter enemies, exacting vengeance for the sufferings their forbears endured. It is estimated that more than a million emigrants from Ireland crossed the Atlantic to North America during the years of the potato blight; and there was an even larger emigration across the Irish channel to Great Britain, to Liverpool, Glasgow, and the ports of South Wales.

Irish emigration elsewhere—to Australia, for example—was negligible. The passage was expensive, and no Irish community as yet existed in Australia, to encourage friends and relations to come out—moreover, anti-Irish prejudice among the Australian colonists was strong. When the Devon Commission took evidence on emigration it wrote, "As . . . America is the attractive destination to emigrants, we shall confine our calculations to it," and the only emigration, of even minor importance, to Australia during the famine years was of female orphans from Irish workhouses, paid for by the British Government.

Before the famine, emigration did not come easily to the Irish. "The warm attachment of the Irish peasant to the locality where he was born and brought up," said Lord Stanley, later Earl of Derby, in 1845, "will always make the best and most carefully conducted scheme of emigration a matter of painful sacrifice for the emigrant." Only during the famine did Irish emigrants leave their country willingly, without the weeping and wailing, the shrieks of anguish, the keening, as for the dead, which could be witnessed in the west of Ireland, at the departure of emigrants in the twentieth century.

The Irish famine emigration is unlike most other emigrations because it was of a less-civilized and less-skilled people into a more-civilized and more-skilled community. Other emigrations have been of the independent and the sturdy in search of wider horizons, and such emigrants usually brought with them knowledge and technical accomplishment which the inhabitants of the country in which they settled did not possess. The Irish, from their abysmal poverty, brought nothing, and this poverty had forced them to become habituated to standards of living which the populations amongst whom they came considered unfit for human beings. Cellar dwellings, whether in English towns or the cities of North America, were almost invariably occupied by the Irish. Poverty, ignorance and bewilderment brought them there, but it must not be forgotten that cellar dwellings resembled the dark, mud-floored cabins in which over half the population of Ireland had been accustomed to live under British rule.

Very few of the poor Irish who fled from Ireland in the famine emigration were destined to achieve prosperity and success themselves; the condition to which the people had been reduced not only by the famine but by the centuries which preceded it was too severe a handicap, and it was the fate of the Irish emigrants to be regarded with aversion and contempt. It was not until the second or third generation that Irish intelligence, quickness of apprehension and wit asserted themselves, and the children and grandchildren of the poor famine emigrants became successful and powerful in the countries of their adoption.

The transport of emigrants from Ireland across the Atlantic has a curious history. During the eighteenth century emigration from Ireland was on a small scale; it is doubtful if the numbers exceeded 5,000 in any one season. The emigrants came mainly from Ulster, they were Presbyterian small farmers of Scottish descent, and not paupers; they took some capital and experience with them and their motive was to better their lot. During this period emigration was not easy, all arrangements had to be made by the emigrant himself, who travelled to the port and bargained personally for his passage with the captain of the ship in which he wished to sail. This practice was abruptly changed as a result of the Napoleonic wars. Before 1807 almost all the imported timber used in Great Britain came from northern Europe. But in that year the Treaty of Tilsit was signed between Napoleon and the Emperor Alexander of Russia; as a consequence, timber from northern Europe was drastically reduced, and had to be imported instead from the British provinces in North America. The trade proved immensely profitable, and after Waterloo heavy duties were placed on European timber, to preserve the market for British North America. By the eighteen-forties, the trade, which had barely existed thirty years previously, had grown to an annual importation of over 925,321 loads of timber and planks, and the 100 ships or fewer which sailed for British North America in 1800 had increased, by 1845, to 2,000 ships, totalling over 1,000,-000 tons.

While the timber trade was rapidly developing, economic conditions in Ireland became disastrous. Agricultural prices, inflated during the Napoleonic wars, slumped after Waterloo, and Ireland became a country in which, with the exception of north-east Ulster, employment for wages virtually ceased to exist. The extraordinary increase in population continued and standards of life became almost unbearably low.

At this point, the peculiar conditions of the nineteenth century timber trade provided an opportunity for escape. Owners of timber ships had a major problem. To find cargoes for the voyage out to British North America was extremely difficult; its provinces were undeveloped and thinly populated, having only about a million inhabitants, compared with approaching twenty-three millions in the United States, and demand for European goods was almost nonexistent. Timber-ships were forced to go out to British North America in ballast, empty, and owners were glad to take such cargoes as coal, or salt for the Newfoundland fisheries.

The solution was to carry "passengers"; the business of conveying emigrants was known as the "passenger trade," and those ships which brought timber across the Atlantic began to go out loaded with emigrants. The traffic had the blessing of the British Government, which was eager to develop British North America, while the expense to the owners of fitting a ship to take emigrants was negligible. Wooden berths were put up between decks, and in the early days no provisions were supplied—the emigrants brought their own food, the owners provided merely fuel and water. Fares were so low that it was possible to get to Quebec for as little as two to three pounds. "Our ships would otherwise go out in ballast," said Mr. Francis Spaight, a well-known Limerick ship-owner, "and the result is whatever we get in the way of emigrants is so much gain to us."

By 1845 the conveyance of emigrants had developed to the point where larger profits were being made by the "passenger trade" than by the carriage of timber or European goods. The passenger trade was described as "one of the great supports of commerce," and had the desirable result of enabling

British North American timber to be sold at a low price.

As the trade developed, instead of the emigrant bargaining for his own ticket, "passage brokers" came into existence, and they or their agents were established in every town of any size in Ireland. The more important firms undertook to supply owners with a fixed number of emigrants on commission, others speculated, booking the whole or part of the space available and then selling passages for the highest price they could extract. Firms of brokers in Liverpool sent agents round the country districts in Ireland to peddle passage tickets; no control was exercised over their activities, and frauds were numerous. *The Times,* for example, described passage-brokers as "unprincipled, heartless adventurers." Nevertheless, through the brokers emigration was made familiar, and an idea was implanted in Ireland that if misery became intolerable the answer was emigration.

Yet, considering the disastrous state of Ireland, the numbers emigrating before the famine were not large—in 1844, the year before the first failure, it is estimated that about 68,000 sailed. The people clung to the land, preferring to starve on it than leave, and the fearful blows of total failure, of fever, of wholesale clearances and evictions were required before they were driven out.

The vast majority of emigrants to British North America landed at Quebec and went up the St. Lawrence to Montreal, a distance of 180 miles. In addition a port in the British North American province of New Brunswick, St. John, received a sufficient number of emigrants for an emigration officer to be stationed there, and had the advantage of remaining clear of ice later than Quebec.

There was, however, very little desire on the part of Irish emigrants to settle in British North America; with an almost frantic longing they wished to go to the United States. At this date the United States, with its nearly 23 millions of inhabitants and its rapidly-developing territories, was immeasurably in advance of Canada. Lord Durham, High Commissioner and Governor-General of Canada, contrasted the two sides of the border in his famous report of 1839: "On the American side all is bustle and activity . . . on the British side of the line, with the exception of a few favoured spots, where some approach to American prosperity is apparent, all seems waste and desolation. The ancient city of Montreal which is naturally the commercial capital of the

Canadas, will not bear the least comparison in any respect with Buffalo, which is the creation of yesterday."

But material advantages were not the only magnet which drew the Irish emigrant away from Canada to the United States. "The Irishman looks on America," wrote Thomas Colley Grattan, "as the refuge of his race, the home of his kindred, the heritage of his children and their children. The Atlantic is, to his mind, less a barrier between land and land than is St. George's Channel. The shores of England are farther off in his heart's geography than those of Massachusetts or New York." The native Irishman had become convinced that no justice or opportunity could exist for him under the Union Jack, and he shrank from the British North American colonies. "It is not well for those who are thinking of leaving their beloved homes in Ireland (wretched though they are) to think of Canada as a home," wrote an Irishman from Boston. ". . . the employment which grows from enterprise and the enterprise which grows from freedom are not to be found in Canada. It is a second edition of Ireland, with more room."

To offset the attractions of the United States the British Government consistently made the passage to British North America cheaper than to United States ports and, in addition, transported poor emigrants who declared their intention of settling in Canada free, in barges, up the St. Lawrence into the interior. The urgent need of the British North American colonies for population was not, however, the British Government's only reason for encouraging Irish emigration. The fear of an enormous poverty-stricken Irish migration into Britain was always present, and eighteen years before the famine, in 1827, a Parliamentary Committee had asserted that the choice was whether the Irish were to be enabled to emigrate to the North American colonies by fares being kept down or ". . . to deluge Great Britain with poverty and wretchedness and gradually but certainly to equalize the state of the English and Irish peasantry."

Nevertheless, it was extremely difficult to reconcile low fares with care for the health and safety of the passenger, and the British laws regulating the transport of persons in ships, known as "Passenger Acts," record a continuous, but not always successful, attempt to combine the two. For instance, an Act passed in 1823 introduced restrictions on the number of passengers carried and enforced improved berthing and provision arrangements; however, these admirable regulations nearly doubled the cost of the passage, and an official statement declared that the Act, though "framed with humane and benevolent views, . . . amounted nearly to a prohibition of emigration to the American colonies." A further Act therefore cancelled the new regulations; disaster followed, and another Act reimposed some of the regulations. After this, Passenger Act followed Passenger Act, alternately stringent and lax, until an Act drafted under specific instructions that there was to be no amendment which raised the cost of the passage and checked emigration became law in 1842. This was the measure under which the famine emigration took place. Requirements for the passenger's health and comfort were reduced to a low level, though the height between decks, where emigrants slept and lived, was to be not less than six feet, no deck for emigrants was to be laid below the waterline, the carrying of life-boats was made compulsory, a stock of medicines must be carried, though not a doctor, and seven pounds of provisions were to be given out weekly and three quarts of water per person daily. The Act also provided that brokers must be licensed by a magistrate, give a receipt for money paid for a passage, and were to be fined if ships were unduly late in sailing.

Conditions in British ships were inferior to those in United States ships, but the all-important object was to keep fares low, and this was attained.

Cheap passages did not result in emigrants settling in British North America. Advantage was taken of the low fare to cross the Atlantic to Quebec in a British ship, and often the emigrant, by alleging that his intention was to settle in Canada, procured free transport up the St. Lawrence, before making his entry into the United States by the simple method of walking across the border.

The percentage leaving Canada was alarmingly high; out of more than 120,000 emigrants from the United Kingdom who arrived at Quebec between 1816 and 1828, some three-quarters were estimated to have crossed, each year, into the United States; in 1843, out of 20,892 emigrants, only 85 settled in eastern townships of Canada and only 208 in Montreal.

To check the exodus the British Government appointed in 1825 an experienced official, Alexander Carlisle Buchanan, who had been engaged in the passenger trade and owned mills in Quebec. It was his duty to board each ship as it arrived, interview the emigrants, and endeavour to persuade them to settle in Canada. In 1835 he retired through ill-health and was succeeded—an appointment which had led to some historical confusion—by his nephew and namesake Alexander Carlisle Buchanan the younger, who was in charge at Quebec during the famine emigration.

At this period however the United States was far from extending an indiscriminate welcome to emigrants. To be acceptable, they must be of good quality, healthy, and possessed of some resources. The United States was very conscious of her growing power and prosperity, and "nativism," America for the Americans, was strong. The inscription on the Statue of Liberty:

"Give me your tired, your poor,
    Your huddled masses yearning to breathe free,
The wretched refuse of your teeming shore," etc.

would have been angrily rejected at this date. In the eighteen-forties the United States was still predominantly Yankee, hard and shrewd, Protestant and anti-Catholic—anti-British, it is true, but also anti-Irish; not, as yet, very far removed from the obstinate Anglo-Saxon dissenters who were the founding fathers.

Crossing the Atlantic in a United States ship to a United States port was more expensive than in a British ship to Canada; the U.S. Passenger Acts were stricter and fewer persons could be carried in relation to the size of the ship. For a man, his wife and four small children emigrating from Belfast to Quebec the fare in 1842 was £6, but if he went to New York it was £21. United States ships were better equipped and safer, and during this period, not only their emigrant vessels but their seamen were superior to the British. A large number of British emigrant ships sank. In 1834, for instance, seventeen emigrant ships were lost in the St. Lawrence and 731 emigrants drowned; and a Committee of Inquiry appointed by the British Government reported that "the ships of the United States . . . are stated by several witnesses to be superior to those of a similar class among the ships of Great Britain, the commanders and officers being generally considered to be more competent as seamen and navigators . . . while the seamen of the United States are considered to be more carefully selected and more efficient

. . . higher wages being given, their whole equipment is maintained in a higher state of perfection, so that fewer losses occur." American captains were usually part-owners, not hired servants, and as a general rule American ships carried no liquor, whereas drunkenness on the part of captain and crew was a frequent cause of disaster in British vessels.

"To the United States go the people of good character and in comfortable circumstances," wrote the American Consul in Londonderry, "to British North America the evil and ill disposed. They go to Canada either because the fare is cheap or their landlords are getting rid of them."

States on the Atlantic seaboard were not content to rely solely on higher fares to prevent the entry of unprofitable persons, and between 1837 and 1840 Massachusetts, Pennsylvania and New York passed statutes forbidding passengers to land until an official had examined them, to discover if any had been "paupers in another country" or were "lunatic, idiot, maimed, aged, or infirm persons." For such persons a bond of 1,000 dollars was required, against the possibility that they might become a charge on any town, city or State, and in addition all passengers were required to pay two dollars "head money" on landing, and this was remitted to the State Treasury and used for the support of alien paupers. The majority of destitute and helpless whom the statutes were designed to keep out were Irish, who arrived with less means than any other emigrants. However, examination and payment of "head money" were both avoided by walking over the border from Canada or landing in small coves on the coast of Massachusetts and going on by foot. Mr. Calvin Bailey, superintendent of alien passengers for the City of Boston, calculated that in 1845 some 17,000 persons arrived in this way, about half as many as came by sea. Of these, the United States authorities sent 715 back to Ireland and 4,706 to British North America, at a cost of more than 20,000 dollars.

At this period emigrant ships sailed to North America only in the spring and summer. The St. Lawrence is generally closed by ice from, roughly, the third week in October to the middle of April, and emigrant ships therefore left English ports for Quebec only after the end of March and before the beginning of September. The Atlantic ports of the United States were not normally closed by ice, but bad weather was so frequently encountered in the Atlantic in winter that crossings by emigrant ships late in the year were almost unheard of, and the "emigration season" was limited.

In the spring of 1846, it seemed as if the first failure of the potato might produce a superior type of emigrant. Many respectable persons who had been debating whether or not to leave Ireland now decided to take the step, and the streets of Westport, County Mayo, were "thronged," throughout April and May, by "comfortable farmers, not the destitute," on their way to emigrate, while in Dublin "vast numbers of well dressed countrymen" were to be seen, "with baggage and sea store" (sea store being food bought to supplement the provisions officially given out on the voyage). Bands of young men and women with their children—thirty to forty at a time—passed through Clare on their way to emigrate to the United States, with their belongings on two or three carts, and anything from ten to thirty pounds in their possession. These emigrants had been engaged in preparations long beforehand. "All the money that could be spared," wrote the Land and Colonial Emigration Commissioners, "was laid by and the Savings Banks were laden, as was well known, with deposits, which the best informed persons did not doubt to be destined to this purpose."

The first emigrant ship of 1846 arrived at Quebec on April 24, and Alexander Carlisle Buchanan reported the emigrants who landed to be well-to-do, healthy, and with a little capital. Through May, though many were poor, a fair proportion were "comfortable": the *Lord Sydenham*, for instance, brought 700 emigrants from Limerick, "all well clad and very respectable looking" and all "going west," that is, probably to the United States.

Several ships brought tenants emigrated by their landlords, and though 120 persons sent by the Hon. Mr. Wandesford, from Kilkenny, were "absolutely destitute," 164 sent by Colonel Wyndham from Clare, and 64 by Mr. Spaight from Limerick, were well provided for, and were pointed out as being an example of the good which could be done by conscientious landlords.

Unhappily the situation was to change all too soon. By the beginning of August it was evident not only that the potato had failed again but that this time it had failed completely; and throughout September and until ice closed the St. Lawrence an "unprecedented" immigration of Irish, of the poorest class, reached Quebec. They had sailed much later than usual; the hard Canadian winter was only a few weeks away; the majority had left without any "sea store," though to depend on the 7 lb. of provisions legally due under the Passenger Act was unheard of; and most, on arrival, did not even possess the sixpence which was the steamer fare from Quebec to Montreal, and had to be assisted by the Government agent. These unfortunates were the first of the panic-stricken thousands who fled from Ireland as the fearful result of the total loss of the potato became apparent. The winter of 1846-47 dragged on; snow fell, the public works failed, food became unprocurable, and desperate appeals came from Ireland. "For God's sake don't let us die of hunger," wrote a small farmer in Sligo to relatives in North America, asking for the loan of passage money.

For the first time in history emigration across the Atlantic continued throughout the winter, the most severe in living memory. Only a small fraction of this emigration went to British North America, because the St. Lawrence was frozen, but about 30,000 persons found the means for a winter passage to the United States, and the condition of destitution in which the majority landed filled the United States authorities with anger. The United States was being made "the poor house of Europe," the worn-out nations of the Old World were trying to get rid of their paupers by throwing them on American shores. Congress took immediate action. In February and at the beginning of March, 1847, it passed two new and severe Passenger Acts: the number of passengers per ton of burthen which a ship might carry to the United States from the British Isles was reduced by one-third, and the price of the passage proportionately increased. The temper of Congress was indeed so irritated, that Lord Palmerston, the British Foreign Secretary, had difficulty in obtaining permission for ships to land passengers who had embarked before the Acts were passed.

The minimum fare to New York for a single passage now rose to seven pounds, but the demand was so great that by early April brokers in Liverpool were closing their offices— all passages to the United States had been sold.

Meanwhile, in Ireland, as the winter of 1846-47 passed into spring, the horror of "fever" was added to starvation. In February, 1847, the headlong flight from Ireland began. The roads to the ports, wrote Trevelyan, were thronged with emigrants. "All who are able," reported a Board of Works' officer, "are leaving the country." "Crowds" were seen "on the roads bound for Liverpool," and an Inspector of Drainage wrote, "Lists are useless. No one answers their names. They have gone . . . or are dead." "All with means are emigrating," wrote the Board of Works' Inspector from Cavan, "only the utterly destitute are left behind and enfeebled labourers"; and Jonathan Pim, one of the secretaries of the Central Relief Committee of the Society of Friends, saw emigrants boarding a ship, for the winter crossing, and "there was nothing but joy at their escape, as from a doomed land." Mr. Monsell, of Tervoe, was begged by his tenants for assistance to emigrate, as "the greatest blessing he could bestow"; and Mr. Kincaid, a well-known agent, was "besieged with requests" from the tenantry on the estates he managed.

In the hurry to get away, a very large emigration, more than 85,000 in 1847, sailed directly from Irish ports, especially in the south and west. Three thousand persons had left Sligo, for the winter crossing, before January 1, 1847; in the early spring, bands numbering as many as 700 persons were seen to pass through Mayo to emigrate, and a total of 11,000 persons eventually sailed from Sligo. A smaller number, 9,000, left from Dublin, and from Waterford only 4,000, because access to Liverpool was easier. Numbers of people—how many cannot be estimated—sailed from small harbours, Baltimore, Ballina, Westport, Tralee, Killala; and in these places a tradition still exists of emigrant ships sailing, only to perish. In Westport a ship is said to have foundered, with the loss of all on board, within sight of land, watched with horror by the relatives to whom the emigrants had just said farewell.

The enforcement of the Passenger Act at small harbours was impossible—the class from which inspectors could be drawn did not exist in Ireland. Ships sailed which were overcrowded, not provided with the legal quotas of provisions and water, and dangerously antique in construction: these were the vessels that were given the name of "coffin ships." A typical example of a coffin ship was the barque *Elizabeth and Sarah,* which sailed from the small harbour of Killala, County Mayo, in July, 1846, arriving at Quebec in September. She had been built in 1762 and was of 330 tons burthen. Her list of passengers, as certified by the officer at Killala, showed 212 names, whereas in fact she carried 276 persons. She should have carried 12,532 gallons of water, but had only 8,700 gallons in leaky casks. The Passenger Act of 1842 required 7 lb. of provisions to be given out weekly to each passenger, but no distribution was ever made in the *Elizabeth and Sarah*. Berths numbered only 36, of which 4 were taken by the crew: the remaining 32 were shared between 276 passengers, who otherwise slept on the floor. No sanitary convenience of any kind was provided, and the state of the vessel was "horrible and disgusting beyond the power of language to describe." The passage from Killala, largely through the incompetence of the captain, took eight weeks: the passengers starved and were tortured by thirst, and 42 persons died during the voyage. Finally the ship broke down and was towed into the St. Lawrence by a steamer sent by Alexander Carlisle Buchanan at his own expense, since Government regulations did not permit such an expenditure. The voyage of the *Elizabeth and Sarah* was a local speculation, and passages had been sold in districts round Killala by means of circulars which were incorrect in almost every particular.

Such dishonest speculators were responsible for the existence of "coffin ships"; but the Irish peasant's wild desire to escape from Ireland, combined with his utter ignorance of the sea and of geography, made him eager to risk himself in any vessel. Passages were bought in small coasting schooners, of under 100 tons, or in vessels so old and so rotten that they were falling to pieces—the brig *Vista,* for instance, preparing to sail from the small harbour of Castletown Berehaven, in County Cork, was observed to have rotten rigging, uncaulked timbers, a leaking hull, and a steerage which was a shambles.

"The desire to reach America being exceedingly strong," wrote Earl Grey, Secretary of State for the Colonies, "many of the emigrants are content . . . to submit to very great hardships during the voyage."

Meanwhile, in Canada in the spring of 1847, intelligent officials and citizens apprehensively awaited the immigration which would fall on them as soon as the St. Lawrence was clear of ice. The steps taken by the United States to prevent the landing of poor emigrants at their Atlantic ports, the unheard-of activity through the winter, and the reports reaching Quebec of the frightful state of Ireland all indicated a very large Irish immigration destitute and in bad health. The idea, however, that "fever," known to be raging in Ireland, constituted a danger crossed no one's mind. What was called "ship fever" was a well-known disease, recognized as being typhus, but considered to arise from overcrowding and dirt in the confined space of a ship. Dr. Griscom, a well-known United States medical authority, told a committee of the United States Senate that ship fever, or typhus, "is the product of a miasm as distinct as that of marshes which produce intermittent fever . . . the direct product of the vitiated excretions of the human body pent up in a small space and made to engender malaria."

Regulations at Quebec required that all ships with passengers coming up the St. Lawrence should stop at the quarantine station on Grosse Isle, thirty miles down the river, for medical inspection; those vessels which had sickness on board were then detained and the sick taken to the quarantine hospital. Grosse Isle, a beautiful island, lying in the middle of the majestic St. Lawrence, had been selected as the site for a quarantine station in 1832, at the time of a cholera epidemic; it is small, and its peculiar charm lies in the number of trees and shrubs which grow down to the water's edge and are mirrored in the St. Lawrence, so that the island seems to float. The brief coastline is diversified by a number of tiny rocky bays; in the interior large trees grow from green turf, and there is a remarkable variety of wild flowers. Near the river the quarantine buildings, which still exist, are low and white, and do not detract from the beauty of the landscape; on rising ground, above them, a small white church nestles in green trees. "A fairy scene," exclaimed an emigrant, as he approached the island. "Exquisite glades, groves, wild flowers and glimpses of the St. Lawrence." In this island paradise an appalling tragedy was to take place.

On February 19, 1847, Dr. Douglas, the medical officer in charge of the quarantine station at Grosse Isle, asked for £3,000 to make preparations for the coming immigration, pointing out that during the previous year the number admitted to the quarantine hospital had been twice as large as usual, and that reports from Ireland indicated that the state of the immigrants this year would be worse.

Far from getting £3,000, Dr. Douglas was assigned just under £300. He was allowed one small steamer, the *St. George*, to ply between Grosse Isle and Quebec and given permission to hire a sailing-vessel, provided one could be found for not more than £50 for the season.

The citizens of Quebec, however, were so uneasy, that at the beginning of March, 1847, they sent a petition to the Secretary of State for the Colonies, Earl Grey, in which they pointed out that the number of Irish immigrants was annually rising, that the present distress in Ireland must mean a further large increase, that they viewed with alarm the probable fate of poor Irish immigrants in the rigorous winter climate of Canada, and that there was also the possibility of such immigrants bringing disease. They begged the Canadian Government to take action.

The *Montreal Gazette,* prophesying that Canada was going to be "inundated with an enormous crowd of poor and destitute emigrants," called for "legislative measures" to meet the coming crisis. Everyone knew, declared the *Gazette,* that Quebec was merely the port where emigrants disembarked for a few hours, to embark again for Montreal, and it was on Montreal that the inundation would descend. However, a meeting of Montreal citizens, called by the Emigration Committee of Montreal on May 10, 1847, to consider what steps should be taken, was so poorly attended that the meeting was adjourned.

There was one man who might have been able to convince the Canadian Government that a catastrophe was approaching, Alexander Carlisle Buchanan. He was the Chief Emigration Officer, he was esteemed in official circles, his reports were studied, his opinion carried weight. Nevertheless, Buchanan, though he anticipated a very considerable increase in sickness, "did not make any official representation to Government" because, as he wrote, "it was a subject that did not come within the control of my department." The Government, therefore, received no official warning that the emigration from Ireland was likely to present any problem, beyond being unusually large; and in April, 1847, the Colonial Land and Emigration Commissioners made their seventh report without any inkling that disaster threatened. In the Canadian Legislature soothing assurances were given; the coming immigration would certainly be large, but the present system was adequate to deal with it; in 1846, 125,000 persons had arrived (this was an exaggeration), but the system had been found to work, "and in general there were no complaints."

The opening of the St. Lawrence was late in 1847; "the

merry month of May started with ice an inch thick," reported
the *Quebec Gazette*, and the first vessel, the *Syria*, did not arrive until May 17. Less than a week later the catastrophe had
taken place, and was beyond control. The *Syria* had 84 cases
of fever on board, out of a total of 241 passengers—nine
persons had died on the voyage, and one was to die on landing
at Grosse Isle. All her passengers were Irish, had crossed to
Liverpool to embark, and had spent one night at least in the
cheap lodging-houses of Liverpool. In Dr. Douglas's opinion,
20 to 24 more were certain to sicken, bringing the total for
the *Syria* to more than 100, and the quarantine hospital,
built for 150 cases, could not possibly accommodate more
than 200.

Dr. Douglas now told the Canadian Government that he
had "reliable information" that 10,600 emigrants at least had
left Britain for Quebec since April 10: "Judging from the
specimens just arrived," large numbers would have to go to
hospital, and he asked permission to build a new shed, to
cost about £150, to be used as a hospital. On May 20, he
received authority to erect the shed provided the cost was
kept down to £135.

Four days after the *Syria*, on May 21, eight ships arrived
with a total of 430 fever cases. Two hundred and five were
taken into the hospital, which became dangerously overcrowded, and the remaining 216 had to be left on board ship.
"I have not a bed to lay them on or a place to put them,"
wrote Dr. Douglas. "I never contemplated the possibility of
every vessel arriving with fever as they do now." Three days
later seventeen more vessels arrived, all with fever; a shed
normally used to accommodate passengers detained for quarantine was turned into a hospital and instantly filled. There
were now 695 persons in hospital and 164 on board ship
waiting to be taken off; and Dr. Douglas wrote that he had
just received a message that twelve more vessels had anchored,
"all sickly."

On May 26 thirty vessels, with 10,000 emigrants on board,
were waiting at Grosse Isle; by the 29th there were thirty-six
vessels, with 13,000 emigrants. And "in all these vessels cases
of fever and dysentery had occurred," wrote Dr. Douglas—
the dysentery seems to have been infectious, and was probably
bacillary dysentery. On May 31 forty vessels were waiting,
extending in a line two miles down the St. Lawrence; about
1,100 cases of fever were on Grosse Isle in sheds, tents, and

laid in rows in the little church; an equal number were on board the ships, waiting to be taken off; and a further 45,000 emigrants at least were expected.

On June 1 the Catholic Archbishop of Quebec addressed a circular letter to all Catholic Bishops and Archbishops in Ireland, asking them to "use every endeavour to prevent your diocesans emigrating in such numbers to Canada." Nevertheless, the numbers continued to mount; ultimately, in 1847, 109,000 are stated to have left for British North America, "almost all," stated the Colonial Land and Emigration Commissioners, "Irish."

By July, more than 2,500 sick were on Grosse Isle, and conditions were appalling. "Medical men," wrote Dr. Douglas, were "disgusted with the disagreeable nature of their duties in treating such filthy cases." Many doctors died; Dr. Benson, of Dublin, who had experience in fever hospitals in Ireland, arrived on May 21 and volunteered his services, but caught typhus and died six days later. Each of the medical officers was ill at some time, and three other doctors died of typhus, in addition to Dr. Benson. At one period twelve out of a medical staff of fourteen were ill; of the two others, one left because he was afraid of catching typhus and one was summoned to a dying parent, leaving Dr. Douglas virtually single-handed. Patients on the ships were often left for four or five days without any medical attention: under the Passenger Act of 1842 ships were not compelled to carry a doctor, and only one doctor besides Dr. Benson happened to have been a passenger.

Nurses, too, were unobtainable, and the sick suffered tortures from lack of attention. A Catholic priest, Father Moylan, gave water to sick persons in a tent who had had nothing to drink for eighteen hours; another, Father McQuirk, was given *carte blanche* by Dr. Douglas to hire nurses, as many as possible, from among the healthy passengers. He offered high wages and told the women that, speaking as their priest, it was their duty to volunteer; not one came forward. The fear of fever among the Irish, said Dr. Douglas, was so great that "the nearest relatives abandon each other whenever they can." The only persons who could be induced to take charge of the sick were abandoned and callous creatures, of both sexes, who robbed the dead.

Equipment in the hospitals hardly existed; bedding had been sent down but no planks on which to lay it—it was therefore spread on the ground and soon became soaked. New sheds had been put up without privies, and the neighbouring brushwood was "disgusting"; the old passenger sheds had never been intended for use as hospitals, they had no ventilation and the smell was intolerable; berths were built in two tiers, and patients with dysentery placed in the upper berth. In some sheds berths had been constructed to hold two or even three persons, and they were filled without distinction between age or sex. The so-called "healthy" were often sick; Father O'Reilly visited the camp for the "healthy," who were quarantined in tents at the eastern end of the island, gave the last rites to fifty dying persons, and did not doubt that many more were dying. On August 18, 88 deaths were reported among the "healthy" during the last week.

In August, Bishop Mountain, the Anglican Bishop of Montreal, visited Grosse Isle. He saw people who had just been brought ashore, and were lying opposite the church, screaming for water. Others were in tents on the ground, without bedding, and it was raining. One woman was dying, in another tent was a dying child, covered with vermin. No relatives could be traced and several other children were unidentifiable waifs. Under a tree was the body of a boy; he had been walking with some others, had sat down for a moment, and died. More than 2,500 fever cases were now in hospital.

The state of the emigrants as they landed was frightful. Arriving vessels "had not one really healthy person on board"; passengers "tottered" on shore at Grosse Isle, "spectre-like wretches," "emaciated," "cadaverous," "feeble." Very many of them had passed the voyage in a state of starvation. The official weekly issue of 7 lb. of provisions was intended to guard against absolute destitution, but "it never could have been expected to be enough to sustain an adult through the voyage," reported the Senate Committee of the United States on Sickness and Mortality in Emigrant Ships. Yet "complete reliance on this issue has been practised to an immense extent by the Irish in voyages to Quebec . . . they arrive so emaciated and prostrate that they had to go at once to hospital." Passage-brokers at Liverpool made a practice of displaying a loaf of bread in their offices to the starving Irish "to delude the poor into the belief that they will be fed at sea."

On the voyage water often ran short, casks leaked; dishonest provisioning merchants bought cheap casks which had previously been used for wine, vinegar or chemicals and made the water they contained undrinkable. When a Government inquiry was held into the disaster at Grosse Isle, Alexander Carlisle Buchanan testified that during the summer of 1847, "the provisions of the Passenger Act appear to have been very generally observed by the masters of Emigrant vessels," and he was no doubt correct. But the Passenger Act of 1842 reduced requirements to such a bare minimum that very little had to go wrong for the emigrant to suffer severely, even if he were fortunate enough not to fall a victim to typhus.

On May 30 Robert Whyte embarked at Dublin in a brig carrying Irish emigrants to Quebec, among them a party of tenants from Meath, who were being sent out by their landlord. Whyte, who travelled as a cabin passenger, kept a diary of the voyage. In one of his earliest entries, on June 1, 1847, he comments that many of the passengers seemed quite unfit for the voyage—one old man was already dying of consumption. However, all had been medically examined and passed by the doctor, although the captain had protested at having to take some of them. The medical examination at the port of embarkation usually consisted of looking at the tongues of the passengers as they passed, in rapid succession, before a little window at which a doctor sat. At the same time the emigrant showed his ticket, but as was later pointed out at an official inquiry, "there was no certainty that the person with the ticket was the person named on it, or that the real owner was not down with typhus and being represented by some conniving friend."

Robert Whyte observed that the emigrants depended entirely for food on the 7 lb. of provisions provided weekly under the Passenger Act. The captain made an issue daily, as otherwise a week's rations would have been eaten in twenty-four hours; a few emigrants had brought one or two salt herrings, but most had nothing.

Cooking, said Whyte, was done on "a large wooden case lined with bricks about the size and shape of a settee, the coals were confined by two or three iron bars in front." This stove was always surrounded by bickering emigrants—"quarrels only ended at 7 p.m. when Jack in the shrouds poured water on the fire, still surrounded by miserable squabbling groups, who snatched up their pots and pans and half blinded by steam descended into the hold with their half cooked supper." The emigrants, however, "never got angry with Jack, however much he teased them." Food was always eaten half raw, and diarrhoea was prevalent. The captain and his wife were kindly enough: she was called "the Mistress" by the emigrants, she dosed the sick with porridge containing drops of laudanum, and a little girl, born during the voyage, was named after her. The ship was a temperance ship, and the crew's rations did not include grog. But a fortnight after sailing water began to run short—two of the casks had leaked, and water in another was undrinkable because the cask had held wine. Meanwhile, the emigrants, with nothing but the regulation 7 lb. of provisions a week, were starving, and their state was so pitiable that the captain and his wife distributed food from their private stores to the sick. On June 15 "ship fever" broke out: "110 passengers," wrote Whyte, "are shut up in the unventilated hold of a small brig, without a doctor, medicines or even water." Next day a deputation of emigrants marched on deck and threatened the captain, demanding food and, above all, water, to make drinks for their sick wives and children; they would, they vowed, rush the provision store and help themselves. On this, the mate went into the cabin, fetched a blunderbuss, and fired it into the air, assuring the deputation there were sufficient fire-arms in store to arm the crew. The deputation then went away. Fresh cases of ship fever occurred daily, and the hold became in a "shocking condition of filth." By bad luck, the wind dropped and progress became almost imperceptible. Since the ship was provisioned for only fifty days the captain was forced to reduce further the issue of water.

On June 27 Whyte was kept awake all night by "moaning and raving from the hold," and cries for "water, for God's sake, some water." The mate, who appeared "frightened and quite bewildered," told him that "fearful scenes" were taking place below—the "effluvium" rising from the hold was so overpowering that it was impossible to go on deck. A medical officer at Grosse Isle recorded that, visiting an emigrant vessel in the morning, "I have seen a stream of foul air issuing from the hatches as dense and as palpable as seen on a foggy day from a dung heap."

By July 9 more than half the emigrants and several of the crew in Whyte's brig had ship fever, and deaths were frequent. All casks had been tried for water, but only some were good, and the sufferings of the emigrants in the hold were "heart-rending."

Five days later the brig entered the St. Lawrence, but the water of the river could not be drunk by the "wretched emigrants" because it was still salt. Only half a cask of good water now remained, and this was reserved for the captain and the crew.

When, about July 25, the ship anchored off Grosse Isle, "a beautiful islet with verdant turf almost down to the water," a doctor paid "a perfunctory visit, remarked sagaciously 'Ha, there is fever here,' and departed," promising to remove the sick "tomorrow or next day," and leaving papers for the captain to fill up. Whyte was told that he might, if he chose, go on to Quebec, but he had become attached to the ship and its company and remained.

The brig was now left, he wrote, "as marooned without skill or help as at sea, still without doctor and no water." Though the St. Lawrence, at Grosse Isle, was no longer salt, it was "a floating mass of filthy straw, refuse of foul beds, barrels containing the vilest matter, old rags, tattered clothes" which had been thrown overboard from vessels when cleaning their holds. The sick were not taken off until August 1, and by then several had died. One was the wife of a Meath emigrant, and Whyte went to her funeral on Grosse Isle: "After the grave was filled up the husband placed two shovels in the form of a cross and said, 'By that cross, Mary, I swear to avenge your death. As soon as I earn the price of my passage home I'll go back and shoot the man that murdered you—and that's the landlord.' "

From the deck of the brig Whyte watched a continuous procession of boats, bringing the sick and dead from the ships to Grosse Isle. There was no pier. "Hundreds were literally flung on the beach, left amid the mud and stones to crawl on the dry land as they could." The priest, who was the Catholic chaplain of the mission, saw thirty-seven people at a time "lying on the beach, crawling on the mud and dying like fish out of water." Boat-loads of dead were taken, four times in one day, from a single vessel; the bodies were wrapped in canvas or boxed in rough coffins, made from the planks of berths.

Whyte then witnessed the arrival of a ship-load of German emigrants. The crowded vessel carried more than five hundred passengers, but there was no sickness and all were "neatly clad." The medical examination took place on deck, and "each comely fair-haired girl laughed as she passed the doctor to join a group of robust young men." As the vessel went up the river "the deck was covered with emigrants who were singing a charming hymn in whose beautiful harmony all took part." Throughout the summer of 1847 vessels crowded with Germans from Hamburg and Bremen were arriving every day at Grosse Isle, "all healthy, robust and cheerful."

Robert Whyte was horrified by the filthy state of the hold in his brig, but he was told by a Canadian priest, one of the courageous Catholic clergy who came on board fever ships to give the last rites to those dying of typhus, that, compared to some, the hold was clean, and the brig was, in fact, an average example of what was endured by emigrants on a transatlantic crossing when their vessel was struck by "the Ocean Plague."

The *Larch*, from Sligo, for instance, sailed with 440 passengers, of whom 108 died at sea, and 150 arrived with fever; the *Virginius* left Liverpool for Quebec with 476 passengers, of whom 158 died on the voyage and 106 were landed sick, including the master, the mate, and all but six of the crew. The *Virginius* had taken nine weeks to cross the Atlantic, and the sufferings, even of the passengers fortunate enough not to catch fever, were appalling. Dr. Douglas wrote, "The few that were able to come on deck were ghastly, yellow looking spectres, unshaven and hollow cheeked . . . not more than six or eight were really healthy and able to exert themselves."

In April Stephen de Vere, of the well-known family of de Vere, Curragh Chase, County Limerick, took a steerage passage on an emigrant vessel to Quebec, in order "that he might speak as a witness respecting the sufferings of emigrants." "Before the emigrant has been a week at sea," wrote Stephen de Vere, "he is an altered man . . . How can it be otherwise? Hundreds of poor people, men, women and children, of all ages from the drivelling idiot of 90 to the babe just born, huddled together, without light, without air, wallowing in filth, and breathing a foetid atmosphere, sick in body, dispirited in heart . . . the fevered patients lying between the sound in sleeping places so narrow, as almost to deny them . . . a change of position . . . by their agonized ravings disturbing those around them . . . living without food or medicine except as administered by the hand of casual charity, dying without spiritual consolation and buried in the deep without the rites of the church." The food, de Vere continued, was seldom sufficiently cooked because there were not enough cooking places. The supply of water was hardly enough for drinking and cooking—washing was impossible; and in many ships the filthy beds were never brought up on deck and aired, nor was the narrow space between the sleeping-berths washed or scraped until arrival at quarantine. Provisions, doled out by ounces, consisted of meal of the worst quality and salt meat; water was so short that the passengers threw their salt provisions overboard—they could not eat them and satisfy their raging thirst afterwards. People lay for days on end in their dark close berths, because by that method they suffered less from hunger. The captain used a false measure for water, and the so-called gallon measure held only three pints; for this de Vere had the captain prosecuted and fined on arrival at Quebec. Spirits were sold once or twice a week, and frightful scenes of drunkenness followed. Lights below were prohibited because the ship, in spite of the open cooking-fires on her decks, was carrying a cargo of gunpowder to the garrison at Quebec, but pipes were secretly smoked in the berths, and lucifer matches used. The voyage took three months, and apart from fever, which does not seem to have been serious, many of the passengers, wrote de Vere, became "utterly debased and corrupted." Yet he was told that the ship was "more comfortable than many."

The worst ships were those which brought emigrants sent out by their landlords, and of all the sufferings endured during the famine none aroused such savage resentment, or left behind such hatred, as the landlord emigrations.

Before the famine, responsible landlords, for instance, Lord Bessborough and Lord Monteagle, advanced money and paid the cost of passages for tenants to emigrate. Lord Monteagle, in particular, believed that in emigration lay the solution of Ireland's population problem, and the Monteagle Papers contain a number of letters from grateful emigrants; he was also responsible for setting up the Select Committee of the House of Lords on Colonization, that is, emigration, in 1847.

Another landlord, Mr. Spaight, of Limerick, a well-known shipbroker, bought Derry Castle, in Tipperary, for £40,000 in 1844, and found "a dead weight of paupers." As he was engaged in the passenger trade, he offered free passage and provisions to those willing to emigrate, and the value of two pounds on landing, provided the tenants "tumbled," that is, pulled down, their cabins. He made the offer only to entire families, and said he had "got rid of crime and distress for £3 10s. a head." The first failure of the potato was followed by a number of landlord emigrations, and a total of more than a thousand tenants from various estates reached Quebec in 1846, those arriving early in the season being reasonably healthy and, on the whole, adequately provided for.

The fatal year 1847 brought a change. In January the Government announced that the whole destitute population was to be transferred to the Poor Law, to be maintained out of local rates at the expense of owners of property, and the only hope of solvency for landlords was to reduce the number of destitute on their estates. Emigration began to be used as an alternative to eviction, and Sir Robert Gore Booth, a resident landlord, was accused by Mr. Perley, the Government emigration agent at St. John, New Brunswick, of "exporting and shovelling out the helpless and infirm to the detriment of the colony." Sir Robert in reply put forward the landlord's point of view, declaring that emigration was the only humane method of putting properties in Ireland on a satisfactory footing. The country was overpopulated, and it was not right to evict and turn people out on the world. To emigrate them was the only solution.

Emigration also saved money; the cost of emigrating a pauper was generally about half the cost of maintaining him in the workhouse for one year, and once the ship had sailed the destitute were effectually got rid of, for they could return only with immense difficulty. In 1847, therefore, the temptation was strong to ship off as cheaply as possible those unfortunates who, through age, infirmity or the potato failure, had become useless and an apparently endless source of expense.

No attempt was made to regulate landlord emigration, but the Colonial Land and Emigration Commissioners did warn landlords that each tenant should have at least one pound landing-money, and provided the necessary organization for remitting money to British North America. No money, however, was sent.

On December 11, 1847, Mr. Adam Ferrie, a member of the Legislative Council of Canada, wrote a furious open letter on Irish landlord emigration to the British Colonial Secretary, Earl Grey. He denounced landlords by name, the best-known being Lord Palmerston and Major Mahon, of Strokestown, County Roscommon, who later was tragically murdered.

Hordes of half-naked, starving paupers, declared Mr. Ferrie, including aged, infirm, beggars and vagrants, had been shipped off to "this young and thinly populated country without regard to humanity or even to common decency." They were given promises of clothes, food and money and told that an agent would pay from two to five pounds to each family, according to size, on arrival at Quebec; when they arrived no agent could be found, and they were thrown on the Government and private charity. Twice as many passengers as the ship should hold were "huddled together between decks"; there was too little food and water and conditions were "as bad as the slave trade."

Nine vessels had left Sligo carrying tenants emigrated by Lord Palmerston from his estates, and additional passages were booked from Liverpool, about 2,000 persons leaving in all. The first vessel to arrive, the *Eliza Liddell*, at St. John, New Brunswick, in July, 1847, raised a storm of protest; it was alleged that she brought only widows with young children, and aged, destitute, decrepit persons, useless to the colony. Another vessel, the *Lord Ashburton*, arrived at Quebec on October 30, dangerously late in the season, carrying 477 passengers, 174 of whom, Lord Palmerston's tenants, were almost naked: 87 of them had to be clothed by charity before they could, with decency, leave the ship. On the *Lord Ashburton* 107 persons had died on the voyage of fever and dysentery; 60 were ill, and so deplorable was the condition of the crew that five passengers had to work the ship up to Grosse Isle. The *Quebec Gazette* described the condition of the *Lord Ashburton* as "a disgrace to the home authorities." Even later in the year, on November 8, 1847, the brig *Richard Watson* arrived, carrying tenants of Lord Palmerston's, one of whom, a woman, was completely naked, and had to have a sheet wrapped round her before she could go ashore.

Most notorious of all was the *Aeolus*—bringing tenants of Lord Palmerston's from Sligo—which arrived at St. John, New Brunswick, on November 2. The St. Lawrence was then closed by ice, the Canadian winter had begun, and calèches, or horse-drawn sleighs, had replaced carriages in the snow-filled streets of Quebec. The captain of the *Aeolus* paid £250 in bonds to be allowed to land 240 emigrants at St. John. They were "almost in a state of nudity," and the surgeon at Partridge Island, the quarantine station, asserted that ninety-nine per cent. must become a public charge immediately:

they were widows with helpless young families, decrepit old
women, and men "riddled with disease." The citizens of St.
John declared that they could not feed or shelter the unfortunate emigrants; notices were posted in the streets offering to all who would go back to Ireland a free passage and
food; and a message was sent to Lord Palmerston that the
"Common Council of the City of St. John deeply regret that
one of Her Majesty's ministers, the Rt. Hon. Lord Palmerston, either by himself or his authorised agent should have
exposed such a numerous and distressed portion of his tenantry
to the severity and privations of a New Brunswick winter . . .
unprovided with the common means of support, with broken-
down constitutions and almost in a state of nudity."

It is unlikely that Lord Palmerston knew anything about the
emigration, beyond the fact that his agents, the well-known
firm of Kincaid and Stewart, had recommended that a certain
sum of money should be laid out on improving his Sligo
estates by emigrating some of the destitute. However, Lord
Palmerston was officially requested for an explanation, and
on December 20, he forwarded to the Governor-General of
Canada, Lord Elgin, a letter from Messrs. Kincaid and Stewart—a letter expressed in curiously insolent language. It was
true, wrote Messrs. Kincaid and Stewart, that over two thousand persons had been sent out from Lord Palmerston's Sligo
estates during the past season. "It is unnecessary to say that
all persons were the poorest class of farmer, very little better
than paupers. If they had been able to retain their small
farms and maintain themselves and their families at home
they would not have entreated your Lordship to send them
to a strange country, nor is it probable that your Lordship
would have incurred so great an expense for the purpose of
removing from your estate a large body of the tenantry
solvent in their circumstances and able to pay their rent."
Dealing with the statement that the emigrants arrived naked,
they wrote, "large sums were expended in providing clothing
. . . but we suppose the hardships of a rough sea voyage
were too much for the inferior kind of clothing to which
the inhabitants of the west of Ireland are accustomed."

As for the last and most miserable ship to arrive, the
Aeolus, Messrs. Kincaid and Stewart stated, shortly, that she
had sailed late because there was difficulty in finding a vessel
to charter, and "it was at the special and earnest request of
the parties themselves that these people were allowed to

emigrate and their passages, etc., paid by your Lordship . . . their entreaties to be sent to America were so urgent that we have seen some of them on their knees in the road praying to be sent out. . . ."

The emigration, as far as Lord Palmerston's Sligo estates were concerned, was a success; by 1849, the number of persons receiving relief had dropped to two per cent. of the 1847 figure; but throughout the winter of 1847 St. John was filled with "swarms of wretched beings going about the streets imploring every passer-by, women and children in the snow, without shoes or stockings and scarcely anything on." J. F. Maguire, the Irish-American journalist, tells the story of a starving half-naked old woman begging in the snow in Broadway, New York—she had come to the New World in a landlord emigration.

Meanwhile at Grosse Isle, by the middle of the summer of 1847, imposing a quarantine for fever had been abandoned as hopeless. The line of ships waiting for inspection was now several miles long; to make quarantine effective, twenty to twenty-five thousand contacts should be isolated, for whom there was no room on the small island. Therefore to carry out the quarantine regulations was, wrote Dr. Douglas, "physically impossible," and at the end of May passengers on ships with fever were allowed to stay, after the fever cases had been removed, and to perform their quarantine on board, the period to be fifteen days instead of ten. Dr. Douglas believed that a simple washing down and airing would make the holds healthy. "After ablutions with water," he wrote, "by opening stern ports and bow ports . . . a complete current of air can pass through the hold, in fact a bird can fly through it." So the passengers remained in the holds, with disastrous consequences.

So great was the number of sick that "a fatal delay of several days" occurred before fever cases were taken away; meanwhile, sick and "healthy" were cooped up together, and fresh infection took place. The *Agnes,* for instance, which arrived with 427 passengers, had only 150 alive after a quarantine of fifteen days.

Dr. Douglas was instructed to let the "healthy" go from the ships without insisting on the full term of quarantine, and by the end of July quarantine had virtually been abandoned. A doctor came on board and inquired how many sick were below. He did not go into the hold, but placed himself at a table and called all emigrants able to walk to come up on deck; they filed past him, and anyone who seemed to him to be feverish was ordered to show his tongue. Those passed as "healthy" were usually taken up to Montreal in a steamer, which picked up passengers at different vessels and had an appearance of gaiety because a fiddler and dancers were in the prow.

The journey up the St. Lawrence, from Grosse Isle to Montreal, took two to three days, and the emigrants were "literally crammed on board the steamers, exposed to the cold night air and the burning sun . . . bringing the seeds of disease with them." A number invariably developed fever on the way, and more than half had been known to arrive at Montreal in a dying condition.

On June 8 Dr. Douglas gave "real fair warning to the authorities of Quebec and Montreal" that an epidemic was bound to occur: quarantine regulations were impossible to enforce, and the division between "healthy" and sick was meaningless. Four thousand to five thousand so-called "healthy" persons had left Grosse Isle on the previous Sunday; out of these, "2,000 at the least will fall sick somewhere before three weeks are over. They ought to have accomodation for 2,000 sick at least in Quebec and Montreal . . . Good God! What evils will befall the city wherever they alight."

Typhus epidemics did occur in both cities, but in Quebec the onslaught was comparatively mild and the victims were almost all emigrants, "emaciated objects" who crowded "the doors of churches, the wharves and the streets, apparently in the last stages of disease and famine." Fever sheds were put up at St. Roch, near the Marine Hospital, in the face of violent opposition from citizens in the district, who threw down the first sheds erected; the Marine Hospital itself, founded at the time of the cholera epidemic in 1832, was filled, and on July 9 there were about 700 to 800 patients in the hospital and the fever sheds, with about 41 deaths weekly. The Governor-General also arranged for a wing of the cavalry barracks on the Plains of Abraham, where Wolfe fought the famous battle which captured Quebec, to be used as a temporary hospital; it contained 100 beds, and was reserved for citizens of Quebec. About 171 cases of typhus were reported by August 20 from the lower town, round Champlain Street. The worst lodging-houses were situated here: "filth turned the stomach with stench," and the cholera epidemic of 1832 had originated in the neighbourhood. However, Quebec may be considered as having been, on the whole, fortunate; and a Board of Health, formed to take "sanitary measures" on May 24, was dissolved on September 10, "the necessity having disappeared."

Montreal was not so lucky. From its geographical position and its commercial importance, it was the destination of most emigrants, and by June 1 completely destitute emigrants with "troops of children" were thronging the city, and showing no signs of moving on. Steamer-loads of emigrants, at the rate of 2,304 in twenty-four hours, were now coming up from Grosse Isle, numbers of them already dying from fever. In this emergency the Montreal Board of Health was formed on June 5. The Board immediately issued urgent recommendations: the "so-called lodging houses," where destitute emigrants went, should be closed, they were hotbeds of infection, more hospital accommodation should be provided, and emigrants should not be allowed to use the harbour in the centre of the city—"the pestilential odour from the emigrants' clothes alone makes it undesirable"; instead, they should be landed at Windmill Point, outside the city, above the Lachine canal. The city must be cleansed; it was cleaned only when the snow was shovelled away, and many of the streets were horribly insanitary. Unfortunately, the Board of Health was "penniless"; it had been given authority but not finance, and having made recommendations was powerless to enforce them.

As fever at Grosse Isle increased an "avalanche of diseased and dying people" was "thrown daily" on the Montreal wharves, the stone wharves of the harbour in the midst of old Montreal, the most beautiful and historic but also the most crowded part of the city. Emigrants were discharged there by the thousand, sick, bewildered and helpless; some, unable to walk, crawled, others lay on the wharves, dying. In the third week in June, Mr. Brown, Secretary of the Montreal Board of Health, accompanied by several doctors, visited the wharves; fever victims were lying in the open, and the "long shed" on the wharf was completely filled with sick. These particular unfortunates were part of a load of 831 persons who had been brought up by the steamer *Queen* from Grosse Isle, and had not been visited by a doctor, either on the steamer or the wharf. Mr. Brown had as many as possible of the sick placed in carts, to be taken to hospital;

two died while being transferred and several others during the night.

The harbour authorities now forbade the landing of emigrants at the stone wharves; but in the bad month of July the steamer *John Munn* landed 400 emigrants, in a sick and dying condition, on the stone wharves. Stringent regulations then compelled all vessels carrying 100 or more emigrants, or with any sick or dead, to land them at the wharf adjoining the outlet of the Lachine canal, beyond the city, on penalty of £500.

⁕

Emigrants were transported by barge up the St. Lawrence into the interior of Canada. Destitute emigrants waiting to leave Montreal were housed in what were known as the Old Immigrant Sheds, which stood near the Wellington Bridge. About 1,500 to 2,000 persons could be housed, and some of the sheds were used as a hospital. Yet these sheds were by no means satisfactory; relic of the cholera epidemic of 1832, they were described as "situated in the heart of Montreal in a foetid bog." Drinking-water had to be carted, and enough to satisfy the burning thirst of the fever patients in the hospital sheds was never brought. The site was too small, there was no room for emigrants to wash and dry their clothes, no space for children to play or for convalescents to obtain fresh air. Above all, the sheds were within Montreal itself, and "troops" of sightseers hung round them. "Between four and five in the afternoon is the favourite hour of promenade," wrote the *Montreal Gazette*. The sick were nursed by the Catholic Order of Grey Nuns, all of whom became ill at some time, and eight of the Catholic priests who ministered to the emigrants died. Deaths of emigrants averaged about thirty a day, and convalescents frequently walked off into the city.

An indignation meeting of Montreal citizens was held in the Bonsecours Market on the evening of July 10 to demand that the "immigrant sheds should be moved to Boucherville Island where the Board of Health and the Emigration Society had found an abundance of excellent water, agreeable shade . . . buildings almost in a state of readiness for occupation and a number of caves." However, a medical commission decided that Boucherville would become another Grosse Isle; it was "hopeless to land the sick where nothing could be got without sending a steamer for it to Montreal." The site finally selected was at Point St. Charles, above the city and above the Lachine canal. It was objected that here the sheds would be a bare mile above the point where pipes for Montreal's drinking-water entered the St. Lawrence, and that the river water would become "poisoned and contaminated" if the refuse of a large body of emigrants and sick persons were thrown into the river. Mr. John Mills, the powerful and popular Mayor of Montreal, pointed out that the "drainings of the whole city of Montreal" were already emptied out into the St. Lawrence, through a creek above the water-pipes, and "with respect to poisoning, the Commissioners have only to relate that the people of Montreal quietly drink the filth produced by fifty thousand of its inhabitants and they do not conceive that the necessary ablutions of, at most, a couple of thousand . . . emigrants would much increase the evil."

Point St. Charles was therefore chosen and the transfer made in the first few days of August. All emigrants were landed at Windmill Point, and the sick taken to hospital at Point St. Charles. For destitute emigrants going further up the St. Lawrence in barges beyond Montreal, open sheds were constructed on the bank with additional sheds for bathing and washing clothes in the river. It was expected that emigrants would be kept waiting for barges at most for "a few hours."

So great, however, was the number of emigrants pouring up from Grosse Isle that the firms responsible for the St. Lawrence barges, far from being able to transport emigrants within a few hours, had not sufficient tonnage to forward them within a few days. The emigrants had no choice but to wait in the sheds if they were destitute, or, if they had a little money, in the low lodging-houses and boarding-houses, where their small assets were soon taken from them. When they did start, the journey entailed greater hardships than the journey from Grosse Isle to Montreal. Space was short, the emigrants were crammed 250 to 300 on each barge, and two or three barges were towed together. The journey to Kingston or Toronto took five or six days, and the summer was hot, the thermometer reaching 96 degrees in Montreal. The state of the emigrants, herded together under the burning sun by day, and in loathsome filth by night, brought protests from the Kingston newspapers—if the emigrants were not sick when they started, they certainly would be by the time they arrived. Apart from sufferings due to heat and exposure, no better circumstances could have been devised for the spread of the typhus-infected louse, and the streets of Kingston and Toronto, like the streets of Quebec and Montreal, became crowded with emaciated, destitute Irish emigrants, many actually in fever; in Toronto on August 16 the hospital, instead of holding about 150, was crammed with 872 patients.

As news of the fever epidemic spread, the Irish emigrant was "dreaded" by the settler; fever might come with him, and even if fit to work he was not hired; in Canada the labourer ate with his employer and his employer's family, and farmers shrank from contact with "cadaverous emaciated emigrants just from hospital or fever sheds."

The new sheds at Point St. Charles were an improvement —deaths were only about twenty-two daily. When Lord Elgin, the Governor-General, visited the sheds, he was "exceedingly pleased with their order and arrangement." They formed "a large square with a court in the centre where the coffins were piled, some empty waiting for the dead, some full awaiting burial." A Montreal citizen describes a visit to the sheds on a Sunday afternoon: he tried the weight of a coffin which appeared to be empty, but on lifting the lid he found a body inside—it was so emaciated that it might have been a skeleton.

Visits of mercy to the sheds cost Montreal valuable citizens. Eight Catholic priests died and the Right Reverend Hudon, Vicar-General to the Catholic Bishop of Montreal, died on about August 14 "from fever caught in the sheds." On about October 5, Dr. Power, Catholic Bishop of Toronto, also died. Finally when the St. Lawrence was closed by ice, the sheds were beginning to empty and winter was at hand, John Mills, Mayor of Montreal, caught fever at the sheds and died on November 12. An attractive, expansive and popular character, John Mills had been born in Massachusetts and made a fortune in the Canadian fur trade. He retained the vigour and geniality of his early days, spoke Canadian-French fluently, and had been Mayor of Montreal since 1845; the "princely hospitality" of his mansion, Beaver Hill Hall, was famous. John Mills regularly visited the sheds, but on the occasion which turned out to be his last and fatal visit his wife had a premonition of disaster, and as he left her she burst into tears.

The Victoria Bridge and the railway sidings now occupy the site of the sheds at Point St. Charles, and at the entrance to the bridge there is a large stone on which is inscribed:

"To
preserve from desecration
the remains of 6,000 immigrants
who died fom ship fever
A.D. 1847-48
this stone
is erected by the workmen
of
Messrs. Peto, Brassey and Betts
employed in the construction
of the
Victoria Bridge
A.D. 1859"

As usual, it is difficult to estimate how many, in fact, died. The figure for the sheds at Point St. Charles given in the official history of the Montreal General Hospital is 3,144, but accurate totals were difficult to obtain. On August 11, 1847, for instance, the *Montreal Gazette* published a letter from one of the medical commissioners stating that 362 emigrants, though interred in the emigrant burial ground, were not included in the burial return from the hospital because they had died outside the sheds.

By September, 1847, the date was not far distant when the St. Lawrence would be closed by ice; the last ships had left Britain in August, and the number of patients in hospital at Grosse Isle had at last begun to decrease. On September 13 the tents were struck, the church and the old passenger sheds, where patients had lain in rows on the floor, were fumigated, and the sick, now numbering about 1,200, sent to the new sheds which had at last been completed at the eastern end of the island. A fortnight later all convalescents were sent up to Point St. Charles. On October 21, when the first snow had already fallen, only sixty patients remained at Grosse Isle, and the authorities announced that the establishment would shortly be "broken up." On October 28, only two patients were left, and on the 30th Grosse Isle closed.

In a wooded hollow, one of the most beautiful of the miniature valleys of Grosse Isle, once the site of the emigrant cemetery, a four-sided monument commemorates those who died. On the first side the inscription runs:

> In this secluded spot lie the mortal remains
> of 5,294 persons, who, flying from pestilence
> and famine in Ireland in the year 1847,
> found in America but a grave.

A second side bears the names of Dr. Benson, of Dublin, and of three other doctors who died while attending the sick; the third, the names of two doctors who died on Grosse Isle during the cholera epidemic of 1832-34; and the fourth records that the monument was erected by Dr. Douglas and eighteen medical assistants who were on duty during the epidemic of 1847.*

Among those who died in Canada, perhaps on Grosse Isle, was the wife of one John Ford, a small farmer from County Cork. John Ford escaped fever and went on, by one of the customary emigrant routes, through the Great Lakes to Detroit, where he carved himself a farm out of the wilderness. He was the grandfather of Henry Ford, inventor and maker of the Ford motor car, and founder of the modern automobile industry.

Those who died at Grosse Isle were, possibly, more fortunate than many who survived. Enfeebled, emaciated, miserably-clad, "like ghosts not like men," the poor Irish emigrants had now to face the harsh, intense cold of the Canadian

---

* There is a second monument at Grosse Isle, a Celtic cross of granite which stands on the summit of Telegraph Hill, 120 feet above the St. Lawrence. The cross rests on a pedestal, on which are three inscriptions, in French, English and Irish.
The first runs:
> 'Sacred to the memory of thousands of Irish immigrants who to preserve the faith suffered hunger and exile in 1847-8, and stricken with fever ended here their sorrowful pilgrimage.'

The second:
> 'Thousands of the children of the Gael were lost on this island while fleeing from foreign tyrannical laws and an artificial famine in the years 1847-8. God bless them. God save Ireland!'

The third inscription states that the monument was erected by the Ancient Order of the Hibernians in America, and was unveiled on the Feast of the Assumption, 1909.

winter. Charity and philanthropy were not lacking, and great efforts were made. Boards of Health were formed, soup kitchens established, almshouses for the destitute prepared; at St. John, New Brunswick, an orphanage was opened, to build up the physique of orphans before attempting to get them adopted; but the fate of many of the "healthy" must have been, after further suffering, to perish. Robert Whyte never met any of the emigrants from his brig again, with the exception of two young men who got employment on the Lachine canal. "The rest," he writes, "wandered over the country, carrying nothing with them but disease and owing to their weak constitutions very few can have lived through the winter."

Over a hundred thousand emigrants left the United Kingdom for British North America in 1847. By the end of that year a modern authority estimates that 20,000 had died in Canada, 5,300 at the lowest estimate on Grosse Isle and 14,706 in Quebec, Montreal, Kingston and Toronto. A further 1,120 died in the province of New Brunswick and 25,000 persons at least had been in Canadian hospitals. Crossing the Atlantic exacted a fearful toll and 17,000 emigrants perished during the voyage, the majority from typhus. "If crosses and tombs could be erected on the water," wrote one of the Commissioners for Emigration in the United States, ". . . the whole route of the emigrant vessels from Europe to America would long since have assumed the appearance of a crowded cemetery."

Chapter XII

No DISASTER comparable to Grosse Isle occurred in the United States as a result of the famine emigration, and the determined measures taken by the United States authorities to prevent their country becoming "a lazar house for the sick and diseased of Europe" were effective.

The Passenger Acts passed by Congress in the spring of 1847 increased the cost of a passage in United States ships, thus discouraging destitute emigrants, and regulations already in existence governing the landing of passengers at the Atlantic ports were stringently enforced. New York and Boston, for instance, had the power to require masters of vessels to give a bond, a financial guarantee that no passenger would become a burden on the community; alternatively, a sum could be put down for each passenger, called a "commutation fee," which released the shipowner from further responsibility. New York, which had adopted commutation, raised the fee to ten dollars for each passenger, while Boston required a bond of $1,000 for each sick, aged, or incapable passenger. Boston also refused to give ships carrying any sick passengers permission even to enter the harbour. The despair of the unfortunate emigrants who, after enduring the hardships of an Atlantic crossing in a crowded sailing-ship, with fever on board, were ordered to put to sea again with their supplies exhausted, broke out in violence. On June 17, 1847, for instance, the British brig, *Seraph*, from Cork, was turned away from Boston; she had 118 cases of fever on board, and her passengers were in such a state of starvation that the British Consul had to go down to her with supplies of food. When *Seraph* was ordered off "to St. John, New Brunswick, or some other British port" the passengers made a rush and tried to "insist on landing," but they were driven back into the ship.

Another ship, the brig *Mary*, also from Cork, was refused permission to land passengers and ordered to go on to the British port of Halifax, in Nova Scotia; the passengers rioted, handspikes were seized, the windlass captured, the captain assaulted and cutlasses drawn before the disturbance was quelled.

Attempts at evading landing regulations were punished by prosecution and fines. For example, the captain of the *Princess Alice* was fined on two occasions—$500 and $271—for landing passengers without paying the commutation fee.

These defensive measures made captains afraid to take "sickly" passengers to United States ports; and the destitute, incapable and fever-stricken were, almost invariably, landed on the shores of British North America. The measures had public opinion behind them, for the citizens of the United States dreaded the effect on the labour market of a great influx of destitute Irish—wages must not be "dragged down to European level." Boston regarded the poor Irish emigrant "with commiseration but also with disgust," and in New

York a newspaper called the *Champion of American Labour* was founded, "to free the American Labouring Classes from the blighting effects of cheap imported labour"—"foreigners will work for what Americans cannot live on."

Dislike of foreign immigration, combined with anti-Catholic and anti-Irish feelings, resulted in riots, especially in Philadelphia and Boston, and in 1844 rioting against Catholics and Irish raged in Philadelphia for three days: many houses and a Catholic church and seminary were burned, 13 persons were killed and 50 wounded; earlier, in Boston, an Ursuline convent and a number of houses had been burned.

The flow of emigrants, "practically all of them Irish," from British North America across the border into the United States provoked angry resentment. United States officials at river and lake ports, and captains of United States ferryboats, turned back poor Irish emigrants; steamboats plying at St. John and on Lake Champlain refused them as passengers, the United States authorities at Ogdensburg "invariably send them back," and the official in charge of the ferry at Lewiston was sent to prison for landing Irish emigrants on the United States' shore. Nevertheless, thousands of poor Irish did cross the border, "notwithstanding the exertions used to prevent their entrance there," wrote Mr. Perley, the emigration officer at St. John, New Brunswick. In his experience half the survivors of the Canadian disaster left Canada and made their way into the United States, and those who went from Canada were able-bodied men who left their wives and young children, their parents and aged relatives behind them, to be maintained by the British Government and the generosity of the inhabitants of British North America. If the men established themselves in the United States, their families joined them; if not, the families remained a permanent charge on British charity.

✑

The poor Irish emigrant was excluded and feared, and by a section of the populace persecuted as well; nevertheless, the generosity and the sympathy of the citizens of the United States for nations in distress was already strong, and when the tragedy taking place in Ireland became known shiploads of food and thousands of dollars began to pour across the Atlantic.

The first organizers of the United States aid for Ireland, on a large scale, were the Quakers, the Society of Friends, and headed by Jacob Harvey, a prominent citizen of New York, an Irishman and a Friend, they became the main channel for the transmission of relief.

Family feeling is stronger in Ireland than anywhere else in Europe, and sending money home was already a characteristic of the Irish emigrant. "I am proud to say," wrote Jacob Harvey, "that the Irish in America have always remitted more money, ten times over, than all the foreigners put together!" He estimated that the total amount sent home by Irish emigrants in America during 1847 amounted to a million dollars, or £200,000 at the then prevailing rate of about five dollars to the pound sterling.

The response of the citizens of the United States to the appeal for starving Ireland was "on a scale unparalleled in history." A great public meeting was held, in Washington, on February 9, 1847, under the chairmanship of the Vice-President of the United States, at which it was recommended that meetings should be held in every city, town and village so that a large national contribution might be raised and "forwarded with all practicable dispatch to the scene of suffering." Meetings all over the country, from Albany to New Orleans, followed; on several occasions Mr. Nicholas Cummins's letter describing the state of Skibbereen was read, and large sums were collected; New York, for instance, sent more than $30,000 and Philadelphia, in spite of the anti-Irish riots of 1844, more than $20,000, with an additional sum of $3,800 which had been raised in 1846. Mayors and Chief Collectors of Customs at the ports of New York, Boston, Philadelphia and Baltimore, with members of the Senate, volunteered to receive local contributions and forward them to Ireland, placing them "in such hands for distribution as they, in their discretion may think advisable." The contributions were entrusted to the Friends, who acted, among other bodies, as agents for money collected for Ireland by Tammany, the central organization of the Democratic Party of the United States. The Catholic churches in New England sent $19,000, and the Catholic church in Brooklyn $13,000. Other contributions included $20,000, sent by Bishop Fitzpatrick of Boston, to Archbishop Crolly of Armagh, on March 1, 1847, and a further $4,000 later; the historian of the Catholic diocese of Boston estimates that a total of $150,000 was subscribed in the diocese for Irish relief.

"Donation parties" for Ireland were held undenominationally; concerts and tea-parties were organized, and young ladies, in select New York boarding-schools, devoted their recreation time to making "useful and beautiful articles," which were sold for Ireland. In Charlestown, South Carolina, the scholars of a "female seminary conducted by Madam du Pree," handed in their pocket-money, amounting to $101.18. "The children of the forest, our red brethren the Choctaw Indians," sent $170, and the Jewish synagogue in New York a "large collection."

A high proportion of contributions was in kind, not in cash, encouraged by an announcement made early in February that the British Government would pay the freight on all donations of food, and that on United States roads and canals no tolls on provisions for Ireland would be charged. In many States, South Carolina for instance, railroads volunteered to carry packages marked "Ireland" free. The amount of freight paid by the British Government on the donations of food consigned to the Society of Friends amounted to the considerable sum of £33,017 5s. 7d. Cities and towns in the United States chartered vessels to go to Ireland. Newark, New Jersey, sent the brig, *Overmann*, at the end of March, to the Committee of the Society of Friends, in Cork, to distribute "without distinction of religious sect or location," and the Irish Relief Committee of Philadelphia sent the barque *John Walsh* to Londonderry, the brig *St. George* to Cork, and the brig *Lydia Ann* to Limerick, to be disposed of at the discretion of the Committee of the Society of Friends. Cincinnati, Ohio, hearing that Miss Maria Edgeworth was engaged on relief work at Edgeworthstown, asked that barrels of corn-meal, to the value of $180, should be delivered to her at Edgeworthstown: "We feel this to be a compliment due to Miss Edgeworth and which we have much pleasure in paying."

In a flood of enthusiasm it was declared that a ship must be loaded for Ireland in every port of the United States, but so many ships were not to be found. Whereas in 1846 the crops had failed in Europe, the harvest in the United States had been exceptionally abundant, and every vessel available was engaged, most profitably, in carrying American food to Europe. "It is heartrending," wrote Jacob Harvey, on February 3, 1847, "to think that whilst our granaries are bursting with food, your poor people are starving . . . Our vessels are not half enough for the wants of the trade. We have a greater surplus of food than can possibly be transported all through the summer." Scarcity of shipping was aggravated by unfavourable weather; ". . . the very winds have been adverse for three months to vessels coming from Europe," he wrote on March 29.

Towards the end of February another crowded meeting was held in Faneuil Hall, Boston, "to consider what Boston should do for Ireland," and an announcement was made that the merchants of Boston had petitioned Congress that, in view of the shortage of shipping, one of the sloops of war now lying in Boston Harbour should be released to sail for Ireland, freighted with provisions. On March 3 Congress granted the *Jamestown,* a sloop of war, lying in Boston Harbour, to Captain Robert Bennet Forbes, a member of one of Boston's best-known families, and the frigate *Macedonian,* lying at Brooklyn, New York, to Commodore George Coleman de Kay, of New York, who had had a distinguished career in the Argentinian Navy.

The plan was to freight the *Jamestown* at Boston, and the *Macedonian* at New York with supplies from the Irish Relief Committees in each city, and as far as the *Jamestown* was concerned the plan proceeded smoothly. By March 27 her cargo was completed, provisions, grain, meal and clothing, to the value of over $40,000, sent by the Irish Relief Society of Boston, and on April 12, after a passage of 15 days 3 hours, she anchored in Cove (Cobh) harbour, to the strains of music, the citizens of Cove having sent out a band. On April 15 Captain Forbes and his officers were given a banquet in Cork, at which anxious inquiries were made about the *Macedonian,* and Captain Forbes promised she would be arriving soon. He was also asked by a gentleman whom he calls Lord . . ., to get him a share of the provisions brought in the *Jamestown;* but, writes Captain Forbes, "as he was building a yacht, I thought I might find a better object with whom to lodge part of my cargo."

On April 21 officers and crew were "at home" on board the *Jamestown* from 12 to 3 p.m. Music was provided, and the refreshments, suitable to an entertainment in a starving country, consisted of best Welsh ship bread, a large piece of ice manufactured from fresh water and kept for the purpose since March 25, lemonade, and a little ginger cake. Several hundred residents attended, and "the ladies danced with the red coats and the blue coats." Next day the *Jamestown* sailed, towed out of harbour by H.M.S. *Zephyr* and cheered by the British marines on Spike Island "in a style never before experienced by me," wrote Captain Forbes. The *Jamestown* anchored off the Navy Yard, Charlestown, Massachusetts, 49 days from the time of leaving, on Sunday, May 16.

The *Macedonian,* however, was still anchored off the Battery, New York, with only 2,500 barrels of meal and flour on board. "As I had said much to the people of Cork as to her coming, I felt much like seeing her go," wrote Captain Forbes.

The *Macedonian* had had an uneasy history. Confusion arose between the present *Macedonian* and her namesake *Macedonian I,* the only British prize-vessel brought into an American port during the war of 1812, when British forces burnt Washington. It was felt that a former British prize-of-war was an improper vessel for charitable relief to a part of the United Kingdom, especially if paid for by British money. Mr. Bancroft, the United States Minister in London, sent assurances that the captain of the *Macedonian* was pledged not to take one penny of British money, but the New York Irish Relief Committee refused to use her and took "other measures to forward their supplies," a course described by the New York *Daily Tribune* as a "most obstinate and unjust stand."

Commodore de Kay then pledged himself to be responsible for all her expenses out of his own pocket, but his career in the Argentinian Navy was frowned on, the New York *Journal of Commerce* declaring that a ship of war, and an ex-commodore who had commanded in foreign service, had "an air not quite in keeping with Republican institutions."

On his return Captain Forbes organized a Macedonian committee; Boston provided 5,000 barrels of Indian corn-meal and the vessel eventually sailed on June 19. On July 28 she arrived at Cove, was met by Father Mathew in the Mayor's barge, and both officers and men were taken for a pleasure-trip in the *Royal Alice* round the famous harbour of Cove; the band of the 1st Royal Dragoons played "Yankee Doodle" as the vessel passed, and a set of quadrilles was got up on deck. A sumptuous dejeuner was also given for the officers in Cork, and the bill of fare makes strange reading, consid-ering that the *Macedonian* was bringing food to a starving country. The dejeuner, which was cold, consisted of turbot, salmon, spiced beef, rump of beef, hares, tongues, pigeon pies, lamb, chicken, duckling, turkeys, lobster salads, veal, haunch of mutton, sponge cakes, jellies, creams, ices, blancmanges, pies, tarts, cheese cakes, tartlets, grapes, apples, plums, cherries, strawberries, champagne, claret, port. Commodore de Kay has not left any comparison between this feast and the barrels of Indian corn-meal he had brought across the Atlantic.

❧

On July 29, 1847, the Treasurer of the New York Irish Relief Committee wrote to the Society of Friends in Dublin, "I think there is now an appearance of an end being brought to this glorious demonstration of a nation's sympathy for poor suffering Ireland." Transport of food across the United States in winter was not possible because the canals, which were then the main arteries of communication, froze; and in the autumn of 1847 the collection of subscriptions for Ireland ceased. Generosity had been astonishing; Cincinnati, for example, had expected to raise $6,000 but had sent $30,000, and New York contributed to the value of more than $200,-000. About £16,000 in cash was forwarded to the Central Relief Committee of the Friends in Dublin, and the food consigned to their committees in Dublin and Cork amounted to all but ten thousand tons. In addition, large quantities of clothing were dispatched, on which no value was put by the donors in the United States. To arrive at any accurate total is impossible; while the Society of Friends formed the main channel, large sums in donations and from collections in Catholic churches were also forwarded to Catholic Bishops in Ireland. A modern United States authority estimates the total value of gifts at $1,000,000, a sum worth many times its value today. This was in addition to money remitted by Irish emigrants themselves.

But while American generosity to Ireland during the famine has, rightly, become a tradition, it should not be overlooked that money was subscribed in England. The British Association for the Relief of Extreme Distress expended about £391,700 in Ireland and the Society of Friends raised £42,906; other societies in England subscribed £70,916. The final total, not including money raised in Ireland, was more than £505,000,

amounting at the rate of exchange at the time to over
$2,500,000.

❧

The magnificent gesture of American generosity to Ireland
came to an end, and the people of the United States were
faced with the appalling quality of the famine emigration. The
poor Irish immigrant had never been welcomed, but because
he was strong and ready to do manual work he had been
important to the development of the country. Thomas
D'Arcy McGee, who had emigrated in 1842 and become
editor of the *Boston Pilot,* reminded the people of the United
States who called the Irish foreigners ". . . that Ireland did
supply the hands which led Lake Erie down to the sea, and
wedded the strong Chesapeake to the gentle Delaware, and
carried the roads of the East out to the farthest outposts of
the West." The canals, the roads, the railways of the United
States, as of Canada, were constructed by Irish labourers;
hard, difficult and dangerous work, dogged by accident and
disease, and rewarded with wages of about a dollar a day.
The Irishman before the potato failed was sturdy; he knew
enough English to pick up directions, and he was sought after
by large-scale employers of labour. Before a large enterprise
began United States contractors were accustomed to adver-
tise in the Dublin, Cork and Belfast papers to tempt men
over; and these labourers became the "shanty Irish," living
in board huts by the side of their work or in shacks thrown
together on the outskirts of towns. But the physical quality
of the famine emigrants made employment in hard manual
labour inconceivable. The thousands who poured over the
Atlantic in 1847 were fugitives, a helpless horde of the kind
which flees from a bombed town, and the authorities never
ceased complaining of the high proportion of old people,
cripples, young children, even idiots and blind.

In the early summer of 1847 Boston was overrun with
destitute, starving, Irish emigrants: ". . . groups of poor
wretches," reported the *Boston Transcript,* "were to be seen
in every part of the city, resting their weary and emaciated
limbs at the corners of the streets and in the doorways of
both private and public houses." Previously, in the nine
years up to 1845, 33,346 emigrants had landed at Boston,
to which must be added another fifty per cent. for those
who came in by land or, illegally, by sea—roughly, an average

of 5,500 a year. In 1847, in a single year, 25,000 emigrants, "three-quarters Irish labourers," landed, and some 12,500 seem to have entered by other methods, making a total for twelve months of something over 37,000 arriving in a city with a population (in 1845) of 114,366. More than 2,500 of the new arrivals were beggars, and they began begging for food as soon as they were on American soil. The Boston authorities were infuriated—Massachusetts, they declared, was being made "the moral cess pool of the civilized world." They were horrified by the hordes of immigrants, by their deplorable physical state and the prevalence of ship fever; and on June 8, 1847, an ordinance passed by the Boston City Council instituted a quarantine station on Deer Island, about eight miles from Boston. All ships were obliged to submit to inspection by the port physician; those with contagious sickness on board were then compelled to proceed to the south side of Deer Island and anchor there for a quarantine of twenty days, while the sick were transferred to hospital sheds and tents. This measure, with the heavy penalties for bringing in fever-stricken passengers, had the desired effect; "sickly" ships avoided Boston, and Deer Island was never overcrowded. The largest total number of emigrants detained was 2,000, in 24 vessels, on July 3, 1847; the largest number of sick in hospital was 790, on July 24; and the largest number of deaths was 19, in the week ending September 19. The number of sick who passed through Deer Island hospital from its opening in June, 1847, until it closed on February 9 of the following year was 2,257, about the same as the number on Grosse Isle for one week. Some cases of typhus occurred in Boston; on July 16 ten cases were reported from Cambridge, all poor Irish immigrants none of whom had been in the country more than five weeks; and later in the year, on October 2, another poor Irish immigrant was found lying dead of typhus in India Street; he had an order to go to Deer Island in his pocket, but had missed the boat. Nothing approaching an epidemic however broke out, and the Boston authorities recorded that the city was saved "from a pestilence fatal to the health and business of the city" by the quarantine station at Deer Island.

The citizens and commerce of Boston were successfully protected, but in 1847 very little was done to assist and protect the newly-landed emigrant, and the first effective emigrant society was not formed until 1850. By a curious piece of reasoning, the Irish starving in Ireland were regarded as unfortunate victims, to be generously helped, while the same Irish, having crossed the Atlantic to starve in Boston, were described as the scourings of Europe and resented as an intolerable burden to the taxpayer.

The Irish had no technical skill to offer; they were not carpenters, butchers, greengrocers, glaziers, masons or tailors; it was not customary for every man to have a trade in Ireland, and the Irishman's agricultural knowledge was apt to be limited to the spade-culture of a patch of potatoes. Once his physical capacity for hard manual work had been lost, as it already had been in the famine—"they are half dead before they start"—the poor Irish emigrant presented a problem which would have been almost insoluble even if strenuous efforts had been made on his behalf. No efforts were made, however, and the poor Irish of the famine emigration were left to assimilate themselves into American life as best they could. The majority drifted into unskilled, irregular, badly-paid work, cleaning of yards and stables, unloading of vehicles and ships, pushing carts, forming a mass of under-paid, casual labour, untaught and ready to be exploited, for whose existence the people of the United States paid dearly in future years.

Low-paid casual labour produced the notorious Irish slum. At this period, sanitary regulations did not for all practical purposes exist, and the speculative builder enjoyed complete licence to convert and erect where and as he chose, not only in the United States but in Canada and Great Britain as well. No laws required specific amounts of light, air and space, drainage was not compulsory, and not a single tap of water need be available to the inhabitants of a tenement house.

Yet the first pioneers in public health were struggling to make themselves heard, and one of the most distinguished was a Bostonian, Lemuel Shattuck, directly descended from William Shattuck, who died in Watertown, Massachusetts, in 1672. Lemuel Shattuck had been in charge of the first census of Boston, in 1845, and he was alarmed at the prospect of large numbers of poor Irish emigrants arriving in Boston and their effect on housing in the city. The emigrant was the prey of the speculative landlord, and unfortunates, of many nationalities, were forced to live in appalling conditions; but no slum was as fearful as the Irish slum, because the degradation endured for generations by the poor in Ireland produced an acceptance of conditions which no other nation would have tolerated. Lemuel Shattuck's alarm was justified, and under pressure from the flood of destitute famine Irish, emigrant housing became a nightmare.

Geographically, at this period, Boston was not suited to receive large numbers of emigrants. To leave the city for the suburbs, it was necessary to cross bridges and pay tolls, which amounted to twenty cents a day; the tolls confined the poor immigrant within the city, and Boston was, in effect, water-locked. The Irish flooded into Ward 8, an area bounded by Hamilton Street, Humphrey Place, Batterymarch, Oliver and Broad Streets, into Washington Square, later renamed Fort Hill, and into the former homes of prosperous Boston merchants on Fort Hill and in the North End. The space was wholly inadequate, and overcrowding on a fantastic scale the result. The gardens and grounds of fine old houses were covered with shacks; backyards and alleyways were built over; rooms were divided and sub-divided; "every vacant spot behind, beside, or even within old houses yielded room for another structure." Before Paul Revere's* house, in Ann Street, was restored, it was so completely encased in tenement structures built on and round it that the house was invisible. When the Committee of Internal Health visited Fort Hill and Broad Street there were up to a hundred inhabitants in each house of three to six storeys: a dollar to a dollar and a half was charged for each room, and failure to pay rent was followed by instant eviction. In Ann, Hamilton and Oliver Streets and the adjoining district "each room from garret to cellar is filled with a family consisting of several persons and sometimes two or more families." These houses, let out by speculators, were "polluted with all manner of bad odours," devoid of cleanliness, privacy or proper ventilation, and inhabited by poor Irish. In August, 1847, in North Square, in one house nine people were living in a single room, in another fifteen persons slept in two attics. Such houses not only swarmed with human beings but "had within them stores, shops and places where fruit, vegetables and refreshments were sold," the "refreshments" usually taking the form of spirits. "Groggeries," or cheap spirit shops, flourished, and

* Paul Revere, the silversmith patriot of Boston, Massachusetts, whose famous ride, during the American War of Independence, is perpetuated in Longfellow's poem. Today his silver is sought by the British with the same zeal but with more success than they sought his person in 1775.

of 1,170 "dram shops" in Boston, which in June, 1847, were open seven days a week, Lemuel Shattuck reports that over seventy per cent. were kept by foreigners, mainly Irish. Disused warehouses, without water or drainage, were hired by speculators and divided up, with flimsy partitions, into compartments, with or without a window, and these were quickly crammed with Irish; rooms in old houses were divided and sub-divided, a space about nine feet by eleven or twelve feet, on an average, being occupied by a family. In the most favourable circumstances water supply in Boston was a difficulty in 1847: a private company supplied water to certain districts from the Jamaica pond to those who paid for it, and the remainder of the city had to depend on wells and the collection of rain-water. For the 1845 census Shattuck collected information on more than ten thousand wells; the water of more than 6,000 of these was not fit to drink. The water supply from Lake Cochituate, "the Cochituate system," did not begin to operate until 1848 and was not fully available until two years later.

A perpetual menace to the health of Boston was the state of Back Bay. The Charles, "a noble river which once flowed round the city," had been dammed up, and its former bed became a "marshy and stagnant pool, increasing ever since by daily accumulation of decaying and offensive animal and vegetable substances." "In fact," wrote a Special Committee of the Board of Aldermen in 1849, "the Back Bay at this hour is nothing less than a great cess pool, into which is daily deposited all the filth of a large and constantly increasing population . . . a greenish scum, many yards wide, stretches along the shores of the basin, while the surface of the water beyond is seen bubbling like a cauldron with the noxious gases that are escaping from the corrupting mass below." A "peculiar smell" of sulphuretted hydrogen emanated from the water of Back Bay, and because the "made land," or land reclaimed under the scheme, was settling, the cellars of houses built in, for instance, South Cove and Harrison Avenue, were flooded with every tide.

Nevertheless, the Irish crowded into cellars. It has been pointed out by Professor Oscar Handlin that without the cellars the Irish population pouring into Boston could not have been housed. Boston cellars were generally entirely below the surface of the ground, without a ray of light or a breath of air, and without drainage or privies. The cellars

of houses built on "made land" were partially flooded with
every tide, while others were flooded from time to time with
two to three feet of water. Yet they sheltered a packed mass
of humanity; one cellar 18 feet square and 5 feet high, was
occupied by eighteen persons; and the normal number of
occupants ranged from five to fifteen. In the cellars, groceries
and vegetables were sold, and "not infrequently a groggery
and dance hall is added"—such places were particularly disreputable and hotbeds of crime.

In 1849 Boston was terrified by an outbreak of cholera;
the first death, on June 3, 1849, was that of an Irishman
living in the notorious Ward 8, at 11 Hamilton Street; the
last, on September 30, was of an Irishwoman living in Wharf
Street, also in Ward 8. As a result the Committee of Internal
Health made an investigation into the sanitary condition of
the Irish quarter of Boston, and were horrified. "During their
visits last summer," they reported, "your Committee were
witnesses of scenes too painful to be forgotten and yet too
disgusting to be related here. It is sufficient to say that this
whole district is a perfect hive of human beings, without
comforts and mostly without common necessaries; in many
cases huddled together like brutes, without regard to age or
sex or sense of decency; grown men and women sleeping
together in the same apartment and sometimes wife and
husband, brothers and sisters, in the same bed. Under such
circumstances self-respect, forethought, all the high and noble
virtues soon die out, and sullen indifference and despair,
or disorder, intemperance and utter degradation reign supreme."

Poor and unfortunate though they were before these people
crossed the Atlantic they had lived in one of the most
beautiful and poetic countries in the world; and to exchange the mountains of Mourne, the majestic sweep of
Galway Bay, the sweet vale of Avoca, for the horrors of an
emigrant slum was in itself a profound psychological shock.
Seldom can high hopes have dissolved into a more terrible
reality. The Irish drowned their despair in spirits, found
compensation for their helplessness in violence and the national weaknesses of drinking and fighting flourished. A return
from the Clerk of the Boston Police Court for 1848 demon-
strates the effect of the recent emigration, three-quarters of it
Irish, on behaviour in the city. During the previous five years
complaints for capital offences had increased 266 per cent.,

attempts to kill 1,700 per cent., assaults on police officers 400 per cent., aggravated assaults committed with knives, dirks, pistols, slingshot, razors, pokers, hot irons, clubs, iron weights, flat irons, bricks and stones, 465 per cent. In addition, 1,500 children between the ages of six to sixteen, 90.3 per cent. foreign, roamed the city, begging and uncontrollable. Mr. Ephraim Peabody, giving the annual address to the Boston Society for the Prevention of Pauperism, at Tremont Temple, declared that the change in Boston was "about equivalent to a social revolution"; emigration had brought violence with it, and "police officers have been knocked down with stones and tied up with handkerchiefs in this once orderly and peaceful city of the Pilgrims."

Very many Irish immigrant girls contrived, however, to preserve the gaiety and chastity which have always characterized Irishwomen, and found a welcome in American homes. The *Boston Pilot* estimated that, by 1850, 2,227 Irish girls were working as domestic servants in Boston, the forerunners of "Bridget," who for nearly a century was the mainstay of innumerable American families.

In the Irish emigrant slum a terrible price was paid by the children. Even before the helpless, half-dead hordes of the famine immigration arrived children were dying in the crowded Irish slums, "with the most terrible mortality the world has ever seen." In his report on the Boston census, Lemuel Shattuck states that among Irish Catholics, between 1841 and 1845, 61.55 per cent. died under the age of five; children in the Irish districts, he wrote, seem "literally born to die," and taking the Irish Catholic population as a whole the average age of persons buried, during the same period, was 13.43 years only.

As a people the Irish have extraordinary powers of survival, they survived the wars of Elizabeth I; they survived extirpation by Cromwell; they survived the fever and the famine, and they survived the mortality of the poor immigrant slum. The birth-rate among the Irish has always been remarkably high: in the Irish quarter of Boston, for example, it was estimated that one birth a year occurred for every 15 persons of population, whereas in England the rate was 1 to 31, in France 1 to 35, and in some non-Irish parts of Boston, 1 to 50. Therefore, in spite of every handicap the Irish population of Boston continued to increase, and eventually the Boston Irish struggled upwards.

∾

The largest number of Irish emigrants to the United States disembarked, and always had disembarked, at New York; half the total of Irish emigration to all ports of the United States, before, during and after the famine, went to New York. Between May 5, 1847, the date when the U.S. Commissioners for Emigration began their records, until the end of the year, a period of just over seven months, 52,946 Irish landed at New York, against a year's total for Boston of 37,000.

New York, however, received no such shock from the Irish famine immigration as Boston. The city was three times the size—the population was 371,223, in 1845—and the immigration into New York in 1847 was not so overwhelmingly Irish.

Between May 5 and December 31 of that year, 53,180 Germans arrived, out of a total of 129,062, of whom the Irish represented less than half.

Moreover, New York was a rougher, tougher, more boisterous town than Boston. In 1847 New York was already a centre of immense wealth, with fine mansions, fine horses and a display of riches; nevertheless, it retained some of the features of a frontier town. Vagrant pigs acted as scavengers, and wandered through the streets at will. They were kept in "hog pens" on vacant lots, usually by Irish owners, and turned loose to forage—there were eight such hog pens on vacant lots on 3rd Street alone. The New York *Sun* declared on August 20 that there were not fewer than ten thousand pigs roaming New York, "dangerous as hyaenas." One pig rushed at a child seated on the steps of her home and snatched a piece of bread from her hand, another charged a "Quaker lady" in the street and knocked her down. On February 4, 1847, an angry citizen complained to the New York *Daily Tribune* of pigs he met "lounging up Broadway." In 1844 the police had been ordered to capture all swine running loose in the New York streets, but their Irish owners resisted so fiercely that the attempt was abandoned, and the pigs continued to "lounge" about New York: "a nuisance," wrote the New York *Sun,* "that can never be got rid of." Other livestock roamed the streets; on January 6 and 7, 1847, the New York *Daily Tribune* advertised for owners of wandering cattle—two fat steers had been picked up and were now in the yard of a house on Mulberry Street; and in the New York

Sun the owner of "a large fat ox, red with a white face," offered five dollars reward for information of its whereabouts —it had last been seen walking up 3rd Avenue. The streets of New York were rough tracks; Broadway was so deeply rutted that on April 12, 1847, "a stage-coach horse slipped into a rut and broke a leg."

New York was not only still primitive, it was in some respects a barbarous and ferocious city. Numbers of stray dogs wandered about the streets, and in hot weather, mad dogs were common. Municipal dog-killers were employed during the summer months to beat out the brains of dogs found without muzzles on the streets, "with an infuriated mob, shrieking, cursing and running behind"; between June 15 and August 25, 1847, 1,510 dogs were clubbed to death. Dogs which slipped out of their homes without a muzzle were chased and killed by gangs of boys, who received fifty cents for every carcass they brought in. The New York *Sun* remarked that the dogs knew the hours when the dog-killers came, and concealed themselves, reappearing later "in droves."

Emigrant and other vessels wishing to enter the port of New York were inspected by the port physician; any passenger or member of the crew found to be sick was sent to hospital at the Quarantine Station, Staten Island, and the vessels detained for thirty days' quarantine as against ten days at Grosse Isle, Quebec. An inquiry into the quarantine station had been held in 1845—the number of emigrants arriving was rapidly increasing—and the arrangements were considered satisfactory. The quarantine buildings at the north-eastern point of Staten Island covered about thirty acres of high ground and consisted of two hospitals accommodating 400 persons with, in addition, a smallpox hospital for 50 cases, a workhouse for the destitute, and auxiliary buildings. The Irish of the famine emigration, however, arrived at New York in the same deplorable state as at Quebec and Boston; scarcely a vessel with Irish emigrants came in without fever; often fifty or more had died on the voyage and more than a hundred sick were sent to the quarantine hospital on landing. Dr. John Griscom, a well-known New York physician and a pioneer in public health, descended from a Quaker family settled in New Jersey since the middle of the seventeenth century, went down into the hold of the *Ceylon*, newly arrived at Staten

Island from Liverpool, and found every horror of the "ocean plague"; scores of "emaciated half-nude figures, many with the petechial eruption still disfiguring their faces, crouching in their berths . . . some were just rising from their berths for the first time since leaving Liverpool having been suffered to lie there all the voyage wallowing in their own filth"; 115 cases of typhus were removed from the *Ceylon*—"The Black Hole of Calcutta was a mercy compared with the holds of such vessels," Dr. Griscom wrote.

William Smith, a power-loom weaver from Manchester and "a thorough republican" disgusted with England, crossed from Liverpool to Staten Island, New York, during the winter of 1847 in the emigrant vessel *India*, and recorded his experiences in a little book entitled *A Voice from the Steerage*. Most of the passengers, he writes, were from the south of Ireland; provisions and water were short and of execrable quality, but the captain, Thompson, was kind. Ship fever appeared before the *India* was a week out and Captain Thompson caught it and died; twenty-six passengers also died, water ran short and the ration was reduced to a pint a day, three of the passengers became lunatics, and one threw himself overboard. Two ships were hailed and implored for a little water; they replied that they had none to spare—ship fever was raging in their own holds. William Smith himself caught fever, and when, after a voyage of more than eight weeks, the *India* arrived at Staten Island, he and 122 others were taken to the hospital. Smith alleges that in the Staten Island hospital the patients were cruelly treated: the beds, grids of iron bars with a little straw laid on the top, inflicted torture on the sick, who were reduced by fever to skin and bone; the doctors were negligent and indifferent, the male nurses took a delight in abusing and thwarting the helpless and struck patients for innocent errors; food was uneatable and conditions horribly insanitary. It was admitted by the authorities that the buildings of the hospital were in "a bad state"—the roofs leaked and the patients' beds were drenched. Nevertheless, William Smith eventually recovered there. Wooden sheds, "shanty hospitals," were put up in 1847 to meet the rush of sick, and the place then held about 1,000 patients. Most fever cases were Irish emigrants from British ships; indeed, a representative of the New York *Tribune* reported that he did not notice one fever patient in the hospital who was not Irish.

As a quarantine station Staten Island had a fatal drawback; it lay only five and a half miles from New York. An unusually beautiful island, covering 57 square miles, well wooded, with rounded hills and gentle valleys, it was early occupied by the Dutch, and many of its buildings date from the seventeenth century. Later, it was used as a summer resort by families from the southern States and New York, and its particular glory is the number of fine Greek Revival mansions, built about 1820-40. For years the only means of communication with New York, apart from private yachts, was a rowing-boat, which crossed with a few passengers twice a day and most of the regular employment on the island was provided by the quarantine station. When winter crossings of the Atlantic were practically unknown and the "emigration season" was confined to spring and summer, workers at the quarantine station during the season gave substantial financial guarantees not to enter New York. But with the rapid growth of the city the inhabitants of Staten Island multiplied; villages and factories sprang up, the staff at the quarantine station itself more than doubled, and the population "was in hundreds where it once was in tens." By 1847 the single rowing-boat had been replaced by a steam ferry, which crossed every hour and was always crowded. Since New York was only 5½ miles away it was impossible to prevent relatives and friends coming to see emigrants in quarantine, "especially the Irish," wrote the committee appointed to report on Staten Island: "Fathers ache to see their wives and families, daughters their parents and brothers, mothers their children." If passengers were forbidden to land at the quarantine station "they went down to New Brighton or Stapleton" (two of the small towns on the coast of Staten Island), "to find every ease of communication." "So great has been the pressure," reported the committee, "that two days in the week have been set apart in which their friends may visit the patients without restraint, and on those days they may be seen by hundreds and thousands, coming and going in the ferry boats, to and from the city to the Island, and the extraordinary spectacle is presented of an unlimited and unrestrained intercourse with an establishment whose great end and aim is to prevent that very intercourse." Entire crews of ships detained in quarantine, bored by restrictions, had been known to take the steam ferry and vanish into New York, while people with money flatly refused to go into quarantine at all; the passengers on the ship *New York,* for instance, "all wealthy persons," would not enter the lighter sent to take them to Staten Island and "escaped in small boats to New York."

The respectable inhabitants of Staten Island, who occupied the seventeenth-century Dutch manors and the Greek Revival mansions, violently objected to the presence of the quarantine establishment and hospital on the island. They complained of the danger of infection, that rubbish of the most disgusting and insanitary nature was thrown from the emigrant vessels and was washed up with the tides, that undesirable persons frequented the quarantine establishment, and that the stench from the Marine Hospital was so powerful that Mr. Robert Hazard had to keep the windows of his house, Nautilus Hall, shut all day when the wind was blowing over the hospital in his direction. Indignation finally came to a head in 1858, when on September 1 the inhabitants of Staten Island rioted and burned down the Marine Hospital.

New York, unlike Boston, did not escape an epidemic. The immense numbers of emigrants arriving, with an unprecedented amount of fever among them, and the fatal proximity of Staten Island to New York, combined to make medical inspection more or less useless. Hundreds of emigrants passed as "healthy" went on to New York and developed fever there; and on May 17, 1847, the Chief of Police announced that "an epidemic of ship fever" had broken out. However, the citizens were assured that there was "no cause for alarm": the epidemic was confined to emigrant hospitals, emigrant boarding-houses, and districts "frequented by that class of person"; unfortunately, later in the year, the disease did spread "among those whose social position was such as to lead to the supposition that they would be exempt." In all, 1,396 deaths from "typhus and typhoid" were reported to the City Inspector in 1847, but the figure is almost certainly an understatement, since though deaths were supposed to be reported to the City Inspector's office no penalty was imposed if they were not. Nevertheless, no epidemic approaching the Canadian disaster occurred.

Fever, however, was only one of the perils which awaited the poor emigrant in New York. He was the predestined victim of swindlers and bullies, and at the port of New York disreputable and fraudulent practices flourished at his expense. "Bonding," for instance, enabled shipowners to evade giving the financial guarantee which by the law of New York must be provided for any emigrant unlikely to be able to earn a living. Professional bondsmen, almost invariably passenger-brokers, gave a bond, promising to assume all future liability for an emigrant, receiving in return a small sum, varying from ten cents to one dollar per passenger, paid to them by the shipowner, in cash. Bondsmen were generally men of low character, "irresponsible from every point of view," and were accepted with the connivance of the city authorities. The shipowner, having received his passage-money, was indifferent to the fate of the immigrant; the broker made a sizeable sum in cash, in which, it was suspected, city officials participated. "The entire business," wrote one of the Emigration Commissioners, "became a private traffic between a set of low and subordinate city officials, on the one hand, and a band of greedy unscrupulous brokers on the other." If the emigrant became destitute, as thousands did, the city authorities disclaimed responsibility and sent him to the broker who had bonded him. As a rule, the broker refused assistance, but if forced to make some provision did so as cheaply as possible. Small brokers made contracts with the cheapest boarding-houses; large brokers maintained "private workhouses," the best known being W. and J. T. Tapscott's "Private Poor-house," at Williamsburg, Long Island. Tapscott's were passenger-brokers on a large scale, bringing over from six to eight thousand emigrants yearly, selling them their passages and bonding them on arrival. Tapscott's were not ashamed of their private poor-house, and when the citizens of Williamsburg wrote that they were uneasy regarding conditions there the firm invited a committee to pay a visit of inspection. On February 3, 1846, a committee of three leading citizens called and reported that "to our utter astonishment, even horror, we found it exhibiting . . . a state of misery and wretchedness not to be borne or countenanced by any civilized community." Among other hideous details, a sick sow was slaughtered in the kitchen for the inmates' meals; the rooms were filthy, the beds full of vermin, and one woman, Fanny Mitchel, was so nearly naked that she was unable to go out and look for employment. The committee took the names of the inmates—all were Irish. Indignant remonstrances were received with astonishment by Mr. Tapscott and his staff, who maintained that their inmates were quite as well off as they deserved to be, and while Mr. Tapscott himself refused even to consider spending a penny more than was necessary on paupers, the visiting physician, Dr. Cooke, assured the committee that the majority of Tapscott's inmates were "as ruddy, able-bodied and healthy looking as any paupers in New York."

"Bonding" was extremely profitable. Eighty thousand dollars were declared to have been received by the passenger-brokers, of which only thirty thousand dollars were spent on assisting destitute emigrants; the rest was profit in that "inhuman trade called the Emigrant Bonding business." Many destitute emigrants had such a horror of private workhouses that, rather than risk confinement in such places, they begged. Old, white-haired women, mothers with children, emaciated men, nearly all Irish, were so frequently to be seen begging that the New York *Tribune* demanded, "Cannot this be stopped?"

Indignation meetings of New York citizens resulted in the appointment of the Board of Emigration Commissioners, on May 5, 1847, "for the aid and protection of emigrants arriving at the Port of New York." The Board was made up of six commissioners; one was Jacob Harvey, of the Society of Friends; others included the Mayors of New York and Brooklyn. A fee of one dollar fifty cents was to be charged for every passenger arriving at New York, and paid over to the Emigration Commissioners, and a bond of $300, not from a professional bondsman but from a responsible citizen, given for each passenger judged likely to become incapable; a surplus from a fund called the Mariners' Fund was also to be placed at the Commissioners' disposal. Out of these funds the Commissioners were to maintain the quarantine establishment and hospital on Staten Island, supply a staff of Emigration Officers, and provide aid for emigrants for five years after their arrival, by indemnifying the State of New York against any expense incurred during that period.

About the same time a Select Committee was appointed to investigate "Frauds upon emigrant passengers arriving in this State." The result took the Committee aback. "Rumours," they wrote, "have fallen vastly short of the reality . . . your Committee must confess that they had no conception, nor would they have believed, the extent to which these frauds and outrages have been practised, until they came to investigate them." Most malpractices centred round villainous touts called "runners." Runners were to be found operating at every port in the United States, in British North America and in

Europe, but it was in New York that their iniquities were at
their worst. Immediately the emigrant reached New York,
even while his ship was still at quarantine, he was accosted by
a runner, speaking in his native language—Irish to the Irish,
German to the Germans, English to the English. Stunned by
the bustle of arrival and, unless he had been met by friends,
frightened and confused, the emigrant listened, and was lost.
The persistency and the boldness of runners were extraordinary; though typhus inspired terror, they went out to
Staten Island and boarded infected ships; when refused admission to the quarantine establishment, they scaled the walls or
rowed from New York in small boats, and there were not
enough police on Staten Island to prevent them.

The runner's first move was to recommend the comfort
and economy of a boarding-house managed by one of his
friends: sixpence only was charged for a good meal, sixpence
for a bed, luggage was stored free. Only too often the
emigrant allowed himself and his luggage to be taken away.

Runners were dangerous men. Thomas Butler Gunn, a contemporary, describes them as "demi-savages of civilization . . .
bigfisted shoulder hitters who pride themselves on travelling
through life on their muscle . . . pimps and caterers for houses
of ill fame, supplying them with victims at so much a head."
They worked in gangs, and each gang had its own bullies;
fights, with bloodshed, were waged for the possession of terrified emigrants, the strongest party carrying off the prey.
Captain Boudinot, Police Captain of the 3rd Ward, in which
the docks were situated, told the Committee that newly-
landed emigrants who refused to fall in with the runners'
suggestions had their luggage seized from them by force,
unless protected by armed police; and at Staten Island an
official confirmed that private persons were powerless to
interfere—armed police were the only solution.

Emigrant boarding-houses were generally kept by men
who had formerly been runners, and they retained one or
more ex-colleagues to bring them victims from the docks. The
Irish emigrant boarding-houses in lower New York, near the
harbour, invariably had an Irish landlord who had become a
United States citizen. A typical landlord was a "thick squat
muscular fellow" with a countenance "equally indicative of
cunning, rapacity and brutality; its general expression being
all the more odious for the mask of blather and blarney. . . ."
The ground floor of his boarding-house was a groggery, selling

the "coarsest and commonest kind of spirit distilled from Indian corn and coloured to represent brandy," and hung, to reassure clients, with cheaply-coloured portraits of O'Connell, Mitchel and Washington and displaying a copy of Robert Emmet's* dying speech. As for the "bedrooms," they were filthy closets into which eight or ten "boarders" were crammed. Once the emigrant was in the clutches of the landlord, there was no escape: baggage was taken away and locked up in a cellar, and an exorbitant sum charged for "storing" it; charges for meals and beds turned out to be three or four times the price quoted. The unlucky emigrant, perhaps from the wilds of Mayo, and helpless in the immensity of a strange city, was bullied, cheated, and sometimes detained by force until all his money had been got out of him, along with his baggage.

Runners also acted as decoys for the sellers of bogus rail and boat tickets, and the Special Committee wrote, "The worst frauds are in the sale of passage tickets." "These tickets," said an Irish journalist, "were of various kinds—tickets sold at exorbitant prices, but good for the journey; tickets which carried the passenger only a portion of his journey, though sold for the entire route; and tickets utterly worthless, issued by companies long-since bankrupt, or by companies which existed only in imagination." The emigrant, illiterate or semi-literate, and in any case a stranger, was handed a ticket "neatly printed" with pictures of a steam-boat, a railroad car and a canal boat. If, as sometimes happened, he was put down three or four hundred miles short of his objective, or when he had completed the first part of his journey—say from New York to Albany, by steamer—the ticket was repudiated and more money demanded if he was to travel on; and most emigrants who had the means paid rather than go back to New York. On the canal boat, instead of the accommodation he had paid for, the emigrant was herded with a crowd of others and told that his ticket was useless because, for instance, it depicted a canal boat drawn by two instead of three horses, and "made to pay again, on the threat of being thrown

* Robert Emmet, Irish Protestant patriot, led an unsuccessful rising in 1803 and was hanged in Thomas Street, Dublin, in the same year, at the age of 25. His speech from the scaffold is a classic of Irish patriotic literature. He was engaged to Sarah Curran, about whom Thomas Moore wrote his famous poem 'She is far from the land where her young hero sleeps'.

overboard by the captain." Inordinate prices were charged for tickets; one "forwarding agent" charged $12 for a $6.50 fare, another, $12 for a $2 fare, and the Special Committee examined an agent who bought tickets at the legal price from the transportation companies and sold them for the highest figure he could get—however, in the course of his evidence he remarked, with pride, that he never "shaved" a lady travelling alone. It was no use being honest in the passage business, the bookkeeper of a forwarding firm told the Committee; all that was wanted was "to get hold of the cattle."

It was easier to disclose frauds and injustices than to prevent them, and the Special Committee investigating frauds was criticized because the abuses they uncovered continued to flourish. The underworld of New York's waterfront, corrupt officials, runners, saloon-keepers, passage-brokers and forwarding agents, was powerful, and frauds were not checked until, in 1855, instead of being landed at different quays in New York harbour, all emigrants were landed at Castle Garden pier, under the eye of the police.

The Commissioners for Emigration were criticized for being extravagant and ineffectual and, unfortunately, gossip connected the names of certain commissioners with the very abuses they were engaged in stamping out. Nevertheless, the Commissioners' achievements were commendable, and so little had been done for poor emigrants in the past that a large expenditure was unavoidable. The destitute did not disappear from the streets, they fled from official assistance, but the less hopelessly submerged were helped; accommodation for convalescents was provided on Ward's, Bedlow's (now Bedloe's) and Blackwell's Islands, the hospital on Staten Island was enlarged, and Fort Lafayette was leased as a fever hospital. Healthy destitute emigrants were boarded in the city almshouses at the expense of the Commissioners for $1.50 a week, and some hundreds were found work on New Jersey farms. Agents were appointed at Albany, where ticket frauds were especially common, and a number of prosecutions were brought against bogus forwarding agents and runners. A start had been made, creditable because the Emigration Commissioners were handicapped by the universal terror of fever; the Special Committee on Frauds wrote that they "showed great energy and perseverance" in carrying through these schemes, "when the fear of the ship fever the emigrants brought with them was so acute." William Smith, the "Voice from the Steerage," was bundled out of his lodgings when it was discovered that he had recently recovered from ship fever—"I never saw persons so scared in my life," he wrote. "They put the bag containing my clothes into the yard among the snow." Later, he was treated with kindness and generosity, settled down in New York, and brought out his wife and children.

There was however one difficulty which no Committee or board of Commissioners could help to solve, the effect of the emigrants on the overcrowding in New York itself.

New York in 1847 was bursting at the seams; tens of thousands of emigrants had poured into the city, and, like Boston, it was confined by its geography, constricted by the limits of Manhattan Island. New York could not spread to East or West; it could extend only North, and at this date it was all but impossible for a working-man to live beyond walking-distance of his work. Public transport was in its infancy, uncertain and expensive, and therefore the new population piled into the streets near the waterfront. A map drawn in 1851 shows a dense population at the south tip of Manhattan, in the Wall Street district, and round the harbour, with a thin scattering in the north; the result was alarming sanitary problems. The neighbourhood of 50th Street had been considered about the limit of the city's expansion; even in the eighteen-fifties maps still divided New York into two sections, above and below 50th Street, and "Potter's Field," the pauper cemetery, had been placed at 4th Avenue and 50th Street in 1825. The neighbourhood became densely populated, and within twenty years the burial ground had to be closed. Still a serious danger to public health remained, bodies were not properly buried, "allowing the most offensive and poisonous exhalations to fill the atmosphere," and in 1849 the coffins were moved, unwillingly, at the rate of 150 a day, by a Mr. Kip, who was nervous of catching cholera. In the following year burials were forbidden to take place south of 86th Street, which was then apparently considered the probable limit of the city's dense population.

What were termed "offensive trades" had been overtaken by the growth of New York; bone-boiling, horse-skinning, slaughter-houses, glue-making, and the manufacture of loco foco, self-igniting matches, originally placed on what were once the outskirts of the city, were now carried on in the midst of a swarming warren of human beings in the 12th and

16th Wards. Hidden away behind the houses, wrote an Inspector, were shanties in which "are boiled up together in large cauldrons the refuse of the streets and markets, the bones and scraps of animal substances found about these places, and every particle of dead and putrefying animal matter that the scavengers of the city collect . . . from these places a most intolerable stench arises . . . so dense and persistent . . that I have been led when ferreting out their secluded abodes for a long distance with no other guide. . . ." In the 16th Ward the disgusting smell was evident "even to those riding through." The business of bone-boiling, however, "is an exceedingly profitable and lucrative one; fortunes have been amassed."

New York had not only outgrown its boundaries but its administration; the system had been designed for a small city, and in the excitement of its expansion the piling-up of vast fortunes, and the growth of fabulous luxury, such considerations as drainage, sewers, housing for poor workers were passed by, and it was not until twenty years after 1847, in 1867, that the first laws relating to the construction of tenement houses were passed.

In 1847 the responsibility for the sanitary condition of the whole of the City of New York was on the shoulders of a single official, the City Inspector. "Ought there not to be in so large and exposed a city some permanent provision by a Board of Medical officers to be in charge of the Sanitary regulations of the city?" asked a Committee of the Senate of the State of New York. ". . . Under the new city charter, the whole subject of Public Health in the City of New York is committed to a department of which the City Inspector is the head, who need not be a doctor. Sources of disease are multiplying and there is urgent need for rigid police." Yet the City Inspector's establishment could hardly be described as a department, since he had, practically speaking, no staff with which to execute his enormous task. "The provisions of the office . . ." the City Inspector complained in January, 1844, "are altogether inadequate to the necessities of the public." He was allowed one hundred dollars a year to hire health wardens, who were unprocurable at the price, and "all duties devolve on the City Inspector with one assistant." Moreover, not only was his staff non-existent but his reports and recommendations were ignored. Again and again the sanitary defects of New York were brought forward in the City Inspector's report—the refuse piled in the streets (a thousand loads of dirt and fi'th were removed from the streets of the 1st Ward alone in 1848), manure heaps round tenement houses, foul smells from o'd cemeteries like Potter's Field, the horrible results of slaughter-houses, bone-boiling and other offensive trades being carried on in crowded districts, the danger to health from vagrant pigs, the want of sewers and drainage. All night-soil, for instance, was allowed to collect in privies and cesspools, then carried through the streets in carts and dumped into the river. Contractors for cleaning the streets heaped up their material on the end of piers and wharves, producing disgusting smells. Yet the City Inspector was unable either to persuade the authorities to construct sewers or, as he begged, to have night-soil and garbage conveyed in scows and discharged into the river at least 300 feet from the wharf or pier.

Presenting his report on March 15, 1847, the City Inspector wrote, "The valuable suggestions offered by my predecessors have met with but little reflection or attention on the part of the corporate authorities . . . whether this report will share the fate of all its predecessors remains to be seen . . . at all events, he [the City Inspector] has the satisfaction of doing his duty."

The familiar history of the emigrant slum repeated itself in New York. Fine old houses near the harbour, the "Knickerbocker" mansions of rich merchants were deserted for "streets beyond the din," and later were taken over and degenerated into filthy tenements, while unsuitable buildings, the school house at the back of Trinity Church, for instance, and an old wooden chapel in Mulberry Street, were seized on and converted into emigrant dwellings.

New York had its own distinctive slums and its own individual features of overcrowding. New buildings of wood, large framehouses of many storeys, known as emigrant "barracks," were run up by speculators and let out, room by room. The construction of these erections was so flimsy that they could not stand alone but leaned together, or on the next house, for support. Philip Hone, a former Mayor of New York, commented in 1848 that two tenement houses in course of erection had just fallen down, "a shameful manner of constructing houses for renting." Wooden barracks were not generally constructed on vacant sites but behind existing buildings. "To reach these tumbling and squalid rookeries," wrote the Committee on Tenant Houses, "the visitor must sometimes penetrate a labyrinth of alleys behind horse stables, blacksmith's forges and inevitably beside cheap groggeries." Any odd corner held a pigsty, rubbish was never collected, piles of "decaying matter" gave off a nauseous smell, and round the buildings were "pools of standing water." A "peculiarly horrible" example, three storeys high, had been built on the top of a stable where the Express Company's horses were kept. The rickety walls were mildewed, portions were breaking off, the building leaked, and in winter the top storey was flooded. All the tenants were Irish. Narrow staircases, steep as a ladder, made emigrant barracks death-traps; at 39 Cherry Street the staircase was hardly twenty inches wide; at 410 Water Street a similar staircase was the sole exit for no fewer than four hundred tenants. In neither case had the staircase any light.

Cellars were eagerly occupied. In 1849, when the first enumeration of "underground dwellings" was taken in New York, 18,456 persons, or four per cent. of the population, were living in cellars. When Dr. John Griscom had made his investigation in 1844 into the sanitary condition of the labour-ing population of New York, he had visited a number of cel-lars. Though his investigation took place three years before the pressure of the famine immigration, conditions were already unbelievably bad. A cellar beneath 50 Pike Street, ten feet square and eleven feet high, with one very small window, was occupied by two families, ten persons in all. Another cellar, visited on the same date, was built against the wall of a churchyard; "Moisture drains in," reported Dr. Griscom, "and the musty smell which exudes from the clothes of the persons inhabiting the cellar is unmistakable." In another cellar below 78 James Street Dr. Griscom found the corpse of a woman who had died of starvation and cold, lying on some wet straw. Her husband and five small children were "moaning" in a corner; there was no furniture of any descrip-tion, not even a chair, no food, and the floor was wet. These people were poor Irish emigrants who had been in New York about three weeks. Beneath No. 17 Baxter Street, 5½ feet below the pavement, the Committee Investigating Ten-ant Houses found two cellars, one a groggery, the other, measuring about 27 feet by 16 feet, a dance hall, with beds for lodgers. In the house above, 75 persons lived in 12 rooms, and the yard was built over with wooden shacks containing an unknown number of occupants, who existed by growing spearmint on the roofs, selling it to bars and hotels.

In these intolerable conditions the vast majority of Irish emigrants settled down, a choice which seems at first glance unbelievable. German emigrants, who arrived in New York in slightly larger numbers than Irish in 1847, "nearly all took passage directly up the river" to Albany, whence they proceeded west. But the Irish remained in the New York slums. "It has been a very strange accident," wrote Thomas D'Arcy McGee, "that a people who in Ireland hungered and thirsted for land, who struggled for conacre and cabin even to the shedding of blood, when they reached the New World, in which a day's wages would have purchased an acre of wild land in fee, wilfully concurred . . . to sink into the condition of a miserable town tenantry, to whose squalor even European sea ports would hardly present a parallel."

The Irish have, in fact, always been a highly social people, gregarious above everything; their virtues are hospitality, good humour and wit. With an immense relish for the company of other people, they depend to an exaggerated extent on human intercourse, especially with other Irish. At home, although their lives were described as being as isolated as the life of any South Sea Islander, the isolation was of small settlements, primitive admittedly but in close proximity to each other. Lord George Hill found his tenants in Donegal unwilling to accept a new and better house if it meant separation from their neighbours. A successful Irish farmer in Missouri who had worked in Ireland for sixpence a day now "rejoiced in land and stock, no rent, light taxes, whiskey without government inspection, free shooting, and, above all, social equality; yet he looked back, regretfully, to the days in Ireland, where, after work, 'I could then go to a fair, a wake or a dance, or I would spend the winter nights in a neighbour's house, cracking the jokes by the turf fire. If I had there but a sore head I would have a neighbour within every hundred yards of me that would run to see me. But here everyone can get so much land, that they calls them neighbours that lives two or three miles off—och the sorra take such neighbours I would say. And then I would sit down and cry and curse him who made me leave home.' "

It is the prevalent idea that an emigrant necessarily possesses some of the qualities of a pioneer, but the famine emigrants were the reverse of pioneers. They had not set out to find wider horizons but had fled from hunger and pestilence.

They were miserably poor, and many were forced to stay where they landed because they had not a penny to go further. Most of them had been, or were at the moment, ill. And though they might be said to have lived by agriculture, since they had tilled their potato patches, they were without knowledge of cultivating other crops and often could not handle any tool but a spade. A group of people can hardly have existed less fitted, physically and mentally, to subdue the wilderness than the Irish of the famine emigration. Only an exceptional few, under ten per cent., it is estimated, became farmers, among them Henry Ford's grandfather, John Ford, who cleared what was then primeval forest near Dearborn, Michigan, and made a farm. "We children," said his granddaughter Margaret Ford Ruddiman, "grew up with those memories of the pioneers in our little settlement as our guide."

The immense majority of the Irish sought employment in towns, and economic conditions throughout United States cities at the time of the famine emigration did not favour the Irish. Immigrants of other nations were pouring in, and employment for the unskilled was difficult to secure. The Irish were advised, warned, implored by newspapers, officials, philanthropists, to leave the cities and go west; but they remained, or if they did leave one city they moved to another, to engage in the lowest type of labour, earn the least wages and live in the worst conditions. Within a short time, almost a few months, the Irish had created a world in New York, and for that matter in every other city in which they settled, that was exclusively Irish. "They love to clan together in some out of the way place," wrote the New York Association for Improving the Condition of the Poor, "are content to live together in filth and disorder with a bare sustenance, provided they can drink and smoke and gossip, and enjoy their balls and wakes and frolics without molestation." The Irish emigrant arriving at New York, or going to cities in the interior of the United States—Albany, Utica, Cincinnati, Louisville—went straight to the Irish quarter, called "Irish town," "Paddy town" or "The Irish Channel," where he associated exclusively with his fellow-countrymen and had no contact with American culture or American ideas. "He is lost in the crowd of his countrymen, who encompass him in such numbers that his glimpses of American manners, morals and religion are few and faint," wrote an American journalist. There was, moreover, a bond which held Irish to Irish which no other nation shared, Irish hatred of England, the burning sense of injustice, resentment, and the feeling of dispossession with which nine out of ten emigrants left their native land. "They feel they have been wronged in their own country," wrote an American observer; "they feel amongst themselves the tie of bearing one common wrong."

It was, however, a hideous world in which the poor Irish immigrant found himself. In suffering and death he paid a terrible price; and the way to forgetfulness was drink. Physical pain, disappointment, bereavement, were dulled with whiskey; birthdays, weddings, christenings, national and political festivals were celebrated with whiskey, until the name of an Irishman and a drunkard became synonymous, and the drunken, fighting, law-breaking Irishman became the Irish image to the citizens of the United States.

How greatly drunkenness held back the rise of the Irish in America can never be estimated, but unhappily it was in the saloon and the bar that the early political role of the Irish in the United States was shaped. United by clannishness, isolated by clannishness from American life, the Irish offered a tool ready to the hand of the political boss, while their long past of subjection, starvation and rebellion had not produced any high degree of political idealism or moral squeamishness. Through the two national passions, for whiskey and political argument, the Irish could be easily swayed, easily inflamed; and once his political boss had arranged naturalization, the vote of the Irishman was as good as the vote of any New England Yankee. So it was, with a glass of free whiskey in his hand, subservient to the orders of a boss, a rioter at elections, a recipient of jobs and favours handed out at political headquarters, that the Irishman first played a part in the government of the United States.

It is a matter of history that the Irish political record has some black spots. Irish emigrants, especially of the famine years, became, with rare exceptions, what their transatlantic environment made them, children of the slums, rebuffed, scorned by respectable citizens and exploited by the less respectable. The Irish were the most unfortunate emigrants and the poorest, they took longest to be accepted, longest to become genuinely assimilated, they waited longest before the opportunities the United States offers were freely available to them.

The story of the Irish in the New World is not a romantic story of liberty and success, but the history of a bitter struggle, as bitter, as painful, though not as long-drawn-out, as the struggle by which the Irish at last won the right to be a nation.

Chapter XIII

IRISH EMIGRATION across the Atlantic has gripped the imagination of the world, but there was another emigration, more numerous though less celebrated, in which the Irish in overwhelming masses crossed the Irish Channel to land at ports in England, Scotland and South Wales. This was the flight of the very poor, those who could not "make out the money" even for a passage to Quebec: a deck passage to England in a steamer could be had for a few shillings. For instance, to go from Drogheda to Liverpool in the well-known steamer *Faugh a Ballagh* cost five shillings; in small sailing-ships engaged in coastal trade the crossing could be made for half a crown, while a large export of coal from Cardiff to Cork enabled vessels to bring passengers back not merely at a very low rate but for nothing at all. Mr. Evan David, chairman of the Board of Guardians of Cardiff Union, stated that a vast influx of Irish from Cork and Waterford were "brought over as ballast without any payment for their passage . . . Captains find it cheaper to ship and unship this living ballast than one of lime or shingle," and until recent years the memory of emaciated, ragged men, women and children, staggering from the holds, more than half dead, lingered in the ports of South Wales. Crossing to Great Britain was a familiar experience for thousands of Irish; they regularly went to work in the harvest, and had done so for centuries; cattle-dealers crossed two or three times a year; labourers, from the beginning of the industrial revolution, had gone over from Ireland in masses, to dig docks and canals, to work on railways and in factories and mills. With luck the sea voyage took only a few hours, and there were regular services of steamers of 300 to 800 tons, daily to Liverpool from Dublin, and weekly, or twice-weekly, to Liverpool from Drogheda, Youghal, Sligo, Cork, Water-

ford and Belfast; from Belfast and Derry there was also a
regular service to Glasgow.

There was an irresistible attraction in England—the starving were given food. Under the English Poor Law, outdoor
relief was permitted in most districts, and the destitute Irish
cottier knew that, once he got himself across the Channel, he
would not be allowed to die of hunger. In addition, from the
end of 1846 the flight of the very poor received an extra impetus from the consequences of a new method of clearing
penniless tenantry from estates.

Landlords were applying not for an eviction order but for
a judgment against the tenant who owed rent; he was put in
prison and his wife and children were left to fend for themselves. The prospect spread terror. Separation is the worst of
evils to an Irish family, and the people did not wait to be
proceeded against; they fled. "An application of this kind is
known throughout a barony as soon as it takes place," wrote
the Head Constable of Liverpool on February 16, 1847, "and
when known the cottier and his family without hesitation put
everything portable on their backs and make their way towards Dublin or some other seaport, determined to reach
England, where they all understand they will not be allowed
to starve. . . ." If they were sent to the workhouse, it was
preferable because the dietary was better. In an English workhouse inmates received certain quantities of sugar, meat, butter and tea, in contrast to stirabout twice a day in an Irish
workhouse, with no "animal food" of any kind. "They have a
great dread of the workhouse in Ireland," stated a relieving
officer in South Wales. The Chief Constable of Liverpool
decided to make inquiries into the flood of poor arriving
from Ireland. He sent over two experienced detective constables who travelled through Kildare, King's County, Westmeath, Roscommon, Galway, Mayo and Sligo. It was better,
wrote the Chief Constable, after receiving their reports, not
to mention names, but certain landlords were pressing very
hard on their tenants, and in one instance notices to appear
in court had been served on 1,400 tenants, of whom 900
fled. "During the progress of the constables . . . they encountered thousands of men, women and children upon the
high roads, moving towards the sea side for the purpose of
embarking for England, most of them begging their way and
all apparently in a state of great destitution." In the west,
at one quarter sessions, held at Ballinrobe, County Mayo,

no fewer than 6,000 applications had been made for judgments for rent, and Jonathan Pim, a secretary of the Relief Committee of the Society of Friends, wrote that a general movement of the people from west to east was in progress; they were leaving their cabins and spreading over the eastern counties, all begging. Their physical condition put work out of the question, nor were they looking towards the future and hoping to establish themselves in Britain; they wanted only one thing—to be fed, and in search of food an army of paupers descended on Britain.

The army entered Britain at three main points, Liverpool, the Clyde, and the ports of South Wales. Glasgow was the town most affected on the Clyde; in South Wales three towns suffered severely, Swansea, Cardiff and Newport (Mon.); but by far the worst shock of the invasion was borne by Liverpool. A seventh of the population of Liverpool was already Irish because, until railways were generally constructed, it was actually easier and cheaper for an Irishman to reach the industrial midlands of England, by crossing to Liverpool, than for an English labourer to make his way there from Devon, Cornwall or Dorset. However, less than fifty years before, Liverpool had still been a comparatively small town, but between 1815 and 1835 enormous growth took place; eight new docks were built, thousands of labourers, very many Irish, were brought in to excavate the sites, and trade expanded with rapidity. But, writes the historian of Liverpool, ". . . the vast commerce which had so suddenly come to the town had not brought civilization in its train. Great wealth had come, but only to the few . . . the great majority of the inhabitants had little share of this golden shower . . . All the new towns of the North which had been created by the industrial revolution were hideous enough, but it is hard to believe that any of them can have been more dreadful than Liverpool."

Liverpool's slums were a byword, produced by the enormously high proportion of casual, unskilled labourers in the working population of Liverpool. The docks employed unskilled labour almost exclusively, and unloading and loading vessels, transference of goods, either to warehouses or to vehicles for transport, involved rushes of heavy work, for long hours, at high pressure, followed by periods of idleness, an existence which proved fatally attractive to the Irish, who disliked routine and, in general, lacked technical skill. Houses

which such casual labourers could afford to rent did not
exist; they were not profitable to build, and the inhabitants of
Liverpool, taking not merely the poor districts but the town as
a whole, were packed together at a density of 100,000 to the
square mile. At one time about 40,000 people lived in cellars,
a notorious feature of Liverpool housing, and half the workers
lived in "courts," houses built face-to-face, sometimes only
nine feet apart, dark, airless, lacking drainage, and evil-
smelling; neither streets nor courts in Liverpool usually boast-
ed drains, and in 1843 not one court had a covered drain to
the street. As usual, the worst housed were the Irish. "It is
they who inhabit the filthiest and worst ventilated courts and
cellars, who congregate the most numerously in dirty lodging
houses, who are least cleanly in their habits and the most
apathetic about everything that concerns them."

During the past few years, however, a remarkable change
had taken place. Housing conditions might be "the worst in
the country," but in public health Liverpool had become the
most progressive town in Britain. This transformation was due
to one man, Dr. William Henry Duncan, M.D., "Duncan of
Liverpool," a correspondent of Lemuel Shattuck of Boston,
Massachusetts. When a fashionable and successful young
Liverpool physician, Dr. Duncan had taken charge of the
South Dispensary, in Upper Parliament Street, a poor district
of Liverpool, and the sufferings he witnessed there decided
him to devote his life to the improvement of public health.
With the support of the Liverpool Town Council he succeeded, before any other city or town of the United Kingdom,
in obtaining the passage of two private Bills through Parliament, the Liverpool Building Act of 1842, which closed the
cellars, and the Liverpool Sanitary Act of 1846, which became
the model for the great British Public Health Act of 1848.
Under the Act of 1846, Dr. Duncan was appointed Medical
Officer of Health for Liverpool, the first time such an office
had ever been created, and through his efforts Liverpool
housing began to improve, sewers and drains were laid down,
no house was built without a privy, nuisances were removed,
and it was made illegal to let any underground cellar for
human habitation.

The arrival in 1847 of tens of thousands of Irish paupers
dealt this work of improvement a shattering blow. The
flood began in December, 1846. ". . .the peasantry are coming
over here by regiments, particularly the women and children

to beg," wrote a Liverpool citizen to Trevelyan, who had a personal connection with Liverpool—his wife's sister had married a Liverpool merchant, Mr. Edward Cropper. ". . . Mr. Rushton, our stipendiary magistrate, who is the milk of human kindness, told me today he was fairly beat. He did not know what to do with the mass of human misery that came before him . . . when returning to my office an Irish steamer having just come in, there was a stream of these poor creatures coming up from the boat to live, if they can, upon English charity. We believe that in some parts of Ireland they are paying their passage over to England to get rid of them, and they will not return at the expense of this parish, preferring to go to gaol, but what is the good of committing them when . . . gaol is a comparative Paradise to them?"

At the end of December, 1846, the Select Vestry of the parish of Liverpool, a body of twenty-eight citizens which in Liverpool performed the functions of a Board of Guardians, sent a petition to Sir George Grey, the Home Secretary. Just a year before, on December 19, 1845, 888 Irish paupers had been given relief in Liverpool, but the figure for December 20, 1846, had swollen to 13,471. The Select Vestry therefore asked that paupers without money or work should be stopped at Irish ports before they embarked, and that Liverpool should be repaid the sums she was being forced to spend on destitute Irish out of the Consolidated Fund. The Home Secretary replied that he had no authority to make any such repayment.

In January, 1847, the numbers of destitute Irish arriving became a deluge. At the census of 1841 the parish of Liverpool had contained about 223,000 inhabitants; in 1847 Dr. Duncan put the population at 250,000, of whom 175,000, a high percentage, belonged to the labouring classes; but during the week ending Saturday, January 23, 1847, 130,795 received relief in Liverpool. Mr. Campbell, Rector of Liverpool and chairman of the Select Vestry, wrote to Sir George Grey, the Home Secretary, that on a single day, Saturday, January 23, 23,866 persons had been given food; 4,483 were men, 4,706 women, and the majority, 14,677 children. This vast crowd was given bread-tickets and "a quart of farinaceous food boiled with pimento and treacle," and the cost to the parish of Liverpool was £378 1s. 10½d. for the week, while during the same week of the previous year only £11 18s. had been spent. The parish of Liverpool, wrote the Rector, was being ruined; there were no funds to meet such a demand; further, the cheap lodging-houses were filled to overflowing, and fever had appeared. From Sir George Grey the Rector received the reply that there was no way of stopping people leaving Ireland who had the fare, just as there were no funds at the disposal of H.M. Government to repay the parish of Liverpool for the expense to which it was subjected. Sir George made no comment on the appearance of fever. Mr. Austin, Assistant Poor Law Commissioner for Liverpool, now wrote, in alarm, to the Poor Law Commissioners. It was quite impossible to house the huge numbers of starving Irish paupers pouring into Liverpool. They had broken into the cellars closed by Dr. Duncan in 1842, and they were again crammed with people—forty persons had been found occupying one cellar. True, a Removal Act existed, under which paupers could be sent back to their parishes in Ireland, but the difficulties of enforcing it were insuperable. A pauper had to appear before two justices for a warrant of removal to be issued; no Irish pauper would appear voluntarily, and the only means of compelling attendance was by a summons. But owing to the multitude of Irish in Liverpool it was impossible to distinguish individuals, and the Act contained no penalties for compelling the attendance of the person summoned. Moreover, in practice it was impossible to keep a large number of persons under a warrant of removal until they could be shipped off. To this letter Mr. Lumley, the secretary of the Poor Law Commissioners, replied that he too considered the Removal Act useless, but made no further suggestion.

On February 1, 1847, Lord Brougham* rose in the House of Lords to present a petition from the Mayor, magistrates and "a number of highly respectable inhabitants" of Liverpool, praying for some relief from the influx of paupers. Thousands of persons at the present moment were begging their way to the seaports of Ireland with the intention of seeking food in Liverpool, and an enormous expense was falling on the Liverpool ratepayers. Three days later he rose again, to tell the

---

* Lord Brougham, Lord Chancellor of England, one of the most powerful orators of his day, was passionately attached to the cause of the abolition of slavery, advocated the improvement of education, the reform of the law, and defended Queen Caroline against the Bill brought against her by George IV for deposition and divorce. In spite of great public services and extraordinary talents, his arrogance, a degree of unreliability and the fact that he was "an indifferent party man," prevented him from achieving the highest honours. He died in 1868.

House that during the past forty-eight hours more than three thousand paupers from every part of Ireland had landed at Liverpool; 240 from Cork, 701 from Sligo, 692 from Drogheda, 272 from Newry, and 911 from Dublin. During the last eleven days no fewer than 198,000 persons had been relieved.

Throughout the spring of 1847 Liverpool continued to petition the Government for assistance, but without success. On March 23 the Liverpool Health of Towns Association urged Sir George Grey to do something immediately "to stop the enormous influx of Irish paupers or there will be a pestilence"; further petitions from the Liverpool Select Vestry were presented by Lord Brougham in the House of Lords, on April 29, and by Mr. Benjamin Hawes in the Commons, on May 7. The Home Office gave the same reply; it was not expedient or possible to prohibit immigration from Ireland, but the attention of Government was being directed to the subject.

On April 3 Dr. Swift, medical officer of the Vauxhall district of Liverpool, sent a desperate appeal to the Home Office. The number of Irish paupers was "baffling all calculation," the poor creatures were crowding into filthy and pestilential dwellings, made worse by the habits of the people; he had visited houses where the floors were covered with bodies, some dead, some dying, and the numbers sleeping in the cellars had now increased, according to Dr. Duncan's calculation, to between 60,000 and 80,000; in addition, "every nook and corner of the already overcrowded lodging houses" was crammed. An epidemic must follow.

Landlords were undoubtedly getting rid of destitute tenants by giving them a few shillings to cross the Irish channel, and priests helped too, out of charity. Mr. Rushton, the Liverpool police magistrate, gave Lord Brougham reports from four police inspectors who had examined Irish destitute landing in Liverpool. Names were given, with statements that sums of from three to five shillings had been handed to them "to carry them over to Liverpool, and that they had received these sums partly from the agents of landlords and partly from the priests." In some cases money intended to buy food for the starving was used to send off the pauper population. For example from Skibbereen, Mr. Hughes, the Commissariat officer, wrote to Routh, on February 12, 1847, that the funds sent for the destitute were being applied by certain persons in Skibbereen "in shipping off the wretched naked creatures to England and Wales," and that the Mayor of Newport (Mon.) had detained a vessel belonging to a Skibbereen grain-merchant because it had been used for landing paupers.

By June 1, 300,000 pauper Irish had landed in Liverpool in five months, descending on a town with a native population of only about 250,000. The town police not being sufficient to control the multitude of the starving, 20,000 citizens were sworn as special constables and 2,000 regular troops brought in and encamped at Everton.

Conditions for poor passengers coming from Ireland were bad; the regulations laid down by the Passenger Act did not apply to vessels crossing the Irish Channel; the decks were dangerously overcrowded; and the wretched deck passengers, herded together, were treated with brutality and contempt. "The pigs are looked after because they have some value but not the emigrants," a witness told the Committee on the Passenger Act. Destitute Irish were landed in Liverpool when they were actually suffering from fever; and by May fever was spreading rapidly.

On the 7th of that month, the Home Secretary informed the House of Commons of the measures the Government proposed to meet a fever epidemic in Liverpool. Two hulks lying in the Mersey, used as quarantine ships for yellow fever and smallpox, were to be converted into hospital ships for Irish immigrants. A Custom House officer would board every vessel carrying passengers from Ireland, and if any fever patients were found a yellow flag would be hoisted; a doctor would then inspect the vessel and fever cases would be transferred to one of the hospital ships. The Mayor of Liverpool, said Sir George Grey, had written that he anticipated the most beneficial results from these precautions. No hope could be held out that any portion of the financial burden imposed on the ratepayers of Liverpool could be removed, but tents for fever patients were to be lent; and without charge on May 14 the Ordnance Board did dispatch a number of tents to Liverpool.

The inspection of vessels proved extremely unpopular; packets were delayed, alarm created, profits reduced. The Mayor of Liverpool begged that inspections should not be carried on in such a way as to cause inconvenience to owners; and Sir Robert Ferguson, Bt., a well-known figure in the shipping industry, declared that the conveyance of Irish destitute was killing the packet trade between Ireland and Liverpool. "Cabin passengers will not go by these steamers crammed with paupers," he wrote to Sir George Grey; "they go Belfast Fleetwood."

Inspection of passengers without quarantine was all but useless. As in Quebec, Montreal and New York, persons were landed at Liverpool who were sickening, they went on into the overcrowded town, fell ill with fever there, and a fever epidemic of enormous proportions broke out. Some 60,000 persons developed typhus, "sometimes called Irish famine fever," and many died; one-seventh of the population of the Vauxhall Ward perished, one-third of the population of Lace Street, ten doctors and ten Catholic priests, and a number of benevolent persons.

Wretched and penniless, the immigrants crept for shelter into condemned and uninhabited houses; Mr. John Johns, of the Liverpool Town Mission, who himself caught typhus and died, found eighteen persons with fever lying on the floor of a condemned and windowless cellar; in an empty house he counted eighty-one persons, in another, sixty-one, lying in corners "in every stage of fever." In these conditions a secondary epidemic of dysentery and diarrhoea developed, no doubt with a proportion of bacillary dysentery. Forty thousand cases were recorded, with 2,589 deaths, and Dr. Duncan "stated distinctly that unless the cellars were cleared and rendered uninhabitable and the influx of destitute Irish checked" no measure could materially diminish the amount of mortality.

Deaths in Liverpool itself, however, were only a part of the damage. Three-quarters of the emigration across the Atlantic sailed from Liverpool, and 95 per cent. of that emigration was Irish, from the low Irish lodging-houses of Liverpool. As no passenger was allowed to board his vessel at Liverpool until it was almost time to sail, because cargo was being stowed up to the last moment, every emigrant who was leaving from Liverpool was compelled to spend at least one night in the town, generally two or three nights. The squalor and filth of the poor Irish lodging-houses were notorious. The emigrant paid about 4d. for what was called a bed, or lay down closely packed with twenty or thirty others in a row on the floor; and thousands who had escaped typhus infection in Ireland were infected in these lodging-houses. Dr. Douglas, the medical officer at Grosse Isle, stated in his report that in his opinion the filthy Liverpool slums, where poor emigrants were forced to lodge before they embarked, were one of the main causes of the ship fever disaster.

But the Government was preparing to take drastic action. A Bill was introduced into Parliament at the end of May and rushed through both Houses, which gave municipal authorities powers to send Irish paupers back to Ireland with the minimum of legal formality and delay. On June 26, five days after it became law, Dublin received a first consignment of two hundred returned paupers. "The Lord Mayor seems puzzled what to do with them," wrote Mr. T. N. Redington, Irish Under-Secretary. Destitute persons actually suffering from fever were returned, and the Mayor of Drogheda complained to the Home Office that the Liverpool authorities had sent five pauper fever cases who were too ill to stand down to the docks in a cart, and forced them on board. The Liverpool authorities disclaimed "having had a hand in this"—they claimed that the five pauper fever cases had come from Wigan. The Lord Mayor of Dublin urged that the same quarantine should be imposed on vessels bringing the destitute back to Ireland as when taking them to England, but this was declared impossible.

The operation of the Act was harsh; the destitute Irish protested they would rather die in Liverpool than be shipped back to Ireland and declared they had no faith in the good intentions of the officials in charge of them. But the measure was successful. In the magistrates' court, orders for summary removal were issued in batches of eighty at a time; as the cellars emptied of population they were filled up with sand, under Dr. Duncan's direction, and a minimum fine of twenty shillings a day imposed on owners for each cellar found occupied. "Early in the autumn the tide of Irish immigration had begun to slacken," wrote Dr. Duncan, "and in November I reported . . . that the inferior lodging houses were not more crowded than in ordinary times." By the end of 1847, as far as Liverpool was concerned, the worst was over.

No other town was struck by such an invasion, but Glasgow, the second point of entry for destitute Irish, repeated events in Liverpool on a smaller scale. In December, 1846, the city became overrun with Irish beggars, ". . . the influx of paupers from the other side of the channel was never so great . . . as it is at present," and statements taken from destitute persons proved they had been sent off by landlords and their agents—"they are coaxed or driven out of the sister kingdom by those who should succour them." Glasgow resorted earlier to deporting the destitute; 130 paupers were sent back to Ireland by the Glasgow and Ardrossan steamers during January, 1847, and nearly four hundred given passages to Ireland by the Glasgow Town's hospital. Nevertheless, in June the streets of Glasgow were "literally swarming" with Irish beggars, and between June 15 and August 17, 26,335 persons, mainly destitute, arrived in Glasgow, many "absolutely without means of procuring lodging even of the meanest description." As in Liverpool, they crept into such shelter as they could find; an old disused barn in the Gorbals was occupied by more than fifty people, and a cellar at No. 95 Bridgegate, measuring ten feet by ten, held eight adults and no fewer than seventeen children. Three times in June the City Parochial Board petitioned that steamers from Ireland should be quarantined, but because quarantine meant a loss to shipowners inspection of passengers on arrival was substituted, with the result that a fever epidemic broke out in Glasgow: 9,290 cases were recorded, of whom 5,316 were Irish. However, a large number in very poor districts undoubtedly remained unknown. The Royal Infirmary put up a fever shed, holding 140 patients, on the green outside the Infirmary, and the Barony Hospital a similar shed for 250.

From Glasgow and the Clyde the destitute Irish took flight into the industrial districts of the Lowlands and Edinburgh. Edinburgh's poorest parts, the Grassmarket, the West Port, the Cowgate, and the Wynds, were crowded with destitute Irish, and by June a fever epidemic had broken out. The Edinburgh Royal Infirmary, which normally held only 300 patients, had 473 fever cases, mainly Irish, on June 10, 1847, and by July 26 there were 608 cases, also mainly Irish; tents were pitched on the green outside the hospital, four buildings requisitioned and an additional fever hospital opened. But by September, in spite of this extra accommodation, it was no longer possible to find beds for fever cases and patients had to be treated "in the crowded warrens that served as homes." The total number of cases and the mortality are not known.

The number of destitute Irish who landed in South Wales, especially at the ports of Swansea, Cardiff and Newport (Mon.), is impossible to estimate with any accuracy. The coast of South Wales abounds in small harbours, then frequented by trading vessels, in addition to the large ports, and Mr. Boase, Poor Law Inspector for Glamorganshire, stated, "Great numbers of Irish landed on the Welsh coast, but the number cannot be ascertained or even guessed." There were those who were brought over as ballast, "huddled like pigs," others were landed secretly on the coast before the vessels reached port and dropped by night, in the mud; many of them were suffering from fever and all of them were exhausted by starvation. At Newport, because there was hostility to captains bringing over destitute Irish, passengers were invariably dropped off before reaching port, and Mr. Evan David, chairman of the Board of Guardians of Cardiff Union, said that the majority of Irish paupers were got rid of somewhere on the coast. They then made their way into the towns, thronging the cheap lodging-houses, "bringing pestilence on their backs, famine in their stomachs." In one instance sixty-one persons, "imported direct" from Skibbereen and Clonakilty, are recorded as having died on landing, from fever and famine. Inevitably, a typhus epidemic broke out in South Wales, but though local tradition in South Wales towns points to houses once used as fever hospitals and describes sudden deaths in streets and on quays, officially the number of victims was not large, and a temporary hospital built in Cardiff admitted only 186 cases. Even allowing for secret landings of unknown numbers, the total of destitute Irish who invaded South Wales cannot compare with the inundation of Liverpool. The number of paupers relieved in Cardiff, the largest port and city in South Wales, in the twelve months from September, 1846, amounted to only 3,555; whereas, in Liverpool on one day on January 23, 1847, nearly 24,000 persons were relieved.

In the spring of 1847 tens of thousands of Irish destitute, carrying fever with them, spread over England, Scotland and Wales, moving on from the ports, afraid of being sent back to Ireland; in Glasgow, for instance, the police rounded up beggars and vagrants daily. Earlier than this the Irish were detested by the British working-man; a large Irish immigration had already taken place, and the part played by the Irish in 19th-century industrial Britain had not been happy. No regulation of wages then existed, trades unions were still struggling to establish themselves; and the Irish were a source of cheap labour. On at least two occasions, at Newton Heath

and Preston, owners of mills brought over bands of immigrants from Ireland for the purpose of strike-breaking.
As a result, it was frequently impossible to get English and
Irish labourers to work together, and economic differences
were further inflamed by religious discords. The inhabitants
of English, Scottish and Welsh industrial towns tended to be
rabidly Protestant, and religious quarrels, even anti-Catholic
riots, occurred. Nevertheless, by 1841 a seventh of the
population of Liverpool and a tenth of the population of
Manchester was Irish. Manchester's experience of the famine
immigration was typical of industrial towns. Manchester already contained a notorious Irish slum, the infamous "little
Ireland," described by Engels in his *Description of the Working Classes in England* (1845) as "the most disgusting spot
of all." The fresh thousands of poor Irish could not be accommodated, whatever the degree of over-crowding. The
Registrar of a Manchester district wrote that starving Irish
were "rambling about the streets in droves," seeking for
shelter. As late as November, 1847, five thousand Irish
paupers were being relieved in a week, and a fever epidemic
broke out which was still raging among the Irish in 1854.
Birmingham was on the verge of an epidemic in May, 1847,
and the number of destitute Irish had resulted in such overcrowding that the Assistant Poor Law Commissioner found
115 women sleeping in three rooms, and three pregnant wom-
en in one bed.

Meanwhile, destitute Irish were streaming into London,
mainly by road from the west. The Secretary of the Mary-
lebone Union, in central London, wrote in February that
applications at the night shelter attached to the workhouse
had increased from 148 to 945; some months later Irish destitute had become a public nuisance. They obstructed the
streets, lay in front of the workhouse gates all day, waiting to
be admitted, and so many had fever that the night shelter
had to be closed. In April the London parishes of St. An-
drew's, Holborn, and St. George the Martyr petitioned
through Lord Brougham, without success, for help from
public funds, to meet the expense of relieving Irish paupers,
who were "being shipped over by persons naturally anxious
to get rid of them." A few weeks later 1,000 Irish paupers
a week were reported to be entering London; in Stepney,
the district lying just east of the City of London, the destitute Irish were proved to have come from Cork, Galway

and Skibbereen; and by the end of May fever had appeared in Stepney and in Poplar, then a riverside parish with fine houses and now a densely populated part of the East End of London.

Chepstow, on the borders of England and Wales, and Cheltenham, a fashionable spa in Gloucestershire, were warned that an "influx" of Irish paupers was advancing on them from South Wales; and Bath reported, as late as November, that the town was "swamped" by new armies of destitute Irish coming in through Bristol and passing on into the West country, where counties in which an Irish beggar had never before been seen were overrun. In December the Clerk to the Guardians of Falmouth, the small port in Cornwall, complained that Irish paupers were being landed with fever actually on them, and the Nottingham Guardians were so much in debt, owing to the cost of relieving Irish paupers at the rate of 337 a week, that they had not been able to pay their last quarter's bills.

Not only were the Irish disliked: any hope that the misery of the destitute might evoke compassion was destroyed by fear of fever. No one dared give poor Irish shelter in barn or stable; the doors of the charitable were closed against them, and the farmer set his dogs on Irish beggars. At York, for instance, when destitute Irish flocked into the city, many with fever, the citizens flatly refused to allow any building to be used as a fever hospital. Just outside the city walls, however, lived the Tukes, members of the Society of Friends; their eldest son, James Hack Tuke, had visited Connaught with William Forster and championed the evicted inhabitants of Erris. Mr. Tuke, senior, was a member of the York Board of Guardians, and considering it his duty to provide some shelter for the unfortunate Irish, he proposed to erect a wooden shed in one of his fields. It comes as a shock to find that the remainder of the field was let to a farmer who sold milk; the farmer objected but after persuasion observed that "the coos would not take the fever," and the shed was duly put up. It was immediately filled with destitute Irish fever patients, who were regularly visited by James Hack Tuke and his father; many died and though Mr. Tuke, senior, escaped, James Hack Tuke caught typhus and his health was permanently damaged as a result.

The tens of thousands of destitute Irish who made their way into the interior of England, Wales and Scotland remained a problem for years. Irish tramps became common in counties where, before 1847, they had been unknown, and fever stayed with them, making them additionally unwelcome. Many, probably the majority, never escaped from destitution; they had no longer the strength to exert themselves, but wandered about the country, existing miserably and precariously on alms and outdoor relief. In June, 1848, the Clerk of the Oxford Union was still complaining to the Poor Law Commissioners of "a huge influx of Irish Paupers."

～

The flood of starving Irish into Britain had important consequences. The realities of the famine in Ireland, emaciated scarecrows, once men and women, skeleton children, dirt, nakedness, fever, and the hideous diseases which hunger brings, appeared on Britain's doorstep; and the British response was one of violent irritation. How had these people been allowed to get into such a state? Why were they invading Britain, bringing fever with them, instead of staying at home? The answer was that Irish landlords were responsible; they had not done their duty, therefore the Irish people were reduced to their present fearful condition, and now these landlords were trying to get rid of the responsibility, by shipping the poor wretches away to Britain.

It was declared in the House of Commons that the "inundation of Irish paupers" had been "cast upon our shores by the desertion of Irish landlords who ought to have maintained them." A Member stated that ten thousand of the inhabitants of Liverpool were at the moment suffering from typhus, brought by the Irish, those "unfortunate and neglected wretches." Members angrily demanded that "the property of Ireland should be made to pay," and declared that "the people of England very generally said that Ireland should be compelled to provide for its own poor."

Admittedly, it was impossible to regard Irish landlords, as a class, with sympathy, but no effort was made to comprehend their dilemma; whatever the wrongs of the past, the majority of Irish landlords were now bankrupt. "Am I to squeeze rent out of the people one day and pay it back in wages the next?" asked Mr. O'Neill, of Bunowen Castle, declaring it was a delusion to think that landlords could possibly raise enough money to save the people, when all they had was unpaid rents. No attention was paid to the many

wretched owners of encumbered estates who, under Irish
law, were burdened with properties hopelessly in debt which
they might not sell. Irish landlords were made the scapegoat,
and when the British Government drafted the new Act,
transferring the cost of relieving the destitute to local rates
and local property owners, they did so in a spirit of reprisal.

Chapter XIV

DURING THIS period, through the spring and early summer
of 1847, as the public works in Ireland began to close down
the state of the people became desperate. "A great deal has
been written and many an account given of the dreadful
sufferings of the poor," wrote Captain Mann, of the Relief
Service, to Trevelyan. "Believe me, my dear Sir, the reality
in most cases far exceeded description. Indeed none can conceive what it was but those who were in it." On March 20
the first reduction of twenty per cent. of those employed on
the works had been carried out, and 140,000 men dismissed;
but almost no disturbance followed. At Dungarvan, County
Waterford, the men turned off, about 2,000, gathered outside
the workhouse with their families and demanded to be taken
in; but troops, the Scots Greys, were ordered out and the
crowd dispersed; at Ballinrobe, County Mayo, "the labourers
retired quietly and in utter despair"; while at Kilnaleck,
County Cavan, all the men on the works were so poor that
dismissals were decided by drawing lots. An eye-witness
reported that "the wretched creatures on whom the lot fell
raised a dreadful cry," but no violence was attempted. "Many
so reduced," reported a Board of Works' engineer, "still
loiter about the works, others linger at home in sullen despair,
and some . . . no longer exist." Richard Griffith, one of the
Commissioners of the Board of Works Relief Department,
told Trevelyan he thought some of those struck off would
have to be taken back, and in a number of districts relief
committees refused to have anything to do with making the
reduction. "Only potatoes with spade work can employ them,"
an inspecting officer wrote of the labourers turned off the

works. In normal times the labourer grew a small quantity
of "green crops," cabbage, peas, beans, with a few turnips
and carrots, on the patch attached to his cabin, but this year
the price of seed was too high. A labourer on the public
works, trying to support a family of six on 10d. a day, was
not likely to buy peas for his garden at 2s. 6d. a stone
or oats at 2s.; and Colonel Jones, travelling about the country,
observed the labourers' patches uncultivated. "Pitiable," he
commented, "and the cost of seed would be trifling—but who
is to give it to them?" Even better-class farmers, especially in
the west, were affected by seed shortage; they ploughed but
had nothing to sow—". . . there is no seed and no one provides it."

The new relief measures outlined by Lord John Russell
on January 25, 1847, included a sum of £50,000 to be spent
in advances to landlords, enabling them to purchase and
distribute seed to their tenants. The scheme was modest;
it was pointed out in the House of Commons that, even supposing the cost could be kept down to the improbable figure
of 2d. an acre, only 125,000 acres could be sown. Nevertheless, seed merchants complained that the Government was
interfering, and Trevelyan, faithful to private enterprise,
felt bound "to give the required assurance" that the "government would no longer disturb the market." The scheme was,
in effect, withdrawn.

A little later the Government was given a striking demonstration of the importance of seed. At the end of May
Routh found that after the Government's withdrawal from
the seed market he had about 40,000 lb. of turnip and green
crop seed left on his hands, and he gave them to the Society
of Friends for distribution. The seed was not sown until well
on in the season, because in many places the land had not
been prepared, and in a few cases the seed arrived too late
for cultivation. However, 39,196 lb. of seed were distributed
to 40,903 destitute smallholders and 9,652 acres were sown,
". . . of which," wrote the Central Committee, "the greater
part, owing to the extreme poverty of the occupiers, would
otherwise have lain waste . . . it is estimated that upwards
of 190,000 tons of turnips were thus raised. . . ." Henceforward the Central Relief Committee of the Society of
Friends considered that distributing seed was the best means of
relief.

Certain landlords made use of the seed shortage to get rid

of their ruined tenantry; they were, Sir John Burgoyne told
Trevelyan, withholding seed from poor tenants "in order to
drive them into greater difficulties" and force them to abandon
their holdings. In Meath, seed was being refused, while in
districts like Skull and Sheepshead, where it seemed inconceivable that the wretched population, spectres too weak to
bury their dead properly, could ever recover and pay rent
again, landlords were refusing seed "because they are afraid
of the difficulty of getting rid of the tenantry next year."

∾

Meanwhile, there was determined opposition to financing the
soup kitchens out of rates, which did not promise well for the
Government's plan of transferring the destitute to the Poor
Law. Ratepayers declared, rightly, that the scheme was the
prelude to a permanent system of outdoor relief, which they
were determined not to accept. In Cavan, the poor rate,
which had originally been 5d., had already increased to
1s. 8d., and ratepayers were "prepared to resist rates to the
point of bloodshed." Though nearly all the ratepayers in
Cavan were Catholic, they were led by a Protestant; "all
differences were forgotten in a determination to escape taxation." Some committees refused to meet at all; others met,
agreed to everything proposed, but did nothing.

On March 23, 1847, three days after the first dismissal
of men from the works, the *Freeman's Journal* declared that
not a single soup kitchen was in operation under the Act.
Nearly a month later, little progress had been made; in
Sligo, one of the most distressed districts, no soup boilers
had arrived; the committees were "getting on very slow indeed," and the state of the country was reported to be "more
frightful than ever." In their official report for May, the
Relief Commissioners admitted that only about half the
electoral divisions, 1,248 out of 2,049, had soup kitchens,
and some districts, Cong, County Mayo, for instance, though
badly distressed, still had no kitchen in June.

On April 10, nevertheless, a circular was issued to all
Board of Works' engineers in charge of works, that on
April 24, 1847, "being more than one month from the period
when the reduction of 20% of the numbers employed was
made you will on that day make a further reduction of 10%,
and on May 1st close the entire of the works in your district,
unless you receive from the Board instructions to the con-

trary." Colonel Jones explained to Trevelyan that the soup
kitchen scheme must be "forced on"; the plan would "never be
brought fairly and fully into operation until we show a determination *coûte que coûte*, to make the new relief scheme the
system." Trevelyan for once was dubious, and he quickly
wrote that the proposals in the circular were "of a very
decided kind," and Lord John Russell wished to have a
report "at the earliest possible opportunity, stating on what
grounds the measure had been adopted, and the means proposed to prevent it falling with unnecessary harshness on any
locality."

Sir John Burgoyne as Chairman of the Relief Commission
then hastened to explain that the circular was merely intended
to give a jolt to the relief committees; something had to be
done to exert pressure "on the listlessness of many committees, some of whom think to *compel* a continuance of
the Public Works by neglecting to prepare under the Act."
In spite of these assurances the only concession was a brief
delay; in some distressed districts, parts of Mayo, Galway,
Tipperary and Roscommon, for instance, only fifty per cent.
of labourers were discharged on May 1, and in a few desperate
cases, one was Upper Fews in reasonably prosperous Co.
Armagh, only twenty-five per cent. Later, however, the blow
fell. By the end of April 209,000 in all had been discharged,
in May a further 106,000, in the first week in June another
318,000 and by June 26, a few days over three months since
the first dismissals on March 20, only 28,000 labourers, instead of 734,000, remained on the works. The 28,000 were
employed not as a measure of relief but to complete works
which, if left unfinished, would be a danger to the public—
they were men chosen by the Board of Works' engineers
"solely for their being able-bodied and skilful."

‌ ‌

The long winter continued into spring; throughout March,
when some amelioration might have been expected, there
were "grating winds, sleet and snow showers, varied by torrents of rain, as raw and inclement as snow." On April 26
The Times Irish correspondent reported "yesterday a hur-
ricane and a storm of frozen hail"; a few days later "a
gale was still blowing and it was piercingly cold." The
hundreds of thousands discharged from the works were penniless; every small possession had long since been sold; except

for private charity, they were bound to starve, and Richard Griffith, who remained dubious about the scheme, wrote to Trevelyan that "a fearful screw had been resorted to." Numbers of landlords were doing everything possible to get rid of destitute tenants, refusing them seed, withholding conacre, and threatening imprisonment when rent was owed. "Oh pity us," runs a scrawl on a rough piece of paper, preserved among the Distress Papers for 1847, "the farmers and land holders of this county will not give a rood or half a rood to the unfortunate poor to put down turnips to keep them alive . . . Oh pity us. Oh what must we do and what will become of us . . . Pity us here scarce half alive."

It is difficult at first to understand why the Irish people, thousands of whom lived near the coast, did not eat fish. They were starving, eating old cabbage leaves, roadside weeds, rotten turnips, while on the coast itself the population lived on dillisk (edible seaweed) and raw limpets. Yet fine fish abounded, especially along the west coast, where distress was most severe. James Hack Tuke, standing on the cliffs of Achill, looked down through the clear Atlantic water and saw "shoals of herring and mackerel in immense quantities," while further out, in the deeper waters, were cod, ling, sole, turbot and haddock. Nevertheless, round him stood starving creatures who made no use of this inexhaustible supply of food.

Fishing was a backward and neglected industry in Ireland. A large part of the Irish coast, in the south-west, west and north-west, is perilous; there are cliffs, rocks, treacherous currents, sudden squalls, and, above all, the Atlantic swell, surging from America across thousands of miles of ocean. By the nineteenth century timber was short in Ireland; in the west, practically speaking, there was none, and fishing-boats were small, the largest being 12 to 15 tons. The national boat of Ireland is the "curragh," a frail craft, often of considerable length, made of wickerwork covered originally with stretched hides and latterly with tarred canvas. The curragh rides easily over the great Atlantic swells, is fast, and with four oarsmen can cover surprising distances. Legend says that Irish adventurers reached Iceland and even America, and today curraghs are commonly used on the west coast, with the addition of an outboard motor.

The curragh was not suitable for the use of nets in deep-sea fishing, and according to an expert writing at the time the fish off the west coast of Ireland lay many miles out at sea in forty fathoms of water. A vessel of at least fifty tons was needed, capable of going out for several days, laden with nets, to face "the frightful swell of the Atlantic." If a gale blew from the east the nearest port of refuge was Halifax, in Nova Scotia. The curraghs and small fishing-boats of the Irish were "powerless in these circumstances"; and an inspector, reporting from Skibbereen, wrote that the failure of Irish fisheries was due to the want of boats suitable for deep-sea fishing, "though this coast and the coast of Kerry abound with the finest fish in the world." Another report commented that the courage and skill of Irish fishermen were remarkable; "the native fishermen" were "out in their frail curraghs whenever an opportunity offers, and in weather when nobody else could think of venturing themselves in such a craft." But the heavy swell off the west and south-west made deep-sea fishing in curraghs impossible. "The poor cottier had a miserable curragh, fished for his family or neighbours and got paid in potatoes."

On Achill, for instance, the fishing "fleet" consisted of four curraghs and one fishing-boat. While James Hack Tuke was in the district a fishing-smack from Scotland fished twenty-five miles off Achill and sold the fish in Westport. In 1847 there were no railways in the west of Ireland and no means of refrigeration; even if great quantities of fish had been caught they could not have been sold. In Galway, when the catch was plentiful, the market was piled with unwanted fish, tons lay everywhere, producing "the most disgusting effluvia."

The finest fishing-ground in Mayo was off Porturlin, a small fishing village in Erris, ". . . to which," wrote Richard Webb, a representative of the Central Relief Committee of the Society of Friends, "the only access by land is over a high and boggy mountain, so wet and swampy that it is difficult to reach it even in summer. It is probable that there is not in Ireland a cluster of human habitations so completely secluded from easy access." Fine cod and ling abounded off Porturlin, but at the time of the year when the fish were most abundant the weather was uncertain and dangerous. Mornings were fine, but the sky then overclouded, a wind sprang up and blew with violence, and certain destruction awaited the curraghs. This "tremendous coast," as Richard Webb called it, is lined with cliffs up to five hundred feet in height; for ten miles the small coves of Porturlin and Portacloy are the only shelter, and it is difficult to enter them in an Atlantic swell.

The most famous fishing-ground in Ireland was Galway Bay, but the fishing of Galway Bay was considered to be their exclusive property by a curious community of fishermen who lived in a settlement called the Claddagh. The settlement of the Claddagh (the beach) dates from an early period, when the "tribes" of Galway, still proud of their descent today, refused to mix with the neighbouring population; the houses were low and thatched with walls of great thickness, and many of the Claddagh people lived in black beehive huts which only recently disappeared. They had their own dialect and their own mayor, a "king" whose laws were implicitly obeyed. Strangers, "transplanters," were not allowed to live in the settlement, and a ring of thick gold, the "Claddagh" ring, was handed down from mother to daughter. These people, fascinating to the archaeologist and anthropologist, were from a practical point of view difficult to deal with. The Society of Friends was asked by the Government to help the Claddagh fishermen, but their representative, William Todhunter, found them exasperating. They are, he wrote, "next to incorrigible," and "some of their laws should be broken through. They will only go out at certain days and times, and if other boats go out the crews would be beaten and the nets destroyed." Some days before he arrived the Claddagh men went out and caught a large catch of fine herrings; they then refused to go out again for several nights, nor would they allow anyone else to go out. Todhunter considered that a naval sloop should be stationed in Galway Bay to protect other fishermen from the Claddagh men. Their carelessness was maddening. It was "really awful," he wrote, "to observe the waste of their property from want of attention and care . . . one sixth the number of boats properly equipped and manned would take a much greater amount of fish . . . Nothing could be more vexatious than to see many boats ruined merely from the circumstances of allowing the large stones to drop from the quays and the boats to rest on them as the tide ebbed."

When the potato failed, fishermen all over Ireland pawned or sold their gear to buy meal. At the Claddagh on January 9, 1847, "all the boats were drawn up to the quay wall, stripped to the bare poles, not a sign of tackle or sail remaining . . . not a fish was to be had in the town, not a boat was at sea." On Achill James Hack Tuke wrote that the waters could not be fished because nets and tackle had been pawned or sold, "to buy a little meal"; the Vicar of Ring, in County Waterford, appealed for help because the Ring fishermen had sold or pledged their fishing-gear to obtain food; and similar reports came in from Belmullet, Killibegs, Kilmoe, the harbours of Clare, and indeed, every fishing port along the coast.

Short-sighted and rash as this proceeding appears, there was a rational explanation. The primitive boats and curraghs in which the Irish fished, combined with the hazards of the "tremendous coast," made regular fishing difficult; the Irish fisherman could never go out in bad weather, and was often kept on shore for weeks at a time. He then depended for food on his potatoes—though the seas might be teeming with fish, they were inaccessible to him. Irish fishermen were reproached for going on the public works instead of going out to fish, but as Mr. Hennell, Fishery Inspector for Donegal, explained, the exceptionally severe winter of 1846–47 made fishing impossible; the Killibegs men (Killibegs was the principal fishing port of Donegal) had not been out for weeks— how were they to live? "Fishermen are on the Public Works and fear to leave them until they can be sure that the weather will allow them to fish continuously."

Some efforts were made by the British Government to assist Irish fisheries, and when the potato failed, Mr. Mulvany, a Board of Works' Commissioner and an Irishman, was appointed Commissioner for the Fishery department; he urged that £100,000 should be spent at once on the construction and improvement of harbours, quays and boatslips, and an additional £10,000 a year set aside for repairs, "to make up for past neglect." He was not successful; under Lord John Russell's relief scheme of January, 1847, only £5,000 a year was to be spent. Mulvany also suggested, without success, that Irish fishermen should be allowed small loans, direct from Government, to finance the improvement of their boats and tackle. Trevelyan characteristically feared that this would be damaging to the fishermen's morale; ". . . experience has proved," he wrote, "that the fishermen are induced by it to rely upon others, instead of themselves, and that they acquire habits of chicanery and bad faith in their prolonged struggle to avoid payment of the loan." The British Association then

offered £500 for loans to fishermen, but this, too, was refused. Next, the Society of Friends proposed to make small
loans to poor fishermen for repairs and replacements of boats
and tackle at the recommendation and under the supervision
of the coastguard. The scheme was rejected by the Treasury,
but the Society of Friends, through local committees, gave
substantial help to a number of fishing communities. In Arklow, for instance, the Vicar estimated that 161 families were
kept alive through the winter of 1847 because the Friends
had lent them money to redeem their boats and nets; the
Ring fishermen were restored to a condition of being able
to support themselves without seeking Poor Law relief, and
the Claddagh men, in addition to being lent money, were
provisioned so that they could remain at sea for several days
and given warm clothing.

Fishing stations were established by the Society of Friends
at Ballinakill Bay, near Clifden in Galway, Achill Sound in
Mayo, and Belmullet in Erris, where a fleet made up of ten
curraghs and other boats fully equipped with nets, lines and
all gear was provided at a cost of £300. At Castletown Berehaven, in west Cork, a fish-curing establishment was set up,
as well as a fishing station, and a trawler, *Erne,* hired for six
months, at £45 a month, to accompany rowing-boats and curraghs to the fishing-grounds. In addition, six fish-curing stations were established by the British Government, at which
fish was purchased at a fair price, and experienced fish-curers
were brought from Scotland to teach their trade.

Unhappily, these measures did not succeed. The difficulties
which had prevented a fishing industry from developing in
Ireland remained: the poverty of the country, the want of
proper boats, the remoteness from a market, the dangers of
the "tremendous coast" in the west. In many places trawling
was declared to be impossible, owing to the rocky and foul
nature of the sea bottom; in others—Castletown Berehaven
was one—for part of the season the fishermen had to row
twenty-five miles to the fishing-grounds; the weather was unreliable, and small boats, curraghs especially, laden with their
catch were difficult to bring in when a squall blew up. Fish-
curing stations could not operate economically when the supply of fish was not regular, nor did it prove easy to dispose
of the finished product; a number of stations had cured fish
left on their hands.

After about two years' operation the fishing stations in

Mayo and Galway were closed, and in April, 1852, Castletown Berehaven as well.

∾€

Meanwhile, Indian corn continued to pour across the ocean,
and prices slumped. By the end of March, 1847, the price
of corn, which had been £19 a ton in February on the Liverpool Exchange, had fallen to £13, and at the end of August
was £7 10s. On March 26 Mr. Nicholas Cummins reported
from Cork, ". . . the continuance each day of food cargoes
here . . . I cannot estimate the fleet this day in our harbours
at less than 250 sail, or the contents at much less than
50,000 tons."

Indian corn was now cheap and plentiful, but the labourers
who were being turned off the public works by tens of thousands weekly no longer had the few pence required to buy,
and though the price of food fell, and fell again, the Irish
people continued to starve.

Lower food prices meant, however, that less money was
needed to establish a soup kitchen, and with added pressure
from the Government's "forcing-on" measures, soup kitchens
became fairly generally established throughout the country.
Indeed, the fall in prices saved so much money that the
temporary relief scheme, the Soup Kitchen Act, ultimately
cost about a million pounds less than had been estimated.

But the food distributed through the kitchens was severely
restricted, both in quality and quantity. The Government
decided that relief given under the Soup Kitchen Act was
to be restricted to cooked food only: "Undressed (raw) meal,"
Trevelyan wrote, "might be converted into cash . . . and
even the most destitute often disposed of it for tea, tobacco
and spirits." Each ration was to consist of one pound of
biscuit, meal or flour, or one quart of soup, thickened with
meal, and four ounces of bread or biscuit. When the ration
was of bread only, 1½ lb. was given. These quantities, stated
Trevelyan, had been "declared by the best medical authorities
to be sufficient to maintain health and strength." Further,
"it was found by experience that the best form in which
cooked food could be given was 'stirabout,' made of Indian
meal and rice steamed, which was sufficiently solid to be
carried away by the recipients. The pound ration thus prepared swelled with the addition of water to three or four
pounds." Each ration had to be collected by the recipient in

person, with the exception of the sick and the infirm and children under nine years of age, who received half a ration; children over nine received the full ration of one pound.

The term "soup" became elastic. On April 8 Mr. Stanley, secretary to Sir John Burgoyne's Relief Commission, circularized the inspecting officer of each Poor Law Union with a definition of what was officially understood by soup. "As the term 'soup' in the instructions seems to have created an impression with many parties that only the liquid ordinarily so called is meant, and that meat must necessarily form an ingredient . . . the Relief Commissioners beg that the general term 'soup' in the instructions may be understood to include any food cooked in a boiler and distributed in a liquid state, thick or thin, and whether composed of fish, vegetables, grain, or meal." Doubt was expressed that "soup" contained enough nourishment, and Mr. Erichsen, the Government agent in the grain market, wrote to Trevelyan that he was uneasy about the effect on the people's health of such a diet. True, in English workhouses the inmates did not always get meat, but were given cheese and pease instead, and though before the famine the Irish labourer had lived all but exclusively on potatoes, he usually drank a certain quantity of butter-milk. The complaint from all sides was that the ration of one pound of meal, biscuit or flour was not enough, even if three or four times that weight in water might be absorbed. Sir Lucius O'Brien, of Dromoland, declared that the people were "only just kept alive" on a pound of meal a day; from Skibbereen a doctor wrote that all the soup kitchens did was to prevent people actually dying of starvation; and in Kinsale the Superior of the Carmelite Convent complained that the starving were being given "soup" made with only ten ounces of meal and rice to a quart of water, and that the four-ounce slice of bread which went with it was very small because the bread was made with one-third Indian meal, which weighed heavy; the Protestant Rector of Killymaule wrote that on soup-kitchen rations his people were starving. All complaints received the same official reply, signed by Mr. T. N. Redington, the Under-Secretary: the ration issued had been approved by the Board of Health.

The method of distribution was detested by the people. Each person was required to bring a bowl or pot and stand in a line until his turn came to have soup or stirabout ladled into it; this outraged Irish pride. The poor inhabitants of

Newmarket on Fergus, County Clare, sent a petition declaring that distribution of food by such a method "debases and demoralizes," and that they could not endure being the bearers of pots and pans. In Ennistymon, when the people were instructed to attend bringing cans, they said they had none. The Inspecting Officer, Captain Gordon, then gave tin cans, free, to four of the poorest men, but only two would use them; the two others refused, though they were in a state of starvation—"such," observed Captain Gordon, "was their pride." In Sligo the people were reported to be "too proud to fetch soup," though they would go any distance for meal; in Tipperary, at Templetouhy, a crowd gathered outside the kitchen, shouted they would not have soup, and "ill treated a female who had been engaged to attend to the soup kitchen"; and at Miltown Malbay a crowd rushed the kitchen and demolished the boiler.

Resistance was in vain; the choice was the soup kitchen or death from starvation, and as the works closed down the number of rations collected soared. 2,253,505 rations were fetched on May 23, 2,689,956 on June 6, and, finally, in July, when 1,826 electoral divisions out of a total of 2,049 were operating the scheme, the number rose to 3,020,712. Trevelyan grew lyrical. "The famine was stayed," he wrote. ". . . Organized armies, amounting altogether to some hundreds of thousands, had been rationed before; but neither ancient nor modern history can furnish a parallel to the fact that upwards of three millions of persons were fed every day in the neighbourhood of their own homes, by administrative arrangements emanating from and controlled by one central office."

In spite of this administrative triumph, however, Sir John Burgoyne was uneasy. He did not agree that the famine had been "stayed" or that the problem before the Government was a problem of famine at all. He knew Ireland well, for he had been chairman of the Irish Board of Works for fourteen years, and he told Trevelyan that the millions of starving who had been saved by the distribution of rations under the Soup Kitchen Act were not all victims of the potato failure; ". . . the enormous amount of destitution that will appear on our accounts," he wrote, "is by no means to be deemed as *all* arising from the potato crisis—had such a measure as this (the Soup Kitchen Act) . . . been adopted *in the best of times* of my recollection of Ireland in the past sixteen years, the numbers that then existed on charity, or on the verge of pauperism, would have afforded heavy lists of families to be supported."

The Poor Inquiry Commission had estimated that approaching two and a half million persons in Ireland starved, more or less, every year; now the administration of the Soup Kitchen Act, under which more than three million rations had been collected daily, showed that since the failure of the potato, and in spite of fever and emigration, the number of starving had increased by more than half a million. These three million persons were "a dead unproductive weight." What was to be done with them, what could be done with them?

In spite of this the British Government considered that their responsibility towards starving Ireland was almost at an end. The Irish Poor Law Extension Bill, legalizing outdoor relief and transferring the destitute to the Irish Poor Law and the Irish poor rates, was now before Parliament; as soon as it passed the problem of Irish destitution would be Ireland's responsibility and the property of Ireland would maintain the poverty of Ireland. Before the famine, the Government's economic experts had declared that outdoor relief was impossible in Ireland; it would "swamp the property of the country" and amount to "entire confiscation," and only a few weeks ago the opposition to the Soup Kitchen Act had demonstrated the enormous difficulties of raising rates in Ireland. Now the country was still in the grip of a major famine, last year's rents had not been paid, great stretches of land lay waste, hundreds of thousands were fleeing from the country, a fearful fever epidemic was raging. Nevertheless, the Irish Poor Law Extension Bill passed the Commons on April 16, the Lords on May 18, receiving the Royal Assent and thus becoming law, on June 8.

The debates on the Bill make curious reading. Very little was said with regard to the wretched, destitute millions of Ireland and their fate; Parliament was obsessed by a rage against Irish landlords and a determination to punish them; Irish landlords were "very much like slave holders with white slaves," "they had done nothing but sit down and howl for English money," they had "so mischievously employed the great powers entrusted to them by law as to have worked themselves to the brink of ruin and the whole people to the brink of starvation"—". . . the landlords of Ireland had not

done their duty . . . England was doing everything. . . ."
Absentee landlords were cited who had never given one
shilling for relief, but "regularly as the 2nd November or the
2nd May came, they sent their agents down for their rent."
Lord John Russell himself felt "bound to state" that, taken
as a whole, the Irish landlords had not done their duty. "I
must say that though great numbers of the resident gentry
have done their utmost, have exerted their best energies and
been contented in some instances to forgo their usual mode
of living . . . yet I do not think that, taken as a whole—as a
body residents and absentees . . . the exertions of property
for relief of distress have been what they ought to have
been . . . Sir, I will not go further into this part of the
subject. I felt bound to state what I have stated, for I felt
it pressing on my mind. . . ."

In vain Lord Mountcashel reminded the House of Lords
that out of an annual rental of thirteen million pounds it
was estimated that Irish landlords paid away nearly ten and
a half million pounds in mortgages and "borrowed money,"
so that the sum actually at their disposal was something less
than three million pounds. Rates were now to be imposed
of at least fourteen million pounds; how could such a sum
be paid?

Parliament refused to listen and ". . . amidst the cry of
famine and death from Ireland, clamour out of doors in
England, and excitement, impatience and noise in the House,"
the Irish Poor Law Extension Bill was passed.

❦

Few classes of men have had so much abuse heaped on them
as Irish landlords, and with justification. It must be remembered, however, that there were many exceptions. For in
Stillorgan Park, County Dublin, an obelisk of green marble
bears the inscription "1847: To Arthur Lee Guinness, Esq.,
Stillorgan Park. To mark the veneration of his faithful labourers who in a period of dire distress were protected by his
generous liberality from the prevailing destitution. This humble testimonial is respectfully dedicated consisting of home
materials. Its colour serves to remind that the memory of
benefits will ever remain green in Irish hearts."

Mr. Arthur Lee Guinness was a member of the famous
family of brewers, bankers and patrons of the arts, whose
history is entwined with the economy of Ireland.

No complaints came from the tenants of the Duke of
Leinster, head of the FitzGerald family, the Geraldines, who
came to Ireland in the twelfth century and became *ipsis
hibernis hiberniores*. Sidney Herbert, the statesman whose
name will always be associated with the work of Florence
Nightingale, obtained Parliamentary powers which enabled
him to grant leases and improve roads, dwellings and buildings on his Dublin estate; in thirty years the rent roll nearly
doubled. A diary kept by Lord Stopford, later the 5th Earl
of Courtown, of County Wexford, gives a picture of what
was done by a responsible landlord. Lord Stopford's father,
the 4th Earl, had built Courtown Harbour in the 1820s to
develop the local fishing industry; the large sums it cost had
an adverse effect on the family finances, but unfortunately
it was not a success, owing to silting. In 1847 Lord Courtown
had a new pier built and a fish-curing establishment set up.
He contributed £1,500 to the Gorey Relief Committee, and
in addition to employing about 100 persons on his estate
gave work to numbers of the Gorey and Riverchapel poor
during the winter of 1846–47, raised two sums of £8,000
and £6,000 for drainage and finally employed every labourer
on his property. Both he and Lord Stopford were active on
relief committees, Boards of Guardians, fever committees
and the magistrates' bench, attending meetings almost daily,
sometimes twice daily, and working in discouraging circumstances. Again and again Lord Stopford and his father found
themselves the only committee members who had troubled
to be present; at the Petty Sessions at Enniscorthy on November 12, 1847, only one other magistrate turned up; at the
Ballycanew Relief Committee meeting on November 2, no
one but Lord Stopford attended, and he had to come home;
meanwhile the relief committee documents were so badly
written that he was forced to copy them out himself.

At Castle Leslie, in Monaghan, the Leslies fed their own
tenants and distributed stirabout and turnips from a huge
cauldron in the courtyard to all who chose to come; at
Carrowmore, in County Mayo, Colonel Vaughan Jackson
broke up his establishment, sold his carriage horses and devoted himself to the destitute. But though few resident landlords did not exert themselves in relief, there was little feeling
of identification with the people. The Irish people starved
and died in one world, the Irish landowning classes inhabited
another. Landlords felt their responsibility was limited, and

when as many tenants as possible had been employed, relief committees supported, and a percentage of rents forgiven, they considered they had done all that could be expected.

During the terrible winter of 1846–47, Richard Monckton Milnes, another friend of Florence Nightingale, came to Ireland to visit famine areas as an eye-witness, and stayed at several country houses. Life went on as usual; at Headfort, seat of the Marquess of Headfort, in County Meath, there was a party and charades in the evening; the Lord-Lieutenant, Lord Bessborough, was a resident landlord noted for generosity, but at Bessborough, his house in Kilkenny, the guests hunted all day and at night got up tableaux vivants and acted a play by Sheridan, for which Monckton Milnes wrote a prologue.

The Dublin season, noted for its gaiety, was as lively as ever in the grim spring of 1847, when fever was raging: labourers were being discharged from the public works in tens of thousands and the desperate flight of the people from Ireland had begun. The Lord-Lieutenant of Ireland, as the Queen's deputy, maintained a court with semi-royal pomp at Dublin Castle, and State functions, levees, drawing-rooms and balls were numerous in 1847; Lord Bessborough, who was not in good health, complained to Lord John Russell that it was the "balls and drawing rooms" which "knocked him up," not the responsibilities of his position.

Lord Bessborough's complaint was unfortunately more serious than an overdose of vice-regal festivities; in the middle of the season he collapsed with an illness, diagnosed as "dropsy of the chest," and on May 16, 1847, he died. ". . . No man ever quitted the world more surrounded by sympathy, approbation and respect than he did," wrote Greville; ". . . he was surrounded by a numerous family, and the people of Dublin universally testified their regard for him and their grief at losing him."

Dublin society, however, regarded the Lord-Lieutenant's illness as a tiresome interruption. "It was sad to hear the ladies wishing him dead that the gaieties might recommence, and the younger A.D.C.s fearing not to be 'clear' in time for the Derby," wrote Mr. Warburton, of Armagh Castle, to Richard Monckton Milnes.

On May 15, 1847, the day before Lord Bessborough's death, Daniel O'Connell, the liberator, died at Genoa, a broken and broken-hearted man, with his life's work in ruins

round him. The cause of Repeal was all but dead, moral force
and constitutional methods had failed, and Ireland herself
lay prostrate, devastated by famine and fever, dependent
on England for her existence, and at England's mercy as
never before. Three months earlier, during the debate on
the Soup Kitchen Act, O'Connell had made a last appearance
in the House of Commons. The once-splendid physical presence had gone, and with it the magnificent voice; he spoke
with difficulty, and his words were audible only to those
nearest him; "Ireland is in your hands, in your power," he
whispered. "If you do not save her, she cannot save herself.
I solemnly call on you to recollect that I predict with the
sincerest conviction that a quarter of her population will
perish unless you come to her relief." The dying Liberator,
broken in health and spirits, was listened to "in almost
reverential silence . . . rancour and party spirit were forgotten
at the spectacle of so great sorrow." Disraeli, however, who
was present, saw only "a feeble old man muttering before a
table," and O'Connell's last appeal for Ireland had no result.

It was now necessary to appoint a successor to Lord
Bessborough, and Lord John Russell offered the Lord-Lieutenancy to George William Frederick Villiers, fourth Earl of
Clarendon. He was universally agreed to be the best man
for the post, and O'Connell, with whom he had been on
good terms, had regarded him as a desirable Lord-Lieutenant.
He was noted for charm and tact, his manners were dignified,
he was industrious, and both a liberal and an aristocrat.
Charles Villiers, champion of cheaper food for the people,
was his brother, and his favourite sister, "my dear dearest
Theresa," had married George Cornewall Lewis, who was
consulted by the Government on Ireland and had written
a book, *On Local Disturbances in Ireland,* pointing out that
Irish disturbances and outrages invariably originated in dis-
putes relating to the occupation of land.

Lord Clarendon was not elated by the appointment and
considered that he was offered the Lord-Lieutenancy abruptly and discourteously. "J.R. [John Russell] sent for me yesterday afternoon and proposed to me to go to Ireland,"
Clarendon wrote, "but it was done in his most cold, short,
abrupt, indifferent manner. Much as if he was disposing of a
tide waiter's place to an applicant" (a tide waiter was a
subordinate customs officer). Clarendon accepted, but without much hope of success in what he called "the terrible

task imposed on me." "I go to Ireland," he wrote, on June 29, "without making myself the smallest illusion as to the more than probability of failure that awaits me . . . almost impossible to do good when all machinery for the purpose is absolutely wanting. Moreover I fear that the distress next autumn and winter will be greater than the last. . . ."

In Ireland, as the summer of 1847 progressed, with magnificent weather, the crops described as "all superb," it was officially considered that the famine must be at an end. In spite of early alarms no blight appeared, though people were quickly agitated, and "inconsiderable traces of disease" which would have "passed unnoticed but for bygone seasons," caused alarm, while "flies and bugs which for centuries lived and died unobserved . . . are now watched with exaggerated fears." But the acreage of potatoes planted, owing to the shortage of seed potatoes, was miserably small; estimates sent in to Dublin Castle by relief officials never exceeded one-fifth of the usual acreage, and in many districts amounted only to one-eighth; and in Dr. Lindley's opinion potato plantings were "insignificant." Though the crop seemed likely to be exceptionally abundant, the reduced acreage of potatoes was not enough to feed the people, and the small farmer dared not eat his grain crops. "The face of the country is covered with ripe corn while the people dread starvation," wrote Mr. Hewetson, senior Commissariat officer in charge at Limerick, to Trevelyan, on September 4, 1847. "The grain will go out of the country, sold to pay rent"; and when Trevelyan wrote that he heard the crops were "magnificent" he was warned "nothing can take the place of potatoes."

Glorious weather, superb crops and cheap food could not help the penniless unemployed masses. In a letter forwarded to Trevelyan, Colonel Vaughan Jackson wrote, "The weather has been lovely . . . the crops are famous . . . food has fallen to one third of what the price was last winter . . . but how are the mass of the people in the country to be supplied and employed?" Captain Pole, an officer who had served in the Commissariat since the first failure, warned Trevelyan that there was still no employment in Ireland. "The price of food is of no consequence to him who has no chance of earning wages . . . though 1847 is a wonderful contrast to 1846, granaries bursting, every outhouse bursting with food, yet because the wages of the Board of Works have ceased the people cannot buy."

Nevertheless, the British Government would not modify their plan. The destitute had been transferred to the Poor Law when the Irish Poor Law Extension Act became law, and relief under the Soup Kitchen Act must end. In a Treasury minute the date was fixed on or about August 15, 1847. "In 1846 the Relief operations were finally closed on the 15th August, with reference to the harvest time of that year, and My Lords think that the period of the cessation of the system in 1847 should be determined by a similar consideration . . . The distressed state of some of the unions in the western parts of Ireland may render some parts of those districts an exception to any rule, but my Lords are of opinion that issues under the 10th Vic. c.7 [the Soup Kitchen Act] should, at any rate, not be continued beyond the end of the month of August."

Trevelyan was anxious to be rid of Irish relief. In his opinion too much had been done for the people, and as a result of this treatment "the people under it had grown worse instead of better, and we must now try what independent exertion will do." Writing to Sir John Burgoyne he admitted that gloomy reports of the state of the country were reaching him, but "whatever the difficulties and dangers may be . . . I am convinced that nothing but local self government and self support . . . hold out any hope of improvement for Ireland." He told Routh, firmly, "This year . . . it will be a real and final close to our commissariat operation and we must dispose of everything to the last pound of meal." Depots in the west were already being closed; Westport had been given up and the lease handed back a few days after the Poor Law Extension Bill passed the Commons, and "outposts" like Clare Island were closed down as they became exhausted. Meal and grain in store was sold, not cheaply, but at current market prices, and remainders were not given away but picked up by Government steamer.

The extreme distress, especially in the west and south-west, made some delay in closing the soup kitchens unavoidable; ". . . remonstrances," wrote Lord John Russell, "were loud and general." On August 15 issues were stopped in 55 unions out of 130; in 26 unions they continued until September 12, and in 49 until October 1, an extra period of about six weeks.

Trevelyan considered the stoppage of rations to have been

accomplished smoothly, successfully and painlessly. Three million persons had been on the Government's hands and had been disposed of without an outbreak of violence. "The multitude," he wrote, "was again gradually and peacefully thrown on its own resources at the season of harvest, when new and abundant supplies of food became available, and the demand for labour was at its highest amount."

Commissariat operations were wound up; ". . . ship off all, close your depot and come away" was the order sent to outlying stations on August 9, and by the second week in August closing was complete. Trevelyan considered his task was finished. "This year is not merely a cessation but a transfer," he wrote to Sir John Burgoyne, ". . . the responsibilities and duties which we lay down have been imposed by the Legislature on the Poor Law Commissioners and the Boards of Guardians."

Trevelyan decided that he might now properly relax, "after two years of such continuous hard work as I have never had in my life"; and he went with his family for a fortnight's holiday to France, travelling through the valleys of the Seine and the Loire and visiting Tours.

Chapter XV

THE FAMINE had brought about a change in the attitude of the British Government towards Ireland. It was impossible any longer to deny that something was dangerously wrong with the state of Ireland, and while there was little to choose between the rebellious people and the irresponsible extravagant landlords—as Lord John Russell remarked, "a plague on both your houses"—England, for her own safety, could not abandon Ireland entirely. Therefore, though direct responsibility for Irish relief was to cease, Lord John wished to lay a "ground work" for "permanent improvement," and on July 17 he wrote, "What we must chiefly look for is advance of money for good profitable works, be they drainage, harbours, railroads, reclamation of waste lands, or what not. In short we must give very little for relief and much for permanent

improvement—that is my programme for next year." The
Government had about a million pounds in hand already
earmarked for Ireland—it had been saved on the Soup Kitch-
en Act, owing to the spectacular fall in food prices—and
it was proposed to devote this million to works of permanent
improvement.

A substantial financial concession was also given to Irish
property-owners when, on July 8, Charles Wood, the Chancellor of the Exchequer, announced that half the money advanced by the British Government to finance public-works
and the soup kitchens would be forgiven, a sum of £4,500,-

∽✲

000. It seemed that a ray of hope for Ireland was becoming
visible, especially as, during the summer of 1847, the position
of Lord John Russell's Government was strengthened by
victory in a general election. But with the ill-luck which
dogged Ireland, at this moment Great Britain was overtaken
by a serious financial crisis, one of the most serious the
country had ever experienced, and the Treasury found itself
dangerously short of money.

During 1846, when famine conditions prevailed not only
in Ireland but throughout western Europe, and wheat prices
rocketed, there was widespread speculation in grain. But by
the summer of 1847 cargoes were pouring in, the magnificent
harvest of 1847 was beginning to show itself, the potato crop
was promising, and the market broke. During May sales of
wheat were made in Mark Lane at 115s. a quarter; by
mid-September the average was 49s. 6d.

Even wilder speculation had been taking place in railways;
"railway mania" rivalled the South Sea Bubble, reckless and
fraudulent proposals were numerous, dubious concerns failed,
and gamblers in railway shares were ruined. The financial
market was already in a state of near-panic when the Bank
of England was forced to refuse further credit, owing to the
straitjacket imposed on its note issue by the Bank Charter
Act of 1844. The financial crisis of 1847 and the relative
importance of the part played in the crisis by the Bank Charter Act have been the subject of debate among political com-
mentators and economists ever since but, roughly, the Bank
Charter Act sought to regulate and strengthen the credit
structure by tying any increase in the note issue to the gold
held by the Bank of England in its Issue Department. In

1847 foreign speculation had increased the need to send gold abroad, and when grain prices and railway shares collapsed a financial crisis occurred. To stem the panic, it was desirable for the Bank to lend freely, possibly at a higher rate of interest, but this could not be done because the drain of gold was reducing the backing required for notes; moreover loans from the Bank would inevitably mean that more notes would be required, and the Bank feared a shortage. Between August 28 and October 30, 1847, notes with the public went up by 2½ million pounds. The Bank therefore refused to lend freely, the crisis was aggravated, and "a great panic in the money market" followed. Early in August failures began in the corn trade. They spread to other branches of commerce, and by the end of September they involved, among first-class firms alone, losses of nine to ten million pounds. In October eleven banks broke and the state of the City of London was described by Lord John Russell as "disastrous." In the House of Commons it was stated that during the course of the panic 117 firms failed.

Eventually, in Lord John Russell's words, "a temporary departure from the Law" had to be sanctioned. In the third week in October a deputation of leading bankers, headed by Mr. Glyn, interviewed Lord John. "Very alarming representations" were made, and the Chancellor of the Exchequer undertook to indemnify the Bank if they issued notes in excess of the statutory limit. Immediately the news was known the pressure eased.

But though the crisis was ended immense damage had been done. Prices of stocks and commodities had collapsed, and in a "week of terror" everything that had to be realized was sold at a loss. Trade remained calamitous, and the falling off in the revenue continued. The Treasury had good reason for anxiety, and it was anxiety which destroyed hope for Ireland.

"The falling off in the Revenue," wrote Lord John on September 10, "still above one million sterling in two months, damages all my views of being able to help Ireland out of the savings of the loan. . . ." Once again urgent domestic affairs in Great Britain pushed Ireland into the background. "I have been so worried about the state of trade in the city," Lord John told Clarendon, "that I have little time to write or think on other matters," and he warned him, "I fear you have a most troublesome winter ahead of you . . . and here we have no money."

Charles Wood, the Chancellor of the Exchequer, flatly refused financial help for Ireland. "I have no money," he told Clarendon. He would refrain from pressing Ireland for repayments due on money already advanced, as he had forgiven £4,500,000 owing for the public works and the soup kitchens, but no fresh money would be forthcoming. "The more bent I am on throwing present expenditure on them, the more lenient I am disposed to be as to what is expended already," he wrote. "I have the most perfect understanding on this subject with Trevelyan. . . ." A few days later he told Clarendon again, "You must not expect that any money will be forthcoming, there will be no money." All hope of using the million pounds must be given up; the only funds available for Ireland would be for works which country gentlemen undertook for themselves under the Land Improvement Act, a recent measure enabling proprietors, under certain conditions, to borrow money at 3½ per cent. for improving their estates. "You cannot have what I have not got," wrote Charles Wood on September 11.

He disliked and distrusted the Irish, wrote angrily of "the safe and comfortable existence our rations have afforded them," and declared, "they have hardly been decent while they have had their bellies full of our corn and their pockets of our money." Sunday, October 17, was set aside as a day of thanksgiving for the magnificent harvest of 1847; and a letter from the Queen, appealing for the destitute Irish, was to be read aloud in every church and a collection made for Ireland. Charles Wood told Clarendon that Delane, editor of *The Times,* had received sixty-two letters by one post from clergymen who objected to making the collection; several had refused to collect at all, and his own preacher in Whitehall "took the opportunity of pointing out the ingratitude of the Irish."

Meanwhile, administrative arrangements in Dublin for putting the new Irish Poor Law Extension Act into effect were not making progress. Up to the present the Irish Poor Law had been administered from Whitehall, but in August a separate Irish Poor Law Board was established in Dublin, consisting of the Chief Secretary for Ireland, the Under-Secretary, and the Poor Law Commissioner, already resident in Dublin, Mr. Twisleton, who was to draw up the administrative scheme.

Mr. Twisleton was a man of considerable experience who had been in Ireland since the first failure of the potato in 1845 and, wrote Lord John Russell, ". . . an abler man and one as well acquainted with Poor Law principles cannot be found," though according to Clarendon he had "some defects, chiefly of manner," and the *Dublin Evening Mail* called him "little Mr. Twisleton, the cockney Poor Law King." Whatever his qualities, the task before him was almost impossibly difficult. Help had been expected from the Treasury, but owing to the financial crisis it was not forthcoming, the country was ruined, hunger and fever were on all sides, the existing Poor Law organization was ineffectual; and Mr. Twisleton failed to produce a plan. On September 10, Lord John Russell rather severely expressed his surprise that no scheme had been sent to the Treasury. No time must be lost, since October 1 had been fixed as the date for the last distribution of rations in any union through the Soup Kitchens.

As a consequence of Twisleton's failure, Trevelyan took charge. "A plan must be made," Trevelyan told Lord John; "if there is more delay it will be impossible to act on any plan." He drafted the scheme himself, though it was, he wrote, "also the opinion of the Chancellor of the Exchequer," and it was under Trevelyan's plan that the new Irish Poor Law Extension Act was put into effect. The scheme drew "the broadest and most impassable line between those unions which, with exertion, could support their own poor and those which never could." Twenty-two unions in the west and south-west were officially listed as "distressed," and these alone were to receive assistance out of "national funds." It was vital to make relief to able-bodied men as unattractive and as difficult to obtain as possible, since there was grave danger that the scheme would be overwhelmed by the number of applicants. Therefore the able-bodied were to obtain relief only within the workhouse. The workhouses were to be emptied of the aged and the infirm, of widows and children, who were to be given outdoor relief in cooked food only. The able-bodied must come inside.

Emptying the workhouses of their present inmates and replacing them with able-bodied men who were destitute was the basic requirement of Trevelyan's scheme, but it proved difficult or impossible to carry out and produced much suffering. Relieving officers, officials new to Ireland, were to investigate all applications, and in the twenty-two unions which might receive "extraordinary assistance" temporary Poor Law inspectors would be appointed to exercise "special and powerful controls." An experienced financial secretary was to supervise the accounts.

In a private letter Trevelyan told Lord Clarendon, "the plan resolved on . . . contemplates *as a last resort,* in order to keep the people from starving, that recourse should be had to the Consolidated Fund; it was therefore necessary that a thoroughly competent financial secretary should be appointed to look after Treasury interests from the first." The Consolidated Fund is the product of various taxes and other branches of the revenue of Great Britain out of which charges, not dependent upon annual vote in Parliament, are paid.

The Commissariat was to return and organize a supply of food in districts remote from markets, while some of the best Commissariat officers, Captain Pole, for instance, who had served at Banagher, became temporary Poor Law inspectors. "This plan," Trevelyan wrote, "affords every scope for the activities of the British Relief Association, the Central Relief Association, and the Relief Committee of the Society of Friends."

Thus Trevelyan was back in control of relief under the new Irish Poor Law Extension Act as he had been in control under previous relief Acts, and the contemplated transfer of relief duties to the Poor Law Commissioners, owing to what Lord John Russell termed "the inefficient state of the Irish Poor Law Board," proved impossible. Copies of all Irish Poor Law correspondence were sent to Trevelyan; in addition, almost daily reports, private as well as official, came in from Commissariat officers in Ireland, as well as from the newly-appointed temporary Poor Law inspectors, many of whom had been writing confidentially to him since 1845. Thus his authority was as great as ever.

~

In the first week of October, 1847, Trevelyan went for a few days to Dublin to confer with Sir John Burgoyne, to "overhaul" the Board of Works, whose accounts were in confusion, and to "come to a full understanding with Twisleton." It was his first visit to Ireland since the famine began, and while he was in Dublin he committed a characteristic indiscretion. Sir John Burgoyne had prepared a letter to *The*

Times explaining the reasons for the continued destitution of Ireland and the need for more assistance. The letter appeared in the newspaper on October 12, accompanied by one from Trevelyan written from the Salt-hill Hotel, near Dublin, which gave details of the Government's new Poor Law plans and drew attention to Trevelyan's standing. He spoke with authority, "having, as you are probably aware, made this subject my principal study for some time past, and being constantly in the habit of receiving information, both written and oral, from all parts of Ireland in reference to it." These statements, published over the signatures of highly-placed Government officials—Trevelyan himself was Assistant Secretary to the Treasury—caused considerable comment, and Clarendon, who disliked Trevelyan and had not been consulted or informed, wrote to Lord John Russell on October 13 that he was "surprised and annoyed to read in *The Times* 2 letters, signed by Trevelyan and Burgoyne about the distress and the necessity for relieving it. Very true but . . . these official statements will increase my difficulty in resisting applications for relief." To Charles Wood, Clarendon used stronger language, sending newspaper cuttings "as a small proof of the enormous scrape which the letters of Trevelyan and Burgoyne have got us into . . . There never was such an invention as a Secretary of the Treasury coming over here and writing a State paper to *The Times* from his hotel without any communication with the Government here or with his own official superiors." Charles Wood, however, merely answered that Trevelyan was "occasionally a little indiscreet, given to writing and publishing what he ought not."

In Ireland Trevelyan's Poor Law scheme was received with misgiving, and in a private letter to Lord Monteagle, Richard Griffith wrote, "I very much fear the new Relief system will not be nearly so effective as it is expected to be by the Treasury, all here are downcast about its working." The Society of Friends who, according to Trevelyan, were to have "every scope for their activities," refused to work through the Poor Law. The Friends had an intimate knowledge of the west and south, and they did not think the Poor Law was capable of relieving the masses of starving in the remote parts of Ireland, where no workhouse existed for thirty or forty miles.

The British Relief Association, on the other hand, sought Trevelyan's advice and agreed to dispose of the balance of their funds by selecting, through the Poor Law Commissioners, "a certain number of Unions in which there is reason to believe that the ratepayers will not be able to meet their liabilities and to appropriate from time to time sums for assisting in giving outdoor relief." In August, the Committee "found itself with a clear cash balance of £160,000," which turned out to be the principal support of the distressed unions.

From this point onwards good intentions on the part of the British Government become increasingly difficult to discern. Making every allowance for the depleted state of the Treasury, and bearing in mind the large sums already expended on Irish relief, sums representing many times their value today, it is still hardly possible to explain, or to condone, the British Government's determination to throw the Irish destitute on the local Poor rate.

Apart from the state of Ireland, the immense size of Irish unions put the establishment of an efficient system of relief, through the workhouses and the Poor Law, out of the question. Of 130 Irish unions, 107 contained 100,000 acres, and of these 25 were over 200,000 acres. No Board of Guardians could conceivably relieve the destitute efficiently and economically in a union of hundreds of thousands of acres. Further, the very large unions were in the distressed districts of Connaught and Munster and contained immense areas of wild, backward, neglected country, without resident landlord or gentry, swarming with "squatters," miserable wretches living in sod or furze huts and bogholes, penniless and starving. An example of such a union was Ballina, in County Mayo.

The Union of Ballina covered 509,154 acres and harboured a population of 120,797 persons. "Let us suppose," wrote James Hack Tuke, "a union stretching from London to Buckingham and Oxford, in one direction, and from London to Basingstoke in another, with a poorhouse at St. Albans, and we shall have a good idea of the extent of the Ballina Union." Ballina, moreover, included Erris, a vast tract of desolate country where distress "wore its most appalling form."

In Erris today there are people who have never seen a train; in 1847 there were many who had never seen a living tree larger than a shrub. Richard Webb, a representative of the Central Relief Committee of the Society of Friends, was told by the innkeeper at Achill Sound, in Erris, that when

his daughter, aged eight, first went out of Erris to Westport
she was frightened of the trees, fearing they would fall on
her as they waved over her head.

In 1847 the population of Erris was estimated at 30,000,
and before the failure of the potato, though life in Erris
was primitive, there was some gaiety and prosperity. On Sundays, market-days and holidays the men wore frieze coats,
red or black, with corduroy or pilot cloth trousers, gaudy
waistcoats and felt hats; the women had stuff gowns, looped
up to show a red or black flannel petticoat, and caps with
gay ribbons; on special occasions both wore shoes and stockings. The failure of the potato brought ruin; frieze coats, red
flannel petticoats, gaudy waistcoats and gay ribbons were
sold, and many thousands of the inhabitants of Erris were
reduced to a state which the Commissariat officer, Mr. Alfred
Bishop, declared was the lowest and most degraded he had
ever met with, even among the Ashantees or wild Indians.
Cabins in Erris were cut out of the living bog, the walls of
the bog forming two or three sides; entrances were so low
that it was necessary to crawl in on all fours, and the height
inside—four to eight feet—made it almost impossible to stand
upright. Floor space was usually from seven to ten feet square,
but James Hack Tuke measured many which were less. Large
families, sometimes of more than eight persons, lived in these
"human burrows"; they were "quiet harmless persons, terrified of strangers."

The Board of Guardians at Ballina regarded Erris with
fear, resentment and dislike. The Erris Guardians did not
attend the meetings of the Ballina Board: they had forty or
fifty miles to travel to reach Ballina, and to collect rates in
Erris was impossible, the parish of Belmullet alone being as
large as the county of Dublin. "The Ballina Guardians," wrote
Twisleton, "detest Erris because Erris does not pay its rates,
and they would see Erris at the bottom of the sea rather
than take any trouble about Erris." On June 12, 1847, two
hundred and sixty starving and destitute persons somehow
made their way from Erris, and appeared at the gates of
the Ballina workhouse. They were turned away, the workhouse
was already full; and in any case Ballina Guardians would
not relieve destitute from districts which did not pay their
rates.

Ballina was not unique. Westport Union included Achill
Island, forty miles from the Westport workhouse; Tralee

Union was seventy miles long, with a population of 90,000, and the workhouse was thirty or forty miles away from several districts; Donegal Union contained the parish of Templecrone, where William Forster, representative of the Society of Friends, found 10,000 persons living in "miserable hovels in a state of degradation and filth which it is difficult to believe the most barbarous nations ever exceeded."

Moreover, though it was officially anticipated that "large bodies" of destitute would throw themselves on the unions for relief, the furnishings and equipment of the workhouses were in a condition which made them totally unable to cope with extra numbers. No improvement had yet been made in the workhouses of the distressed unions since the Board of Health issued their shocking report on Cork, Bantry and Lurgan in March, 1847. Scariff urgently required "large quantities" of bedding and clothing: the miserably poor population of the union amounted to more than 53,000 persons, and it was £6,000 in debt. Westport, after a chequered finnancial career, "lingered on," but by August 4 the workhouse was again being maintained by "the bounty of the Marquess of Sligo." The Guardians had all but given up the attempt to collect rates; between March 1 and June 30 only £111 was collected out of £4,400; meetings of the Board of Guardians seldom took place, and on August 4 both the Master and the Clerk of the workhouse were out in the town all day, trying to buy food on credit for the following week.

Castlebar was in hopeless disorder; the organization had broken down in January, 1847, and never been re-established; by July 31, for example, no entry had been made in the weekly relief list since January, and no record of purchase of clothing existed since September, 1846. At Ballina the lack of food in the workhouse was so great that on July 5, 1847, the doctor told the Guardians that the inmates were starving and that in his opinion some of them had actually died of starvation. On one occasion during the past week there had been no food in the workhouse for twenty-four hours; and beds, blankets and clothing for the destitute, who came in half naked, were all wanting. A small quantity of clothing had been sent by the Board of Ordnance in February, but was not paid for. It was difficult to buy clothing cheap enough to give to Irish paupers; all the really cheap clothing had been made for slaves on the West Indian plantations and had gone off the market after emancipation. Sailors' clothing rejected by the Admiralty was suggested, but Routh considered it "much too good for the Irish poor." On July 1 Ballina owed more than £6,000, and on August 28 bailiffs entered the workhouse and seized its goods in distraint for a debt.

The story was repeated again and again, not only in the twenty-two unions officially listed as distressed, but in almost every union in Ireland. On August 12, Lord Clarendon wrote that only eight unions of the 130 in Ireland had any money in hand, and the sum they possessed was only £3,600, while the debts of the 122 others amounted to over £250,000. He estimated that relief, under the new Poor Law Act, must cost at least £42,000 a week, and "the largest sum ever collected in any one *month* has been £64,000." As for the £160,000 balance of the British Association, which was to be expended on outdoor relief, it would not even cover the debts incurred by unions before the new Act was passed.

As October 1 approached, ominous descriptions of the state of the country came in. Harvest time was the best, indeed the only, period of employment in Ireland, and this year the harvest was superb. But on September 27 Mr. Lecky, a Guardian of the unions of Castlebar and Westport, told the Poor Law Commissioners that he had seen crowds of able-bodied men standing in the streets of Castlebar, reaping-hooks in hand, offering themselves for from 8*d*. to 10*d*. a day, but such was the universal poverty there was no one to hire them, "though the corn is ripe and falling on the ground. If this is the state of the labour market at the height of the harvest, what will it be in the winter?" he asked. "Something *must* be done by landlords, or the Government, to give labourers wages, or the whole population will come on the parish," that is, the rates.

It was, however, an article of faith with the British Government that rates could be collected in Ireland if pressure were used; apply the screw with sufficient force and the money would appear. Lord John Russell told Clarendon that he would not propose giving any relief to Ireland out of "imperial resources" until a rate of 15*s*. in the pound had actually been levied and Twisleton must be instructed to find out "in what places there are no funds to collect the rate . . . I expect they are very few." The landlord was to be compelled to pay, but what if no landlord were available to be compelled? "There are whole districts in Mayo and Donegal and parts of Kerry where the people swarm and are even now starving and where there is no landed proprietor to levy on," Clarendon wrote, on September 20. "He is absent or in Chancery and the estate subdivided into infinitesimally small lots . . . What is to be done with these hordes? Improve them off the face of the earth you will say, let them die . . . but there is *a certain amount of responsibility* attaching to it."

Charles Wood remained unbending in his determination to throw present and future expenditure on Ireland; no fresh money was to be provided by the Exchequer for relief, and on September 10 a circular informed Poor Law inspectors that after October 1, the date on which the distribution of food under the Soup Kitchen Act finally ceased, no more advances of money for temporary fever hospitals would be made by the Treasury: "all necessary funds" must be provided by Boards of Guardians, "whose attention should be drawn in time to this very important object."

The announcement was received with consternation. Fever was still widespread, and 26,378 patients were in fever hospitals at the date when the circular was issued. "Nothing creates so much alarm in my mind as this subject," wrote Sir William Somerville, the leading Irish liberal who had succeeded Labouchere as Chief Secretary, to Trevelyan, on September 18, "knowing as I do that the cessation of the accustomed funds even for one day may cause effects the most deplorable and disastrous . . . When I think of the difficulty of raising rates and the confusion which will accompany the change, I tremble at the thought of what may happen." Trevelyan supported Charles Wood. "A trial of strength," he wrote, was about to take place, to decide "whether the necessary measures for relief are to be taken by the Poor Law Guardians, or all thrown back on Government."

Boards of Guardians now tried to escape from their thankless position. The new Poor Law Act provided that inefficient Boards of Guardians might be dissolved by the Poor Law Commissioners, who could then appoint paid Guardians in their place, and Guardians wrote in asking to be released. On July 12 the Board of Guardians at Granard wrote that if they were expected to provide funds "to relieve the destitute poor who are now supported by monies . . . advanced by government, we beg, most respectfully but most decidedly to inform you that such will be impossible . . . Notwithstanding all the efforts we have made and the proceedings we have taken against our collector, we find it impossible to expect

anv large amount of rate to be paid in, and, were the whole
of the arrears at present due upon rate paid in, they would
not cover our liabilities." The Granard Guardians were "convinced that bankruptcy and confusion . . . will be hastened
by the course you are pursuing . . ." and therefore requested
to be dissolved. In the same week the Carrick-on-Shannon
Guardians wrote that the union was bankrupt: there were
only sufficient provisions to feed the paupers in the workhouse for three days, merchants refused to send in further
supplies until they were paid, and it was "utterly impossible
for the Collectors to get in rates sufficient to provide food for
the inmates." They accordingly resigned and asked for paid
Guardians to be appointed, since it was "no longer in their
power to conduct the affairs of the Union."

But Boards of Guardians were not to be allowed to escape.
"It is very important that we should give the Guardians no
excuse for escaping from their responsibilities and evading
the performance of their duties," Trevelyan wrote, and Clarendon cautioned Poor Law inspectors never to threaten unsatisfactory Boards of Guardians with dissolution because
they would behave worse than ever, in the hope of being
relieved of their task. If paid Guardians were sent in it would
be considered that "the government are the parties administering the relief of the poor in those places," and the British
authorities might find themselves saddled with Irish relief after
all.

Boards asking to be dissolved received a sharp reproof.
The Granard Board of Guardians was informed that the
Poor Law Commissioners did not "think it to be their duty
to relieve the Guardians from the difficulties and responsibilities of their present position"; further, it was useless for
them to hope for financial help from the Government—"the
Lords Commissioners of the Treasury have not sanctioned
the remittance of any further advance." In the opinion of
the Poor Law Commissioners "the present difficulties of the
union have arisen in great part . . . from the neglect here-
tofore to provide sufficient rates to meet the current expenditure . . . the only course which the Commissioners can
recommend to the Guardians is . . . to insist upon their
collectors proceeding for the recovery of the rates by every
available legal means and power of recovery. . . ."

Meanwhile, Charles Wood had warned Trevelyan, on September 12, to "look sharp after the rates, one of the inspecting

officers tells me that all the corn in Galway has been seized for rent." The landlord had forestalled the rate collector and was already stripping the unfortunate Irish small farmer of any crops he had managed to raise; and on September 16 Twisleton confirmed to Trevelyan that it had been reported from several districts that landlords were seizing crops. On this Routh declared angrily that the Poor Law officials were to blame; there was a "want of energy in Poor Law arrangements," he told Trevelyan; "landlords are grinding their tenants so as to be in advance of rates," but he neither saw nor heard of "anything doing" on the part of the Poor Law. Captain Gordon, temporary Poor Law Inspector in the distressed union of Bantry, told Trevelyan that rates should not have been left "until now, the landlord having collected what he could, leaving nothing in the hands of the small occupier." Trevelyan asked, "Is there no power of securing the rates out of the produce of the crops seized for rent?" But the rate collector, it appeared, had no power to compel the landlord to divide his spoil. In every other respect, however, the law gave the rate collector very summary powers indeed. On October 9 Mr. Stott, an Inspecting Officer of the Coastguard, wrote indignantly to Trevelyan describing scenes he had witnessed in the distressed district of Connemara: two-thirds of the population were destitute, many ratepayers had become paupers, some were actually in the workhouse, yet "collectors, aided by police, are out daily, seizing wearing apparel and tools even." Rate collectors were officially recommended to ask for troops, but not even the whole strength of the British Army could wring rates from places where nothing was left to seize. In Sligo, for instance, Mr. T. N. Redington, the Under-Secretary, told Trevelyan, on October 20, rates would not, because they could not, be collected, and Lord Sligo wrote, "Public funds must feed our poor or they must die, and how are these funds to be produced? Not in Sligo, for a stone is not bread." In Swineford, County Mayo, no fewer than nine properties were being administered by the Court of Chancery, and "out of 60–70 names returned as ratepayers, 50–60 are non-resident," reported Captain Delves Broughton, the temporary Poor Law Inspector. "The tenantry are proportionately neglected, or, I might say abandoned, for in few instances is the Agent resident either, and, in some cases no one but a driver is left as the representative of a Proprietor." A "driver" drove away cattle seized for rent or rates and forced evicted persons out of the ruins of their homes. During the previous week, finished Captain Delves Broughton, £25 only, out of a rate of £2,600, had been collected in Swineford.

Clarendon had already put this problem to Charles Wood; ". . . if it can be clearly proved," he wrote, "not by the assertions of Guardians but by the reports of Assistant (Poor Law) Commissioners that in certain localities the power to pay rates is absolutely and bona fide wanting—and that such localities exist there is no shadow of doubt—I ask how we are to deal with such cases?" He was not, he assured Charles Wood, raising premature objections, or popularity hunting, but if the Poor Law, under which the unions depended for maintenance on rates collected locally, was rigorously insisted upon, "the Poor Unions in the West must close and the inmates starve . . . it is right that you should understand the consequences."

Charles Wood was not to be moved; and so relentless was the severity of the rate collection that during the six months following the introduction of the Poor Law Extension Act of June 1847 £961,356 in rates was collected from a people who had not yet recovered from one of the worst famines known to history.

The first of October, when the last distribution from the soup kitchens ceased, passed without disturbance, but on October 23 Lord Clarendon made an urgent appeal to Lord John Russell: "There is one thing I must beg of you to take into serious and immediate consideration," he wrote, "which is, whatever may be the anger of people or Parliament in England, whatever may be the state of trade or credit, Ireland *cannot be left to her own resources,* they are manifestly insufficient, we are not to let the people die of starvation, we must not believe that rebellion is impossible." Lord John replied, coldly, "The state of Ireland for the next few months must be one of great suffering. Unhappily the agitation for Repeal has contrived to destroy nearly all sympathy in this country."

If the new Poor Law was to be effective, the workhouses must be cleared of the infirm, the old, the helpless widows and children and filled with able-bodied men who were destitute; but to clear the workhouses proved impossible. Guardians were unwilling to turn the helpless out; at Galway, for instance, they indignantly refused, while at Tralee, the immense distressed union which contained two estates under the Court of Chancery, the workhouse inmates had no clothes to put on and no shelter to which to return, for landlords customarily took advantage of destitute persons being forced to enter the workhouse to pull their cabins down. A proposal was made that outdoor relief to the helpless poor, in addition to the ration of meal, should include a halfpenny a day for an adult and a farthing for a child, to help them to obtain shelter; but the Tralee Guardians declared that the finances of the union "could not bear even so small an allowance." The Poor Law Commissioners reported that, when the helpless and infirm were turned out, those who had nowhere to go "were often compelled to part with a portion of their food to obtain a lodging," and in consequence "the cabins became crowded with ill-fed, ill-clothed and sickly people, and epidemic disease found victims prepared for its attack." If the "impotent poor" were allowed to remain there was no room for able-bodied, destitute men; and on November 5, a mob of starving labourers gathered outside the workhouse at Tralee, broke down the gates, and marched into the yard carrying a black flag marked "Flag of Distress," declaring they would enter the workhouse by force. Troops were called out, and with their help the police dispersed the mob, who did no damage.

Some unions had collapsed; Clifden, in Galway, was bankrupt, had closed down and the "wretched inmates" had been expelled. When James Hack Tuke visited Clifden in the autumn of 1847 he reported that "many of these poor creatures had taken up their abode in some holes or cavities in the hillside, where gravel appeared to have been dug." A poor lad of about fourteen begged for "a little meal to keep the life in me"—he was "a breathing skeleton wasted with hunger and sores." At Scariff, on November 21, an auction of workhouse property took place in the house, the first of a series, because the Sheriff held seventeen executions for goods supplied and not paid for. Mr. T. N. Redington, the Under-Secretary, asked Trevelyan, "What is to be done in these circumstances to make the Poor Law efficient for the relief of destitution in this Union? . . . Home Office and Treasury will have to act."

The Treasury had no intention of acting nor any doubt what should be done—rates must be collected, more force must be used. "Arrest, remand, do anything you can," wrote

Charles Wood to Clarendon on November 22; "send horse, foot and dragoons, all the world will applaud you, and I should not be at all squeamish as to what I did, to the verge of the law, and a little beyond." Meanwhile, Trevelyan was instructing Twisleton, "The principle of the Poor Law as you very well know is that rate after rate should be levied, for the purpose of preserving life, until the landlord and farmer either enable the people to support themselves by honest industry, or dispose of their estates to those who can perform this indispensable duty."

The problem, however, was not as simple as Trevelyan appeared to suppose. A good landlord who lived on his property, exerted himself to keep his tenants from starvation and the workhouse, gave employment and paid out a large sum in wages, frequently found himself in the same electoral division as an estate swarming with neglected, destitute paupers whose only refuge was the workhouse. Yet good and bad were put together for rating and paid the same, the good landlord being penalized for the bad landlord's neglect. As Colonel George Vaughan Jackson, considered by the Society of Friends to be one of the few good landlords in Mayo, wrote, "No men are more ill-fated or greater victims than we resident proprietors, we are consumed by the hives of human beings that exist on the properties of the absentees. On my right and my left are properties such as I allude to. I am overwhelmed and ruined by them. These proprietors *will do nothing*. All the burden of relief and employment falls on me. . . ."

Relentless severity in rate collecting increased evictions, since on holdings valued at £4 and under, the landlord was liable for the rate. On December 19 Captain Hellard, Poor Law Inspector at Galway, reported that "no less than eleven boats, loaded with destitute persons" had come into Galway Harbour from Connemara, "most from the estate of Christian St. George, our county member, who, I am told is ejecting them without even a rag to cover them." Captain Mann wrote that after about 200 persons had been evicted near Kilrush, County Clare, the district became disturbed, and on December 22 the steamer *Alban* brought in extra troops. The most notorious example, however, was supplied by the unhappy district of Belmullet, in Erris, on the estate of a Mr. Walshe. He lived at Crossmolina, and was a magistrate, but had taken no part in relief work during the famine. The inhabitants of three villages were evicted by Mr. Walshe, with

the help of a company of the 49th Regiment: their houses
were thrown down and they were turned out, in the depth
of the winter, to exist as best they might. The largest of
these hamlets was Mullaroghe, on the peninsula of the Mullet;
Mr. Hamilton, the temporary Poor Law Inspector at Belmullet, brought Mr. James Hack Tuke to the site, and a woman
who had been evicted made a statement "in the presence of
three most respectable witnesses, including a clergyman of
the Church of England." She had been, she said. "living in
Mullaroghe with her husband, when young Mr. Walshe and
two 'drivers' came, about ten days before Christmas . . . The
first day they made a 'cold,' a make-shift, fire, the second
day the people were all turned out of doors and the roofs of
their houses pulled down. That night they made a bit of a
tent, or shelter, of wood and straw; that however the drivers
threw down and drove them from the place . . . It would
have 'pitied the sun'," she said, "to look at them as they
had to go head foremost under hail and storm. It was a
night of high wind and storm, and their wailing could be
heard at a great distance. They implored the drivers to allow
them to remain a short time as it was so near the time of
festival [Christmas] but they would not . . ." Mullaroghe
was "literally a heap of ruins," wrote James Hack Tuke; the
Townland assessment book showed that, in 1845, 102 families
were rated there, but only the walls of three houses now
stood. Mr. Higgins, of the British Association, who wrote that
he would like to be a dictator in Erris, with power to shoot,
told Trevelyan that Mr. Walshe wished the troops to return
the next day and "finish his work, but Captain Glazebrook
of the 49th, an excellent officer and a most humane man,
was so disgusted at what he and his men had witnessed that
he contrived to baffle him, by putting all manner of obstacles
in the way as to getting the troops out again." "The horrors
of that wretched place," concluded Mr. Higgins, "you can
never describe." Two more hamlets on Mr. Walshe's land,
Tiraun and Clogher, were destroyed in the same way: the
inhabitants were driven out with the help of troops and their
cabins demolished. The people, timid by nature, were stunned.
Tuke saw "miserable objects" lingering helpless and bewildered round the ruins of their homes, while outside their few
possessions disintegrated in the rain. Between Mullaroghe and
Clogher, Mr. Hamilton, the Poor Law Inspector, set up a
"feeding station," where more than three hundred persons

gathered "in various stages of fever, starvation and nakedness"; many, too weak to stand, lay on the ground; the worst,
however, said Mr. Hamilton, did not appear; they were too
ill to crawl out of their hiding-places and shelters.

Officials in Dublin began to be uneasy—perhaps the Irish
people were being pushed too far. And Mr. Sheean Lalor,
a well-known figure in Irish life, warned Mr. Redington that
the people would not endure much more. Since the Government was determined to stop the issue of rations and there
was no employment of any kind, "the consequence must be
death from starvation, and will the people put up with it? . . .
The people have openly said they will not endure a repetition
of the spring and summer." On October 10 Clarendon told
Lord John Russell, "A great social revolution is now going
on in Ireland, the accumulated evils of misgovernment and
mismanagement are now coming to a crisis."

A month later Twisleton wrote despondently to Trevelyan,
"The Irish Poor Law is going on as satisfactorily as can be
expected"; but the fact was that the struggle had not yet
begun. Without Treasury aid the Poor Law could contrive
to get along only "as long as we stave off relief to the able-
bodied . . . with much fighting and some hardness we have
put off the evil day for a while. Only two unions have outdoor
relief . . . but others must in time and then the great battle
will commence."

The Poor Law Inspector for Ballinrobe, Castlebar and
Westport warned the Poor Law Commissioners that in the
west the amount of destitution was unbelievable—the people
would come up 20,000 at a time. "All calculation," he wrote,
"is set at defiance."

Routh meanwhile had been making some disturbing calculations, and early in November he wrote anxiously to
Trevelyan. Confidential reports made to Sir John Burgoyne
by inspecting officers showed that about 360,000 men would
require relief, which was to consist of 1 lb. of meal daily—
that is, about 4,800 tons a month. The Government might
be relying on the funds of the British Association, but the
cost would be £270,000 at least, whereas the funds of the
British Association amounted to about £160,000. What was
to be done?

Trevelyan disagreed; the demand for relief, in his opinion,
would more resemble the scale required in the first failure
of 1845-46 than the huge demands of last year; the Govern-

ment had in hand, in the Commissariat depots after the soup kitchens closed, about 20,000 tons of Indian corn, valued at £200,000. The position as regards food was far better than last year, and it was important to "avoid disturbing the market." Something would have to be done for such places as Belmullet, in Erris, but the "great need was for a bona fide active administration of the Poor Law"; rates must be collected, and the difficulty of the collection would be increased if there was any indication that relief might be paid for out of public money.

However, in a few days Routh wrote again, even more anxiously; Father John O'Sullivan, at Kenmare, was pressing for general outdoor relief at once though, Routh added, he himself had hopes of holding off until January. A terrible report on the state of the south-western distressed unions had been received from Mr. Crawford, the Poor Law Inspector, so terrible that it had been thought wiser not to circulate it. Mr. Crawford urged general outdoor relief at once, and wrote that the state of the children was particularly bad: "Fathers say, feed the children, we do not care about ourselves." Trevelyan, in reply, repeated once again that rates must be collected, and that "no other assistance will be given until every practicable local effort has been made"; if relief was provided through any other channel but the Poor Law, ratepayers would feel freed from their responsibilities.

The British Association, however, refused to let children suffer. They were "determined to give direct relief," wrote Trevelyan disapprovingly by feeding and clothing pauper children in schools in the distressed unions. In one of the most successful relief schemes stirabout and bread was distributed to schoolchildren and £12,000 was allocated from the Association's funds for clothes.

By the middle of December the number of destitute, half-naked, and starving who were besieging the workhouses made it evident that outdoor relief could not be "staved off" much longer. "The great stress on the Poor Law is now commencing," wrote Trevelyan to Twisleton on December 10, "and I sincerely hope that under your and Redington's able management and with the zealous assistance of your Inspecting officers, permanent and temporary, it will bear the strain." From Tralee, on December 15, Mr. Dobree, of the Commissariat, reported that the able-bodied were "coming up in masses to be refused," 700 to 800 at a time. The workhouse, which held 1,400, was full—"the labouring class have no visible means of existence." Ballina workhouse on December 11 had 500 more inmates than it had been built to contain; Kilrush on December 14 had 500 to 600 too many; Galway on the 19th had 500, of whom 200 were fever cases; Erris was "out of control," with three-quarters of the population urgently requiring relief.

Orders permitting outdoor relief to certain unions were now issued, and Erris received one on December 18. But these orders were good for only two months, and on December 24 a circular from the Poor Law Commissioners reminded such unions that the outdoor relief orders were "merely temporary," and instructed Guardians to give relief only within the workhouse. "Every possible exertion must be made to render the workhouse available almost exclusively for able-bodied men and their families . . . and to provide further workhouse accomodation by every means the union may present . . ." Disused buildings of every sort, old breweries, empty warehouses, derelict stores, without sanitation or means of heating or water, were now hired, dignified by the name of "auxiliary workhouses," and in this way additional accommodation for 150,000 persons was provided. The inmates of the auxiliaries were generally women, children, the aged and infirm, "impotent poor" who were turned out to make room for destitute able-bodied men but had nowhere to go. Buildings which served as auxiliary workhouses are still pointed out in the west of Ireland; a gaunt warehouse in Killala, for instance, and the stores, which until a few years ago still stood, on the road to the harbour at Westport. To this day stories are told of windows filled with the half-starved, wild faces of the unhappy creatures shut up inside.

Meanwhile, Routh's anxiety over supplies of food to the distressed unions was proving justified. "He is at issue with Trevelyan and has drawn up a memorandum," wrote Sir William Somerville. Routh wanted the Government to purchase "large supplies" and send cargoes, by steamer, up the west coast of Ireland. Though rates were being collected with all possible severity, though troops were freely used and every conceivable pressure applied; in Scariff even the ration given by the British Association to starving children was withdrawn until "some progress had been made in the collection of the rate," none the less rates were not collected and the workhouse authorities had no funds to feed the crowds

in the workhouses and auxiliaries. On December 24 Major
Halliday, Poor Law Inspector, reported that in Sligo workhouse the people were "actually beginning to starve." Three
coroners' verdicts of death from starvation within the workhouse had been returned, "quite justly," and the mortality
among the younger children, attributed to dysentery, was
really due to starvation. In a burst of feeling he added to his
report, "When I go to the workhouse I see such sights of
suffering and wasted humanity, I cannot wash them away
from my imagination."

The sufferings of the people began to approach the horrors
of the winter of 1846–47; the country, generally speaking,
was ruined, pauperism was spreading, there was no employment, and though the yield of the potato crop was superb
the quantity planted was inadequate. Dead bodies were found
lying by roadsides and in fields; men who had tramped many
miles to a workhouse, only to be refused admittance, died
at the gates; a man turned away from Tipperary workhouse
died after lying outside the gates for twelve hours.

Clarendon became alarmed. "Distress, discontent and
hatred of English rule are increasing everywhere," he told
Lord John Russell; and his alarm became acute during the
autumn and winter of 1847, when in a succession of assassinations landlord after landlord, seven in all, were shot in
less than two months, six being killed outright and the
seventh horribly injured. The most notorious of these murders
was the tragic and confused case of Major Mahon, a terrible
illustration of the insuperable difficulties which confronted
Irish landlords when famine suddenly brought the accumulated
evils of centuries to a crisis.

Denis Mahon, a handsome, amiable and well-intentioned
young man, who had held a commission in a crack cavalry
regiment, the 9th Lancers, had inherited the property of
Strokestown, in County Roscommon, about two years previously. The former owner, Lord Hartland, had been a lunatic
for some time, and during this period the estate had been
badly managed. £30,000 arrears of rent had been allowed
to accumulate; sub-division had flourished unchecked, the
population swarmed; only about a third of the land was
properly cultivated, and rates were three years in arrears.
Almost at the moment Major Mahon inherited, the potato
failed, and famine followed. New management of the property
must be introduced, and Major Mahon proposed that any

tenant who would peaceably give up possession of his patch
of land, on which he could not hope to exist now that the
potato had failed, should not be turned out of his house but
given work and then a passage to Canada. Eight hundred
and ten tenants agreed, and in the late spring of 1847 Major
Mahon chartered two vessels to take them to Quebec: extra provisions were supplied to an "extravagant amount,"
and the cost of the emigration to Major Mahon was £14,000.
The legend in the west of Ireland is that "coffin ships" were
chartered, when one foundered, and all aboard were lost,
Major Mahon was shot by the lover of a girl who had been
drowned. In fact the ship did not founder, although she was
forced to put back to port in distress; both ships eventually
reached Quebec, but in a very bad state. In one vessel 268
persons were alleged to have died at sea. It must be remembered that the emigrants were poor, unsophisticated people, unaccustomed to observe any rules of hygiene, and
typhus had raged during the voyage.

These formed a minority of Major Mahon's tenants. The
majority would "neither pay nor go," and 3,006 persons
evicted, including 84 widows, according to the Catholic Bishop
of Elphin. Murmurs that Major Mahon was a "tyrant" began
to be heard. Now, most unwisely, since he was a Protestant,
he quarrelled over the local relief committee with the parish
priest of Strokestown, Father MacDermott, who was accused of having denounced him from the altar, saying "Major
Mahon is worse than Cromwell." Father MacDermott stren-
uously denied he had said anything of the kind, and Mr.
Ross Mahon, Major Mahon's cousin and agent, declared the
reports were "so conflicting and various that he could not
be sure what had been said, or if a denunciation had happened at all." However, Major Mahon was shot by two
men on the high road on November 2, 1847, while seated
in an open carriage travelling back from a meeting of the
Board of Guardians of the Roscommon Union, which he
had attended in the hope of finding some way of keeping
the workhouse open. That morning he had addressed a meeting of his tenants and been cheered. Nevertheless, reported
a Board of Works' engineer, "the exultation of the country
people at Major Mahon's death was general and undisguised
. . . As soon as it was dark . . . signal was given of the
deed having been perpetrated by lighting straw upon some
of the hills in the neighbourhood of Strokestown, and on

the following evening, when the people were better prepared, bonfires were to be seen on the hills for many miles in extent."

In addition to the six landlords, ten other persons, occupiers of land but not "gentlemen of property with large bodies of tenantry," were murdered.

Lord Clarendon was almost beside himself. "There never was," he wrote to his brother-in-law, G. Cornewall Lewis, M.P., "so open or so widely extended a conspiracy for shooting landlords and agents, and my fear is this will spread (there are already symptoms of it) and that the flame which now rages in certain districts will become a general conflagration." He was convinced that the murders were part of a rebellious campaign. "The intention," he told Sir George Grey, "is to shoot landlords and agents this winter, drive away resident gentry from the country and make the management of property so dangerous that the occupiers [the tenantry] will be able to keep possession"; and on November 10, 1847, he asked for an Act to give him "extraordinary powers." First, authority to impose a fine on any district where crime was committed; second, authority to prohibit the possession of arms, except under registered licence from the police; third, the Act must contain "penal clauses" against men, disguised or with blackened faces, going about at night.

Lord John Russell, whose prejudice against Irish landlords had already been made clear in the House of Commons, answered coldly. "I am not ready to bring in any restrictive law without, at the same time, restraining the power of the landlord. . . . It is quite true that landlords in England would not like to be shot like hares and partridges . . . but neither does any landlord in England turn out fifty persons at once and burn their houses over their heads, giving them no provision for the future."

Clarendon, in a fury, threatened to resign. He could not understand, he wrote, "how any Government can think it expedient to leave 300,000 arms in the possession of some of the most ferocious people on earth, at the commencement of a winter when there will be great poverty and little employment, when armed outrages are increasing every day . . . if I do not see any reasonable ground for believing I can perform the duties of Government, in maintaining the law and according some protection to life and property, I cannot, and I am sure you would not ask me to, remain here when I feel my power of usefulness is gone."

This threat, he said, "produced an immediate change." The Lord-Lieutenancy of Ireland was not a popular post; Clarendon had accepted with reluctance, and in the present state of Ireland to replace him would be all but impossible. A compromise was effected, and on November 29 Sir George Grey introduced a Bill in the House of Commons, the Crime and Outrage (Ireland) Bill. The Lord-Lieutenant was given power, at his discretion, to draft police, up to any number, into a district, such a district to be punished by being required immediately to repay the cost of the drafting. Arms were to be carried only by persons already licensed or holding official positions, J.P.s, naval and military officers, etc.; game-keepers were allowed a gun, and householders might keep firearms within the house, for protection. When a murder had been committed all male persons in the district between the ages of sixteen and sixty were liable to be called upon to assist in finding the criminal, and failure to assist was a misdemeanour, punishable with two years' imprisonment.

In common with most compromises, the Act, which received the Royal Assent on December 20, 1847, "appeared to almost everybody insufficient for the object," and the Irish Members of Parliament were "evidently surprised and had expected much more stringent measures . . ." However, extra troops were brought to Ireland, and three bodies of five thousand men each sent to Arklow, Clonmel and Limerick City. But Lord John Russell refused to attempt general disarmament: "the government did not have enough force at their disposal," nor was he "ready to adopt like Mr. Pitt, 'ripening' measures to force on a rebellion." Pitt, by the use of secret agents, when he was Prime Minister, is alleged to have caused the rebellion of 1798 to break out before the preparations of the leaders were complete.

In Ireland fear spread through the upper and middle classes, and a number of landlords left the country. At Nenagh, County Tipperary, Mr. Bayly, chairman of the Board of Guardians, had been attacked and horribly wounded, the result, it was said, of his "spirited resistance to a mob of applicants at the workhouse," and when the Board of Guardians at Rathkeale were directed by Poor Law Commissioners to refuse outdoor relief, they declined to obey and resigned, saying that they were "alarmed for their lives"; while in

Leitrim the Guardians could not be got to meet at all, because they were afraid of being shot at on the roads. The
country appeared quiet enough; Colonel Vaughan Jackson
wrote that Mayo had never been more quiet; but in the
general atmosphere of alarm the quiet was declared to be
"deceptive." In Sligo and Leitrim alone, at the end of December, the sub-inspector of police could give the names of at least
ten landlords who were marked men, "their lives are not
worth a sheet of paper"; and Captain Pole, of the Commissariat, reported, "The personal insecurity of all property
owners is so hideous that the impression is of being *in an
enemy country"*; this was true not only of certain counties
but was universal. From Carrick-on-Shannon, the temporary
Poor Law Inspector, "a most talented engineer and surveyor-
general in Hong Kong," wrote, "Not one of the proprietors or
their agents dare go out alone, even in daylight, and everyone
is armed to the teeth. On Friday I saw a gentleman at his
sister's funeral, three policemen with him and himself armed.
The man who is hired to shoot him was walking on the road
with a gun in his hand. Pleasant state of things that!"

The condition of Ireland, declared Clarendon to Lord John
Russell, was that of a "servile war," a rebellion of slaves.
The Irish people had risen many times before; now, driven
to desperation by hunger, he believed they were about to rise
again.

So with fifteen thousand extra troops in the country, a
campaign of terrorization being waged, workhouses enlarged
to take 150,000 additional inmates and, in the distressed
unions, people dying of starvation, both inside the workhouses and outside them, with rates impossible to collect,
employment non-existent, fever still raging and the people
pauperized and wretched as never before, Ireland passed from
1847 into 1848.

Chapter XVI

IN SPITE of the sufferings, the rage and the despair of the
Irish people, the popular rising which the British Govern-

ment feared was not being planned, and when a revolutionary movement did come it originated not among the starving
masses but with the intellectual and middle classes.

Lord Clarendon had misread the situation. The murders
which horrified and alienated public opinion had no insur-
rectionary significance and were not related to any political
conspiracy. They were produced, as similar horrifying murders had been produced in the past, by land hunger. A special
Commission of Judges sent down in January, 1848, to
counties where murders had taken place declared that, in
every case, "circumstances connected with the possession of
land . . . were the primary cause of the crime." Tenants had
been evicted or land had been disposed of over the occupier's
head, and "the motive for all," said Lord Chief Justice
Blackburn, "was the wild justice of revenge."

Apart from these terrible acts of individual vengeance, the
mass of the Irish people lay helpless and inert; indeed, as
blow after blow fell, they appeared too weakened to protest.

Yet a powerful organization, the Repeal Association, existed which should have been the mouthpiece and champion
of the Irish masses. The Repeal Association had been "the
real government of Ireland," with branches in every town
and village and "Repeal wardens" and "Repeal police" in
every parish, but during this critical period the officials of
the association, turning their backs on the terrible realities of
the famine, became absorbed in party politics and party
intrigues.

The explanation of this situation lay in the secession, in
July, 1846, of the Young Ireland party from the Repeal
Association. The Young Irelanders had left because they
refused to pledge themselves never, in any circumstances, to
resort to physical force and armed rebellion; but behind the
apparently simple issue lay a tangled story. Owing to Daniel
O'Connell's tragic decline, his son John gained control of the
Repeal Association. John O'Connell has been described as
"uniting a stealthy ambition to a narrow intellect"; he was not
the man his father had been, in mind or nature, and he
detested the Young Irelanders; while they, on their part,
believed he had worked upon the Liberator to state the
physical force issue in terms which compelled Young Ireland
to leave the association. The bitterness which accompanied
the secession was so intense that when the potato failed total-

ly the disaster took second place to the struggle within the Repeal Movement.

There was, however, a difference between Old Ireland as the O'Connellites were called and Young Ireland, more fundamental and more important than the question of using physical force. The tradition of the Repeal movement was a Catholic tradition, and its strength was derived from the "great silent masses" of the Irish people, led by their priests. The Young Irelanders were not in the Catholic tradition. It was not merely that several of their leaders were Protestants —a larger number were Catholic, and Protestant patriots have always been numerous in Irish history. But the Young Irelanders tended to be intellectuals, and if not positively anticlerical they were not inclined to be submissive to ecclesiastical authority. They alleged that John O'Connell had instigated a "whispering campaign against them to render them odious to the people," declaring that they were atheists and "the secret enemies of the Liberator and the church."

As the fearful winter of 1846-47 went by the all-absorbing issue in the Repeal Association was not the failure of the potato but the crushing of Young Ireland. "The Famine and Repeal," wrote a Young Ireland leader, "were forgotten . . ." However, the Young Irelanders also failed to come forward with a policy or a plan to meet the famine; they were absorbed in trying to find a new method to force the British to grant Repeal of the Union.

The leader of the Young Irelanders, William Smith O'Brien, was forty-five years of age, a Protestant patriot landlord who had sat in Parliament for more than fifteen years pleading the cause of Ireland. The O'Briens are one of the few native Irish aristocratic families still in possession of their estates and trace their descent in an unbroken line from Brian Boroimhe, popularly known as Brian Boru, King of North Munster, who became supreme Monarch of Ireland in 1002 and was slain at the Battle of Clontarf, in which he vanquished the Norsemen, in 1014. William Smith O'Brien was the brother of Sir Lucius O'Brien, of Dromoland Castle, and has been described as stepping straight from the pages of Burke's *Landed Gentry*. Tall and wonderfully handsome, though grave and frigid in manner, he was a throw-back to 1782, when the Protestant patriots of the landlord class, ostensibly for the defence of Ireland, raised 80,000 armed volunteers commanded by the Duke of Leinster in Leinster, and by the Earl of Charlemont in Ulster, and coerced the English Government into granting Ireland a new constitution, the event which called forth Grattan's celebrated exclamation, "Ireland is now a nation!" First and foremost an Irishman, William Smith O'Brien was a member of the Catholic Association and a Repealer, in spite of being a Protestant.

Smith O'Brien and three other men led the Young Irelanders. Charles Gavan Duffy, son of a Catholic grocer and bleacher in Monaghan, was one of the founders and editor of the newspaper, the *Nation,* the mouthpiece of Young Ireland. Thomas Francis Meagher, son of an Old Irelander who was Catholic Mayor of Waterford, had won fame at the time of the secession by a fiery oration in favour of armed rebellion and been christened "Meagher of the Sword"; he was twenty-four years of age.

The third was John Mitchel, the most remarkable and the most formidable of the Young Ireland leaders, the son of a Presbyterian minister in Ulster and the principal leader-writer on the *Nation.* His abilities were outstanding, and his *Jail Journal,* a minor masterpiece, has won him immortality. John Mitchel possessed an extraordinary capacity for hatred directed at the British Government, and an equal talent for burning invective. He had also the gift, which the other leaders of Young Ireland lacked, of arousing the masses of the people and inspiring them with intense devotion.

On January 13, 1847, when the famine was reaching its full horror, the Young Irelanders founded a new militant organization, the Irish Confederation, compelled, they declared, to take this step by the inadequacy of the Government's relief measures.

The plan was to form Confederate "clubs" in every city, town and parish: militant organizations capable of exerting enough pressure to force the British Government to concede Repeal immediately; only Repeal of the Union and an Irish Parliament could save the country from destruction.

The Young Irelanders did not succeed. The unfortunate masses of destitute were crushed by hunger; the more prosperous were an inert mass of lower middle-class Catholic respectability; and "Old Ireland" was powerful and hostile. In Cork, for instance, it was impossible to start a club; in Belfast the attempt resulted in a riot. The campaign, which was to have been revolutionary, dwindled away into educational articles, debates, committee meetings. Feelings of failure became universal. "Our agitation so far has been a very eloquent high-toned sort of business," wrote a Young Irelander. "I think it will have to become a more democratic style of work, and that at once too."

The Repeal Association, meanwhile, had become all but extinct. In March, 1847, Daniel O'Connell died at Genoa, but before his death the Repeal "rent," the voluntary contributions out of which the expenses of the movement were paid, had almost ceased, and Lord Clarendon reported to London that its meetings became "gradually uninfluential and unimportant." Duffy blamed John O'Connell. "His father," wrote Duffy, "began with a dozen followers, and increased them to millions, he began with millions and reduced them to a score or a dozen."

At this moment of depression a new and revolutionary force appeared in Irish politics. Fintan Lalor had lived, for nearly forty years, secluded on a farm in Queen's County, a "poor, distorted, ill-favoured, hunchbacked creature" brooding over the misfortunes of his country; and he had realized the truth, which escaped both Old and Young Irelanders, that the famine had swept away all past values. A new situation had arisen, and previous issues, including the crucial issue of Repeal, had lost their significance.

In January, 1847, about the date when the Irish Confederation was founded, Lalor, unknown, even by sight, to the leaders, sent Gavan Duffy a long letter so remarkable that Duffy at once invited him to expound his doctrines at length in the *Nation*. "A new tribune—a new policy!" exclaimed Duffy exultingly.

". . . a new adjustment is now to be formed," Lalor wrote, ". . . a new social order to be arranged; a new people to be organized." The issue of over-riding importance was the land, beside which Repeal "dwarfs down into a petty parish question"; and Lalor rejected Repeal. "I will never contribute one shilling, or give my name, heart or hand for such an object as simple Repeal by the British Parliament of the Act of Union." The future of Ireland lay in possession of the land; "forever henceforth, the owners of our soil must be Irish," and the importance of the famine was that it opened the way for an agrarian revolution. ". . . unmuzzle the wolf dog," wrote Lalor. "There is one at this moment in every cabin throughout the land, nearly fit to be untied—and he will be savager by and by."

The call to an agrarian revolution was new; it promised action in place of frustration, and it grew directly out of the famine. If it should mean armed insurrection, the sufferings of the Irish people were so frightful that armed rebellion had lost some of its terror. Among the Young Irelanders and their leaders, Lalor's doctrines created a sensation, and throughout 1847 he gained adherents.

Lalor exercised a particular fascination over John Mitchel. Yet side by side with outstanding qualities of leadership, courage, integrity and fanatical sincerity, Mitchel possessed fatal defects. He was wildly unpractical, he was obstinate, he did not foresee the consequences of his actions, he did not merely lack organizing ability, he regarded method, organization and system with lofty contempt.

Mitchel now adopted Lalor's plan "in its entirety, as completely as a man adopts a new religion," but while Lalor admitted the necessity of armed rebellion with reluctance, Mitchel enthusiastically welcomed the prospect of a resort to arms. Mitchel had been a constitutional Repealer, opposed to violence, but all he had previously believed was thrown overboard; he desired, he wrote to Duffy, ". . . to turn men's minds away from the English Parliament and from Parliamentary and constitutional agitation of all kinds . . . The Nation and the Confederation should rather employ themselves in promulgating sound instruction upon military affairs . . . in order that the stupid legal and constitutional shouting, voting and agitating . . . should be changed into a deliberate study of the theory and practice of guerilla war."

Mitchel had a vision of the Irish peasantry rising as one, breaking their fetters, raising the green flag, and irresistibly—because morality and justice were on their side—sweeping the British into the sea; and this vision became a fixed idea. ". . . a kind of sacred wrath," he wrote, "took possession of a few Irishmen at this period. They could endure the horrible scene no longer, and resolved to cross the path of the British car of conquest, though it should crush them to atoms. . . ."

Duffy, William Smith O'Brien and other leading Young Irelanders held back, they shrank from provoking the most terrible of all insurrections, a peasant war; moreover, Duffy was dubious of the real existence in Ireland of the persons Lalor described as "angry peasants chafing like chained tigers"; in his opinion the Irish people were too enfeebled by hunger, too demoralized and pauperized by Poor Law relief, to be capable of rising.

Within a few weeks Mitchel had broken away from the Young Irelanders and formed a party dedicated to armed rebellion. Lalor planned that the first step towards agrarian revolution should be an organized refusal, all over Ireland, to pay rent. A "strike" against rent would rouse the country districts; the high rents being mercilessly extorted were a universal and burning grievance. Mitchel suddenly proposed that, instead, there should be a general refusal to pay poor rates.

The Young Irelanders were aghast. After the public works had been closed by the British Government, poor rates and the relief they provided, miserable though it was, alone stood between tens of thousands and death from starvation, and Duffy declared he would rather perish than be a party to stopping the collection of poor rate, until some other method of feeding the destitute was provided. Mitchel refused to retract. At the end of January, 1848, he left both the *Nation,* the newspaper edited by Duffy, and the Young Ireland party, and on February 12 Mitchel began to publish the short-lived *United Irishman,* "to prepare the country for rebellion." With characteristic contempt for subterfuge, Mitchel declared that he scorned to conceal his purpose; there was to be no secret plot, he would state his intentions openly in the *United Irishman* each week, and offered, if it would be any convenience to His Excellency Lord Clarendon, to entertain a Castle detective in his office, provided the man was sober and honest, who could make daily reports to the Castle. Further, there was to be no one leader; public wrath and indignation would suffice, at the first signal, to sweep the English out of Ireland.

The Government was unmoved by these declarations—considerable verbal licence was allowed in Ireland. The "public mind," wrote Clarendon, "was inured to political excitement and the people habituated to the system of associating together for the redress of grievances, real or supposed, to an extent unknown in any other country in Europe." At the moment, he went on, the famine had created "general discontent" and a feeling of opposition to the Government, because the people thought and, declared Clarendon, he agreed with them, that the Government had not done all that might have been done to relieve their distress; however, he did not think that there were "feelings of desire for revolution."

When the political situation in Ireland had reached this point the news burst on Europe that a great popular rising had taken place in Paris on February 22, 1848. The French Government, which had consistently refused parliamentary reforms, had been overthrown in an all but bloodless revolution, and the King, Louis Philippe, forced to fly to England in disguise. A few hours later came further news; a Republic had been proclaimed, with Lamartine, the famous poet, as Minister for Foreign Affairs.

The dawn of a golden age of liberty and progress was hailed. Workmen, philosophers, priests and artists fraternized, and "the triumphant insurgents seemed to be as magnanimous as they were valiant": no excesses were committed and private property was as safe as when the streets swarmed with police.

Comparison with Ireland was irresistible, and to the Irish leaders, wrote Duffy, "with the wail of the famishing people in their ears, the news . . . sounded like a message from heaven." "Frenchmen we do exult," declared the Sarsfield Club, at Limerick; "we feel as if the victory were our own . . . Victors of the barricades . . . your glorious achievement came to cheer us with the assurance that freedom is ever within the grasp of those who manfully seek her." Bonfires were lighted to celebrate French freedom; in forty-eight hours, on March 10 and 11, they were reported at Wexford, Listowel, in King's County, in Meath, at Tuam and on the sacred ground of the rebellion of 1798, Vinegar Hill. In Waterford and Limerick banners waved, inscribed "Honour to France" and "Despots beware." Mullingar and Kells were illuminated, Cork displayed a lighted transparency "France is free—an example to the world," and crowds in the streets cheered the new Republic.

In a torrent of enthusiasm, hesitations were swept away, and the Young Irelanders embarked on armed rebellion. "Ireland's opportunity, thank God and France, has come at last!" Duffy wrote. "Its challenge rings in our ears like a call to battle and warms our blood like wine . . . We must answer if we would not be slaves forever . . . We must resist, we must act, we must leap all barriers . . . if needs be we must die rather than let this providential hour pass over us

unliberated." On March 18 Meagher "of the sword" wrote in
the *Nation,* ". . . if the Government of Ireland insists upon
being a government of dragoons and bombardiers, of detectives
and light infantry—then up with the barricades and invoke
the God of battles."

Meanwhile, Mitchel's paper, the *United Irishman,* was
printing ferocious, if vague, directions for street fighting in
Dublin. Windowpots, brickbats, heavy furniture, logs of
wood and pokers, were to be cast down on the heads of the
troops: cavalry, the inhabitants of Dublin were told, cannot
charge over broken bottles, and therefore a wide use of
broken glass was recommended. Home-made grenades could
be manufactured from empty soda-water bottles, and vitriol,
boiling water and boiling grease were also to be poured from
above on the troops' heads. Soldiers were to be tempted into
narrow streets, where such methods would have their maximum effect. Molten lead from spouts and roofs, however, was
to be saved for bullets.

But while the Irish people, or a portion of them, were
dancing round bonfires and preparing home-made ammunition, the state of their country remained as appalling as ever.
Famine was still devastating Ireland, worst in the west, but by
no means confined to the west. The destitution, Lord Clarendon told John Russell, was "horrible even beyond that of last
year," and even if the rates were collected "to the uttermost"
the money would not be sufficient to feed the starving. From
Kilrush, County Clare, Captain Mann reported, "The poor of
this union are decidedly more distressed than they were last
season," and Captain Jules Routh, Sir Randolph Routh's son,
wrote from Carrick-on-Shannon, "Never in my life could I
have imagined such distress could exist in a Christian country."
Meanwhile, homeless beggars continued to stream into the
towns; in Galway, for instance, three thousand starving
beggars roamed the streets, "children, mere animated skeletons . . . screaming for food." Jails had become a refuge: the
food given in prisons was better than in workhouses, people
were "most anxious to be committed," and 13,000 persons
were shut up in jails intended for 5,000. "Such sufferings as
the wretched prisoners are subjected to, arising from insufficient prison accommodation, disease, cold and nakedness,
were never even heard of in any country on the face of the
globe," wrote a chaplain. Only potatoes could save the Irish
people, and there were not enough potatoes. "I have not

overcoloured the frightful picture," wrote a resident magistrate; ". . . distress not only continues unabated but seems
every day to be increasing."

Nevertheless, the faith of the Young Irelanders in armed
rising was unshaken, though William Smith O'Brien, who had
been active in relief work on his estate, must have had first-
hand knowledge of the exhausted state of the people. Lalor's
eloquence was intoxicating; "Will Ireland perish like a lamb,
or will she turn as turns the baited lion?" he demanded; and
now that a policy of armed insurrection had been adopted,
Mitchel was again prominent in the councils of Young Ireland.
Mitchel, of all the leaders, knew least of the Irish masses and
was the most optimistic. He was an Ulsterman, his life had
been spent in towns, he had never lived among small tenant
farmers, and he regarded the famine-stricken, enfeebled Irish
peasantry, mainly unaccustomed to the use of firearms, and
armed only with cudgels, as if they had been "Calabrians
and Tyrolese with rifles always in their hands and ammunition
in their pouches."

Meanwhile, events in Europe were causing the British
Government anxiety. All over the Continent in the spring of
1848 oppressed peoples were rising, governments falling
and kings and despots fleeing. In January, 1848, insurrection
in Sicily forced the King to concede a constitution; in
Piedmont, the people secured a constitution; on March 13,
about two weeks after the flight of Louis Philippe the population of Vienna rose, routed the troops and forced the re-
actionary Metternich to fly. The people of Milan drove the
Austrians out of the city, and the people of Venice seized the
city arsenal and proclaimed a provisional government.

The collapse of government after government, however
corrupt and inefficient, was unnerving; any "display of the
power of a people over constituted authority," wrote Lord
Clarendon, "was dangerous." In England times were bad,
unemployment prevalent, and the Chartists, a working-class
association so-called from the charter in which they embodied
their demands, had increased to millions and were threatening revolution. The Chartists were led by an Irishman and a
Repealer, Feargus O'Connor, M.P., and a vast mass meeting,
announced for April, was anticipated with anxiety by the
Government. A rising in Ireland might touch off an explosion,
and a rebellion of Catholics would be peculiarly embarrassing
at the moment: Lord Minto, Lord Privy Seal, and Lord John

Russell's father-in-law, had been sent to the Vatican on a private mission to the Pope. To be in communication with the See of Rome was still a crime by the law of England, and though diplomatic intercourse was in fact carried on by means of an attaché at the Florence Legation resident in Rome, Lord Minto's mission was nevertheless a startling innovation and extremely delicate.

The British Government decided that steps must be taken to prevent any embarrassment in Ireland. At the end of March Lord Clarendon wrote, "the time to suppress the public preaching of sedition had come," and measures were concerted to nip any insurrection in the bud. The Law Officers of the Crown conferred to devise methods of repression, a stream of military reinforcements began to proceed towards Dublin, the Duke of Wellington advised on military dispositions, Colonel McGregor, Inspector-General of the Irish Constabulary, was warned to be ready; and as the formidable power of Britain moved into action it became evident that the chained tiger and the baited lion of Irish rebellion, if indeed they existed at all, were only made of paper.

The events which followed, known as "the '48," make painful reading. Seldom can a revolutionary movement have been conducted with more idealism and less sense of realism. "These men are honest," Lord Stanley told the House of Lords. ". . . They are not to be bought off by the government of the day for a colonial place . . ." Their programme, Mitchel declared, was "honest, outspoken resistance to oppression," while Meagher cried, "It is a policy which calls forth the noblest passions . . . it is far removed from the tricks and crimes of politics—for the young, the gallant, the good, it has the most powerful attractions."

But sincerity, highmindedness, nobility are not the sole materials of revolution; careful and cunning preparation is needed, secrecy, plotting, the establishment of an underground organization, and in these the revolutionary movement of Young Ireland was utterly deficient; " . . . never in all history," says a modern Irish nationalist historian, "was an insurrection conducted so ineptly."

Duffy laid the blame at Mitchel's door: ". . . method was what he altogether rejected . . ." He was "contemptuous of every expedient but stimulating the popular feeling. Preparation, pre-concert, a military leader, a plan—all these were idle and dilatory . . . Were not Paris, Berlin and Vienna sufficient evidence of what a spontaneous rising could effect? We reminded him," writes Duffy, "that in these continental cities the population had long been organized and armed by secret societies, but that . . . there was not a week's supply of food in Dublin . . . there was no depot of arms and ammunition . . . they did not know with certainty where to lay their hands on the first barrow and pickaxe to throw up the first barricade. . . ."

In addition, the Young Irelanders were incorrigibly un-businesslike. Duffy complained that not one letter in ten was dated, nor was the address stated—William Smith O'Brien alone was accustomed to transacting business, and always dated his briefest note.

Meanwhile, in the columns of the *United Irishman*, Mitchel, with no organization, no support, no arms and no ammunition behind him, hurled threats and curses at the Lord-Lieutenant and the British Government. Lord Clarendon was addressed as "Her Majesty's Executioner General and General Butcher in Ireland," "High Commissioner of Spies and General Suborner in Ireland," the "holy hatred of foreign dominion which nerved our noble predecessors fifty years ago (to rebel in 1798) . . . still lives, thank God," Mitchel declared, "and glows as fierce and hot as ever." He was dedicated, he vowed, "to educate that holy hatred, to make it know itself and arm itself . . ." He spoke of "ten thousand fighting men in Dublin" and the "crash of the downfall of the thrice accursed British Empire."

1782 had been bloodless, and William Smith O'Brien clung to the hope that 1848 would also be bloodless, and that support, as in '82, would come from the landed gentry. "What we desired," wrote Duffy, "was another and better '82." By Mitchel, however, "the constitution of 1782 was covered with ridicule and scorn."

On March 15, 1848, a meeting was held at the Music Hall, Abbey Street, Dublin, at which William Smith O'Brien and Meagher spoke. Smith O'Brien invited names for service in an armed National Guard, announced that an Irish Brigade was to be recruited in the United States, and reminded his audience that one-third of the British Army consisted of Irishmen, and that there were ten thousand Irishmen serving in the constabulary. Meagher supported him, and it was agreed, with enthusiasm, that an address of congratulation

to the infant French Republic should be taken to Paris by
these two and a representative Irish working man.

The Government had now poured 10,000 troops into Dublin, and during the summer of 1848 17,000 stand of arms
with 1,500,000 rounds of ammunition, were sent to Ireland.
The Inniskilling Dragoons were brought up from Newbridge,
the Castle garrison was strengthened by two squadrons of
Light Dragoons, quartered in the riding school in Lower
Castle Yard, two pieces of ordnance were brought into the
Castle, and the fleet, which had been off Lisbon, was ordered
to proceed to the Cove of Cork (Cobh).

Some disturbance was expected on St. Patrick's Day, 1848,
but the weather was wet and stormy and the streets more
than usually empty. On March 20 a mass meeting was
announced, at the North Wall, to express admiration of the
heroic conduct of the French people and to address Her
Majesty "respectfully" on the necessity for an immediate
Repeal of the Union. The attendance was not as large as had
been expected, about 3,000 persons only; no rioting followed,
but a mob marched to the Castle gates, which were closed
and guarded, and there the Lord-Lieutenant was "groaned
most heartily."

On March 21 William Smith O'Brien, Meagher and
Mitchel were summoned by the police; O'Brien and Meagher
were charged with having made seditious speeches at the
Music Hall meeting, Mitchel with publishing seditious articles
in the *United Irishman*. Having made an appearance in court
and given bail, they were remanded.

This respite was due to the fact that the British Government was not ready with preparations for dealing with Ireland.
A prosecution for high treason under existing laws was felt
to be impossible. The savage barbarity of the punishment,
hanging, drawing and quartering, coupled with the fact that
in France the death penalty had recently been abolished,
would arouse an outcry; therefore the Law Officers of the
Crown had drafted a new Act, known as the Treason Felony
Act, which passed through Parliament "with the speed of an
express train" but did not receive the Royal Assent until
April 22, 1848. It recognized a new offence: "any person
who, by open and advised speaking, compassed the intimidation of the Crown or of Parliament was made guilty of
felony," punishable with transportation for fourteen years or
for life. "Thus," wrote Lord Campbell, a former Irish Lord

N

Chancellor, presenting the measure to Lord John Russell, "while you would have the glory of mitigating the severity of the penal code, you would be armed with the effectual means of sending Messrs. Mitchel, Meagher and Smith O'Brien to Botany Bay."

William Smith O'Brien and Meagher were released on bail and were able to leave for Paris, as arranged, with the address of congratulation, while Mitchel addressed a meeting on March 24, adjuring his audience "for the love of God to get themselves guns . . . he understood a very good serviceable rifle could be had for £3 . . . The King of France had run away from Paris, the King of Prussia was hiding at Potsdam, the Emperor of Austria was packing his portmanteau to run away from Vienna, but Lord Clarendon still sat in Dublin Castle. He meant to call on them, if they would not remain slaves for ever, to rise up . . . at an early day, or perhaps an early night, and smash through the Castle of Dublin and tear it down." The speech was received with "deafening cheers" and interrupted with cries of "Pikes!" "Pikes!"

Five companies of the 52nd and the 57th, and the Regiment of the Carabiniers, were now added to the Dublin garrison, and two ships of war were detached from the fleet anchored at the Cove of Cork and brought round to Kingstown.

The British Government also stretched out a long arm and took action further afield. When Smith O'Brien and Meagher reached Paris the interview with the poet-President, Lamartine, was "a great disappointment." Lamartine had been warned by Lord Normanby, the British Ambassador, that if he encouraged agitation within the British Empire it might be necessary to withdraw the British Embassy. His official response to the Irish delegation was that though France had infinite goodwill towards Ireland she could not interfere with the internal affairs of Great Britain. The text of the reply was reprinted by the British Government and received the distinction of being posted on all police barracks in Ireland.

Meanwhile, discouraging events were taking place. In addition to their courage and devotion during the period of the penal laws, the Irish Catholic priesthood had taken part in all movements for Irish freedom. Patriot priests were "out" in '98; in the Repeal movement O'Connell was "supported and assisted all over Catholic Ireland by the priesthood," and the vast correspondence by which the Repeal organization was maintained was largely conducted by them. During the famine, parish priests were solidly the champions of the Irish people. "The priests," testified Count Strzelecki, of the British Association, "often endured the same privations as their people . . . no food but stirabout, no tea and sugar. The wind blew, the snow came in, the rain dripped. . . ." In Ireland the influence of the parish priest was incalculable; he was at once the spiritual guide, the practical adviser, the leader and the comrade of his flock.

But John O'Connell's whispering campaign against Young Ireland had had a fatal effect. Dr. Cane, Mayor of Kilkenny, described it to Duffy as "the long pre-arranged blackening of all your characters in the eyes of the Catholic clergy, who are hereabouts to a man opposed to you . . . this is an immense power you have to encounter, and any public meeting anywhere in Ireland would, by its majority, rule against you . . ."

Nevertheless, a certain number of priests had supported Young Ireland; Duffy gives the names of twenty-three, but says that, after the French Revolution of 1848, "it was no longer possible to count their supporters among the younger priests." This support, however, was not evident. One of the few important clerical adherents of Young Ireland was Father Kenyon, of Templederry, known as the patriot priest of Tipperary. An eccentric, but a man of culture and intellect, Father Kenyon exercised immense influence in Tipperary, and had given a pledge to the Young Ireland cause on behalf of twenty parishes. He had consequently been elected to a seat on the council, and the Young Ireland leaders had implicit faith in him.

However, at the beginning of February, 1848, any hope of clerical support for an insurrection vanished. In a Papal Rescript dated February 5 Pope Pius IX admonished the Irish priesthood and forbade political activities. The Rescript was the result of "intense British pressure" and was connected with Lord Minto's mission. The Rescript began by stating that Irish clergy were accused of giving "provocation to murder." These reports had been so frequent as to awake the solicitude of the Sacred Congregation of Propaganda, which "cannot believe that these reports so extensively noised abroad are true." "Satisfactory and speedy information" was required in order that the Sacred Congregation might know what

importance it should attach to the damnatory reports, and
meanwhile the Catholic prelates of Ireland were required by
the Sacred Congregation to admonish the clergy, to sedulously
apply themselves to watch over the spiritual interests of the
people, and in no way to mix themselves up with worldly
affairs." Father Kenyon was reprimanded by his Bishop and
suspended; but he did not inform the Young Ireland leaders
either of the reprimand or the suspension.

On April 10, 1848, the great Chartist meeting took place
on Kennington Common near London—it was a failure. A
monster petition with, it was alleged, more than five million
signatures was to be carried to the House of Commons by a
gigantic procession. But to meet the Chartists' threat tens
of thousands of upper and middle class citizens enrolled
themselves as special constables, 9,000 troops and four bat-
teries of field artillery were brought into London and posted
at strategic points, and the bridges across the Thames were
held. The Chartist leaders were informed that the meeting
would be permitted only if the giant procession were cancelled. The offer was accepted, the meeting split into sections
and was addressed by various delegates, while "the petition
was humbly taken over Battersea Bridge" and handed in at
the House of Commons. Repeal of the Union was an article
of the Chartists' "Charter," but a meeting subsequently held
in the Princes Theatre, Dublin, with Mitchel in the chair, to
form an alliance with the Chartists, was attended by fewer
than three hundred persons, and was a "dead failure."

The trial of William Smith O'Brien for sedition, however,
ended in unexpected triumph. On Monday, May 15, ten
thousand men, marching in "military formation," were
said to have escorted him from his lodgings in Westland Row,
Dublin to the Law Courts, and though the jury which tried
him was "packed," that is selected under the influence of the
Government, it proved impossible for it to reach agreement.
Of the three Catholics allowed two obediently voted for a
conviction, but the third, converted, it is said, by a brilliant
speech for the defence made by Isaac Butt, later celebrated as
the leader of the Home Rule party, refused to convict, and
William Smith O'Brien was freed. On the following day
Meagher was tried. Once more the jury was "packed," though
on this occasion only one Catholic was allowed on it: there
was, however, a member of the Society of Friends. Isaac

Butt again defended, the Quaker refused to convict, the jury disagreed, and Meagher in turn was freed.

Now it was Mitchel's turn to be tried, and he was not to be allowed to escape. "The Lord-Lieutenant," wrote an official historian, "could not go on for ever allowing a newspaper to scream out appeals to rebellion and to publish, every week, minute descriptions of the easiest and quickest way of killing English soldiers." There was no procession marching in military formation from Mitchel's lodgings to the Court; he had been arrested and imprisoned in Newgate (Dublin) on May 13, under the Treason Felony Act, and he was tried on May 25 at the Court House, Green Street, where an underground passage led from the prison to the dock. The jury was so flagrantly "packed" that out of 3,000 Catholics on the jury list not one was selected; outside the courthouse the streets were filled with troops.

Imprisoned though he was, Mitchel's conviction of the swift approach of insurrection never wavered. ". . . for me, I abide my fate joyfully," he wrote, "for I know that whatever betide me my work is nearly done . . . the music my countrymen now love best to hear is the rattle of arms and the ring of the rifle. As I sit here, as I write in my lonely cell, I hear, just dying away, the measured tramp of ten thousand marching men—my gallant Confederates, unarmed and silent but with hearts like bended bows, waiting till *the time* comes."

Mitchel's faith in armed rebellion was shared by the British Government; a rising was expected hourly; Lord Clarendon's nerves were described as being "in a condition of diseased sensibility," and he sent his children to England for safety. In England the Duke of Wellington "expected an outbreak," and *The Times* made arrangements for receiving dispatches via Cork and Bristol in case Dublin should fall into rebel hands.

More and more troops were poured into Dublin; the 71st Highland Light Infantry from Scotland, the 48th Regiment of Foot from Belfast, the 31st from Manchester. *The Times* reported that the streets "swarm with red coats varied by the blue uniforms of the Artillery and the Light Cavalry. Barracks . . . are rearing their fronts in quarters hitherto devoted to the peaceful purposes of science and commerce." Leinster House, the Linen Hall, the Tenterhouse in the Liberties were requisitioned, and under the direction of the Duke of Wellington Trinity College, the old Parliament House, the Post Office

and the Custom House became strongpoints. Civilians, however, were not allowed to arm, and the Protestants, fearing
a massacre, were brought almost to the point of rebellion by
this decision; John Pitt Kennedy, the Secretary of the Devon
Commission and an improving landlord, then bought 500
stand of arms at his own expense and secretly distributed
them to Protestants, maintaining that he had prevented an
outbreak by his action.

The Government was convinced that an attempt to rescue
Mitchel would follow his conviction, but the truth was very
different. Meagher had made a personal inspection of the
Dublin Confederate clubs and "sought information from all
sources" with a view to Mitchel's rescue; his reluctant
conclusion was that "the people were unprepared, unorganized,
unarmed and incapable of being even roughly disciplined for
such an attempt." More than 10,000 regular troops, with
constabulary in addition, thronged Dublin; against them were
some thirty clubs, numbering, at an optimistic estimate, between 6,000 and 10,000 men, almost totally unarmed and
lacking even pikes. Outside Dublin the situation was worse.
In Cork City, though the position had improved since the
news of revolution in France, there were only eleven clubs;
in the neighbourhood of Cork, about six; Kilkenny had only
four, Tipperary ten, Wexford four, Ennis one and Galway
one. In all Ulster only three clubs had been formed, in spite
of the fact that Mitchel had held office, as Inspector of Clubs
for Ulster, for a year. In all, including Dublin, not eighty
clubs existed in the whole of Ireland and, most significant of
all, though the insurrection was to be an agrarian rising, not
a single club existed in the agricultural districts. Moreover,
the Young Irelanders had no treasury, there were "no funds
whatever" to buy arms, ammunition or food. "The insensate
policy of deriding preparation had borne its natural fruit, no
one was prepared," wrote Duffy; and not only was rescue
impossible, but any scheme for a rising must be postponed
until the autumn, after preparations had been made and the
harvest gathered in.

◦◦◦

Mitchel's trial was short and the result a foregone conclusion.
The jury retired between four and five o'clock, and before
seven a verdict of guilty was returned. Next day Mitchel was
brought, by the underground passage, into the dock at Green

Street, and received a sentence of fourteen years' transportation. His friends made a desperate rush for the dock, the judges retired from the court, and he was hustled back into the underground passage. A warship was waiting in Dublin Bay, and within an hour he was chained and on his way to Spike Island, the convict depot off the Cove of Cork, to be transported to Bermuda. Orders from the Castle directed that he should not be treated with unnecessary harshness; "as regards food and exercise he should have such indulgence as the state of his health might seem to require"; he did not wear a convict's uniform, and on his way to Spike Island was allowed the use of the ship's chart room for his meals and recreation, which angered the Tory Members of the House of Commons.

On the morning after Mitchel's deportation, May 27, "for the first time commenced a formal conspiracy," writes Duffy. "Then and there, for the first time, measures were taken to obtain money, arms and officers from abroad." As far as money was concerned, during the '48, the Young Irelanders had only £916, most of which was contributed by the leaders. It was agreed that an executive committee should be appointed, and an insurrection was "pledged" to take place after harvest and "before the year closed."

"Examined by the light of practical sense," wrote Duffy later, "nothing more wildly hopeless than this scheme can be found among the extravagances of political literature."

Preparations for armed rebellion now began, with complete lack of concealment—they were known in detail to the police and fully described by the newspapers. *The Times* reported that the formation of clubs was rapidly proceeding and their organization being tightened up; youths of sixteen were no longer being accepted, and persons were not admitted to meetings without showing their cards of membership. At a mass meeting at the Music Hall on June 6 Meagher announced that "the fate of Ireland must this year be determined, the end was at hand, so get arms and prepare," upon which *The Times* sarcastically inquired, "when is the rebellion going to come off? . . . There are to be clubs formed in the utmost silence all over Ireland; and those clubs are to be prepared for rebellion, we presume, in similar silence."

By the end of June, however, enrolment began to increase; the system of clubs, wrote Routh to Trevelyan, was spreading "fast and unchecked"; he thought there might be

50,000 men, "more or less, preparing and drilling," and he had been instructed to plan Commissariat arrangements for troops on active service. "Rapid increase" in the clubs was reported, and "wholesale enrolment . . . all accounts concur from town and country." In Dublin the number of clubs increased to twenty-six in the city, with eight in the suburbs.

John O'Connell now "intimated to William Smith O'Brien that he was ready for a reconciliation on the most accommodating terms." Without the sanction of the name of O'Connell, which swayed the Irish masses as Napoleon's name swayed the French peasantry, nothing could be done in the rural districts, and a conference of Young and Old Ireland met in the office of the *Freeman's Journal* and debated terms for several days.

For a time it looked as if a new national organization might be born, but events outside Ireland abruptly ended any possibility of a coalition. The dream of a liberal and idealistic government in Paris came to a bloodstained conclusion as the extreme left wing rose against the Republican government. Hundreds of barricades were erected, fierce fighting took place, and the Archbishop of Paris, who crossed the barricades in an effort to negotiate a truce, and was unmistakable, because he wore his canonical robes, was shot dead. A shudder of horror and repulsion went through Europe.

News disturbing to Catholics now came from Italy. The reign of liberalism and idealism was over in Rome. Pius IX, the liberal Pope, was forced, by extreme republicans, to dismiss his ministers, his temporal power was threatened, and the Catholic clergy became more antagonistic to the ideas held by many of the Young Irelanders than ever before.

Meanwhile, in Dublin, Clarendon's existence had become nerve-racking. "No Tipperary landlord ever received more threatening notices than I do . . . as to when and where I am to be assassinated," he told Lord John Russell; "I only go out in the carriage for a short walk in the Park which makes me nearly a State prisoner . . . the life I lead is hardly endurable."

Nevertheless, the British Government was steadily moving forward, preparations were now complete, and in July arrests began under the new Treason Felony Act. One of the first victims was Duffy, who was arrested on July 9, 1848, as he came home to dinner; he was put in a car and conveyed to the Dublin Newgate. An "immense crowd" collected, shouts arose of "take him out, take him out." and D'Arcy McGee, who had come over from America in 1847, got up on the step and whispered, "Do you wish to be rescued?" Duffy replied, "Certainly not," adding, with singular candour, since a detective and two policemen were in the car with him, ". . . you must wait for the harvest."

On July 12, when Meagher was arrested in his native city of Waterford, the church bells were rung, a "vast" crowd rushed into the streets, and the bridge over the river Suir, on the Dublin road, was barricaded with baulks of timber. But in the river, "within a stone's throw," lay three warships, *Dragon*, *Merlin* and *Medusa*, capable of knocking the town into rubble in an hour, while the crowd "had not a gun or a mortar." Standing on the roof of the carriage in which he was to be taken to Dublin, Meagher forbade an attempt at rescue, and was driven away. Duffy was kept imprisoned in Newgate, but Meagher, with others arrested at the same time, was released on bail until his trial, fixed for August 8. "It was the policy of the Government to show forbearance towards political agitators to its utmost limits, so long as it could feel assured that the preservation of order was secure."

At this point John O'Connell prudently departed for a continental holiday, having first ordered Conciliation Hall, the headquarters of the Repeal Association, to be shut up and barricaded, while Father Kenyon, the patriot priest of Tipperary, failed to appear at a meeting held in Duffy's cell in Newgate. Duffy was allowed by the Dublin Corporation to see his friends and edit the *Nation* and hatch plots against the Government in his cell. Father Kenyon now denied that he had left the movement: "I cannot get up [to Dublin] at present unless I resign my benefice," he wrote to Duffy, "and that I am not prepared to do unless in a very last extremity." Duffy took this to mean that when the crisis came Father Kenyon would be in "the place he was pledged to occupy."

Meanwhile, troops were encamped near towns, in the sight of the inhabitants, to discourage rebellion; 500 men were encamped at Waterford, 400 at Kilkenny, and the 75th Regiment bivouacked in Phoenix Park, Dublin. Formations, called "movable columns," prepared to "scour the country"; one, which left Dublin for Thurles, consisted of 800 infantry, two companies of Rifles, a demi-brigade of Artillery and two troops of cavalry, and the city of Cork was described by

Routh as being "occupied." The troops, however, were not entirely reliable, largely because a high percentage of the soldiers of the British Army were Irish. Men of the 7th Fusiliers pelted the Protestant cathedral at Cork with stones and shouted for O'Connell, Smith O'Brien and Meagher, while a private in the 88th, the famous Connaught Rangers, was court-martialled for assaulting a constable, and at an exercise another Connaught Ranger shot a constable in the leg.

William Smith O'Brien now embarked on a tour of the south and south-west, to ascertain the state of feeling in the country. His tour was reported to be "a continuous triumph." The Young Irelanders claimed that 150 clubs had been formed, representing 50,000 men, and Smith O'Brien declared that the pulse of the country "beat passionately for action." Meetings were held in Meath and at Limerick during the third week in July, and in each case 10,000 men were said to be present; while at a meeting on the mountain side at Slievenamon, in Tipperary, the attendance was alleged to be 50,000, "all men, there were no women or children."

Ten days after the arrests under the Treason Felony Act, the Government exerted another of its powers. Dublin, Cork, Waterford and Drogheda were "proclaimed" by Lord Clarendon under the Crime and Outrage Act, that is, they were placed under semi-martial law. All persons not holding a police permit were ordered to give up their arms within four days, on penalty of a year's imprisonment with hard labour. The walls of buildings in Dublin were covered with proclamations, which groups of people read in silence, while "leaders of the Confederation were observed posting in hot speed from one lodge to another."

Lord Clarendon, who, according to the Home Secretary, was "over-frightened," did not consider these measures sufficient, and he demanded the suspension of Habeas Corpus, to enable him to arrest and detain, without charge or trial, any persons who might be suspected of conspiring against Her Majesty's person and Government. "Nothing has been left undone which could inflame the people," he wrote, and "an early opportunity will be taken to break out into open rebellion." He had "used all his powers," he told Sir George Grey, and he must be assisted by a suspension of Habeas Corpus.

The Government, advised by Sir George Grey, refused, upon which Clarendon once more threatened to resign. Once

more the Government gave way, and on Saturday, July 22, a
Bill, suspending Habeas Corpus in Ireland until March 1, 1849,
was rushed through the House of Commons, passing all its
stages in one day; and on Monday it was similarly rushed
through the Lords.

The news was received in Dublin by telegraph on Saturday afternoon, "and had a thunderbolt fallen on the city, it
could not have created greater dismay or terror," though
dismay might seem inexplicable, since Habeas Corpus had
repeatedly been suspended in Ireland, and the Government
was not likely to neglect a weapon so powerful.

The Young Ireland leaders were now on the horns of a
dilemma: they must either submit to arrest, and fail, or try
to raise the country before preparations for rebellion were
complete. William Smith O'Brien was out of Dublin—he had
reached Wexford on his provincial tour. But at a meeting of
Young Irelanders it was agreed that, in spite of all deficiencies,
"the one honourable course" was to fight. The strength of the
garrison put insurrection in Dublin out of the question, but
an attempt might be made to seize Kilkenny, "the old
historic seat of government," centrally situated, easy to
defend and lying on the borders of the three best fighting
counties in Ireland, Tipperary, Wexford and Waterford.

The Young Irelanders believed the people were massed
behind them, thirsting for action, but the police had no very
high opinion of the crowds who attended their meetings.
The 10,000 who marched in "military formation," to escort
William Smith O'Brien to his trial were "Dublin rabble," and
"no respectable people" were present at the Limerick meeting; in Meath, William Smith O'Brien was described as "addressing the mob"; in Tipperary, Meagher was greeted by "the
lower orders," while a meeting to form a club at Knockeevan,
Tipperary, was "composed of servant boys"; the solid mass
of lower middle-class respectability remained inert.

Further, the Young Irelanders had no organization, no
general, no military command, no central authority, no
headquarters, no specific plan of insurrection, no treasury,
no store of munitions or arms, no accurate information as
to the strength of the Confederate clubs. However, when William Smith O'Brien was joined in Wexford by the other
leaders he too agreed that the only honourable course was to
fight, and the Young Irelanders set about raising the country.

On Sunday, July 23, 1848, William Smith O'Brien, with

the other leaders, drove into Enniscorthy, County Wexford, and called a public meeting. Large crowds attended, but there was only one club in Enniscorthy, and that did not number more than 150 members; a local priest, Father Parle, warned Smith O'Brien that the people were not prepared for war. Though Wexford was one of the fighting counties of Ireland, and the people had fought with desperate gallantry in '98, the Young Ireland movement had made little progress. The memory of '98, of its bloodshed and brutality, and of the atrocities and reprisals which accompanied the suppression of the rising, was too recent. Moreover, British ships of war were lying in Wexford Harbour, as well as in Waterford.

William Smith O'Brien and his companions drove on to Kilkenny, where the Mayor, Dr. Cane, was a leading Young Irelander, and sat on the council. He met them with discouraging news: no attempt to seize Kilkenny had any chance of success without the assistance of substantial forces from outside the city. The garrison of British troops had recently been strengthened, and the Old Ireland party within the city was hostile. The strength of the clubs in Kilkenny, estimated at 1,700 men, had been misprinted in the newspapers as 17,000 and though the Young Irelanders can hardly have credited such a figure they had anticipated a more favourable situation. Dr. Cane assured them that if the Kilkenny clubs rose at this moment they would certainly be defeated, and he advised William Smith O'Brien and his companions to leave Kilkenny, raise as large a force as possible in the chief towns of Tipperary, and return with reinforcements in a few days.

The Young Irelanders drove on to Callan, where a band, green boughs and bonfires awaited them, and an enthusiastic meeting was held. Many of the Royal Irish Hussars, who were stationed in the town, attended and appeared to be "among the most delighted of the audience." After warning the people to be ready for an early summons to arms, the leaders proceeded to Carrick-on-Suir. It was now evening, and the whole population of the town was abroad, delirious with excitement. There was, writes Meagher, "a torrent of human beings, rushing through lanes and narrow streets, whirling in dizzy circles and tossing up its dark waves with sounds of wrath, vengeance and defiance . . . eyes red with rage and desperation . . . wild half-stifled, passionate, frantic, prayers of hope, curses . . . scornful exulting defiance of death. It was the revolution, if we had accepted it."

There were, however, only 300 rifles and muskets in Carrick-on-Suir, and though the clubs claimed they could turn out about 3,000 men, they were armed only with pikes. British troops in or near Carrick had recently been reinforced, and there were now 1,200 men, with artillery, two howitzers and two field-pieces, either in the town itself or within an hour's march. The local Young Irelanders refused to attempt a rising —it would be "drowned in blood." William Smith O'Brien then asked for a force of 600 volunteers, to be ready, provisioned and equipped, "within an hour," to march back to Callan with him. This, too, was declared to be impossible, and O'Brien, with the other leaders, was urged to conceal himself for the present, to allow time for arrangements to be made. He refused, and Meagher became much cast down by the "want of alacrity" among the local leaders. However, another enthusiastic meeting, attended by large crowds, was held, and the Young Ireland leaders drove on once more, this time to Cashel.

Meanwhile, the news had reached Duffy, in Newgate, that William Smith O'Brien was out raising the country. Duffy was thrown into a state of intense excitement; he was devoted to O'Brien, and if there was to be fighting, Duffy longed to be present. He decided to attempt an escape, and a silk ladder was smuggled into the prison, concealed in a basket of clean clothes. Duffy calculated that, with assistance from outside, he, with two others, could pass under cover of darkness through one of the courts, which was badly lit, empty and unguarded and not occupied by prisoners at the moment, and fly from Dublin.

"But where should we fly to?" Duffy asked himself. There was no headquarters, no agency to supply information, no means of contact with the leaders. The newspapers were full of contradictory reports of what was happening in the south, and it was not likely that escaped prisoners, well-known to the police, would remain long at liberty, wandering about the country in search of an insurrection. No letter or news came from O'Brien, and though, Duffy writes, "the fever of impatience in which we tossed would add a new horror to Dante's 'Purgatory,' " he remained in prison.

Meanwhile, William Smith O'Brien and his party had reached Cashel, a famous shrine of ancient Ireland and the former capital of Munster. Cashel, remarkable for the Rock of Cashel, a startling mass of limestone which rises abruptly

from the plain, crowned by a magnificent group of ecclesiastical ruins including a cathedral, was a principal stronghold of
Brian Boroimhe (Brian Boru), the ancestor of the O'Briens.

The Young Irelanders were convinced they would find the
green flag flying from the Rock of Cashel, "sentinels and
watch fires, columns of sturdy peasants, carts laden with
provisions, flaming smithies where strong men were hammer-
ing iron and steel into serviceable weapons." Instead, Cashel
was like a city of the dead, not a soul was to be seen in
the streets. The project of raising Cashel and southern Tipperary had failed.

Since Kilkenny, Carrick-on-Suir and Cashel had, all three,
declined the responsibility of striking the first blow, the
Young Irelanders decided to attempt raising the rural districts,
and on Tuesday morning, July 25, drove north, to Killenaule.
Here, according to an eye-witness, "the reception of Mr.
O'Brien was most enthusiastic, bouquets fell in showers on
him and addresses were read for him, but that there was . . .
any effective addition to his strength I did not hear." Once
more the leaders took to the road, this time west, to Mullinahone.

In Mullinahone there appeared to be eagerness, though
only three members of the club turned out. However, the
chapel bells were tolled, and by midnight it was estimated that
6,000 men had gathered. Pikes were hammered out at the
local smithy—the first pikes made in that part of Tipperary
since '98—and barricades thrown up, though William Smith
O'Brien forbade the felling of trees for road-blocks without
the permission of the proprietors on whose lands they grew.
Throughout the night the 6,000 armed with impromptu pikes,
pitchforks and a few fowling-pieces, were kept busy practis-
ing rudimentary drill, but when morning came the crowd
began to melt away. There was no sign of food, and it
transpired that the majority had come in the expectation of
being fed. William Smith O'Brien bought and distributed
some bread at his own expense, giving a warning that, in
future, his followers would have to provide provisions for
themselves. "This announcement," reported an eye-witness,
Father Fitzgerald, "gave a death blow to the entire movement." Tipperary was starving.

Wholesale desertion now reduced the 6,000 to 500, but
that morning, Wednesday, July 26, William Smith O'Brien,
with two others, went to the police barrack in Mullinahone

and called on the occupants to surrender and hand over their
arms. Six constables and a sergeant were taken by surprise;
two were cooking breakfast, the others were shaving. The
sergeant begged O'Brien not to humiliate them: "Oh, Sir, if
we give in to three or four men we'll be disgraced for ever.
Bring a force and we'll submit." Smith O'Brien agreed, and
withdrew, upon which the police, without waiting to surrender,
fled to a stronger station, "taking their arms with them."
A Young Irelander from Carrick-on-Suir, who was present,
recorded that this chivalrous treatment of the police "filled
him with despair."

Placing himself at the head of the remaining 500, William
Smith O'Brien now marched north, to Ballingarry, endeavouring, but without success, to raise the hamlets as he passed.
At Ballingarry a large crowd collected, but he was forced to
make an announcement from the chapel wall that he could
not supply food; he instructed volunteers to go home and
provide themselves with "at least" four days' provisions, suggesting "oatmeal, bread and hard eggs." The effect of this
announcement was disheartening; the majority of his audience were existing on Government relief, a pound of Indian
meal a day. His instructions seemed a mockery. Local priests
remonstrated with the people, warning them that they were
"rushing on ruin"; Smith O'Brien's 500 followers dwindled to
50, and he was seen to shed "silent tears of shame and
despair."

At Ballingarry, he was joined by Terence McManus, a
native of Liverpool, a prosperous young merchant who had
crossed the Irish Sea as soon as he had heard the insurrection
had begun—"a tall dashing soldierly fellow . . . with a ringing
and uproarious laugh."

On Thursday, July 27, the chapel bells at Ballingarry tolled,
all possible recruits were collected, and between twelve and
one o'clock, the Young Irelanders prepared to march, with
"about a hundred and fifty slashing fellows tolerably well
armed." The intention was to pass again through Mullinahone
and raise the country round Silevenamon, where a recent
meeting was alleged to have been attended by 50,000 men.
The recruits were without food, and McManus bought some
bread. While a hasty meal was being eaten, the parish priest
"got among them," and when the order to march was given
about a third went home. "To our mortification," writes
McManus, ". . . desertion continued at every opportunity, so

that while we were still five miles from the rendezvous our party did not exceed a score." Weary and depressed, the leaders paused for the night at Killenaule.

Early next morning there was a sudden alarm—cavalry were advancing on Killenaule. It was assumed their object was to seize William Smith O'Brien; barricades were hastily constructed, and O'Brien was persuaded to retire to a distance. The insurgent force now numbered about thirty men—their armament consisting of one rifle, two muskets and some pikes and pitchforks—followed by a considerable crowd of women and children. The cavalry proved to be the 8th Royal Irish Hussars, who had already shown themselves by no means hostile at the meeting at Callan; the officer in command gave his word of honour he had no warrant for Smith O'Brien, they were on their way to provide an escort for the Judge of Assizes at Nenagh. They were allowed to pass the barricade, one by one. The regiment was Irish, popular, and the people gave them a cheer as they passed through.

Subsequently, the Young Ireland leaders were reproached for allowing the Hussars to pass, but to engage a troop of fully-equipped cavalry, numbering at least 100 men, with one rifle and two muskets would have been suicide. William Smith O'Brien now took a count of all his men with arms; one or two additional recruits had come in, but the total number with "arms of any description," including pikes, was, at the most, fifty.

At the head of this small force, William Smith O'Brien, accompanied by McManus, marched on to the neighbouring colliery district of Castlecomer, where large numbers of men were employed. He was well received, but the people were "without arms" and "in a state of semi-starvation"; destitution round Castlecomer was especially severe because the population, owing to the collieries, was dense, and work in the pits had been suspended. "They seemed," noted McManus, "to have had much of their physical courage starved out of them"; this attempt, too, was a failure.

Failure indeed was universal. Carrick-on-Suir and Waterford had lost their enthusiasm, an attempt to march from Dublin to a rendezvous at Blanchardstown and seize Navan collapsed, and when the failure at Cashel became known at Limerick "it was intimated . . . that nothing could be attempted there."

An effort by D'Arcy McGee to raise recruits in Glasgow

and Greenock was unsuccessful—only 400 volunteers enrolled; he was recognized and compelled to leave at once.
He managed to reach Sligo, but nothing was to be accomplished there. The Catholic Bishop of Sligo had circulated
a letter directing parish priests to restrain their parishioners
from joining clubs and to exhort them to keep the law, and
though D'Arcy McGee got into communication with the head
of a secret society, the "Molly Maguires," the Mollies refused
to move until news of a rising came from the south.

On the evening of Friday, July 29, Meagher caught up with
William Smith O'Brien and Terence McManus, and the party
went to "the village on the commons," Ballingarry, for a
council of war. Their position was grave.

It was even graver than the insurgents, who were devoid of
an intelligence service of any kind, were aware. All attempts
to raise the country had failed, and under the suspension of
Habeas Corpus Young Irelander after Young Irelander was
being arrested by the Government. Every figure of note in the
movement was named for arrest in a hue and cry published
that day, the total reaching 120; Lalor had been arrested
on the 28th and Dr. Cane, the Mayor of Kilkenny, that morning.

The British Government was still convinced of the serious
nature of the rising, and the wildest rumours circulated in
Dublin. William Smith O'Brien was said to have raised 20,000
men and to be marching on Kilkenny, and the Duke of Wellington advised that 10,000 troops should be concentrated in
Kilkenny, Waterford and Carrick-on-Suir, to catch the rebel
force in a bag. Something like a panic occurred on Thursday,
when *The Times* reported that Thurles, Clonmel, Carlow and
Kilkenny were in the hands of the rebels, railway lines had
been torn up, and Thurles station was in flames. The report,
received by "electric telegraph" from Liverpool, proved to be
a hoax.

❦

At Ballingarry the Young Ireland council of war began at
8 p.m. on July 29 and lasted for an hour and a quarter. After
"severely censuring" everything that had been done up to
date, the Council proceeded to consider what could be done
now. The vote of the majority was to go into hiding and make
a fresh attempt later, but William Smith O'Brien refused. "I
won't hide," he declared. "I won't be a fugitive where my

forefathers reigned . . . I will continue to appeal to the people, as I have been doing, until we gather enough support to enable us to take the field." The leaders then agreed to separate. Meagher went off, to try again to raise the country; McManus remained with O'Brien at Ballingarry.

Meagher went first to Templederry, on the borders of Tipperary and Limerick, and called on Father Kenyon to fulfil his promises, toll his chapel bells, call out the twenty parishes he had promised, and, placing himself at their head, to march to join Smith O'Brien. To the "consternation" of Meagher he was received by Father Kenyon "with coldness and irony." Father Kenyon was prepared to fight if the people were also prepared to fight, but not to begin a "bootless struggle." If the Young Ireland leaders thought his parishioners were in a fighting frame of mind, he suggested they should raise a green flag anywhere in the district and see how many men would gather round it. Having received this ironical counsel, Meagher took his departure.

Abuse has been heaped on Father Kenyon for treachery, and it is true he had come to a private understanding with his Bishop, Dr. Kennedy of Killaloe, not to take any action. Nevertheless, to lead the inhabitants of twenty parishes into a hopeless armed insurrection was a responsibility which he could only refuse.

The hopes entertained of the Slievenamon district also proved vain; 50,000 persons were reported to have attended the previous meeting, but recruits with arms who came in did not amount to "more than a bodyguard."

It was now Saturday, July 30, just one week since William Smith O'Brien had begun the attempt to raise the country, at Enniscorthy, and in a field at Ballingarry, McManus inspected the insurgent force. It consisted of about thirty-eight armed men—some observers put the figure as high as forty-four—of whom about eighteen had "rudimentary" pikes and about twenty guns, mainly fowling-pieces or pistols, with one charge of powder each. In addition, about eighty men and women were prepared to throw stones. As McManus was addressing this force a messenger came galloping towards them, shouting that a large body of police was advancing on Ballingarry.

The insurgents were thrown into such a state of confusion and excitement that "it was a quarter of an hour before the butts of our rifles could get us room enough to consult together." It was then decided that Ballingarry must be defended, as to retreat would be fatally disheartening, and a barricade was hastily thrown up. William Smith O'Brien, with two or three of the twenty-odd men who possessed firearms, posted himself in front of the barricade, the remaining men with firearms were placed in houses which overlooked it, the stone-throwers concealed themselves on the left, the pike and pitchfork men were also on the left, but nearer the barricade. They were instructed to "lie close" until the police had passed and received the first fire, then the pike and pitchfork men were to spring up and charge down on the police rear, while the stone-throwers let fly "a volley of stones." Meanwhile, any men with firearms fortunate enough to possess a second charge were to reload.

As the police advanced the Inspector in command, Inspector Trant, received the impression, and stated it later in print, that a hostile crowd of about 3,000 persons was waiting to attack; no doubt there were spectators. The police lost their heads, broke rank, and ran for a farmhouse, standing on a hill about a mile to the left, belonging to a certain Widow McCormack.

At the time the Widow McCormack herself was out; she had started a few moments before for Ballingarry, leaving her five or six children, of whom the eldest was about ten years of age, alone in the house.

With a yell the insurgents abandoned their positions and dashed in pursuit of the police, carrying William Smith O'Brien along with them, while McManus, "very sullenly," he writes, followed. The Widow McCormack's house, which still exists, is a solid stone building, two storeys high which stood in a cabbage garden. The police barricaded the front windows on both storeys, using Mrs. McCormack's mattresses and furniture, tearing down her mantelpieces, pulling her doors from their hinges and her dresser from the kitchen wall. They then posted ten to twelve men, armed with carbines, in each window, while about twenty others manned the windows at the back. McManus made a reconnaissance, creeping round the house on his hands and knees, and reported that it could not be taken without a piece of artillery. William Smith O'Brien declared that nevertheless he was determined to attack; in that case, said McManus, the only way was by "smoking them out," and followed by about forty men he dashed into the stackyard, at the back of the stables, and

ordered each of his followers to get a load of hay on his
back and pile it against the back door. The men refused;
they would not risk being exposed to the fire of the police
while crossing the yard, so McManus carried the hay himself, piled it against the door, and fired into it, to ignite it.
The hay began to smoke.

At this point the Widow McCormack, who had been fetched
back when half-way to Ballingarry, appeared in a state of
frenzy. "Herself was shut out from her children and they
were prisoners within." She had managed to make herself
heard by the police, and William Smith O'Brien ordered Mc-
Manus to stop firing the hay. "Here is the Widow McCormack," he said, "she has been sent round by the police to
say they will make terms." O'Brien, McManus and one or
two others then went round to the front of the house, opened
the garden gate, and walked up the path, an act of considerable courage. William Smith O'Brien climbed on a window-
sill, thrust his arm in, over the top of the barricade, and
shaking hands with the constable inside said, "it was not their
lives but their arms we wanted." While he was in this dangerous position some insurgents, "the fellows who before refused to do anything," writes McManus, angrily, "commenced
from under cover of the walls to throw stones . . ." The
police instantly fired a volley from about forty carbines, two
men fell beside McManus, one dead, one severely injured,
and a second volley followed. McManus was knocked down
by a spent bullet striking him in the leg, but William Smith
O'Brien refused to move, saying, "An O'Brien never turned
his back on an enemy." The rebel force, however, fled in
utter disorder, urged on by a neighbouring priest, and could
not be rallied. Many, probably the majority, had come in
hopes of food, and they hastily concealed themselves in
neighbouring limekilns and a sunken road; they had, after
all, no ammunition. Within a few minutes the insurgent
"army" had vanished. William Smith O'Brien was persuaded
to retire, mounted on a captured police horse, and the insurrection of 1848 was over.

The unbridled threats, the invective, the boasts ended in a
scuffle between a handful of half-armed, undisciplined peasants
and a few police, in the Widow McCormack's cabbage garden,
and the lamentations of the Widow over the damage to
her furniture and her cabbages were the epitaph of the '48.

In a moment of bitterness Smith O'Brien wrote, "It matters

little whether the blame of failure lies on me or upon others; but the fact is recorded in our annals—that the people preferred to die of starvation at home, or to flee as voluntary exiles to other lands, rather than to fight for their lives and liberties."

No statement could more clearly reveal how completely Smith O'Brien and the Young Ireland leaders failed to grasp the effect of the famine. Starvation hardly seems to have entered into their calculations, and while it is true that hunger drives men to desperation, the moment of desperation in Ireland had spent itself in the food riots, the hunger marches, the headlong emigrant flight from Ireland of 1846 and 1847; what was left was apathy and despair. "Famine," wrote an "ex-Young Irelander" in October, 1848, ". . . effected a revolution very different from that Mr. O'Brien sought to accomplish . . . The lower classes . . . are broken down both in body and spirit. A ration of yellow meal is the highest object of their ambition, and so they can procure this, they care for naught else. . . ." Taking Tipperary as an example, he wrote, "famine has wrought a transformation . . . The Tipperary of 1848 and 1845 are as dissimilar as black and white." In 1845, before the famine began, the people were "ripe and ready for any enterprise, however desperate"; now, travelling between Roscrea and Clonmel on a Sunday, he saw "men, women and children looking as if they had been for the previous six days the inhabitants of an ash pit. Fine materials, truly," he commented, "for an army designed to 'squelch' the 'bloody old British Empire.' " *

But the last few weeks had brought news more terrible and more important than the scuffle in the Widow McCormack's cabbage garden. The shadow of another fearful catastrophe fell over Ireland; the blight, the same potato disease as in 1846, appeared all over the country, and there was every indication that a total failure of the potato was about to occur again.

---

* See Appendix. II, p. 413.

Chapter XVII

THE SPRING of 1848 was cold in Ireland; throughout February there were falls of snow, and the country people believed that snow would prevent the reappearance of blight. In 1847 only a small acreage had been planted, though the potato crop had proved superb, and now potatoes were planted all over Ireland, in what Lord Clarendon described to Lord John Russell as a "frenzy of confidence."

Severe sacrifices were made to obtain seed potatoes: clothes, bedsteads, tables and chairs were sold, and a Poor Law inspector reported that small occupiers, "already reduced to a state of all but pauperism, are straining every nerve to plant potatoes as largely as possible as a last desperate venture." Potatoes were "stuck in everywhere they could be planted and everyone's hopes were raised at the idea of a return to the old system." Landlords looked forward to rents being paid, the people to having enough to eat. "Please God it will be a blessed season . . . the olden times are coming back," the Poor Law inspector was told in Kells. "Next season, please God, we shall have potatoes as plentiful as ever," people said in County Clare. Reports coming in to the Board of Works in Dublin estimated the amount of land put down to potatoes, compared with the previous year, as twice as much in some districts, in others three times, four times, five times, and even ten times as much. Almost no "green crops"—cabbages, beans, carrots, kale—had been sown; an official travelling through the west saw "green crops" only on the experimental farm of the Society of Friends, at Pontoon, County Mayo; the resident magistrate at Ballinasloe reported that the "small farmers have abandoned attempts at any other kind of crop and have staked all they possessed or could borrow" on potatoes.

Through May, and until half-way through June, the weather was favourable. A few cases of blight did appear, as early as April 15. in County Monaghan, but caused no anxiety. Cases of blight had been reported early in 1847, and the crop had proved superb. Potato blight, like typhus, was endemic in Ireland, and an odd case or two could always be found.

But from the middle of June, 1848, the terrible story of 1846 was repeated, blow after blow. The weather changed and became continuously wet; by the middle of July the catastrophe had begun. "We were all in the greatest spirits at the approach of plenty," wrote Father John O'Sullivan, parish priest of Kenmare, on July 16, "but blight has made its appearance. On the morning of the 13th, to the astonishment of everyone, the potato fields that had, on the previous evening, presented an appearance that was calculated to gladden the hearts of the most indifferent, appeared blasted, withered, blackened and, as it were, sprinkled with vitriol, and the whole country has in consequence been thrown into dismay and confusion."

Skull, Castletown, Galway, Carlow, Parsonstown (now called Birr), Mayo, Sligo, Limerick all reported disease, "as in 1846." At Clifden a Poor Law official saw "four acres blackened as if steeped in tar." At Bantry, not a garden had escaped for nine miles, and Mr. Twisleton, the Poor Law Commissioner, noticed the characteristic "intolerable stench." Meanwhile, Dr. Lindley sent Trevelyan a report, "which tells its own unpleasant story"; blight was also appearing throughout England and Scotland, "from the Isle of Wight to Banffshire."

Trevelyan was not greatly disturbed. "The matter is awfully serious," he wrote, on July 19, "but we are in the hands of Providence, without a possibility of averting the catastrophe, if it is to happen; we can only await the result." He refused to be alarmed, and on July 25 noted in a memorandum, "I have read today and yesterday numerous answers to circulars addressed by the Poor Law Commissioners to their Inspectors about the potato disease, and the general result is that, although blight has appeared in many places, it has not done much damage as yet . . . The accounts from the South and West of England are worse than from Ireland."

At the end of July a report from Dr. Lindley showed that almost every district in Ireland was affected. This was the week when William Smith O'Brien was out trying to raise the country, but, said Colonel Jones, of the Board of Works, the people were not interested in sedition, they were too intent on watching their potatoes. Through August, rain fell "in one continuous cataract," "incessantly night and day";

hay was "actually floating"; "torrents" descended; "as bad as 1846." Blight, as in 1846, made rapid progress, and on August 8 Father Mathew wrote to Trevelyan that the worst fears had been realized and the potato crop was all but destroyed, while Lord John Russell told Clarendon he was "lost in despair about the potatoes . . . we must prepare for a calamitous winter."

At the end of the second week in August Dr. Lindley warned Trevelyan, "an Irish famine in 1848–9 is, I think, inevitable." Wheat and corn crops were poor, wet weather had produced maggot, and "Hessian fly" had caused the wheat to sprout on the stalk and produced "smut" in the oats; in the second week of September it was estimated that half the wheat crop was lost. By October, as in 1846, the fungus of *phytopthera infestans* was reducing potatoes, apparently sound when dug, to a stinking mass of rottenness in a few days; in many districts "no portion of the crop remained for the people's food," and Lord Clarendon told Prince Albert that he looked forward to the winter "with perfect dismay"; he was afraid that "a great part of the population must die of absolute want." The failure of the potato crop in 1848 was as complete as in 1846, and coming as it did upon a people already impoverished and enfeebled by distress, the results must be even more disastrous.

Even before the crushing blow of the new potato failure, the condition of the people, in those parts of Ireland which depended on the potato, was worse than in the previous year. The excellent yield in 1847 did not help them because an inadequate acreage was planted, and in addition to the acute shortage of potatoes, distress this summer was increased for two reasons. In May, 1848, the "Quarter acre clause," which had forbidden relief to any member of a family while the head of that family remained in possession of a quarter of an acre or more of land, was relaxed, and relief to the destitute wife and dependent children of a man holding a quarter of an acre or more was permitted. The decision was based on an opinion given by Mr. Henn, Q.C., in which the Irish Attorney-General concurred, but Trevelyan wrote, "I think this is a very doubtful measure"; he was in favour of "making the applicant for relief give up everything." An eye-witness testified that "many lives were saved, which would certainly otherwise have been lost."

Far more numerous were the applications for relief, the

result of a sharp increase in evictions due to the liability
of the landlord for rate on holdings rated at £4 and under,
whether the rent was paid or not. The Earl of Clancarty,
giving evidence before the Select Committee on the Irish
Poor Law, stated that a landlord might be without any rent
for years and still pay rates on the holdings valued at £4
and under. "It is absurd to suppose," said Lord Clancarty,
"that the landlord should be compelled to pay where he
has not the power of receiving. He will, of course, get rid of
that class of tenantry. He will not pay £500 a year in rates
for tenants from whom he receives no rent. He will direct
an ejectment . . . and the tenants will be turned out. It
is forced on the landlord by the £4 clause."

With good intentions towards his tenantry, a landlord
found it difficult to avoid clearance. The Marquess of Sligo
was twenty-eight years of age and, according to *The Times*,
was in receipt of £7,200 a year from his estate in Westport,
on which, however, there were charges of £6,000 annually.
He had been active in relief work, had twice supported the
insolvent Westport workhouse for a period at his own expense,
and since the famine kept "no establishment, not even a carriage." On October 8, 1848, he wrote to Lord Monteagle
that he had "struggled hard not to eject," but was now being
forced to do so. He had received no rent for three years,
had had to borrow £1,500 to pay the rates, and now found
himself "under the necessity of ejecting or being ejected . . ."
"The landlords," wrote Lord Clanricarde, a large Irish landowner, to Clarendon, "are *prevented* from aiding or tolerating
poor tenants. They are compelled to hunt out all such, to
save their property from the £4 clause"; and since the majority of smallholders in Ireland were tenants at will, the
landlord was able to get rid of them when he chose.

In the spring of 1848 Captain Kennedy, the able temporary
Poor Law Inspector in County Clare, reported "An immense
number of small land holders are under ejectment or notice
to quit, even when the rents have been paid up, the universal
and minute sub-division of land may make this necessary,
but the immediate effect must be disastrous." In February
120 houses were "tumbled" in the townland of Moyarta,
about the same number in Carrigaholt, and 575 families
were turned out on the world. The "few respectable residents"
were helpless. The following month 200 houses were "tumbled" on an adjacent estate and the dispossessed occupiers,

"wretched, houseless, helpless," were wandering about the country, "scattering disease, destitution and dismay in all directions . . . the most awful cases of destitution and suffering ever seen. When the houses are torn down, people live in banks and ditches like animals, until starvation or weather drives them to the workhouse. Three cartloads, who could not walk, were brought in yesterday."

At the end of March, cabins were being thrown down in all directions, and the workhouse at Kilrush was full. "I cannot think where the evicted find shelter," Captain Kennedy jotted down in his diary. A thousand cabins had been levelled in three months.

On April 13, at the request of the Poor Law Commissioners, Captain Kennedy sent in a report on oath. "The great mass are tenants at will, and dare not resist"; many evicted in County Clare had taken refuge in "bog dens," holes in the living bog roofed over with sods. "Several of these wretched dens," which contained sick persons, "were without light or air and I was obliged to light a piece of bog fir to see where the sick lay, while many good substantial houses lay in ruins round them. Whatever future good these clearances may effect, they are productive of a present amount of suffering and mortality which would scare the proprietors were they to see it." The evicted were dazed; they "don't know where to face, linger about localities for weeks or months burrowing in ditches or among the rafters of their former dwellings . . . the poor are hunted off land, when perhaps they have never been five miles away."

The second complete failure of the potato fell on a people already ruined; and not only were they ruined but the landlords were plunged still more deeply into insolvency. It was one of the peculiarities of Irish law that for a bankrupt landlord to sell his estate was extremely difficult; mortgages and loans in Ireland were raised, not on separate items of property, a farm, a piece of woodland, a mill, but on the whole estate, and a property could not be transferred to a new owner until all encumbrances and debts had been satisfied. A large part of Irish land was thus practically unsaleable, an insolvent owner was unable to get rid of his property, and his tenants suffered. In the summer of 1848 an attempt was made to facilitate the sale of estates burdened by debts by passing an Act under which a sale might be effected with the authority of the Court of Chancery, or an estate might be sold and the money paid into the Court of Chancery and distributed by it among persons with a claim. It proved useless. Owing to the immensely slow procedure of the Court of Chancery, delays could extend to five years, and purchasers did not come forward. In the coming crisis the ruined landlord must continue to hold his property, and his tenantry must pay the price.

❧

On August 13 John Russell wrote to Charles Wood, "Clarendon in his letter today asks what we propose to do in the event of a deficiency (almost certain) of the potato crop." The answer was, as little as was conceivably possible. Generosity was hardly to be expected after the attempted insurrection and the denunciations of the "thrice accursed British Empire." As John Russell warned Clarendon, "The course of English benevolence is frozen by insult, calumny and rebellion," and *The Times*, reporting the potato failure, remarked that the frame of mind created by the recent attempt at insurrection was "not a good atmosphere for compassion for Ireland." In a leading article on August 30 *The Times* declared, "In no other country have men talked treason until they are hoarse, and then gone about begging for sympathy from their oppressors. In no other country have the people been so liberally and unthriftily helped by the nation they denounced and defied, and in none have they repeated more humble and piteous supplications to those whom they have previously repaid with monstrous ingratitude. As a matter of state economy, some relief will be given to Ireland, in case she needs it, but we warn her that such relief will not be carried to the extent, or dealt forth, after the measure of former years."

Mitchel's wild boasts and insults and the folly of the insurrection were now to be paid for by the helpless victims of the new potato failure, and when Clarendon pressed for food supplies and relief plans, Lord John Russell told him, "Neither assistance from public works nor a general system of rations are to be looked to for any large portion of relief," repeating, in a second letter, that it was "impossible for the Government to do much to relieve distress."

Eight million pounds, wrote Lord John, had been advanced, after the failure of 1846, "to enable the Irish to supply the loss of the potato crop and to cast about them for some less

precarious food. The result has been that they have placed
more dependence on the potato than ever, and have again
been deceived. How can such a people be assisted? No
one in their senses would think of repeating the outlay to
lead to a similar improvidence." The fact that the Government had refused to supply seed, to enable the people to
grow some crop other than the potato, was forgotten.

Trevelyan was already determined on ruthless economy.
The £160,000 which the British Association had agreed to
spend on distressed unions was melting away; by May 28,
some months before the potato failed, the Association's agent,
Count Strzelecki, was giving out £13,000 a week, and the sum
increased each week. "Terrible," wrote Routh, the funds
would soon run out. On the same date the distressed unions,
with a population of half-starved paupers, already owed
£264,000; a very large sum of rates was in arrear, and
it was useless to attempt collection. Twisleton told Trevelyan
that a number of unions would soon be asking for loans,
and in a crushing reply Trevelyan told him there would be
no loans. "I hasten to remark," he wrote, "that you appear
to contemplate a much more extensive system of assistance
to the unions than the government has any idea of according.
. . ." Nothing was to be advanced out of public funds; ". . .
the assistance given by the Treasury will be in the form of
grants, which should be doled out in the proportions absolutely necessary to enable the worst class of distressed union
to feed the paupers dependent on them until harvest . . . and
a detailed report should be made to the Treasury of the circumstances of every such case previously to any assistance . . .
I have thought it right," concluded Trevelyan, "to state clearly
what is intended without loss of time, for half the embar-
rassments which take place are for want of knowing beforehand the wishes and intentions of the Government."

On July 1 the funds of the British Association were exhausted, and their help ceased. Two hundred thousand children were being fed by the Association, and Lord John Russell
promised that this relief should continue; ". . . the government
will take up the charge when the British Association lays it
down," he wrote.

At the end of August the Commissariat left Ireland, and
this time for good. Though the potato failure was now all
but certain, Trevelyan decided that "Commissariat operations
ought to be discontinued even if the potato does fail"; by

August 31 final reports had been submitted and the Commissariat relief service in Ireland was over.

One after another, familiar figures disappeared. Sir Randolph Routh left Dublin for London and wrote to Trevelyan from Bangor, North Wales, that he did not find the Welsh as handsome a race as the Irish, though, he remarked, Irish women were "passionless." Mr. Dobree, who had been Commissariat officer at Sligo, went to clear up at Dublin Castle. Captain Mann left Kilrush for Plymouth, "disappointed because he has not been promoted," wrote Routh. On September 12, Count Strzelecki, a good friend to Ireland, left Dublin, refusing any payment for his services. "I never could justify myself to my inner tribunal if I were to take money for what I have gone through," he told Twisleton.

Ireland was left to face a winter of total failure, bankruptcy and starvation, supported only by the Treasury, the Poor Law, and some help from the Society of Friends. The armies of starving half-naked paupers in the distressed unions were almost overwhelming; nine-tenths of the population of Clifden, for instance, were receiving outdoor relief, and more than forty thousand persons in Ballina; in Castlebar, where the Poor Law organization had collapsed, not a single entry was made in the Guardians' minute book between March 13, 1848, and May 25, 1850, the applications were equal in number to the entire population of the union.

After the second potato failure, it was hopeless to expect rents to be collected in the west and south-west, and more ruthless clearances resulted. In Kilrush Union, County Clare, Captain Kennedy wrote that by November 7, 1848, the evicted were "swarming all over the union, living in temporary sheds, unfit for human occupation, from which they are daily driven by the inclement weather." Huts were made by roofing ditches with boughs and sods, or leaning sticks against walls and covering them with turf and furze, and here whole families huddled for shelter.

Between August and December 1848 in the Kilrush Union alone 6,090 persons had been evicted; by January 22, 1849, 880 more had been evicted, nearly 7,000 in less than six months and evictions were continuing at the rate of 150 persons a week.

The evictions in Kilrush were duplicated all over the west. Sir William Butler describes an eviction and a "tumbling" which he witnessed as a boy in Tipperary: "The sheriff, a

strong force of police, and above all the crowbar brigade, a
body composed of the lowest and most debauched ruffians,
were present. At a signal from the sheriff the work began.
The miserable inmates of the cabins were dragged out upon
the road; the thatched roofs were torn down and the earthen
walls battered in by crowbars (practice had made these scoun-
drels adepts in their trade); the screaming women, the half-
naked children, the paralysed grandmother and the tottering
grandfather were hauled out. It was a sight I have never
forgotten. I was twelve years old at the time, but I think if
a loaded gun had been put into my hands I would have fired
into that crowd of villains as they plied their horrible trade."
"The winter of 1848–9," he goes on, "dwells in my memory
as one long night of sorrow."

Many years later Captain Kennedy, by then Sir Arthur
Kennedy, C.B., was staying with Lord Carnarvon at High-
clere Castle. "One day," writes a fellow guest, "the conversa-
tion turned upon Ireland and the Irish famine . . ." Turning
full towards his host, Kennedy said, "I can tell you, my Lord,
that there were days in that western country when I came
back from some scene of eviction so maddened by the sights
of hunger and misery I had seen in the day's work, that I
felt disposed to take the gun from behind my door and shoot
the first landlord I met."

∿

In July Twisleton had told Trevelyan that the Poor Law
would have to find a minimum of £12,000 a week for grants
to distressed unions and £2,700 to feed the children, and that
in the distressed unions no rate "worth mention" could be
collected for several months. On September 14, however,
Trevelyan sent a letter to the Poor Law Commissioners in
Ireland, informing them the Treasury had decided that a
5s. rate was to be collected. Referring to the total failure of
the potato, he wrote that extensive relief would probably be
required during the coming season, and that the Lords of
the Treasury could not sanction "a smaller rate than will be
needed for the Poor Law expenditure . . ." Twisleton wrote
back a furious letter. To collect a 5s. rate was "morally and
physically impossible." There was universal opposition from
the magistrates, and from all the Government officials in
Dublin.

Twisleton and Trevelyan were not on good terms. Twisleton sent angry letters to Trevelyan, asking him to observe "the usual official procedure" and give explanations before he cast "slurs" on the Irish Poor Law Commission, and Trevelyan harried Twisleton, as he had harried Colonel Jones of the Board of Works, requiring detailed information, analyses and returns to be sent to the Treasury when the Irish Poor Law Commission was overwhelmed with work. "A heavy and most complicated task," wrote Twisleton of a request for analysed accounts. "The gentlemen of the Statistical Department were up all night as well as Sunday," but "The statistical Department . . . found themselves beaten by the work."

The alliance between Trevelyan and Charles Wood had become closer, and Sir Charles now sent Trevelyan jovial little notes scribbled in his own hand and signed with his initials. On September 14, 1848, for instance, ridiculing a scheme, organized by Lord Clarendon, to send agricultural instructors round Ireland, he wrote, "Clarendon seems fond of his hobby, and if the Irish are grateful for them, it is more than they are for anything else. C.W."

Clarendon, meanwhile, complained to Sir Charles Wood that the Treasury would not give a "civil answer" and "won't listen." Above all he implored Wood to fix a rate at 3s., not 5s. To collect a 5s. rate was utterly impossible now that the potato had failed again. This, wrote Clarendon, was Twisleton's opinion, and Redington's opinion and his own opinion. Making an almost frantic appeal to Lord John Russell, Claredon urged that famine was approaching and that at the prospect of such taxation "the people will be rendered desperate and abscond."

For once, Charles Wood and Trevelyan were defeated. On September 16, 1848, Trevelyan wrote to Charles Wood, "These letters from Twisleton . . . show clearly what the Irish Poor Law Commissioners are about . . . they have taken upon themselves, without our leave but with the connivance, I suspect, of Lord John and Lord Clarendon, to reduce the maximum rate from 5/- to 3/- . . . ."

Rumours of the 5s. rate had already "spread terror" among farmers. Mr. Richard Bourke, permanent Poor Law inspector of ten unions in Mayo and Galway, reported a "panic." Ratepayers who had managed to keep solvent knew that the 5s. rate was only a beginning; double or treble the amount would not bring distressed unions through the year, and rates would be collected with merciless severity, troops and police used to seize property by force, and special collectors, devoid of local sympathy, sent down from Dublin.

On September 30 another blow fell; as the potato failure was spreading despair and ruin throughout Ireland, Trevelyan informed Twisleton that Treasury grants to distressed Irish unions were to cease. The Chancellor of the Exchequer had rather less than £3,000 in hand, out of the sum allocated, and the issues were to stop. A few weeks later Twisleton was informed that there would be no issue of condemned and unwanted Ordnance clothing to Irish workhouses, as there had been last winter. "It is a great object not to revive the habit of dependence on Government aid," wrote Trevelyan, and to encourage independence further he stopped feeding destitute children, in spite of Lord John Russell's pledge, and wrote informing applicants that the British Association's funds were now exhausted and the Government could do nothing.

A wave of alarm and foreboding swept over the country; everyone who could scrape the money together prepared to leave Ireland, and a new emigration began.

The emigration of 1848, however, was of a very different quality from the disorganized flight of 1847. New Canadian legislation had followed the disaster of 1847, to prevent helpless and diseased pauper emigrants being landed on Canadian soil, the cheapest passages were no longer available, and the ruined small farmers who had made up the bulk of the emigration of 1847 had no choice but to remain in Ireland, nor could landlords afford to emigrate their pauper tenantry.

The emigrants of 1848 were farmers of a good class whom Ireland could ill afford to spare. "A new emigration is developing of the most fatal kind," wrote Lord Monteagle on October 30, and he gave an example of a man who had just announced his intention of leaving, an excellent tenant of thirty acres on his estate who had paid his rent regularly and put up good buildings and a house on his farm. In Sligo and Donegal a Poor Law inspector reported that "the better, more energetic farmers are selling up and going." In Cork, wrote Mr. Nicholas Cummins, the quays were "thronged with emigrants as in spring," a thousand a week were leaving; and on November 28 "comfortable farmers" from Meath and Westmeath were said to be arriving in Dublin daily by the hundred, "apparently all of substantial class and well provided for the transatlantic journey." But

Charles Wood wrote to Monteagle, "I am not at all appalled
by your tenantry going . . . that seems to me to be a necessary part of the process": larger holdings were essential in
Ireland, and holdings could not be enlarged until the number
of holders was diminished. Trevelyan agreed. "I do not know
how farms are to be consolidated if small farmers do not
emigrate," he wrote, "and by acting for the purpose of keeping them at home, we should be defeating our own object. We
must not complain of what we really want to obtain. If small
farmers go, and then landlords are induced to sell portions
of their estates to persons who will invest capital, we shall
at last arrive at something like a satisfactory settlement of
the country."

Ireland, however, was assuming an appearance unlikely to
tempt investors. In the huge union of Ballina thousands of
acres looked as if they had been devastated by an enemy;
in Erris seventy-eight townlands were without a single inhabitant or four-footed beast; in Munster the landlords could
not deal with the farms abandoned and thrown on their hands,
and large tracts of arable land were either deserted or squatted
on by paupers, living in a "hut in a ditch" and with "no chat-
tels whatever distrainable for poor rate," Barrington & Co.,
well-known land agents in Dublin, were stated to have land
to the value of over £300,000 on their hands for which they
could not find a purchaser; and on Saturday, October 7,
the well-known Ballydowlan estate, Galway, was put up for
sale at Ballinasloe and withdrawn, "there being scarcely any
bidders" and not one reasonable offer received. In Clare, an
owner of eighteen farms was preparing to abandon his
property. Fourteen farms had been thrown on his hands by
emigration, destitution and death; he received nothing in
rent, and meanwhile arrears of poor rate piled up against
him. Once a rate was levied it became a debt, attached to
the land for ever. Mr. James Martin, one of the famous
Martins of Galway, stated in evidence that he himself had
a debt for rates of £11,000 on his property, and when land
was sold the purchaser became liable for the debt.

Substantial towns were becoming deserted. In Athlone, for
instance, the best shops were closed because the owners had
emigrated, and all the respectable part of the population was
leaving. In the finest streets in Dublin, shops had their
shutters up, and broken windows were stuffed with paper.
All over Ireland trade was almost at a standstill, and markets

were reported "glutted with all kinds of provisions at fear-fully unremunerative prices to the producer, but there is no money among the indigent poor to pay even the lowest prices." "Everyone who can get out of the country is trying to do so," and Colonel Knox Gore added that the land left waste was not poor land but some of the richest; the occupiers, being reasonably prosperous, were able to find the money to get away. "Honest farmers are going, fraudulent farmers are absconding," wrote Monteagle to Lord John Russell on November 3. "We shall be left a pauper warren . . . the Queen being the matron of the largest union workhouse ever yet founded.

Meanwhile, the wretched hordes of destitute were being treated with increasing harshness. Trevelyan would have liked to abolish outdoor relief; and by the exercise of ruthless severity, in spite of the failure of the potato, numbers on outdoor relief had been reduced to 200,000 in October, though by December they all but doubled, to nearly 400,000. In Mayo, wrote a landowner, "thousands are brought to the workhouse *screaming* for food and can't be relieved." The starving people became violent; Shanagolden, Co. Limerick, Lord Monteagle's own union, was described as "greatly above the average," but the Board of Guardians, of which Lord Monteagle was chairman, had to sit under police protection all day because of the crowds of starving, who threatened to riot if they did not get food; and on November 3, in spite of "armed police, an attempt was made by the excited mob of paupers to break into the house . . . ." Lord Monteagle told Lord John Russell, "The pressure for outdoor relief from the paupers, the relieving officers and the elected guardians is very strong, and will be irresistible. Last year we had 13,000 . . . this year they speak of more than double on a population of 68,000 . . . We have taken auxiliary work-houses in the central town, and I now propose leasing three others in more distant places, seven, nine and eleven miles apart. But how are these to be governed and kept in order?"

Lord Sligo declared the Government responsible for creating the crowds of paupers. He pointed out, in a letter to *The Times* on December 16, that in 1847, under the Soup Kitchen Act, 26,000 persons had received free rations in the Westport Union, "on the express condition that they should make no provision for the future . . . There are now there-fore, at this moment, in obedience to the law, 26,000 people

in Westport who are destitute of food, fuel and clothing . . .
The long account of money spent will not feed the crowds
of destitute, the rates cannot do it, and if the union be left to
that fund alone, these myriads must perish by famine."

Meanwhile, the resident landlords and resident gentry, the
class on whom Trevelyan had repeatedly declared any relief
scheme for Ireland must depend, were rapidly being ruined
by rates and no rents. Lord Monteagle warned Lord John
Russell, "The crack of the gentry is going on right and left";
a Poor Law inspector spoke of "the dread of the breakup
of all society . . . the state of the gentry is awful," and *The
Times* prophesied, "A tremendous crash must come in which
all interests and all classes will be swept away."

Lord Clarendon implored the Government to make advances to the distressed Irish unions. "I dread some wholesale
calamity," he wrote to Sir George Grey, the Home Secretary,
on December 7, "some hundreds dying all at once of
starvation, which would not only be shocking but bring
disgrace on the Government." Sir George Grey, an ally of
Trevelyan and Charles Wood, administered a snub in his reply.
"It may be that if numerous deaths should occur the Government would be blamed," he replied, "but there is such an
indisposition to spend more money on Ireland, that the
Government will be assuredly and severely blamed if they advance money to pay debts. . . ." At this Clarendon became
angry, citing Trevelyan, who in accordance with the principles
of *laissez-faire* had produced a phrase, "the operation of
natural causes," to which he considered Ireland should be left.
As for "the operation of natural causes," Clarendon told Grey,
it meant "wholesale deaths from starvation and disease, and
John Bull won't like that, however cross he may be at paying."
Charles Wood, however, denied that the state of Ireland was
as frightful as Clarendon represented—". . . there had been
exaggeration last year and there was probably exaggeration
now." Trevelyan was now said to be all-powerful with the
Chancellor of the Exchequer, and Greville reported that
Clarendon "attributes a great part of the obstacles he meets
with to Charles Wood, who is entirely governed by Trevelyan;
and C.W. is to the last degree obstinate and tenacious of
the opinions which his Secretary puts into him."

Meanwhile, numbers on relief continued to increase; nearly
200,000 persons were crammed into workhouses intended for
114,000. Fever—typhus and relapsing fever—was still prev-

alent, and Routh's son, Captain Jules Routh, of the Welsh
Fusiliers, who had become a temporary Poor Law inspector
in Newcastle, County Limerick, caught "fever" in December
and died.

Poor Law instructions were applied with the utmost strin-
gency. In Gort, to take one example, a distressed union, but
not one of the worst, the workhouse was emptied of women
and children, old and infirm persons, even convalescents,
before being filled with able-bodied men; and before outdoor
relief was given the labour test was carried out "in the most
stringent manner." This test required all able-bodied men to
attend and remain at work for the full period of eight
hours every day. "Many of them have to travel considerable distances morning and evening," wrote the Gort Vice-
Guardians, "and we have observed some without shoes of any
description working at the drain leading from the workhouse
site. All clothing is in a very bad state, insufficient to stand
the present cold weather." Only those persons who were
completely destitute qualified for relief: "All applications
are rigidly scrutinized, and the Relieving Officers, when visiting houses of applicants, make a careful examination of all
boxes, bundles and parcels they may observe"—in case property of some description was concealed. The applicant, who
had been stripped of every scrap which might be regarded as
property and subjected to a degree of hardship which must
prove injurious to health, received as his reward about one
pound of meal a day, on which he was just kept alive; it was
estimated that £1 would cover the cost of keeping one person
for thirty-four weeks. Twisleton told Trevelyan he had thought
it better to omit from the Annual Report of the Poor Law
Commission (Ireland) any statement as to how much each
pauper cost, in case people should say "we were slowly
murdering the peasantry by the scantiness of our relief."

At the end of the year, on December 27, 1848, Lord
Clarendon wrote to Trevelyan in despair. "How," he asked,
"are the next six months to be got through in the South and
West? I am at my wits' end to imagine. The reports of our
own officers are bad enough, heaven knows, but the statements I have received from (credible) eyewitnesses exceed all
I have ever heard of horrible misery, except perhaps that
of shipwrecked mariners on a yacht or desert island." On
these words Ireland entered the year 1849.

⋘

The answer was that Ireland was to be abandoned to Trevelyan's operation-of-natural-causes system. On February 9, 1849, Clarendon, "quite disheartened," told Lord John Russell that he was unable "to shake Charles Wood and Trevelyan, that the right course was *to do nothing* for Ireland, and to leave things to the operation of natural causes." Three days later he wrote that he had now given up all hope and was convinced that "the doctrinaire policy of Trevelyan, reflected through C. Wood, and supported by Grey, would prevail." Lord John's reply was that a loan for Ireland could not be obtained from Parliament—"rage against Ireland on account of its faction, its mendicancy, its ingratitude, is extreme." The attempted rising of 1848, and the violent abuse which accompanied it, had done immense harm. "We have subscribed, worked, visited, clothed, for the Irish," wrote Lord John, "millions of money, years of debate, etc. etc. etc. The only return is rebellion and calumny. Let us not grant, lend, clothe, etc., any more, and see what that will do. This is the great difficulty today—British people think this." Officially, it was declared that no deaths from starvation must be allowed to occur in Ireland, but in private the attitude was different. "I have always felt a certain horror of political economists," said Benjamin Jowett, the celebrated Master of Balliol, "since I heard one of them say that he feared the famine of 1848 in Ireland would not kill more than a million people, and that would scarcely be enough to do much good." The political economist in question was Nassau Senior, one of the Government's advisers on economic affairs. Meanwhile, the British Exchequer was still struggling with financial difficulties; the revenue accounts, wrote Lord John, were "very bad," and the first three months of 1849 showed a deficit of more than a million pounds.

The emigration of farmers from Ireland began to cause alarm. "The U.S. will have gained enormous wealth and resources by the Irish famine and the Irish Poor Law," wrote Lord Clanricarde to Clarendon. "All who should have tilled, or should be tilling Irish soil in Mayo and Galway, which is left untilled, have been carried off to clear land in America—this is the *direct* consequence of the Poor Law." Landlords tried in vain to persuade good tenants to stay; for example, near Clonmel, County Tipperary, a year's delay in paying the rent was offered and rejected, tenants saying, "if they didn't go this year, they would have to go next"; one landlord had been forced to take up 300 acres, another 180 acres, others 150 to 200 acres, and for ten miles along the high road to Kilrush, County Clare, no cultivation whatsoever was to be seen.

Jails had already become a refuge, and men had committed crimes to be transported out of Ireland. Destitute young people, even children of twelve, now courted transportation to escape from Ireland. In Mayo, for instance, Mr. Michael Shaughnessy, the Assistant Barrister (in Ireland the Assistant Barrister was a judicial officer appointed by the Crown and independent of local influence) was repeatedly asked, by young persons under eighteen years of age, for sentences of transportation. At Westport, Dominic Ginelly, aged 17, was charged with stealing hemp ropes; he said he wanted to be transported and would do the same again; he was transported for seven years. John Austin and Charles Ruddy, 12 and 15 years old, "honest people's children from Clare Island," where there had been 576 deaths from starvation out of a population of 1,700, were found guilty of sheep stealing; transported for seven years. Michael Gavin, Thomas Joyce, Martin McGinty, John McGrene, John English, all about 17, guilty of stealing, asked to be transported. A youth named Owen Eady, asked if he knew what transportation meant, said even if he had chains on his legs he would have something to eat; anything was better than starving and sleeping out at night. Mr. Shaughnessy said, "I am satisfied that they had no alternative but starvation or the commission of crime." He found, he added, the state of young people, as he passed from town to town on his circuit, "afflicting." Some months had now gone by since feeding the children had been stopped, and they were "almost naked, hair standing on end, eyes sunken, lips pallid, protruding bones of little joints visible." He asked himself, "Am I in a civilized country and part of the British Empire?"

The authorities in London and in the penal settlements were embarrassed by the deluge of youthful convicts. "Your transportation returns are indeed appalling," Sir George Grey told Clarendon, on February 5, 1849. "More were sentenced to transportation, at these last two sessions, than were transported at all the assizes . . . in a year before 1846. It becomes absolutely impossible to carry the sentences into effect with such numbers." Governors of penal settlements, he went on, complained that many of those sentenced were "wholly unfit for ordinary convict association and treatment, owing partly to their youth and partly to their general good conduct."

The first few months of 1849 saw as much, if not more, suffering than at any time since the potato failed. The Irish Poor Law Commissioners, in their second annual report, stated that the misery and distress was equalled only by the worst months of 1846–47, and Count Strzelecki, consulted as an expert, declared that 1849 was the worst of all. The effect of the famine, he pointed out, was cumulative; in 1849 the people were enduring a fourth year, and they were "skinned down to the bone" by workhouse and relief tests, by the economic consequences of the Quarter Acre clause and evictions. After they had gambled every last vestige of any value they possessed on a good potato harvest, they had been confronted with a new total failure of the potato. A "singular and melancholy state of depression," Count Strzelecki said, brooded over the western unions, and the people declared "the land is cursed."

Distress was worst in the twenty-two "ruined" unions, but those unions were not merely plague-spots in a country otherwise restored to prosperity. On April 9 Lord Monteagle estimated that there were forty to fifty further unions "which are on the very verge of ruin and which must be absorbed in the whirlpool before harvest. I am astonished to see some of the Leinster and Ulster names included in the list." It was, he wrote, "a most frightful picture," and by English standards the whole of Ireland was ruinous, dilapidated and starving.

In 1849 Carlyle paid a visit to Ireland. Carlyle was not a compassionate man, he was squeamish; and the beggary, dirt and disease of famine-stricken Ireland repulsed him. He found Dublin patched and dilapidated, the harbour at Kingstown empty, and the swarms of beggars little short of terrifying; leaving Dublin, he considered the small town of Kildare, in Leinster, the most prosperous part of Ireland, to be "a wretched, wild, village . . . like a village in Dahomey . . .

beggars, beggars . . . wretched streets . . . the *extremity* of raggedness."

At Waterford he found commerce ruined; the bacon-curers had left the town, owing to the poverty consequent on the potato failures; for the same reason, the butter trade and cattle trade had ceased, and numbers of warehouses on the quays, at one point three in a row, were empty and shuttered. Indeed, trade in Ireland seemed to be at an end; when he did meet carts going to and fro on the road, "alas, when you look it is mostly, or all, meal sacks, Indian corn sacks—workhouse trade . . . I didn't, in all Ireland, meet one big piled carrier's cart, not to speak of a carrier's wagon, as we see here." Some small country dealers were furtively prospering, but "by workhouse grocery and meal trade, by secret pawnbroking—by *eating* the slain." These individuals were the curse of Ireland, the "gombeen men." The crammed workhouses and auxiliary workhouses of distressed unions with their wretched pauper inmates Carlyle dismissed as "human swineries . . . pity dies away into stony misery and disgust in the excess of such scenes."

Landlords who owned thousands of derelict acres were shut up in their mansions, existing on rabbits shot in their overgrown parks, and gossip said that Lord Sligo was living on the proceeds of an opera box belonging to his family in the Covent Garden Opera House, London. In conclusion, Carlyle wrote, ". . . the whole country figures in my mind like a ragged coat, one huge beggar's gabardine, not patched, or patchable any longer. . . ."

The state of Ireland began to cause uneasiness in England, and on February 8, 1849, *The Times,* a consistent and stubborn opponent of help for Ireland, "with great reluctance," announced a change of heart. There must be some "exceptional relief." *The Times* had been converted by the fearful reports from places like Ballina, which owed more than £18,000, had nearly 21,000 destitute on outdoor relief, and where persons, previously paying 13s. in rates, were now asked for £13; and from Bantry, where 2,327 persons and 600 children were huddled in the workhouse and auxiliary workhouse, naked, except for filthy rags, half starved, and without the common decencies of life. Four hundred and thirty-one persons, according to official figures, died of starvation in Ireland between January and May, 1849. "Nobody knows what to do," wrote Greville, on February 9. ". . .

Charles Wood has all along set his face against giving or lending money . . . and he contemplates (with what seems very like cruelty, though he is not really cruel) that misery and distress should run their course; that such havoc should be made among the landed proprietors, that the price of land will at last fall so low as to tempt capitalists to invest their funds therein. . . ."

In accordance with this policy the Government now came forward with a scheme, of which Trevelyan was the "real author." A rate-in-aid was to be levied, by which the more prosperous unions in Ireland were to be forced to contribute to the support of the unions listed as distressed; and an additional rate of 6d. in the pound was to be paid by every union, against which the Treasury would make advances, not exceeding £100,000, for relief. The duration of rate-in-aid was limited to December 31, 1850, and the Bill was accompanied by a vote, authorizing the Treasury to advance £50,000 immediately for the distressed unions. "There must be a stop put to these drains on the Treasury," wrote Sir George Grey, on March 8. ". . . some means must be found *in Ireland* of making whatever provision is indispensable for certain parts of the country the local means of which are clearly insufficient to support their population." Lord Lansdowne, however, "a great proprietor" in Ireland, said the rate-in-aid filled him with "horror and dread." It was "nothing less than a scheme of confiscation, by which the weak would not be saved, but the strong be involved in general ruin." Supporters of the rate-in-aid regarded it as a disciplinary measure. George Nicholls, who had drawn up the recent Poor Law Act, wrote of the "necessity for compelling the Irish people to abandon the treacherous potato . . . The rate-in-aid was calculated to effect this object, by casting the consequences of the failure entirely on Ireland herself." In Ireland the announcement of the new Act provoked fury, and Ulster was strongly resentful at being called on to support Munster and Connaught. But uniting all parties was the anger felt at England's attitude to Ireland; was, or was not, the Act of Union a reality? Catholic and Protestant came together, and on February 23 a joint meeting of Orange and Green—Protestant and Catholic—was held at Fermanagh, the largest meeting that had been held in the north for many years. After protesting against the rate-in-aid the meeting declared that if the Union was a fact, and Ireland an integral part of the Empire, then the Imperial Exchequer should contribute.

Trevelyan, Sir Charles Wood and Sir George Grey were still determined not to give Ireland a penny more than would prevent a scandal, and the immediate advance of £50,000 offered against the security of the rate-in-aid was painfully small. In 1848, Count Strzelecki, on behalf of the British Association, had distributed nearly £160,000 in less than three months, and his distribution had been made before the new potato failure.

For Twisleton the rate-in-aid was the last straw, and on March 12 he resigned. "He thinks," Clarendon told Lord John Russell on the same day, "that the destitution here [in Ireland] is so horrible, and the indifference of the House of Commons to it is so manifest, that he is an unfit agent of a policy which must be one of extermination . . . Twisleton feels that as Chief Commissioner he is placed in a position . . . which no man of honour and humanity can endure." He was succeeded by the Assistant Poor Law Commissioner, Mr. Alfred Power, a successful solicitor, described by Lord Clanricarde as "a man of landed property and *well to do*"; Lord John Russell and Sir George Grey, however, had not "a high opinion of his capacity." Mr. Power soon fell out with Trevelyan; his appointment was gazetted on May 8, and by August he was at war with the Treasury, complaining of its interference, of the tone of Trevelyan's letters, the unfair statements made in them, and going so far as to take legal advice on the extent of Treasury authority.

Nevertheless, on May 24, 1849, the Rate-in-aid Act passed, and a general order of June 13 assessed the sum to be levied in each union; the total was to amount to £322,552 11s.

Before the Act was put into operation yet another terrible misfortune fell on Ireland; an epidemic of Asiatic cholera broke out. On December 2, 1848, a man had arrived by sea at Belfast who a few days previously had left a part of Edinburgh where cholera was raging. The vessel and the route by which he came are not mentioned, but it is certain that he was for some hours in a Belfast workhouse, before he was removed to the hospital, where he died. Some days later cases of Asiatic cholera occurred in the workhouse and extended to the town of Belfast; and travellers then carried it to the overcrowded workhouses and auxiliary workhouses, the pauper hospitals, the crammed jails and military barracks all over Ireland.

In spite of this new blow the British Government remained adamant—the Irish unions were not to be helped. Boards of Guardians were warned that a cholera epidemic was imminent, and in successive circulars the Central Board of Health, in Dublin, issued instructions for nursing, accommodation, setting up special dispensaries, medical treatment, necessary drugs, and even, on March 22, the treatment of convalescent patients. But, wrote the Central Board of Health, "Guardians shall defray the expenses incurred . . . out of the funds of their respective unions." The instructions were a mockery—funds in distressed unions had ceased to exist. Clarendon now became frantic: he had, it was reported, completely turned against his former political allies for their treatment of Ireland. ". . . it is enough to drive one mad, day after day, to read the appeals that are made and meet them all with a negative," he wrote to Lord John Russell on April 26. "At Westport, and other places in Mayo, they have not got a shilling to make preparations for the cholera, but no assistance can be given, and there is no credit for anything, as all the contractors are ruined. Surely this is a state of things to justify you asking the House of Commons for an advance, for I don't think there is another legislature in Europe that would disregard such suffering as now exists in the west of Ireland, or coldly persist in a policy of extermination." No advance was granted, but the Irish Poor Law Commissioners went so far as to record their regret that, in the cholera epidemic, "a want of means had crippled their efforts"; in some districts, where every penny was needed to save the destitute from starvation, money had to be diverted from the purchase of food to make some provision for cholera victims.

The epidemic originated in January, became serious in March and April, reached a peak in May, and in most parts of the country declined in June; but little sympathy was felt for Ireland; her misfortunes were too frequent, too hopeless, too impossible to remedy, and, moreover, the attempted insurrection of 1848 had not been forgotten. Even the total failure of the potato in 1848 had not been much noticed, though the failure of 1846 had been universally reported as a horrifying and shattering catastrophe. In the winter of 1848–49 no subscriptions were raised, no philanthropic persons knitted or sewed for the Irish destitute. Compassion for Ireland was dead.

The consequences of a total failure of the potato, compli-cated by the extra and unexpected destitution arising from the cholera epidemic, had to be met; but if destitute persons must be rescued from death by starvation, they were to be rescued in a workhouse. Harsh conditions would prove the extremity of their need, and confinement keep them under control. Buildings to serve as auxiliary workhouses were hired wholesale, and ultimately accommodation for 250,000 persons was provided. In addition, the ration given to persons who did succeed in obtaining outdoor relief was reduced to under a pound of meal a day. By June, 1849, numbers on outdoor relief had risen to 768,902, and the debts of Irish unions amounted to more than £456,000, Munster alone owing near-ly £250,000.

Horrifying reports of the state of the destitute in the work-houses came in. The Guardians had funds enough to supply only what were termed "the necessaries of life," which meant just enough food to avoid death from starvation. Inmates of female wards were reported to be more than half naked, since one of the measures of economy had been to stop the issue of clothing to Irish workhouses. In a number of workhouses, in auxiliaries in particular, which were frequently isolated and difficult to supervise, discipline broke down. Spirits were passed in, young men climbed into the wards at night, inmates and workhouse officers became intoxicated together, and con-finement within the workhouse became a farce—in Westport, for instance, paupers were to be met strolling boldly about the town. Fever, dysentery, and an epidemic of ophthalmia were general: 13,812 cases of ophthalmia were reported in 1849, and in 1850 the figure rose to 27,200. The disease was especially severe among the young, and the number of one-eyed children became noticeable.

As a result of shocking reports, a private subscription was launched by members of the Government in the second week of June, each Minister subscribing £100 and the Queen £500; about £10,000 was collected, and Count Strezelecki returned to Ireland to take charge of the distribution.

And now Ireland lost her last remaining friends; for in June, 1849, the Quakers gave up relief work. On June 2 Lord John Russell offered the Central Relief Committee a donation of £100 towards any plan the Society of Friends might be draw-

ing up for the relief of the distress in the west of Ireland. In
reply, the Central Relief Committee wrote that there would be
no plan, and with their habitual courtesy and restraint administered a few home truths. There was "great and increasing
distress prevailing in many parts," but the problem of relief
was "far beyond the reach of private exertion, the Government alone could raise the funds and carry out the measures
necessary in many districts to save the lives of the people . . .
and we are truly sorry that it is now out of our power to
offer ourselves as the distributors of Lord John's bounty to
our suffering fellow countrymen." In the opinion of the Central
Relief Committee, ". . . the condition of our country has
not improved in spite of the great exertions made by
charitable bodies," and could not be improved until the land
system of Ireland was reformed, which was a matter for
legislation, not philanthropy.

The "operation of natural causes" must now, it seemed, be
Ireland's fate; but there was a remedy in which Lord Clarendon had great faith, and one that might justly be termed a
sovereign remedy. Through his efforts, it was now to be
applied—Ireland was to receive a visit from Queen Victoria.

Chapter XVIII

IT SEEMS, in retrospect, a remarkable determination. Ireland
was in the grip of famine in the west and south-west, and
deaths from starvation were occurring daily; less than a year
before, there had been an attempt at armed insurrection, and
British journals and spokesmen in both Houses of Parliament
never ceased to reproach the Irish for their rebelliousness,
ingratitude and "dogged dissatisfaction with British rule."
Assassinations were notoriously frequent in Ireland, and already, in May of this year, a pistol had been fired at the
Queen, when she was driving in London, by a man from
Adare, County Limerick. "Half-way down Constitution Hill
the report of a pistol was heard . . . Her Majesty stood up, and
said to the page accompanying her, 'Renwick, what is that?'
'Your Majesty has been shot at,' replied Renwick." The Queen

then, he stated in his evidence, "resumed her seat." True, the
pistol had been either improperly loaded or not loaded at all,
the man mentally deficient, and the Queen calm, but the inci-
dent was not reassuring.

In addition, there was a risk from Asiatic cholera, which
had broken out in Dublin, where she intended to stay.

Lord Clarendon, however, believed that a visit from the
Queen would act as a tonic for trade, and certainly a tonic
was badly needed—trade was almost at a standstill in Dublin.
In the middle of June demand for "many important articles"
had fallen so low that the correspondent of the London *Times*
had difficulty in getting prices to quote for the newspaper's
commercial columns. Cholera was spreading out of the filthy
courts and alleys for which Dublin, in spite of its beauty, was
infamous, had indeed broken out in the garrison, among the
troops in the Ship Street barracks, and in the ranks of the
75th Regiment, who were encamped in Phoenix Park. In
the country trade was disastrous; the famous cattle fair at
Ballinasloe, for instance, was a total failure in 1849, and
beasts, kept alive and fed at what sacrifice only their owners
knew, were either sold at a loss or driven away unsold. In
Dublin on the last day of Trinity Term, the Court of Queen's
Bench had risen before noon, "there being literally no business"; and during the previous week seventeen Queen's
Counsel were counted "walking the hall," unemployed.

The original plan had been for the Queen to come to
Ireland in 1848: she was to visit Dublin for a few days, after
Parliament rose, in August. That plan was given up only
because an insurrection was expected, and even after the
insurrection Lord John Russell, who believed in the magic of
the Royal Presence as devoutly as Clarendon, wrote that he
would have advised the Queen to go all the same, if the
people had been "penitent and sobered, but they are not."

The attitude of the Irish people to the Queen was, on the
surface, all admiration; the Repealers were professionally loyal, perhaps, however, with tongue in cheek; O'Connell's trib-
utes to the "darling little Queen" and the fervid protestations
of Repealers in the House of Commons and Conciliation Hall
must be treated with reserve. Nevertheless, Clarendon could
write, in October, 1847, "Distress, discontent, hatred of
English rule, are increasing everywhere," yet add, in the same
letter, "Whatever may be the political feelings or animosities
of the Irish, their devotion to the Queen is unquestionable

and whenever Her Majesty shall think proper to come to Ireland I am convinced she would be received with enthusiastic loyalty."

Complete separation from England had not yet become the only solution for Ireland. Most Irish patriots, as in 1782, wanted freedom for Ireland to conduct her own affairs and settle her own destiny—they asked for a Parliament in Dublin, the equivalent of Dominion status; and the long road to an independent Irish republic had yet to be trodden. The Queen was still young, just thirty, agreeable, and the Queen of Ireland, and as such the people of Ireland were ready to give her a cheer. At one of the largest meetings of the Young Ireland party, in the Music Hall, Dublin, on April 15, 1848, when John Mitchel's invective was at its height, the health of the Queen, as Queen of Ireland, was proposed and drunk in tea, and "God Save the Queen" played on an Irish harp.

On June 6, 1849, in a letter marked "Confidential," Lord John Russell informed Clarendon that the Queen intended to visit Dublin that summer. "She will live at Vice-Regal Lodge for a week in some splendour and hold a levée and a drawing-room . . . Carriages and horses must be sent over, but she will make no visits, what will it cost?" A little later the visit was extended to include Cork as well as Dublin, but "in such a manner as to occasion the least display and expense"; and Clarendon was asked to "consider what the Board of Works should do at the Vice-Regal Lodge"; he was to "forward an estimate of the total cost of the Queen staying for four days and holding a drawing-room, with music, refreshments, etc."

The official intimation, dated June 23, emphasised that the visit was not to be a State visit. "The general distress, unfortunately still prevalent in Ireland, precludes the Queen from visiting Dublin in state, and thereby causing ill-timed expenditure and inconvenience to her subjects." For the sake of economy, she would travel by sea, in the Royal yacht, *Victoria and Albert,* first, across the Irish Channel to the Cove of Cork, and then along the coast to Dublin, "at some sacrifice of personal convenience," wrote Lord John Russell —the sacrifice was genuine, as the Queen was a very bad sailor and always "suffered dreadfully" while at sea. As a further demonstration of the Queen's wish for economy and informality, Sir Charles Wood, as Chancellor of the Exchequer, sent an intimation that Her Majesty "does not desire State beds."

The announcement received a mixed reception in Ireland. The *Freeman's Journal*, remarking that one visit to a hut in Connaught, one view of a "cleared" estate in the south, a pencil sketch, of the kind Queen Victoria was fond of executing, showing an unroofed cabin with the "miserable emaciated inhabitants cast out and perishing on the dung-heap beside it," would be a better portrait of Ireland than the beauties of Killarney.

The Dublin *Evening Mail*, a Tory paper, representing the landlord's interest, was sarcastic; since it was desirable that Her Majesty should see as little as possible of the decay of Ireland, the houses in the Dublin streets through which she would pass should be occupied, for the time at least, by decently dressed people; "the greater number of good houses in Dame Street, Grafton Street and other principal thoroughfares are in a dirty and dilapidated condition, the windows broken, patched with brown paper, or here and there . . . stuffed with an old hat, the shops closed and the wooden shutters covered over with auction bills, railway tables, quack advertisements and notices from the Poor Law Commissioners or the Insolvent Court." It would also be "highly expedient that such houses were cleaned as well as the short time allows and fully furnished with window curtains, muslin blinds and flower pots." The Queen was going to travel from Westland Row railway station, and the newspaper suggested that as there were "sundry back settlements in the purlieus which will not fit with the magnificent carriage provided for her" there should be a screen of boards "from the first flourishing suburb at Beggar's Bush all the way to the platform."

A letter in the *Evening Mail* also demanded, "Is it possible that Her Majesty could be gratified by a wretched display of wealth when thousands of her subjects are starving?" One huge lie was to be acted, and this the Queen would find out "if she goes one mile from the places prepared for her."

Lord Monteagle and Lord Fitzwilliam refused to have anything to do with the visit. "If you will not go to the pageant in Dublin Castle I think you are quite right," wrote Lord Fitzwilliam, "a great *lie* is going to be acted there . . . false impressions are going to be made and false conclusions will be drawn . . . then false government will ensue . . . I would not have had her go *now* unless she went to Killarney workhouse, . . . Galway, Connemara and Castlebar. *That* would have been my tour for her instead of Cork, Dublin, where she will have nothing but falsehoods, unless she draws the right conclusion by seeing the Cove of Cork without a ship in it."

Some patriotic hotheads contemplated a plot to seize the Queen's person and hold her as a hostage in the Wicklow mountains. The scheme was communicated to Charles Gavan Duffy, who pointed out that there were ten thousand British troops in Dublin, and even if the Queen was successfully snatched out of their hands there would not be a glen or a dell in the Wicklow mountains which, within twenty-four hours, would not be as well-trodden as Sackville Street (now O'Connell Street). However, "a muster of volunteers," to carry out the deed, was announced for 9 p.m. on the banks of the Grand Canal. Only about two hundred men came to the rendezvous, and as this was considered insufficient to beat the garrison, "they dispersed and the adventure came to an end."

Mr. Timothy O'Brien, Lord Mayor of Dublin, "hailed the Queen's visit with joy and satisfaction," offered his house for the use of members of her suite, and hastened to propose festive plans, including illuminations and a banquet at the Dublin Mansion House; £300 from the Borough Fund was to be spent on the Mansion House, to make it "clean and decent," and a further £1,000 allowed for food and wine. It was suggested that he hoped for a baronetcy.

Ireland was hardly in a condition to rejoice. On the day the Mansion House banquet was proposed, the Marquess of Kildare, eldest son of the Duke of Leinster, head of the Geraldine family, announced that the Dublin Central Relief Committee, a different body from the Central Relief Committee of the Society of Friends, had "completely exhausted" their funds, while they had over 200 urgent applications from all over the country waiting for attention, and local secretaries, had been instructed to bring before the public "the present frightful state of the country." Two-and-sixpence, the Marquess stated, would keep alive a family of five for a week, by enabling them to buy a little meal to mix with cabbage and other vegetables. "If we have funds to spare let them be spent not on illuminations but on Her Majesty's starving subjects," declared the *Evening Mail*.

Among the tradesmen and middle classes of Dublin, opinion was divided. At a meeting of the burgesses of the Post Office Ward, which included Sackville Street, one member, Mr.

Coyne, said he would rather have his windows smashed than illuminated; another, however, declared that the Queen's visit would be "a great godsend to raise the country from its present deplorable condition." At a meeting of the Linen Hall Ward a speaker pointed out that there was scarcely a poor family in Dublin who had not lost a cholera victim, and what family, in the Linen Hall Ward, could look forward, as a certainty, to daily food? Why should the people be called on to rejoice when gaunt famine and cold poverty reigned? It was an insult to the misery of Dublin, and illuminations and festivities should be repudiated. Another speaker, however, reminded the meeting of the deplorable condition of trade in Dublin and the good effect which would be derived from the money spent during the Queen's visit. "Give Her Majesty a charming and loyal reception which would induce her to forget any prejudice she might entertain, and perhaps fix royal residence for a definite period every year in Dublin."

Gradually the advantages expected from a royal visit won the day. On July 17 the Dublin Corporation, a Repeal body, convened a meeting to pass a resolution informing the Queen that ". . . the people of every class are suffering many privations, and . . . the humblest of your Majesty's subjects here are dying for want of food . . . we still feel the only hope left is in a Parliament which shall be local . . . we most solemn protest that we do not seek for separation between the two countries but we cling with anxious hope to you our beloved Queen and sovereign." Only eighteen members attended, and the meeting was not held. "So much for the Repeal Corporation," remarked *The Times*.

The once-powerful Repeal movement was now, in fact, extinct, and the contents of the committee rooms at Conciliation Hall, the headquarters of the movement on Burgh Quay, had been autioned off.

On July 25 a meeting of "influential citizens of County Dublin of every shade of opinion," called by the High Sheriff, passed a unanimous motion of welcome to the Queen, proposed by Viscount Monck, a Conservative and a Protestant, and seconded by the Hon. Mr. Preston, son and heir of Lord Gormanston, a Whig and a Catholic.

Plans were now made and notices issued; the Queen was to be welcomed by an "undress procession" of gentlemen wearing white trousers, blue coat with silver or silver-plated buttons, and a blue sash over the shoulder—a pattern of the sash might be inspected at the Mansion House. Gentlemen intending to join the procession were requested to state whether they would be on foot or on horseback, and an organizing committee was formed to make the arrangements.

Tiers of elevated seats were raised at the Rotunda and Rutland (now Parnell) Square, and six triumphal arches erected between Ball's Bridge and the Phoenix Park Gate. Five hundred pounds was advanced out of the Borough Fund to pay for welcoming the Queen, and £300 for repairs to the Mansion House; £200 was placed at the disposal of the Lord Mayor for "general and public demonstrations." "Devices," letters and crowns for illuminating with gas, and "illuminating candles" were offered for sale, and "several thousand bucket lamps" were for hire. Some protests continued; at an "aggregate meeting of the Trades of Dublin," in the Fishamble Street Theatre, Dublin citizens were besought to show that "they would not have an illumination over the corpse of Repeal," and a member asserted that "if his own family attempted to waste tallow he would smash his windows." The Lord Mayor felt uncertain whether he should issue an official order for illuminations, and though the "general illumination of the city on the night of Her Majesty's entry" had been advertised a week before, the official announcement was not made until August 3.

Meanwhile, Lord Clarendon's own preparations were not going smoothly. There were, in his own words, "a vast many kind friends, both here and in England . . . denouncing the 'premature and hazardous experiment,' and declaring that I alone was responsible for whatever mischief happened." Moreover, he had at his elbow Charles Wood, the Chancellor of the Exchequer, insistent on economy, and supported by Prince Albert.

Lord Clarendon had begun his preparations in a spirit of optimism. The furniture of Vice-Regal Lodge, he wrote to Charles Wood on June 27, "is not handsome but it is clean and good, and I am sure the Queen and Prince will be as comfortable as if the Board of Works was allowed to run up an enormous bill . . . Our children will be sent away, but Lady Clarendon and I shall probably remain in some corner or other; for I should not think things were properly superintended if I were living in another house . . . And then as to the expense—I shan't give myself the airs of a millionaire or pretend I am not a poorer man for being Lord-Lieutenant, but I don't mean to bring you in a bill for entertaining the Queen here. The refreshments for the Drawing-room are not strictly my department, and the Chancellor of the Exchequer may take cognisance of them, but as I am to have the charge of providing them, they won't ruin you."

The arrangements for the Royal party, however, turned out more complicated than Lord Clarendon anticipated. True, the visit was to be private, the Queen wished it to be without any state or expense whatever, there was to be no banquet at the Mansion House in Dublin, and the "compliment of a *déjeuner*" was declined at Cork. Nevertheless, the Queen's landing at the Cove of Cork was not to be private; as many people as possible were to be "gratified" by the opportunity of seeing her, and though the State coach was not to be brought over for the entry into Dublin, a special carriage was to be built in Dublin and a "cortège like that at Ascot," the famous racecourse, arranged. The Queen expressed herself as quite ready to receive "any demonstrations of loyalty the people of Dublin may wish to display."

In addition, while Lord Clarendon was informed that both the Queen and the Prince were anxious that the visit should be "well done," at the same time Colonel Phipps, the Queen's secretary, sent a warning that no bills were to come in afterwards. Moreover, the number of persons attending the Queen turned out unexpectedly large; four Royal children were to accompany their parents, and the total of the party, with servants, was thirty-six. Thus when, at the end of July, Lord Clarendon went over the Vice-Regal Lodge with Mr. Owen, of the Irish Board of Works, he looked at the house with different eyes. ". . . I am always most anxious to avoid putting the public to any expense in which I am personally concerned," he wrote to Charles Wood, "and it may be partly owing to this . . . that the furniture, etc., of this house is in a condition I should not have tolerated in my own . . . I found the carpets and chintzes in such a disgusting condition from dirt and old age that they were quite unfit for decent people, let alone a Royal family requiring seventeen *lits de maître* and bringing with them nineteen servants!" He had done his best to be economical, taking care that existing furniture was made use of in "inferior apartments," and had "only allowed three rooms to be new papered where our children had been with the whooping cough."

The Vice-Regal Lodge was not the only neglected building

in Dublin. Though the Lord-Lieutenant of Ireland lived and
gave entertainments at Vice-Regal Lodge, his official residence
was Dublin Castle, and State functions were held in the
magnificent State Apartments. Since the Queen was going to
hold a levée and a drawing-room in Dublin, the Castle itself,
now dirty and dilapidated, St. Patrick's Hall, where the
Knights of St. Patrick were invested and installed, and the
adjoining apartments must be redecorated and repaired. No
investiture of the Knights of St. Patrick was to be held,
however, on account of the expense involved.

The estimate Clarendon received from the Board of Works
was £2,500 for the Castle and the Vice-Regal Lodge, with
two additional items, £500 for erecting a "tent," a pavilion,
for the Queen's reception when she landed at Kingstown (now
Dunleary), and £400 for "illuminations"—£3,400 in all.

Charles Wood was horrified; ". . . we never dreamed of
anything like this," he wrote to Clarendon. "The Prince's idea
was some £500 to cover everything, beyond eating and drinking." Clarendon became discouraged; he was, he told Charles
Greville, "considerably disgusted," as the preparations proceeded, at the "petty difficulties" raised and the "want of
consideration" he felt was being shown him by the Queen and
the Prince.

Eventually, Clarendon submitted a bill for under £2,000,
but Lord John Russell, though admitting he had expected as
much, or more, wrote, "I do not know where it is to come
from."

The private means of Clarendon, never more than moderate, were, he wrote, being "heavily drawn upon" to meet the
expenses of the Lord-Lieutenancy. "I have no prospect but
the Watford Workhouse before me when I leave this," he
told his brother-in-law, George Cornewall Lewis, "particularly
as I have now to undergo another Dublin season at £3,000
a month." The Grove, Lord Clarendon's country house, was
near the town of Watford in Hertfordshire.

Nevertheless, at the end of July, 1849, an army of workmen
appeared in Dublin, preparations started in earnest and excitement began to mount. "Triumphal arches, platforms,
devices, meet you on all sides," reported *The Times*. The
exterior of the Castle was being given "a clean face" and the
windows repainted; St. Patrick's Hall was to be entirely
redecorated and all State Apartments "put in order." The
number of workmen employed was reported to run into

hundreds, men and materials both being Irish. Windows, to view the Queen's entry, were hired out at six guineas, lists of noblemen coming to Dublin were published almost daily, an "influx of visitors" flowed into Dublin, and accommodation in hotels was "at a premium."

. The Queen's carriage for the visit which was being built at Messrs. Hutton Summerhill, Dublin, was a light barouche, to take two persons only, royal blue in colour, with royal blue wheels interlined with white; the Royal arms were painted on the panels and the interior was lined with royal blue silk tabinet. It was to be drawn by four horses, with postilions and outriders. The Four Courts were to be illuminated with gas on the night of Her Majesty's arrival, and the Nelson Pillar by electric light, under the superintendence of Professor Gluckmann, "a grand feature." The Pillar was being railed in, and a platform erected inside the railing for the apparatus—the light was expected to be so dazzling that, from time to time, it was to be turned off, to avoid spoiling the effect of the other illuminations.

Meanwhile, extra troops to line the route marched in and encamped in Phoenix Park. Though the visit was to be private, notice was issued that the Queen's Levèe and Drawing-room, at the Castle, would be full dress, and that the Drawing-room, in accordance with Irish custom, would be held in the evening; further, no lady or gentleman could be presented "except by someone who has been himself or herself presented to Her Majesty"—presentations to the Lord-Lieutenant at the Vice-Regal Court were not to be recognized for the Queen's Dublin Drawing-room. This announcement caused "a perfect panic." Nevertheless, milliners and dressmakers continued to be in urgent requisition, and Mr. J. Hart, of 81, Regent's Quadrant, London, dispatched to Dublin "a splendid stock of Court dresses, regimentals, naval uniforms, swords, epaulets, etc., for Her Majesty's levées and drawing-room."

&

At 9 p.m. on August 1 the Royal yacht, the *Victoria and Albert,* was reported to be passing Portland Bill, on her way down channel to Cork; the weather was clear, but at sea there was what the Queen described as "a dreadful swell." It had been expected that a call would be made at Plymouth or Falmouth, but the voyage was made direct, and at 10 p.m. next day, "to the great surprise of everyone," the

Victoria and Albert steamed into Cove. Ships of the Royal Navy in Cove harbour, including the *Ganges,* were illuminated, rockets were sent up, blue lights burned, a *feu de joie* fired, and bonfires lighted by the owners of houses and villas overlooking the harbour. Through over-enthusiasm in the use of tar and kindling wood, the servants of Mr. E. B. Roche, M.P. for Cork, set alight fourteen acres of fir plantation, so that the Royal yacht was bathed "in a blaze of light, which was more like what we read of the sheet of flame in which an American prairie is sometimes enwrapt, than the usual murky appearance of bonfires, when viewed at any distance from the shore. Her Majesty, we understand, was much pleased with the effect."

Next day, Friday, the Mayor of Cork hurried off to the *Victoria and Albert* to beg the Queen not to land until Saturday; it was feared that the preparations in Cork, triumphal arches, etc., would not be ready. Delay was impossible, he was told: the Queen's time-table made it essential for her to move on to Dublin, and she would visit Cork that afternoon at 4 p.m. This announcement created "consternation."

During the morning, numbers of small craft circled round the *Victoria and Albert,* with passengers waving laurel branches; about noon the *Fairy* tender was observed to be getting up steam, and at 2 p.m., to loud cheers, the Queen showed herself, and stepped on board the *Fairy.* The fleet of the Cork Steam Packet Company, crowded with cheering passengers, now "swept down" the harbour and saluted the Royal yacht, and "thunders" of artillery were heard. The Queen first toured the harbour in the *Fairy,* with yachts and boats circling round, then landed on Columbine Quay, Cove Harbour, where a "marine villa," or pavilion, had been fitted up, consisting of two rooms, each 60 feet by 40 feet. Loud cheers and huzzas broke out as she stepped on Irish soil, the first British sovereign ever to set foot in the county of Cork, and the roar of the cannon, which had been placed rather too close, shook the pavilion.

"The Queen, the virtuous and honoured embodiment of fashion, steps on . . . shore . . ." reported the *Freeman's Journal,* by no means reconciled to the visit as yet, "Prince Albert follows, honoured and revered of course but at the same time suggestive of ideas of taxation." ("Ideas of taxation" referred to the humiliating affair of the Prince's annuity, settled on him by Parliament on his marriage to the Queen;

£50,000 a year was asked for, but the House of Commons objected and the Prince had the "mortification" of being granted only £30,000.)

∾

However, a totally unexpected development followed: the Queen and the Irish people fell in love with each other. The affection was brief, the participants unsuited, the episode soon forgotten and the course of history uninfluenced, but for a few days in August, 1849, the attraction was a reality.

Within the marine villa at Cove addresses were presented to the Queen, who announced, "I have much pleasure in giving my sanction to the change of name which has been sought by the inhabitants and directing that this town shall in future be called Queenstown"; and at that moment a flag bearing the name Queenstown was run up over the pavilion. Since Ireland became independent the town has reverted to its native Irish name, Cobh.

The Queen then re-embarked and steamed up to Cork, the *Fairy* keeping as near the shore as possible. Houses and villas were decorated, and the gunfire from the shore and from steamers on the river was continuous; the Queen commented on the amount of firing and the beauty of the richly-wooded landscape. A pause was made at Blackrock Castle to receive "a salmon and a very pretty address" from the fishermen of Blackrock, and the *Fairy* came alongside at the Custom House, Cork Harbour. The whole of the side of the Custom House which faced the water was covered with a rich scarlet cloth worked in gold, with the shamrock and the rose and the thistle; above the entrance the famous Irish greeting, Cead Mille Failte, "a hundred thousand welcomes," was surmounted by a handsome golden crown. The steps to the water were covered with scarlet, a triumphal arch had been erected on the quay, flags floated both from the arch and the building, and on the quay a stand for 400 ladies, crowded with county notabilities, was covered with an awning of scarlet cloth. Within the Custom House two "magnificent Grecian vases" stood on pedestals of scarlet, on which the letters V and A were raised in gold, "supported on true lovers' knots in the same brilliant hue."

The Mayor, Corporation and other dignitaries came on board the *Fairy* and presented addresses, and the Queen knighted the Mayor of Cork, *"on deck* (on board the *Fairy*) like in times of old," she wrote to her uncle, King Leopold of the Belgians; she then passed across the quay and through the Custom House, cheered by "thousands congregated on the wharfs and on board steamers," and at 4 p.m. precisely entered an open landau, drawn by four grey horses, and drove round Cork for two hours. She was accompanied by the Prince and preceded by two outriders, while the Earl of Bandon, Lieutenant of the county, and General Turner, with their aides-de-camp, rode on either side of the carriage, all mounts and chargers being grey. A detachment of the 12th Lancers escorted, and a long procession of carriages and horsemen followed. The shops were closed, the streets decorated with arches, evergreens and banners, a favourite inscription being "Hail Victoria, Ireland's hope and England's glory." The Queen had expressed herself to Sir George Grey as being most anxious that no accident should occur to anyone, through excessive crushing, during her progress through the streets, and had asked that special care should be taken to prevent any danger of the people being trampled or hurt by the horses, *The Times* correspondent described the order as "admirable" and the welcome "enthusiastic," though "many of the people who crowded the streets looked poor and haggard." The Queen herself commented that the heat and dust were great, the streets decorated and densely crowded, and that "Cork is not at all like an English town and looks rather foreign. The crowd is a noisy, excitable, but very good humoured one, running and pushing about, and laughing, talking and shrieking. The beauty of the women is very remarkable and struck us much; such beautiful dark eyes and hair, and such fine teeth; almost every third woman was pretty and some remarkably so."

At 6 p.m., with a punctuality which was to cause some surprise in Ireland, the Queen returned to the Custom House, and rejoined the *Victoria and Albert* at 7 p.m.

Next morning, by 9 a.m., preparations for sailing were visible on the *Victoria and Albert,* and numbers of small boats and yachts put off and sailed round her, upon which "the Royal party . . . with an evident desire to gratify an excusable and even laudable curiosity, came on deck repeatedly and leant over the side of the yacht so that the sightseers should be sent away perfectly satisfied." The Queen wore a morning dress and plain bonnet, with a green veil, the Prince a military cap with gold band, light trousers and shooting-jacket.

The Prince of Wales, in a sailor suit, was observed "bounding about." At 10 a.m. the *Victoria and Albert* weighed anchor for Kingstown.

The weather was fair, but with "a head sea and a contrary wind which made it rough and me very sick," wrote the Queen, and it was decided to put into Waterford Harbour for the night. Prince Albert, with the two boys, went up to Waterford, a distance of about ten miles, in the *Fairy,* but the Queen felt too "giddy and tired."

Next morning the weather had not changed, the wind was still contrary and the sea rough. "However we went out as it could not be helped and we might have remained some days for no use." The *Victoria and Albert* got under way at 8.30 a.m.; "for three hours it was dreadfully rough, and I and the poor children were very seasick," wrote the Queen. However, after the yacht passed the Tuskar Rock, off the coast of Wexford, the weather improved, and towards evening the Queen was able to admire the beauty of the Wicklow Hills.

Meanwhile, in Dublin a rehearsal of the illuminations had been held on Saturday night, including the *pièce de résistance,* Professor Gluckmann's electric illumination of the Nelson Pillar. The Bank of Ireland, which occupied the old Parliament building, was said to have spent £1,000, and was considered the best effort. For the first time for more than a year the Castle Guard trooped with full band; a false report that the Queen would arrive that day brought crowds into the streets. It was then officially announced that the Queen would make her entry into Dublin on Monday, August 6, at 10 a.m.

Meanwhile, outside Dublin Bay, the *Victoria and Albert* had been met by the steamers *Sphinx, Stromboli, Dragon,* earlier employed in the relief service, and the steamer *Trident,* and at seven o'clock on Sunday evening, "with this large squadron," wrote the Queen, "we steamed slowly and majestically into the harbour of Kingstown which was covered with thousands and thousands of spectators, cheering most enthusiastically . . . altogether it was a noble and stirring scene. It was just seven when we entered, and the setting sun lit up the country, the fine buildings and the whole scene with a glowing light which was truly beautiful. We were soon surrounded by boats, and the enthusiasm and excitement of the people were extreme."

Monday was cloudless and sunny. The Queen disembarked

"as the clock struck ten," stepping on shore from the yacht accompanied by the Prince and her four children, the ships in the harbour saluting and bands playing. At Kingstown an old woman shouted, "Ah, Queen dear, make one of them Prince Patrick and Ireland will die for you."

The *Freeman's Journal*, which remained highly critical, reported that the Queen wore a red plaid shawl and a plain Dunstable, i.e. a straw bonnet, and the Prince a blue pilot coat, buttoned high, and a hat of the kind known as "the Albert hat." Trains, according to the newspaper, brought comparatively few visitors from the city, and the procession was "scant, formal, cold." There were about 200 horsemen and not very many carriages, and the whole passed in about fifteen minutes. The stands were only about a quarter full; there were cheers from windows, but no crowds followed the procession, and the first greeting at Kingstown was the warmest the Queen was given.

The Queen herself, however, received a very different impression; she wrote of immense multitudes, most enthusiastic and excited, flowers strewn in her path, masses of human beings waving hats and handkerchiefs, bursts of cheering which "rent" the air: the crowd was the most good-humoured she had ever seen, "noisy and excitable beyond belief," given to "shrieking instead of cheering," and "talking and jumping." The scene was "wonderful, striking, never to be forgotten," she wrote. "Our entrance into Dublin was really a magnificent thing." At the same time, the poverty of Ireland did not escape her. "You see more ragged and wretched people here than I ever saw anywhere else," she wrote that evening, and commenting again on the good looks of Irishwomen added, "*En revanche* the women are really very handsome—quite in the lowest class . . . such beautiful black eyes and hair and such fine colour and teeth."

Dublin delighted her—Dublin was a very fine city, she wrote that evening; Sackville Street and Merrion Square remarkably large and handsome; Trinity College and the old Parliament House noble buildings. "At the last triumphal arch a poor little dove was let down into my lap, with an olive branch round its neck, alive and very tame." The heat and dust were "tremendous," but when the Vice-Regal Lodge at Phoenix Park was reached at noon, the Queen was again appreciative; the view of the Wicklow Hills was "very beautiful" and "we are most comfortably lodged and have very nice rooms."

Queen Victoria possessed a remarkable capacity for enjoyment and a remarkable readiness to appreciate what was offered for her to enjoy. That afternoon she drove out, incognito, and visited the Botanical Gardens at Glasnevin, "followed by jaunting cars and riders and people running and screaming," which amused and did not irritate her. That evening the illuminations were lighted; unfortunately it rained, but a vast multitude filled the streets, and no disturbance took place. The inhabitants of Dublin eagerly welcomed diversion, for a long series of drab years lay behind them: Dublin had lost her splendour following the Union, now she was sunk in the despair of the famine, and Dubliners responded with excitement to lights, flowers, band music, uniforms.

That evening there was a dinner at the Vice-Regal Lodge; next morning the Queen rose early and drove into Dublin, in Lord Clarendon's carriage, with the Prince and two ladies, "without any escort," visiting the Bank, where she admired the old Parliament buildings, the Model School, where she was received by the Catholic Archbishop of Dublin, Archbishop Murray, whose fine, venerable looks she also admired, and Trinity College, where she was once more all admiration. In the library she and the Prince signed their names on a blank sheet of vellum, which was subsequently bound with the Book of Kells. The legend, current in Dublin, that the Queen and the Prince wrote on the illuminated manuscript is not correct.

The crowd in the streets, wrote the Queen, was immense, and cheered a great deal. She got back to the Vice-Regal Lodge at a few minutes past one, lunched, wrote letters, heard the children at their lessons and then set out again, this time for the Royal Hospital, Kilmainham, an institution for old soldiers, conducted on the same lines as Chelsea Hospital. Again, there was no escort: the Queen drove with her ladies and Lord Clarendon in a carriage, the Prince rode behind, and five or six mounted police went ahead, to see that the road was clear. At Kilmainham, the Queen inspected the veterans, admired the hall and made a little speech. "I am glad indeed to see you all looking so comfortable." Instead of going back to the Vice-Regal Lodge she then drove, informally, round "all the principal parts" of Dublin, "at a leisurely pace," making a circuit of St. Stephen's Green, College Green, the Four Courts and the famous streets and squares. Although she was not expected, large crowds gathered at several points. As the Queen drove slowly through Parkgate Street, Mr. T. Nugent, a guardian of the North Dublin Union, approached the carriage and exclaimed, "Mighty Monarch, pardon Smith O'Brien." The pace of the carriage was then quickened. The Queen, however, did not return directly to the Vice-Regal Lodge, she remained in Dublin city; and that night there was another dinner and a ball.

The Queen's simplicity, lack of stiffness and touchiness, and her admiration of Dublin were having their effect. Queen Victoria at this time was pretty, eager, and with a great deal of vitality. Few people can visit Dublin without forming an affection for the most beautiful and hospitable of cities, and the Queen's evident enjoyment and her quick response to the efforts made for her entertainment were irresistible.

On August 8 the *Freeman's Journal* succumbed. "The personal demeanour, the frank and confiding manner of the Queen, have won for her golden opinions," declared a leading article, adding, "The more the citizens of Dublin see Queen Victoria, the more she wins their affections"; and the *Dublin Evening Mail,* which had also been hostile, observed that the Queen's early rising and habits of punctuality . . . held forth to her sex an example worthy of all imitation." From this point onwards the Queen's visit to Dublin became a triumph.

On Wednesday, August 8, after an early luncheon, the Queen left the Vice-Regal Lodge at twenty minutes to one for the first full-dress State occasion of her visit, the levée at the Castle. The Queen and her ladies wore evening dress, the Queen's being of green Irish poplin lavishly embroidered with gold shamrocks; she wore the blue ribbon and star of St. Patrick, and a brilliant diamond tiara; the gentlemen were in full-dress uniform.

The levée was held in the magnificent throne-room of the Castle, with the Queen seated on the great gilt throne; more than 4,000 people were present, 2,000 were presented, and the levée was of inordinate length, lasting "without intermission until twenty minutes to six o'clock," wrote the Queen. Everything was done exactly as at Buckingham Palace and St. James's, and the Lord Chamberlain had come over especially, to supervise procedure. The indefatigable Queen then returned to the Vice-Regal Lodge for a dinner, an evening party and a concert.

Next day, Thursday, August 9, the streets of Dublin were astir at dawn, as a "human tide" began to flow towards Phoenix Park for the most popular event of the Queen's visit, described by the Queen herself as the "great and brilliant review." Carriages had remained on the ground all night, to secure a good position, and by 9 a.m. not one disengaged carriage or car was to be found in Dublin, for any price; vehicles which had acted as hen-roosts since the Union when, after the suppression of the Irish Parliament, society deserted Dublin, once more took the road, and the crowds continued "swelling as every hour advanced until the streets were one compact mass of men on horse and foot and every type of vehicle."

The Queen left the Vice-Regal Lodge punctually at 10 a.m., with the four children and Lady Clarendon, in an open barouche, drawn by four horses, with postilions and outriders; the Prince, in the uniform of a major-general, rode a magnificent chestnut. The march past began at 11 a.m.; cavalry evolutions by Hussars and Lancers, "the butterflies of war," were followed by infantry movements, an artillery display, and two grand charges by cavalry. The whole body of troops then marched to the extreme end of the review ground, the infantry formed into line, the cavalry in squadrons to the right and left, the artillery took up a position in the centre rear, and the entire mass, about six thousand men, moved forward to the music of their regimental bands. When within view of the Queen, the infantry fixed bayonets and charged forward, in double quick time, to a "terrible cry, half British cheer, half Irish hurrah," coming to a dead halt about twenty yards from the Royal carriage, when the colours were advanced and three cheers given for the Queen.

The enthusiasm was tremendous; very many of the troops were Irish, as in almost every British regiment, and that "terrible cry," half English cheer, half Irish yell, had resounded on every battlefield of the century in which British troops were engaged. Not only was it many years since the citizens of Dublin had seen such a show, but no show was more to their taste—few Irishmen are not soldiers at heart, and more than three hours after the Queen had driven away, the roads to Phoenix Park, and the quays, were still blocked, so great had been the number of spectators.

The same evening, at 8.30, after dining alone, the Queen and Prince drove into Dublin for the most important social occasion of her visit, the Drawing-room: "the Queen of the United Empire holding her court in the second city of her dominions" was the phrase of *The Times*. Carriages had begun to set down at the Castle as early as 7 p.m., the night was fine, the illuminations "blazing," with "every object almost as discernible as if it were day." Dense crowds, "perfectly orderly," thronged the streets, the Queen was enthusiastically cheered as she entered the Castle gates— and she sent a request to the Castle authorities that the people might be allowed closer, to have a better view. The Queen and her attendants occupied three State carriages, and were escorted by the Inniskilling Dragoons. The Queen again wore Irish poplin, "a superb pink poplin dress elaborately figured with gold shamrocks," and the number of ladies at the Drawing-room was very large; the Queen estimated that between two and three thousand passed before her, and 1,700 were presented. After the presentations the Queen walked through St. Patrick's Hall, and other State apartments, conversing with the guests, while the bands of the 2nd Regiment and the 60th Rifles played. Soon after midnight the Queen left; the streets, she noticed, were still densely crowded, and she was loudly cheered.

The four days of the Queen's visit, days of "continual jubilee," were now coming to an end. But before embarking at Kingstown the Queen was to visit Ireland's "only Duke," the Duke of Leinster: and had consented to accept a *déjeuner* at his seat, Carton, in Co. Kildare, about an hour's drive from Dublin.

The Duke threw open the demesne of Carton to the public, and from the early hours of the morning lines of carriages, cars and pedestrians streamed towards Carton, special trains were run from Dublin by the Midland Great Western Railway Company to the nearest station, Maynooth, and long before the time of the Queen's arrival every vantage-point in the demesne and along the road where she would pass was crowded with spectators. On this occasion the Queen appeared in some state. An advanced guard was followed by two mounted servants in Royal livery, next, several files of the 8th Hussars, then two Royal carriages, with postilions and outriders, escorted by more files of Hussars, and, finally, the remainder of the regiment bringing up the rear.

The Queen drove along the valley of the Liffey; at every vantage-point along the route cheering crowds gathered, and students from the Catholic seminary at Maynooth cheered the Queen at Leixlip. About half-way, the Hussar escort was relieved by the 17th Lancers.

The day was brilliantly fine, the sun had shone during almost the whole of the Queen's stay, and a "vast but orderly" crowd waited in the demesne. Six or eight marquees had been erected for the Duke's guests at the rear of the mansion, an "elegant entertainment" was spread out on tables, and the bands of the 1st Carabiniers and 2nd Royals played. Precisely at the hour named, the Queen's cortège swept through the gates of Carton; the picturesque spectacle of the Royal carriage "dashing along over hill and dale through the demesne with its scarlet outriders and lancer escort," was much admired, and "with her usual punctuality" the Queen drew up before Carton at one o'clock. Simultaneously, the Royal standard was run up over the house.

The Queen wore a "beautiful pink silk dress" and a blue silk bonnet, both covered with Limerick lace, and carried a parasol. The sole disappointment was that the children did not accompany her. The Queen walked round the garden, and it was observed with pleasure that she leaned on the arm of Ireland's only Duke, while the Prince walked on the other side; the Duke was, she wrote, "one of the kindest and best of men." After luncheon some of the Duke's tenants danced jigs to Irish pipes, which the Queen found "most amusing"; she was struck by the thick blue coats the men wore, with short breeches and blue stockings, and the way one dancer wore his hat tilted over one ear. The Queen and the Duke, the Queen again leaning on the Duke's arm, next ascended a tower which commanded a view of the demesne, then drove in a carriage, with the Duchess of Leinster, to a rustic *cottage orné* which overlooked a lake made by a tributary of the Liffey. The people, the Queen noted, "were riding, running and driving with us," but this did not irritate her—they were "extremely well behaved; and the Duke is so kind to them that a word from him will make them do anything." It had been intended that the Queen should return to Carton by water, and a pleasure-boat waited, with the Royal standard at the stern; but the Queen had named an hour for her return to the Vice-Regal Lodge, and punctual arrivals entailed punctual departures, so she drove back through the

demesne to Carton in a jaunting-car, sitting between the
Prince and the Duke. The Queen was delighted with the
experience, subsequently commemorated in a popular song a
line of which runs, " 'Be me sowl,' says she, 'I like the joultin'
of yer Irish jauntin' car,' " and the Duke of Leinster had a
car built in Dublin and sent over to the Queen which she
accepted with evident pleasure and amusement. Soon after
4 p.m. the Royal cortège left, this time taking the Lucan
road, and driving rather faster than in the morning, as the
Queen did not want to be late; however, she particularly
noticed the fine decorations in the village of Lucan, with
arches of bay and laurel, "every possible demonstration of
affection and respect was given by . . . persons along the
road and as cordially acknowledged."

Meanwhile, in Dublin, a "vast concourse" of people awaited
the Queen's return at the Knockmaroon Gate to Phoenix Park,
including "vast numbers of fashionably dressed persons in
cars and carriages," and she was cheered until she had disappeared into the demesne of the Vice-Regal Lodge. The
crowd then hurried round to line the route to Westland Row
station, where the Queen was to take the train for Kingstown
and re-embark in the *Victoria and Albert*.

The Queen reached Phoenix Park a little after five, and
appeared again at six; to the delight of the crowd the four
Royal children now accompanied their parents; the two elder
boys were in the first carriage with the Queen, the Prince and
Lord Clarendon.

The Queen's visit reached its climax in her departure. It
was a personal triumph. For the four days of jubilee Dublin
had been "like a city risen from the dead," and it was then
the second city in the Empire, and perhaps the most beautiful.
The Queen had, plainly, been delighted with Dublin; she had
admired its people, she had driven about almost unattended,
she had betrayed no irritation at the people pressing and
chasing after her; indeed, at the Drawing-room, she had
requested the authorities to let the crowds come closer. She
might well exclaim with Charles II, as he passed through the
crowds on his way to London at the Restoration, "How is it
they and I have been kept so long apart?"

The Queen's interest and delight were not assumed as a
matter of policy. Lord John Russell wrote that she left
Ireland with "real regret." She would never, she declared, forget the affection and enthusiasm with which she had been

received, and at the end of August, at Balmoral, he noted that she was still speaking of her journey to Ireland with "real delight."

From the moment the Queen's carriage left the Vice-Regal Lodge the cheers were deafening; the Prince took off his hat and remained uncovered all along the route to Westland Row. The quays were crowded, dense masses of people had gathered on Carlisle (now O'Connell) Bridge, banners and flags were flown from larger buildings, roofs and windows were crowded, and the rigging of ships in the Liffey clustered with people. The Queen "appeared extremely gratified at the enthusiastic reception which awaited her . . . and we can have but little doubt that Her Majesty's present visit is the forerunner of many others of much longer duration" wrote an observer, hopefully.

Crowds had been gathered at the Westland Row railway terminus from ten o'clock in the morning; the station entrance was decorated with scarlet cloth, a white awning trimmed with scarlet had been put up, the band of the 48th Regiment played, and a guard of honour was provided by the 71st Regiment. The Queen left Westland Row at about twelve minutes past six, preceded by a pilot engine, and was cheered all along the line. "The Queen," wrote Macaulay, who was in Ireland about a week after she left, "made a conquest of all hearts."

At 6.30 p.m. Kingstown was reached. Every pier, every wharf, every roof in Kingstown was black with people, every boat in the harbour was crammed. The Dublin *Evening Mail,* noting the "tremendous enthusiasm," could not "think where the crowds came from." As the Queen's railway coach drew in, the Royal standard was run up over the station, and a tremendous cheer burst out, first from the ships nearest in the harbour, then taken up, from ship to ship, as all yards were manned. The Queen and Prince appeared on the upper terrace with the children, were "recognized by the vast crowd below and throughout that great assemblage one thrilling cheer broke out . . . the peals of hurrahs floating from the manned yards like echoes across the water, whilst in the distance the shout was taken up by the dense crowds that thronged the ends of the piers."

The Queen, with her family, paused: and advancing to the end of the terrace overlooking the whole scene she bowed repeatedly and raised and waved her right hand "in cordial salutation to her people."

Below, with steam up, the *Victoria and Albert* was waiting. After some minutes the Queen stepped on board, and the vessel at once moved off. For some time the Queen, with the Prince and the children, stood aft, where she could be distinctly seen by the people standing on the pier. Her Majesty then "paced the deck for a little time and, on approaching the extremity of the pier near the lighthouse where vast numbers of people had congregated, she . . . looked towards the crowd, ran along the deck and, with the sprightliness of a young girl and with the agility of a sailor, ascended the paddlebox." On the summit she was joined by Prince Albert and, taking his arm, "gracefully waved her right hand towards the people on the pier . . . After some time she appeared to give an order to the Commandant and immediately the paddles ceased to move and the vessel floated on with the impetus it had already received. Her Majesty remained in this position (the vessel moving very slowly and as near the pier as was compatible with safety) waving her handkerchief and receiving the plaudits of the thousands who crowded the extremity of the pier. An occasional revolution of the paddles kept the vessel in motion and in this way the *Victoria and Albert* drifted rather than steamed past the pier, and until the Royal vessel had passed full half a mile from the pier the speed was not altered, nor did Her Majesty leave the paddle-box. . . ."

"The departure," said Lord Lansdowne, who was present, "was quite affecting and he could not see it without being moved"; and John Bright, Radical Member of Parliament for Birmingham, said he would not for the world have missed seeing the embarkation at Kingstown, for he had felt just the same enthusiasm as the rest of the crowd. "Indeed," he told Lord Clarendon, "I'll defy any man to have felt otherwise, when he saw the Queen come upon the platform, and bow to the people in a manner that showed her heart was with them."

A huge crowd of spectators waited until, as evening closed in, the smoke of the last ship of the Royal Squadron sank below the horizon.

～⚜～

The idyll had been charming, but it brought no result. The

days of "continual jubilee," the enthusiasm, the sympathy, had no effect whatsoever on the fate of Ireland. The Queen had prestige, importance and social authority, but political power belonged to her Ministers, and Ireland remained in the hands of the Cabinet, above all, with the Chancellor of the Exchequer and his department, the Treasury.

The Queen returned to Ireland three times, in 1853, 1861 and 1900, but the enthusiasm of the first visit was not recaptured. The Queen was less eager, less accessible, and the Irish people, abandoned to *laissez-faire* and the operation of natural causes, had learnt the frantic detestation and distrust of everything and everyone English which made total separation from England, not merely an Irish Parliament in Dublin, the only solution.

And meanwhile, year after year, decade after decade, hunger continued to stalk through Ireland.

The famine was never "over," in the sense that an epidemic occurs and is over. The poverty of the Irish people continued, dependence on the potato continued, failures of the potato, to a greater or lesser extent, continued, and hunger continued. Trevelyan had considered the famine to be "over" in the summer of 1847, when an abundant harvest succeeded the scarcity of 1846; ". . . the downward progress of the country," he wrote, "has been mercifully stayed," and his book *The Irish Crisis,* dealing with the Government's relief measures, ends in August, 1847; but in 1848 the potato failed totally again, and in the opinion of experienced relief officials the people suffered more than in 1846. At the end of 1849, Mr. T. N. Redington, Under-Secretary for Ireland, an Irish Poor Law Commissioner and a landlord in Galway, again pronounced the famine over. At that time there were about a million destitute in the workhouses and on relief, and the philanthropist, Sidney Godolphin Osborne, travelling in the west, "frequently" saw dead bodies lying by the side of the road. In 1852 Harriet Martineau, the political writer, found blight flourishing round Belfast; the people were digging up their potatoes in hopes of finding a few fit to eat, and on the way to Dublin the potato fields were blackened.

In 1879 a disastrous failure occurred; a Mansion House Committee was formed in Dublin, subscriptions raised, and a report published, deploring the state of Ireland, in words which might have been written in 1846.

When Irish people refer to "the famine," however, they mean the years of concentrated disaster in which blight first appeared; and in rapid succession the partial failure of 1845 was followed by the total failure of 1846 and the second total failure of 1848. The history of what then occurred is deeply engraved on the memory of the Irish race; all hope of assimilation with England was then lost, and bitterness without parallel took possession of the Irish mind.

❧

The treatment of the Irish people by the British Government during the famine has been described as genocide—race murder. The British Government has been accused, and not only by the Irish, of wishing to exterminate the Irish people, as Cromwell wished to "extirpate" them, and as Hitler wished to exterminate the Jews. The eighteen-forties, however, must not be judged by the standards of today; and whatever parsimony and callousness the British Government displayed towards Ireland, was paralleled seven years later by the treatment of their own soldiers which brought about the destruction of the British Army in the Crimea.

The conduct of the British Government during the famine is divided into two periods. During the first, from the partial failure in 1845 until the transfer to the Poor Law in the summer of 1847, the Government behaved with considerable generosity. An elaborate relief organization was set up, public works were started on a scale never attempted before, and what was, for the time, a very large sum of money indeed, more than eight million pounds, was advanced. Not enough was done, considering the size of the catastrophe, but it is doubtful if any Government in Europe, at that date, would have done more.

But during the second period, after the transfer to the Poor Law in the summer of 1847, the behaviour of the British Government is difficult to defend. Lord John Russell and his advisers, in particular Sir Charles Wood and Trevelyan, were aware of the state of the Irish Poor Law. They knew that most of the distressed unions were bankrupt, that the worst unions had never been anything else, that in those districts where poverty, destitution and starvation were greatest the workhouses were badly equipped, or not equipped at all, dirty,

understaffed and disorganized. They knew that, in the most
distressed unions, rates, in normal times, had been virtually
uncollectable, while in others they had to be collected with
the aid of police, troops, and sometimes ships of war and,
even then, were only partially gathered. They knew that
Ireland was, at the moment, in the grip of a major famine,
described by Lord John himself in January, 1847, as "such as
has not been known in modern times; indeed I should say it is
like a famine of the 13th century acting upon a population
of the 19th."

Yet, with these facts before them, the Government threw
the hordes of wretched destitute on their local Poor rates,
refusing assistance when the second total failure of the
potato occurred and even breaking Lord John Russell's pledge
to feed the starving children. Since Britain was passing
through a financial crisis, the justification of the Government's
actions was expediency, but it is difficult to reconcile expediency with duty and moral principles.

The most serious charge against the British Government,
however, is not the transfer to the Poor Law. Neither during
the famine nor for decades afterwards were any measures
of reconstruction or agricultural improvement attempted, and
this neglect condemned Ireland to decline. A devastating
new disease had attacked the potato; nothing to equal the
total destruction of 1846 had been seen before, yet no
serious effort was made to teach the people to grow any
other crop; and when Lord Clarendon tried to effect improvement by means of "agricultural instructors," his scheme
was ridiculed, Charles Wood writing contemptuously of Clarendon's "hobby." Seed rose in price, far beyond the reach of
the famine-stricken Irish, but the Government would not
assist with seed, in spite of the successful distribution by the
Society of Friends. The Irish small tenant was inevitably
driven back on the potato; he was penniless, starving, ignorant;
the only crop he knew how to cultivate was the potato; generally speaking, the only tool he owned, and could use, was a
spade. He had no choice. Yet when the potato failed totally
again, in 1848, the Government exploded in fury. "In 1847,"
Lord John wrote, angrily, "eight millions were advanced to
enable the Irish to supply the loss of the potato crop and to
cast about them for some less precarious food . . . The result
is that they have placed more dependence on the potato

than ever and have again been deceived. How can such a people be assisted?"

As nothing was done to improve agriculture, so nothing
was done to improve the system under which land was
occupied in Ireland. Tenants at will remained tenants at will;
twenty years after the famine, Isaac Butt was still writing,
"The vast majority of the occupiers of land in Ireland are at
this moment liable to be turned out at the pleasure of their
landlords"; and improvements carried out by the tenant
continued to become the property of the landlord. Two Bills,
introduced respectively by Sir William Somerville and Mr.
Sharman Crawford, in 1848 and 1850, to give tenants a
measure of security and some benefit for improvements, were
dropped. The Government's one important measure affecting
the land, the Incumbered Estates Act of 1849, proved disastrous to the people.

The first Incumbered Estates Act of 1848 was a failure
and, almost in desperation, a further Act was passed in July,
1849. This Act was drastic: under its provisions an estate
could be compulsorily sold on the petition of a creditor or
of the landlord himself. "At a time of unprecedented deprecia-
tion of the value of land, it caused a general auction of Irish
estates." Properties were sold for prices which did not cover
the mortgages and debts, and creditors and owners were
alike left penniless. No legislation protected the tenant, estates
were bought in at bargain prices with a view to profit, and
the new landlords proved very hard masters. Many of the old
owners, though insolvent and unbusinesslike, had retained
traces of feudal feeling, some like the famous Martins of
Connemara, who were sold up under the Act, had a great
deal, whereas the new mercantile owners of the land had
none; rents were raised and estates cleared more ruthlessly
than ever before.

These misfortunes were not part of a plan to destroy the
Irish nation; they fell on the people because the government
of Lord John Russell was afflicted with an extraordinary
inability to foresee consequences. It has been frequently
declared that the parsimony of the British Government during
the famine was the main cause of the sufferings of the people,
and parsimony was certainly carried to remarkable lengths;
but obtuseness, short-sightedness and ignorance probably
contributed more.

To take only a few instances, it did not occur to Lord John

Russell and his advisers that, by forcing the famine-stricken applicant for relief to give up every possession, they were creating fresh armies of paupers, even though Lord Clarendon had inquired if it were wise to compel a man to become a pauper, when he was not one already, in order to be saved from starvation. It was not apparently anticipated that refusing to assist the famine-stricken small tenants with seed would result in holdings being left unsown, nor that, unless some means of subsistence were provided, men with families who had lost their winter food must drop the cultivation of the land and crowd on the public works. Even the self-evident truth, that Ireland is not England, was not realized by the Government in Whitehall; the desolate, starving west was assumed to be served by snug grocers and prosperous merchants and to be a field for private enterprise; bankrupt squireens, living in jerry-built mansions, with rain dripping through the roof, became county gentry, and plans for sea transport were made as if the perilous harbours of the west coast were English ports. The ruthless clearances which followed the Incumbered Estates Act of 1849 and subsequent Acts were not planned by the British Government; it was not foreseen that such clearances were bound to happen.

Much of this obtuseness sprang from the fanatical faith of mid-nineteenth century British politicians in the economic doctrine of *laissez-faire,* no interference by government, no meddling with the operation of natural causes. Adherence to *laissez-faire* was carried to such a length that in the midst of one of the major famines of history, the government was perpetually nervous of being too good to Ireland and of corrupting the Irish people by kindness, and so stifling the virtues of self reliance and industry. In addition hearts were hardened by the antagonism then felt by the English towards the Irish, an antagonism rooted far back in religious and political history, and at the period of the famine irritation had been added as well. The discreditable state of Ireland, the subject of adverse comment throughout the civilized world, her perpetual misfortunes, the determined hostility of most of her population, even their character, provoked intense irritation in England. It is impossible to read the letters of British statesmen of the period, Charles Wood and Trevelyan for instance, without astonishment at the influence exerted by antagonism and irritation on government policy in Ireland during the famine.*

It is not characteristic of the English to behave as they have behaved in Ireland; as a nation, the English have proved themselves to be capable of generosity, tolerance and magnanimity, but not where Ireland is concerned. As Sydney Smith, the celebrated writer and wit, wrote: "The moment the very name of Ireland is mentioned, the English seem to bid adieu to common feeling, common prudence and common sense, and to act with the barbarity of tyrants and the fatuity of idiots."

How many people died in the famine will never precisely be known. It is almost certain that, owing to geographical difficulties and the unwillingness of the people to be registered, the census of 1841 gave a total smaller than the population in fact was. Officers engaged in relief work put the population as much as 25 per cent. higher; landlords distributing relief were horrified when providing, as they imagined, for 60 persons, to find more than 400 "start from the ground."

In 1841 the population of Ireland was given as 8,175,124; in 1851, after the famine, it had dropped to 6,552,385, and the Census Commissioners calculated that, at the normal rate of increase, the total should have been 9,018,799, so that a loss of at least 2½ million persons had taken place. The figures available, however, must be regarded as giving only a rough indication; vital statistics are unobtainable, no record was kept of deaths, and very many persons must have died and been buried unknown, as the fever victims died and were buried in west Cork, as bodies, found lying dead on the road, were buried in ditches, and as the timid people of Erris perished unrecorded.

In the four provinces of Ireland the smallest loss of population was in Leinster, 15.5 per cent., then Ulster, 16 per cent., Connaught's loss was greatest, 28.6 per cent., and Munster lost 23.5 per cent. In some respects, death and clearance improved Ireland; between 1841 and 1851, nearly 360,000 mud huts disappeared, the greatest decrease being 81 per cent. in Ulster, which then included the distressed county of

---

* For a summary of the subsequent careers of Trevelyan and Charles Wood, see Appendix I, p. 411.

Donegal, followed by Connaught, with a decrease of 74 per cent., Munster 69 per cent., and Leinster 62 per cent. Small-holdings under five acres were nearly halved, and holdings over fifteen acres doubled. No advantage, however, was taken of the reduction of small tenants, agriculture was not improved, and in 1866 Isaac Butt wrote, "Ireland has retrograded . . ." Between 1848 and 1864, however, thirteen million pounds was sent home by emigrants in America to bring relatives out, and it is part of the famine tragedy that, because no adequate measures of reconstruction were undertaken, a steady drain of the best and most enterprising left Ireland, to enrich other countries.

The famine left hatred behind. Between Ireland and England the memory of what was done and endured has lain like a sword. Other famines followed, as other famines had gone before, but it is the terrible years of the Great Hunger which are remembered, and only just beginning to be forgiven.

Time brought retribution. By the outbreak of the second world war, Ireland was independent, and she would not fight on England's side. Liberty and England did not appear to the Irish to be synonymous, and Eire remained neutral. Many thousands of Irishmen from Eire volunteered, but the famous regiments of southern Ireland had ceased to exist, and the "inexhaustible nursery of the finest soldiers" was no longer at England's service.

There was also a more direct payment. Along the west coast of Ireland, in Mayo especially, on remote Clare Island, and in the dunes above the Six Mile Strand are a number of graves of petty officers and able seamen of the British Navy and Merchant Service, representatives of many hundreds who were drowned off the coast of Ireland, because the Irish harbours were not open to British ships. From these innocents, in all probability ignorant of the past, who had never heard of failures of the potato, evictions, fever and starvation, was exacted part of the price for the famine.

APPENDIX I

TREVELYAN'S work in the Irish famine, for which in April 1848 he was made Sir Charles Trevelyan, K.C.B., was followed by the undertaking on which his reputation chiefly rests. In 1853 he investigated the system of admission into the civil service, and published with Sir Stafford Northcote, a report entitled "The Organization of the Permanent Civil Service." As a result the civil service was reformed, posts ceased to be, as had too often happened, at the disposal of influential aristocratic families, and the scholastic standard required was sharply raised. The modern civil service may be said to be largely Trevelyan's creation. He has been portrayed at this period by Anthony Trollope as Sir Gregory Hardlines in *The Three Clerks*. Since his early service in India (1826–38) he had maintained his interest in Indian affairs, possessed remarkable proficiency in Indian dialects, and in 1858, immediately after the Indian Mutiny, was appointed Governor of the Presidency of Madras. He conducted himself with a fearless sense of justice, instituted land reforms and won the esteem and confidence of the native population, who, through his administration, became reconciled to government by the British. He was abruptly recalled in 1860 owing to differences with the authorities on financial policy, which he made public and found their way into the newspapers; an indiscretion which was condemned even by his old ally Sir Charles Wood, then Secretary of State for India. However in 1862 he was appointed Financial member of the (India) Council, in effect Finance Minister, and again went to India. The appointment was a triumphant vindication of his financial views and his term of office was marked by an improvement in the financial position of India and by valuable administrative reforms. Periodic famines occurred during his Indian service, his letters reflect a less rigid and more humanitarian attitude than he exhibited in Ireland and his Irish experience may be said to have had a softening effect. Returning to England in 1865 he devoted himself to the

411

reform and amelioration of social grievances, especially the system of purchasing commissions and promotion in the British Army and died at 67 Eaton Square, London, in 1886.

SIR CHARLES WOOD, like Trevelyan, became engaged in Indian administration. On the fall of Lord John Russell's government in 1852 he was appointed President of the Board of Control (of the East India Company), and after a short term of office in Lord Palmerston's Cabinet as First Lord of the Admiralty, during which he was made a G.C.B., became Secretary of State for India in 1859. While holding this office he strongly supported the censure on Trevelyan in the House of Commons, following Trevelyan's recall from Madras. As Secretary for India in 1859, Wood's task was difficult; the Indian Mutiny had taken place, the East India Company had ceased to exist, the government of India had passed to the Crown and the administration and finances of India were to be adapted to the new state of affairs. Wood was criticized, often without justice, since the problems confronting him were almost insoluble. In the autumn of 1865 a serious hunting accident forced him to resign the Indian secretaryship and retire from strenuous official work. In 1866 he was raised to the peerage as the first Viscount Halifax of Monk Bretton, but was not prominent in the House of Lords; he was a poor speaker and owed his influence to his knowledge and experience of public affairs, his industry and talent for business. He died at his country seat Hickleton in Yorkshire in August 1885.

APPENDIX II

WILLIAM SMITH O'BRIEN, Meagher and McManus, after about a "week on the run," were arrested. O'Brien, fearing to bring reprisals on persons who concealed him, decided to make for his property, Cahirmoyle, in Limerick, and was taken at Thurles station, on Saturday, August 5, 1848. All three were tried for high treason and formally sentenced to be hanged, drawn and quartered. The sentence was not executed, but delay followed, because the law did not give the Sovereign power to commute a sentence for high treason. Special legislation had to be passed through Parliament before the sentence could be commuted to transportation for life, and it was not until July 9, 1849, that the three Young Ireland leaders were transported to Tasmania.

Smith O'Brien was released in 1854, his health having broken down. He took no further part in public life and died in 1864 at Bangor, North Wales.

Mitchel, who had been transported from Bermuda to Van Diemen's Land, escaped to the United States in 1853, founding a newspaper in New York, mainly in the interests of slave owners; he not only defended slavery but regarded the emancipation of the Jews as an unpardonable crime, and become a bitter critic of his former comrades. Mitchel was inspired not by love of liberty but hatred of England.

Meagher and McManus escaped in 1852 to the United States; McManus settled in San Francisco; Meagher, proved to possess considerable military ability, rose to be a general in the Union Army during the Civil War, but in 1867 was accidentally drowned in the river Missouri while on his way to take up his appointment as Governor of Montana.

James Fintan Lalor was imprisoned, first in Nenagh jail and then in Newgate, Dublin; after some months his health broke down and he was released. He immediately embarked on a conspiracy and attempted to found a new journal, unassisted, however, by Duffy, who wrote that "an insurrection more futile than the last was ripening, and my plainest duty was to

tell the people there was no hope or safety in that direction."
Nevertheless, on September 16, 1849, Lalor and three others
led what was termed a "rising" in Tipperary and Waterford;
it was so small and hopelessly unsuccessful that scarcely a
memory of it survives, and the majority of Irish historians do
not mention it. In Tipperary the "rising" was abandoned for
want of support; in Waterford an attack was made on the
police barrack at Cappoquin, in which a constable and one
of the insurgents were killed. The leader of the attack then
fled to America, the insurgent "troops" dispersed, and Lalor
returned to Dublin, where he died of bronchitis on December
27, 1849.

Charles Gavan Duffy remained imprisoned in Newgate,
Dublin, throughout what he calls the "palpitating days of July
and August 1848," but was subsequently tried, no fewer than
five times, under the Treason Felony Act. He defeated Government efforts to obtain a conviction by his skill in challenging
"packed" juries, and in 1849 his prosecution was dropped.
Having tried, in vain, to revive the *Nation* and the Young
Ireland movement, he was elected to Parliament in 1852 as
Member for New Ross, and flung himself into Land Reform,
working for a Bill which gave the Irish tenant compensation
for improvements and protection from eviction. The Bill
twice passed the House of Commons, but on each occasion
was thrown out by the Lords. Despairing and broken in
health and heart, Duffy emigrated to Australia in 1854, where
he had a distinguished career, became Minister of the Province
of Victoria, was knighted by the Queen in 1873, and ended
his life in an aura of respectability as Sir Charles Gavan
Duffy, K.C.M.G.

ACKNOWLEDGEMENTS

In writing this book I have received most generous help. I should like first to record my gratitude to the late Dr. Constantia Maxwell, formerly Lecky Professor of Modern History, Trinity College, Dublin. I wish she had lived to see the book in print.

I am especially indebted to Dr. R. B. McDowell, junior Dean of Trinity College, Dublin, who assisted me with his unrivalled knowledge of the nineteenth-century administration of Ireland and gave up many hours to reading the final draft of the manuscript.

I should like to express my gratitude to the group of Irish scholars who collaborated to produce *The Great Famine*. Professor Dudley Edwards of the National University, Dublin, has given me permission to make use of this authoritative volume. In addition I owe a special debt to Mr. Thomas P. O'Neill, Librarian of the National Library of Ireland, whose knowledge and patience have been inexhaustible, and to Dr. Kevin Nowlan who drew my attention to material I should otherwise have missed. I am also greatly indebted to Professor James Delargy and Dr. T. Wall of the Irish Folklore Commission, University College, Dublin. The encouragement and expert help I received from Mr. Roger Machell of Hamish Hamilton during the preparation of this book and his patience with innumerable telephone calls have given me the greatest support.

I should like to thank Mr. Kenneth Timings of the Public Record Office, London; his knowledge of nineteenth-century records was invaluable. I am also grateful to the staff of the State Paper Room at the British Museum and the State Paper Office at Dublin Castle.

In Canada I received valuable assistance from Dr. Kay Lamb, Dominion Archivist, and the staff of the Public Archives of Canada at Ottawa, to whom I gave a considerable amount of trouble. I should also like to thank Professor John Irwin Cooper of McGill University, Montreal, who made me acquainted with the topography of the city, and Mr. James Thom of Montreal, who answered a number of troublesome queries. I was able to visit Grosse Isle through the kindness of Dr. Charles Mitchell and I owe a debt of gratitude to Mr. Vincent Massey, who gave me the best possible start on my Canadian inquiries.

In the United States I should like to thank Professor R. K. Webb of Columbia University, who has helped me with information for a number of years. I am indebted to Mr. A. K. Barganawath of the New York Municipal Gallery, who kindly read through the New York section and I have received valuable information from Mr. Seymour Peyser and Mr. Russell Lynes. I am grateful to the Information Bureau of the *New York Times,* who solved a number of problems for me and I should like to record my appreciation of the helpfulness and courtesy of the staff on the New York Public Library, at 42nd Street, 25th Street, and West 125th Street and the staff of the New York Historical Society, 170 Central Park West.

I owe a great deal to Mr. Walter Muir Whitehill, Director and Librarian of the Boston Athenaeum, who placed his remarkable knowledge of the topography and history of Boston at my disposal and read through the Boston section. I am indebted to Mr. and Mrs. Murray Forbes, and to Mrs. Phyllis de Kay Wheelock for family information, and to Professor Oscar Handlin of Harvard for information and several years of kindness and encouragement.

Emigration material of great interest was lent me by Dr. M. A. Jones of the Department of American Studies, University of Manchester, and by Dr. Oliver MacDonagh, of St. Catharine's College, Cambridge. I have permission to quote from Dr. MacDonagh's recent work, *A Pattern of Government Growth.*

I am also indebted to Mr. Michael Perrin, C.B.E., chairman of the Wellcome Foundation, Dr. S. N. L. Poynter, Librarian of the Wellcome Historical Library, and Colonel C. A. Bozman, C.I.E., Director of the Wellcome Museum of Medical Science, who took an immense amount of trouble in answering what must have been, to them, elementary questions.

The debt I owe to Lieut.-General Sir William MacArthur, K.C.B., to Mr. Geoffrey Samuel, Mr. E. C. Large, and Dr. N. Robertson is acknowledged in the text.

I have been fortunate in being given permission to use a large number of private papers. I should like to thank the Marquess of Anglesey who lent me the letters of Sir John Burgoyne from the Plas Newydd Papers, the Earl of Clarendon who has given me permission to use the Irish Papers of the fourth Earl of Clarendon, and the Earl of Halifax, who has allowed me to use the Hickleton Papers, including the correspondence and papers of Charles Wood, first Viscount Halifax of Monk Bretton. I should also like to thank Mr. T. Ingram who guided me through the great mass of the Hickleton Papers. I have permission from Lord Monteagle to use the Monteagle Papers and from the Earl of Courtown to quote from a manuscript diary written by the fifth Earl; Sir Fergus Graham, Bt., has given me permission to use Sir James Graham's Papers. I am grateful to the late Sir Charles Trevelyan, Bt., for allowing me to use Sir C. E. Trevelyan's private Letter Books. I am much indebted to Mrs. Jenifer Hart of St. Anne's College, Oxford, who informed me of the existence of the Private Letter Books, assisted me in obtaining access to them and guided me in their use. I should like to thank Dr. R. W. Hunt, Keeper of Western Manuscripts and the staff of the Bodleian Library, Oxford.

I owe a special obligation to Mr. E. C. W. Tuke, who lent me the important Tuke Papers, notes, drafts, correspondence and pamphlets, collected by James Hack Tuke, and to Mrs. Corbett who first told me of their existence.

The Pitt Kennedy Papers are used by kind permission of Mr. J. Winthrop Young, and the extract from Lord Arthur Russell's M.S. notes by permission of Miss Flora Russell.

I should like to thank Mrs. Olive Goodbody, who arranged for me to use the historical collection at the Society of Friends Meeting House, Eustace Street, Dublin, and lent me her own collection. I am grateful to the Taoiseach of the Republic of Ireland for permission to use papers in Dublin Castle.

Professor Denis Gwynn has given permission to make use of his excellent work *Young Ireland and 1848*. I have also permission to quote from *Ford, the Times, the Man, the Company* by Alan Nevins, and from *Monckton Milnes, The Years of Promise*, by James Pope-Hennessy.

In dealing with the financial crisis of 1847 I received valuable help from Sir George Bolton, K.C.M.G., Mr. John Hogg, and Professor R. F. Sayers, and on the subject of Irish coin from Mr. J. H. James, Deputy Master of the Royal Mint.

Among very many people who have kindly helped me with information I should like to thank Dr. G. Kitson Clark, Professor George O'Brien, the Earl of Pembroke, Lord Rothschild, G.M., Mrs. Beatrice Grosvenor, Mr. John Horgan, Mr. Alec Wallace, Dr. N. Marshall Cummins and, once again, Mr. Michael Egan of Castlebar, Co. Mayo.

Illustrations proved difficult to find. Perhaps because the years of the Great Hunger were a period of economic pressure, paintings and drawings of contemporary events, with the exception of the wood-cuts in the *Illustrated London News,* temporarily at least disappear. I should, however, like to thank the staff of the department of Prints and Drawings at the British Museum, of the New York Public Library, the Municipal Gallery of New York and the Folklore Commission, Dublin, who searched in vain. For the portraits with which the book is largely illustrated I am indebted to their present owners, to Mr. Kingsley Adams, C.B.E., and the staff of the National Portrait Gallery, London, and to Dr. McGreevy and Miss Murphy of the National Gallery of Ireland: I am afraid I gave them an immense amount of trouble.

It was with the co-operation of the Mayo County Council that I was able to see the interesting collection of workhouse minute books which were then stored in Castlebar.

I am under an obligation to Mr. Leonard Russell who has once more read through my manuscript and given me the benefit of his advice, and I am again deeply indebted to the helpfulness and patience of the staff of the London Library. Finally I want to record my obligation to Miss Phyllis Woodham-Smith who has been as indefatigable as she has been long suffering in checking references and verifying facts.

INDEX

INDEX

421

The Easter Rebellion
By Max Caulfield

'Never had man or woman a grander cause,
never was a cause more grandly
served.' **James Connolly**

Here is the hour-by-hour account of the fantastic
week of an impassioned struggle with all its
heroes and martyrs. A week of bloody slaughter and
an orgy of revenge: a week whose effects are
still felt today half a century later.

At noon on Easter Monday, April 24th 1916,
a handful of Irish volunteers slipped through the
guard of the British and took up positions
on the Dublin streets. They commandeered the
post offices and cut the wires to England.
They ran up a flag—a green flag with a
golden harp in the centre. Written across it in
bold Gaelic lettering, half-gold half-white
were the words IRISH REPUBLIC.

Within a week it was over: 1,351 people killed
or severely wounded; 179 buildings totally ruined and
one third of the population needing public relief.
But only in death could they achieve victory.

'You cannot conquer Ireland, you cannot extinguish
the Irish passion for freedom.' **Pearse**

'Utterly absorbing.' **Sunday Times**

'Impressive . . . exciting.' **New Statesman**

'Conscientious and lively . . . gift of creating
atmosphere. Readable, judicious . . . makes clear the
confused strategy.' **Times Literary Supplement**

'Highly valuable.' **Punch**

THE NEW ENGLISH LIBRARY 6s. 0d.

NEL BESTSELLERS

F.2373	THE DOCTOR DARES	Elizabeth Seifert 5/–
F.2231	THE NEW DOCTOR	Elizabeth Seifert 4/–
F.2159	HARRIET HUME	Robecca West 5/–

Science Fiction
F.1233	THE OCTOBER COUNTRY	Ray Bradbury 3/6
F.1234	THE SMALL ASSASSIN	Ray Bradbury 3/6
F.1803	STARSHIP TROOPERS	Robert Heinlein 5/–
F.2124	STRANGER IN A STRANGE LAND	Robert Heinlein 7/6

War
F.2423	STRIKE FROM THE SKY—THE BATTLE OF BRITAIN STORY	
		Alexander McKee 6/–
F.1686	EASTERN APPROACHES	Fitzroy Maclean 7/6
F.1875	THE LONGEST DAY (illustrated)	Cornelius Ryan 7/6
F.2146	THE LAST BATTLE (illustrated)	Cornelius Ryan 12/6
F.1270	THE RED BERET	Hilary St. George Saunders 5/–
F.1943	REPORT FROM No. 24	Gunnar Sonsteby 5/–
F.1084	THE GUNS OF AUGUST—AUGUST 1914	Barbara W. Tuchman 5/–
F.1880	END QUIET WAR	Hedger Wallace 5/–

Western
F.2134	AMBUSH	Luke Short 3/6
F.2135	CORONER CREEK	Luke Short 3/6
F.2142	THE ALAMO	Lon Tinkle 3/6
F.2063	THE SHADOW SHOOTER	W. C. Tuttle 3/6
F.2132	THE TROUBLE TRAILER	W. C. Tuttle 3/6
F.2133	MISSION RIVER JUSTICE	W. C. Tuttle 3/6
F.2180	SILVER BUCKSHOT	W. C. Tuttle 3/6

General
F.2420	THE SECOND SEX	Simone De Beauvoir 8/6
F.2117	NATURE OF THE SECOND SEX	Simone De Beauvoir 5/–
F.2234	SEX MANNERS FOR MEN	Robert Chantham 5/–
F.2060	SEX AND THE ADOLESCENT	Maxine Davis 5/–
F.2136	WOMEN	John Philip Lundin 5/–
F.2333	MISTRESSES	John Philip Lundin 5/–
F.2382	SECRET AND FORBIDDEN	Paul Tabori 8/6
U.2366	AN ABZ OF LOVE	Inge and Sten Hegeler 10/6
F.2374	SEX WITHOUT GUILT	Albert Ellis Ph.D. 8/6
F.2358	CANDY	Southern and Hoffenberg 10/6
F.2511	SEXUALIS '95	Jacques Sternberg 5/–

Mad
S.2955	A MAD LOOK AT OLD MOVIES	3/6
S.3523	BOILING MAD	4/6
S.3496	THE MAD ADVENTURES OF CAPTAIN KLUTZ	4/6
S.3158	THE QUESTIONABLE MAD	3/6
S.2385	FIGHTING MAD	3/6
S.3268	HOWLING MAD	3/6
S.3413	INDIGESTIBLE MAD	3/6

NEL P.O. BOX 11, FALMOUTH, CORNWALL

Please send cheque or postal order. Allow 9d. per book to cover postage and packing (Overseas 1/– per book).

Name...

Address ....

....

Title ....
(MARCH)